*Routledge Library Editions*

# THE THEORY OF MARGINAL VALUE



ECONOMICS

# HISTORY OF ECONOMIC THOUGHT
In 23 Volumes

| | | |
|---|---|---|
| I | A Select Bibliography of Modern Economic Theory | *Batson* |
| II | Early British Economics | *Beer* |
| III | Nassau Senior | *Bowley* |
| IV | The Theory of Marginal Value | *Birck* |
| V | Ricardo and the Theory of Value Distribution and Growth | *Caravale & Tosato* |
| VI | Productive Labour and Effective Demand | *Coontz* |
| VII | London Essays in Economics | *Gregory & Dalton* |
| VIII | Capitalism and the Historians | *Hayek* |
| IX | The Origins of Scientific Economics | *Letwin* |
| X | The Individual in Society | *Macfie* |
| XI | Essays on Hayek | *Machlup* |
| XII | The Economics of Physiocracy | *Meek* |
| XIII | Karl Marx | *Mehring* |
| XIV | Marx's Critique of Political Economy I | *Oakley* |
| XV | Marx's Critique of Political Economy II | *Oakley* |
| XVI | J R McCulloch | *O'Brien* |
| XVII | A Key to Ricardo | *St Clair* |
| XVIII | Roads to Freedom | *Streissler* |
| XIX | Economics in the Twentieth Century | *Suranyi-Unger* |
| XX | Elements of Pure Economics | *Walras* |
| XXI | The Common Sense of Political Economy I | *Wicksteed* |
| XXII | The Common Sense of Political Economy II | *Wicksteed* |
| XXIII | Social Economics | *von Wieser* |

# THE THEORY OF MARGINAL VALUE

L V BIRCK

Routledge
Taylor & Francis Group
LONDON AND NEW YORK

First published in 1922

Reprinted in 2003 by
Routledge
2 Park Square, Milton Park, Abingdon, Oxon, OX14 4RN
or
270 Madison Avenue, New York, NY 10016

First issued in paperback 2010

*Routledge is an imprint of the Taylor & Francis Group*



The publishers have made every effort to contact authors/copyright holders of the works reprinted in *Routledge Library Editions – Economics*. This has not been possible in every case, however, and we would welcome correspondence from those individuals/companies we have been unable to trace.

These reprints are taken from original copies of each book. In many cases the condition of these originals is not perfect. The publisher has gone to great lengths to ensure the quality of these reprints, but wishes to point out that certain characteristics of the original copies will, of necessity, be apparent in reprints thereof.

*British Library Cataloguing in Publication Data*
A CIP catalogue record for this book
is available from the British Library

The Theory of Marginal Value
ISBN 978-0-415-31324-7 (hbk)
ISBN 978-0-415-60716-2 (pbk)
ISBN 978-0-415-31320-9 (set)

Miniset: History of Economic Thought

Series: Routledge Library Editions – Economics

# THE THEORY OF MARGINAL VALUE

BY

L. V. BIRCK, DR.SC. POL.,

*Professor of Economics at the University of Copenhagen*

Routledge
Taylor & Francis Group
LONDON AND NEW YORK

DEDICATED TO

ALFRED MARSHALL, CAMBRIDGE ;

HORACE WESTERGARD, COPENHAGEN

AND FRIEDRICH VON WIESER, VIENNA.

# PREFACE

THE purpose of this treatise is not to give an entire system of economics, but to initiate the student in the methods, notions, or fundamentals of the marginal theory, and at the same time to carry him so far as to enable him to work out the problems for himself. Hence the first part of this book has been worked out in great detail, contrasting the rather condensed exposition of the difficult 4th and 5th parts, where the student, in a lesser degree, needs the guidance of his teacher. This book does not contain anything about the mechanics of economics, being reserved for a second volume.

In order to avoid delay the diagram blocks, used in the Danish edition, have been utilised in the English version ; in some of the diagrams Danish words appear, and although their general sense is obvious, I would note the more important cases : In Diagram XIIa and XIIb, " maengde curve " stands for " curve of quantity ; " Nödvendighedsvare " for " necessary," and " luxusvare " for " luxury." In Diagram XVI. (pp. 185–6) " arbulyst " stands for " disutility of labour," and " varens Nytte " for " utility of the commodity," and " pengenes-nytte " for " utility of money." In some cases the diagrams have been drawn in terms of " Danish Krone," but these have been interpreted in the text in terms of " English shillings."

I am indebted to Messrs. Fred Zeuthen, M.A. (Copenhagen), Hugh Dalton, M.A., Cambridge, and Thomas A. Joynt, M.A., Edinburgh, for valuable advice both as to form and matter, and to the latter for his patience and courtesy in reading of the proofs.

Dr. L. V. BIRCK.

# CONTENTS

**Book III. Relations of Subjective Prices**

# BOOK. I

# UTILITY.

## CHAPTER I

### The Disutility of Labour

**1. The Economic Motive.**—Mephistopheles does not appear to have grown wiser by experience when he agrees that his claim to Faust's soul shall be conditional upon the learned doctor becoming so much enraptured by the pleasures provided by the fiend that he must exclaim : " Oh ! stay, stay for ever, happy hour ! " For nobody has felt the happiness of a moment so intensely that he wishes to stay the fleeting seconds. Memories and anticipations make themselves present, throwing us out of our momentary happiness. Ascetic and pessimistic philosophy teaches happiness as depending on the subjugation of our desires ; by killing every germ of human desire we attain a state of happiness, the complete mental equilibrium in which our mind, drained of all desire is ready to merge in the " Nirvana." The optimistic, hellenic view of life is that happiness is attained through positive enjoyment and the avoidance of pain.

These two opposite theories of life have one truth in common : that a state of happiness is brought about by exterminating our desire, whether by killing it in its embryonic state or by drugging it with satisfaction.

Happiness, then—in so far as it can be defined—is identical with the cessation of desire, and the state of happiness is that point of complete satisfaction, of harmony of body and mind, in which state we are pained by no desire, because desire either has not yet been aroused or has already been satisfied. The further we are from this harmony the more pain we feel, and the greater is our discontent.

It is not a matter for economic science to decide, which of the two theories of life—the ascetic or the epicurean—is the right one ; only this—in our mind life we experience this striving to attain harmony, which is a characteristic of all life. The classical school of economists have, however, experience on their side when they maintain that human beings, from an egoistic point of view, regard happiness positively as the satisfaction of our desire, and negatively as the avoidance of pain, *i.e.*, the satisfaction of as great demands as possible in return for the smallest possible sacrifice. This is the basis of the fundamental economic postulate—the rule that *our economic motive is maximum satisfaction and minimum sacrifice.*

**2. The Working Hour.**—In relation to his economic activity man is *the end* in his capacity of consumer, and *the means* in his capacity of producer. From this it must not be concluded that each individual is the end in view of his own activity, for we are only units in a community of many; but even the existing community is not the end in view, as every generation living in the present interval between the two eternities—the past and the future—is in itself a link in the chain of humanity. "Public welfare" has a longer range than thirty years; economic ethics cannot acknowledge benefit for the individual as an indicator of the correctness of an economic action

As a means man is a *working machine* which creates and supplies *energy*; our consumption refunds us the energy expended by our activity; part of the energy supplied through our consumption is expended merely in keeping alive—in "preserving the machine." We know from feeding-experiments that the functions of life consume a great part of the calories of the food, and that only part is transformed into muscle; only part of the energy supplied is converted into productive work. Progress, whether individual or universal, is founded upon the existence of a surplus of energy; part of the energy at our command we invest in the productions of our labour. The *workman* is possessed of *working-power* which produces "doses" of *energy*. These doses of energy may be useful in themselves (personal services) or be incorporated in things (*substances*); substances as well as services are thus economic goods. We now have the circle: Human energy—production — economic goods — consumption — satisfaction — energy. Compare: want—effort—satisfaction.)

Labour has two dimensions—*time* and *intensity*. As a third dimension quality might be mentioned (for instance, mental in contrast to manual labour), but this is in another plane and compares with the other two dimensions, as movement in time with movement in space.

As the correct unit of measurement—the unit of energy—cannot be defined, it is necessary in the following pages to employ *the working hour*, by which is meant something similar to Karl

Marx's reduced normal working hour, which is the product of average intensity and average skill.

By economic work we mean exertion of energy through the incentive of mainly economic ends, even if the object need not be the worker's personal benefit. The work must be *necessary for the purpose,* in the sense that the object would not have been attained without performance of the work in question or *equal* work. The singer who beats rhythm to the reapers is as productive as they by accelerating their speed; the government official who creates safe working conditions, the inventor who improves working-methods, and the manager who organises production, all perform indispensable work themselves. Not all indispensable work is remunerated, and much superfluous work is paid for—the wages thus being no indicator of the productivity of work; the relative indispensability of the individual *worker, not of the work,* determines wages.

By production—*i.e.*, applying working energy to substance—(the active and passive element respectively) we *produce* economic goods. To produce means converting substance into a shape in which it is *useful* and thus able to satisfy our demand. To *consume* means transforming goods into such a state that they are no longer able to satisfy our demand (destruction in an economic sense—not to be confused with destruction in a physical sense; a chair without legs is consumed, destroyed economically, without being destroyed physically).

**3. The Curve of Productivity of Labour.**—It is natural for a healthy human being to exercise energy, and when Simon Patten speaks of the "joy of work" he states something more than a paradox. What makes labour disagreeable is its monotony, and the fact that too much of it is required—the presence of an element of compulsion, breathless routine (specialising kills the joy of work) and often special aversion against repeat work. Unemployment is felt to be an evil, not only for economic reasons, but because idleness is tedious (there is a distinction between idleness and leisure); the joy of work is furthered by change of work, but the product of labour is increased by uniformity of movement.

The exercise of energy involves fatigue, which has objective as well as subjective effects. After conquering the sluggishness, the yield of labour may increase during the first few hours, but afterwards it will decrease every hour (although a pause may again increase the yield) until it perhaps becomes negative; as far as piece-work is concerned the decrease in yield can be directly measured, but where the worker is adjunct to a machine and must follow its movements, the mistaken policy of long working-hours is proved by breakdown of machinery, accidents, and sometimes by the disappointing quality of the product (for instance, weaving-faults). This may be illustrated by diagram 1.

Along the abcissa or lateral axis in a system of co-ordinates we mark out the units of time, while the working intensity during the periods of time in question is marked out along the ordinate or perpendicular, the rectangles thus drawn up indicating the quantities produced during each unit of time (intensity multiplied by time).

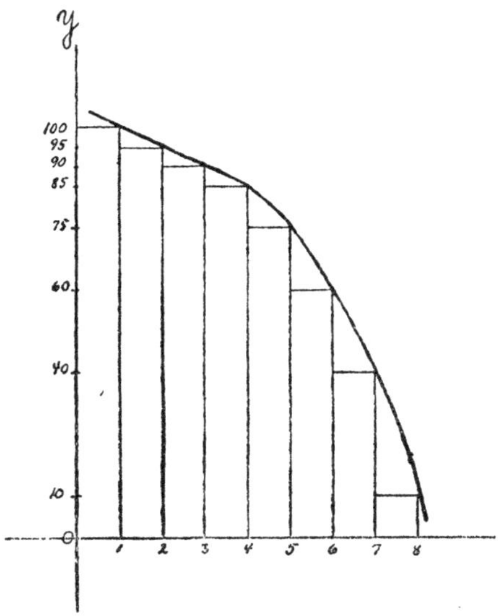

Diagram I

If the units of time chosen are sufficiently small, the connecting-line between the corners of the rectangles will form a continuous curve—the curve of working-intensity, which starts high and declines—thus illustrating the decreasing productivity of labour.

**4. The Curve of Disutility.**—The subjective effect of fatigue is a feeling of disinclination for work, and this may be increased by other elements, as, for instance, a loathing for the kind of work in question, monotony, etc. This disinclination is akin to pain. Few men can work for the sake of work itself; the work of the scientist or the poet need not, however, be attended by any disinclination; he is often driven on by a kind of demonic power (Socrates' "daimon").

But where this is not the case, and where work has ceased

to be a natural and spontaneous exertion of energy, it throws us out of our physical and mental equilibrium, and is felt as something onerous, varying in degree according to how far we are from our equilibrium, from the scarcely noticeable disinclination at the first dig with a spade, to the stinging pain after sixteen hours of work. The disutility of labour is thus dependent upon how much work a person has previously performed, and is not alike for all working-hours.

Supposing the disutility of the first instalment of work to be $u_l \cdot q_1$, the disutility of the second instalment will be somewhat larger, the worker being more fatigued after performing one instalment of work than before. The disutility of the second instalment might be described as $u_l q_1 \cdot q_2$, in which $q_2 > q_1 > 1$; the disutility of the third instalment is still larger; this is denoted by $u_l q_1 \cdot q_2 \cdot q_3$, in which $q_3 > 1$, and so on down to the $n$-th instalment, the disutility of which accordingly amounts to $u_l \cdot q_1 \cdot q_2 \cdot q_3 \cdot \cdots \cdot q_n$. That $1 < q_1 < q_2 < q_3$, etc., is in accordance with the *rule of gradually increasing disutility of the work* to produce the article in question. If we *assume* that the difference between $q_1$ and $q_2$ and between $q_2$ and $q_3$, between $q_3$ and $q_4$, etc., between $q_{n-1}$ and $q_n$ are small enough to be regarded as negligible quantities, we have $q_1 = q_2 = q_3 = q_4 = \ldots = q_n$. Thus we arrive at the following assumption :—

The disutility of the first instalment of labour amounts to $u_l \cdot q$, of the second to $u_l \cdot q^2$ of the third to $u_l \cdot q^3$, of the fourth instalment to $u_l{}' q^4$, etc.

By assuming that the difference between $q_2$, $q_3$, $q_4$, $q_n$ is infinitesimal we arrive at the hypothesis, that *the burdensomeness of work increases in geometrical progression corresponding to the arithmetically progressing increase in the quantity of work performed*, and that $q =$ the rate of increase of this disutility—varies inversely with our capacity for work and proportionally with our susceptibility to pain or fatigue.

Without attempting to judge the correctness of this hypothesis, we must maintain that to adopt it will lighten our task without doing any harm. The formula $u_l \cdot q^4 > u_l \cdot q^3$ expresses clearly to the eye that we are comparing the third and the fourth working hour, and that the disutility of the fourth hour's work is greater than that of the third. Further, I shall not be tempted to draw any other conclusions from the designation of the disutility of the two first working hours as $u_l(q + q^2)$, than I can if it was written $u_l(q + q\cdot q^2)$. If $u_l\cdot q$ is the disutility of the first hour the disutility of the $t$-th hour will thus be $u_l\cdot q^t$, that of the $(t-1)$ *th* hour will be $u_l\cdot q^{(t-1)}$. Assuming that I work $t$ hours in all, we describe the $t$-th hour as the *marginal* hour, the work of *this* hour as the *marginal* labour, and the specific burdensomeness of this hour's work as the *marginal disutility* of labour. The *total* disutility of $t$ hours work is, then :

$$u_l\cdot q + u_l\cdot q^2 + u_l\cdot q^3 \ldots\ldots\ldots u_l\cdot q^t = u_l\ (q + q^2 + q^3 \ldots\ldots + q^t)$$

for which sum I use the contracted term $u_{l\cdot t}$.

From this it is immediately apparent that $t\ (u_l\cdot q^t) > u_{l\cdot t}$, *i.e.*, that the total disutility of the labour is less than the product of the time of working and the marginal disutility. This can be graphically represented (Diagram II.) by a system of co-ordinates, in which the hours are marked out along the abscissa and the disutility attending the work along the ordinate; in this case also we arrive at a curve, which illustrates the disutility of labour. The curve of disutility starts low, near the base, and ends high, thus indicating the increasing disutility of labour.

To compare time with pain, for instance, by writing the first + the second hour equal to $u_l(q + q^2)$ would be incorrect. Apart from the fact that the equation is misleading, because the disutility of four hours of work is more than twice as much as that of two hours, we are not justified in comparing quantity with feeling because physical quantities and mental conditions are incommensurable.

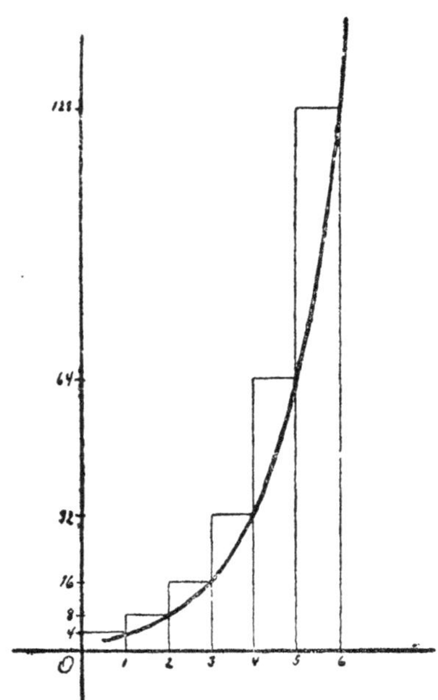

Diagram II

Work reveals itself in three ways : (1) as an objective quantity of work, (2) as the result of work, and (3) as a feeling of onerousness by the person who performs the work. Quantity and onerousness (disutility) are like two quite different pictures of the same thing in two differently prepared mirrors—the retina of our eye and our feelings. Quantity of work applied and result cannot be compared either, even if the latter can be measured by the former.

The conditions of our work, then, are hard: objectively the yield decreases with increased working-hours, subjectively it causes us greater and greater discomfort each hour. If we add to this, that nature also grows more and more unwilling to yield the substance—the raw material—to which we apply our labour, and thus makes increasing resistance, we see that each human being as well as humanity generally in a sense works under the law of decreasing return. Capital and human ingenuity can mitigate this, for us, unfavourable fact.

**5. Professor Lehman's Responsum.**—The hypothesis of the logarithmic proportion between the quantity of work and the feeling of onerousness is far from unreasonable; Jevons quote several treatises, and has himself made some experiments with the object of measuring the increasing fatigue of uniform work, and his results confirm the hypothesis. Professor Dr. Phil. Alf. Lehmann has sent the following responsum to my inquiry:

"In reply to your inquiry concerning the variation in intensity of sensations and their relation to outside influences, I am able to give you the following particulars:

"Concerning the feelings of inclination, of desire, no experimental investigations are available. This is quite obvious, as any attempt to establish a formula for the proportion between the intensity of this feeling and outside influences must fail, because of the fact that we have no indicator of the intensity of the feeling. We cannot directly judge that the sensation at the present moment is a certain number of times more or less intense than at a certain previous moment. Bernoulli's mathematical expression of '*la fortune morale*' is therefore—as I have pointed out in my book, *Principal Laws of Human Emotional Life*, p. 195—a hypothesis, which in any case cannot be verified by experiment. But this does not preclude the possibility of testing it in a different way, *i.e.*, from practical life instead of through the laboratory. Here the external actions accompanying the feelings will certainly in many respects be available as indicators of the intensity of emotions, and for this reason I do not by any means consider it impossible to verify Bernoulli's hypothesis, or even to find a more exact expression. I support this assumption on the fact that it appears to be actually possible to measure a certain feeling of disinclination.

" For feelings of disinclination generally the case is similar to that of feelings of inclination—we have no measure for them. But for that state of discomfort which accompanies physical and mental fatigue, it will in any case not be difficult to establish a certain measure without being too arbitrary. Fatigue itself, as a purely physiological state, can easily be made the subject of experimental investigation and be measured exactly through the decrease in the production of labour, either in quantity or quality.

" A rule may thus be established for the increase in fatigue in proportion to the quantity of work performed. When this rule becomes known, and we are able to form a not altogether improbable hypothesis as to the increase in fatigue, the outcome of this will evidently be a rule for the increase in disinclination in proportion to the quantity of work performed.

" The progress of fatigue has been examined repeatedly, for physical as well as mental labour; I have some time ago adapted a couple of experiments with a view to the question before me. Through a series of ergographic measurements of muscular fatigue I have found that fatigue measured by the number of maximum exertions required for the performance of certain work increases approximately in geometrical progression, as the work performed increases in arithmetical progression. By adapting a series of pedagogic experiments concerning intellectual fatigue—fatigue from mental labour—I arrive at approximately the same rule. A rather large class of children have been kept working for several hours without a break, and their fatigue has been measured at the end of each hour, through the number of mistakes made in test work (exercises from dictation, etc.). Here also it is proved that fatigue approximately increases in geometrical progression when the work performed—measured by the number of working hours—increases in arithmetical progression. (Compare Körperliche Aeusserungen Psychischer Zustande 2 Teil, Leipzig, 1901, Pg. 147–52).

" If now we dare assume that the disinclination accompanying fatigue increases proportionally with the latter, we would arrive at exactly the rule mentioned: that the onerousness, the disutility of work increases in geometrical progression proportionally with an arithmetical increase in the quantity of work performed. But this assumption is directly at variance with experience. By ergographic measurements, where a number of maximal muscle-contractions are performed in a certain time, it is easy for the person subjected to the test to perceive that the onerousness to start with increases, and that simultaneously the work performed in each contraction continually decreases. But if the work is continued, the effort will finally be reduced to an almost constant quantity, which can be maintained for a very long time, and then the work is no longer disagreeable. Something similar is known from everyday life; for instance, on a long walk, where fatigue is also easily conquered by decreasing the speed of the walk; when the muscles are adapted for the work, the feeling of fatigue ceases. In this case there is no increase in the disinclination, which can be described as proportional with the increase in the work performed.

"The feeling of fatigue is, however, not the only deciding factor. When working to perform a certain task, the activity will be less satisfactory as the quantity of work, which can be performed per second, decreases. If the yield of work on account of fatigue has dropped to half the original quantity, we will not hesitate to say that the work is only half as satisfactory, and the smaller the performance per second, the greater the dissatisfaction with the work. This presumably applies more particularly to mental labour, where the dissatisfaction of the worker with his own performance increases, the greater the quantitative or qualitative decrease in the yield. Then there is really a disinclination, which can be said to increase proportionally with fatigue—that is, in geometrical progression—when the quantity of work performed increases arithmetically. And this disinclination may cause the worker to stop, even if the feeling of fatigue is only slight, for the sole reason that the result does not correspond to the effort. As this disutility, however, is not the only one resulting from the work—fatigue proper and possibly also other disutilities as well making themselves felt with varying intensity—the 'disutility of labour' is probably rather complex, and it is then only as a rough approximation that the above rule can be said to apply.

" While these experiments concerning fatigue have fairly well elucidated the relations of disutility to the quantity of work performed, by employing a measurable consequence of this psycophysiological state as an indicator, I must accordingly assume that similar proceedings may be feasible in any case as far as certain of the feelings of inclination are concerned."

(Signed) ALFR. LEHMANN.

COPENHAGEN, *October 10th,* 1916.

# CHAPTER II

## Utility and Wants

**6. Desire and Utility.**—As work entails discomfort, which, furthermore, is increasing, there must be some motive for subjecting oneself to this pain, and this motive arises from the still greater discomfort which is created in us by our *unsatisfied wants.* Our wants are thus the "ultima ratio" of our efforts. If we cannot kill our desire by commonsense and self-control, we must buy the satisfaction thereof by means of a *sacrifice*; for instance, the disutility of labour. Already this shows that economic relations must be treated as *problems of equilibrium;* economic motives as well as economic forces continually tend towards a state of equilibrium which, scarcely attained, is again disturbed.

The consumption of energy in living creates our wants; they become evident as a feeling of discomfort, strong or weak, varying from a hardly distinguishable awakening discomfort to the pangs of hunger.

We *desire* to cause this pain to cease. The greater the need, the stronger is our desire and the further we are from happiness; he who is able to resign comes nearest to being happy, but "the coveting character bears Hell in his own heart." Consumption (actual consumption or use) of certain goods may cause our want to cease. Consequently we desire such goods; the pain caused by the want (*i.e.*, the pain we would feel by continually being without the goods) and the desire for the goods, will thus become equal. As soon as we desire a thing, a certain desirability or, to use an accepted term, utility, derived from our desire is attributed to it. A thing has only utility for us as long as we desire it, and we only desire it as long as we feel the pain of wanting it; only a hungry man cares for bread. This quality, which is equal to our desire, is termed *Utility,* which thus means a quality attributed to the goods and derived from our desire, which in turn has been created by our feeling of discomfort arising from the want—in other words, *Utility, Desire* and the *Pain of Want* are identical conceptions, covering one another and all measured by the strength of our feeling of pain The greater the pain caused by our need, the greater our desire for those goods, the enjoyment of which allay the feeling of pain, and the greater the utility which our desire attributes to them.

Utility is thus not an objective quality of a thing ; whether a thing has utility for me, depends upon my desiring it or not, and, consequently, the *amount* of utility depends upon *the strength* of my desire. Goods are only of importance for us if we come in relation to them, and economically they have only the importance we ourselves attribute to them. The individual measures the pain or disutility of labour against the utility of the thing, consequently pain is the basis of the conception of utility ; but utility and pain would be incommensurable if both were not physical states.

**7. Utility and Usefulness.**—In contradistinction to utility—the subjective and, consequently, varying quality of a thing—we often speak of the objective and unchangeable quality of *usefulness* in a thing—which is this inherent, technical quality in a thing, that it *may* satisfy a possible want. Bread has always usefulness, because it has a certain taste, is digestible and nutritive ; but it only has utility for me if I am hungry. A loaf of bread may save me from starvation, and its utility is immense ; the same loaf would cause me disgust when satisfied, and has thus negative utility (*i.e.*, disutility). Utility is thus contingent upon, but cannot be measured by, usefulness. We might compare utility with the energy possessed by a piece of matter which has been raised to a certain height from the level, while we compare usefulness with the properties inherent in the matter because of its weight or form.

In economics we only deal with utility, the property attributed by the individual, ***at a given moment***, to a thing according to his desire. The actual utility of a thing thus is an expression for how far the individual at a given moment is from the equilibrium of satisfaction as far as that thing is concerned. By the expression utility in the following pages we always mean the actual utility covered by the expressions " Utility " (Jevons) ; " rarèté " (Walras) ; " Nutz " (Wieser) ; " ophelimité " (Pareto) ; " Nytte " (Westergaard and Aschehoug), or the expression of daily talk—desirability.

It is misleading—as some authors do—to use the expressions subjective value and utility indiscriminately. While subjective value is a possible proportion of exchange between two goods employed by the individual to express a comparison between the utility of those two goods, utility is a kind of incorporeal substance, *i.e.*, a mental state of a certain intensity.

**8. Measurement of Utility.**—We treat utility (desire, pain of want) as if it were measurable ; but ought we do to that ? We can certainly not find any direct measurement for the strength of the feelings of other individuals, no more than of our own—in any case, never exact enough to find out how many units of pain we really suffer at a given moment. Edgeworth's hope of becoming able to measure the feeling of disinclination as we are able to measure the strength of the electric current is at the least sanguine. Even if we are able to measure certain physiological phenomena accompanying the feelings, as, for instance, to prove that feelings of fatigue are accompanied by a falling off in the pulse and the volumen of the arm, the existing apparatus only show us the direction and do not provide an exact measurement. But, anyhow, I know that I am able to compare, *i.e.*, measure and estimate my own feelings in as far as I know that my desire for one thing is stronger than for another. I have daily the alternative put before me, *to be without a thing I desire, or to make a sacrifice to obtain it*, or I have the choice between two things ; and, consequently, I base my choice on an estimate of the difference between the strength of my feelings, at times to a nicety. If two feelings thus compared are of exactly the same strength, my fate will be the tragic one of Buridan's ass.

We are therefore entitled to presume that every individual is capable of measuring his *own* feelings and, presuming this, we might say that if a certain desire (and consequent utility) is estimated at a strength of 20 units, my desire for another thing, if felt with double the strength, will be 40 units. We make this measurement of our desire and of the *utility* of the thing in question every time we compare, *i.e.*, in production and exchange.

But to compare the feelings of two different persons, as done by many adherents of the subjective school, must be regarded as being inadmissible and, furthermore, superfluous. If the individual must buy or sell, he has his considerations of the proportion between two goods *for himself* fixed in the *subjective ratio of exchange* ; he knows how much he at the utmost will give, and the least he will accept. At the market he meets with other individuals, who also have fixed *their* subjective ratio of exchange ; the mental process is the secret of the individual, hardly revealed to himself. We may compare the ratios of exchange ; if, for instance, A calculates that a pair of boots will render him the same actual utility as three pairs of stockings, and B that they will have the same utility to him as six pairs of stockings.

But to compare the feelings direct will only lead us astray. If many economists are sceptical towards the mathematicians, one reason is that this comparison between the feelings of two persons only leads to elegant formulae. Walras' theory would certainly have predominated, if he had turned aside in time and dealt with subjective values. For utility is to us only the means to find the subjective value and, inasmuch as this is dependent upon the fluctuations in utility (*i.e.*, desire), to gain a starting point for the comprehension of the fluctuations in subjective prices. Once this is found we do away with all the psychological scaffolding (the conception of utility) and operate with tangible factors, the respective, subjective ratios of exchange of buyer and seller, in order to find what we are looking for —the ratio of exchange attained in an actual market.

**9. The Law of Diminishing Utility.**—Our desire decreases as we increase our supply of a commodity, and ceases when we are fully satisfied ; consequently, the utility diminishes as we come nearer to the point of satisfaction ; utility thus starts high and is finally nil. This rule of the *gradually decreasing utility* of goods was first advanced by *Gossen*. We know the rule from psychology as *Fechner's* rule ; the influence must increase in geometrical progression in order to make the feeling increase arithmetically. That the utility of a certain increment is dependent upon the place it takes in the succession might be confirmed by anybody from his own experience If we describe the utility of the first unit as $u_1$ (or $u_{d1}$ if we want to indicate that it is the first unit of the commodity *D*) and the utility of the second unit as $u_2$, and that of the third as $u_3$ and the $n$-th as $u_n$, we know from the rule of decreasing utility that $u_1 > u_2 > u_3 \ldots\ldots > u_n$ (the later the unit, the larger index, the less utility).

**10. The Rate of Decrease in Utility.**—The symbols $u_1$, $u_2$, $u_3$ . . . $u_n$, placed in succession, are termed a series of utility. The difference between them is termed the rate of decrease in utility; if this was alike at every point of the series and equal to the fraction $\frac{1}{r}$, the utility would consequently decrease in geometrical progression—a regularity which would only exist as an exception, and then only for a certain part of the series.

Suppose the following utility-schedule 64, 51, 41, 33, 26, 21, 17, etc., units of utility for respectively the first, second and third, up to the seventh unit of the commodity; if we continue, we would finally have a unit, the utility of which is nil or even negative (King Midas' experience). This schedule is expressed graphically in Diagram III.

The units of the commodity are marked out along the abscissa, while the different ordinates show the utility yielded by the different units.

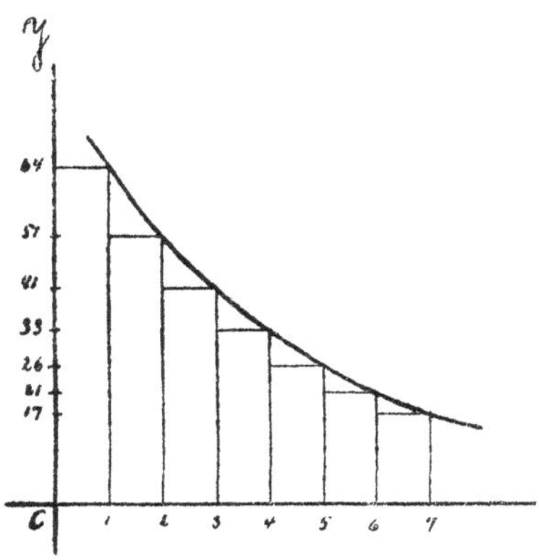

Diagram III

We may here note that the curves for different goods *do not start at the same level.* The first unit of bread meets with a very strong demand, that of butter with a somewhat smaller demand, and an article of luxury with a much smaller one, because we might do without it altogether. Diamonds meet with a very small demand, because a number of other demands must be satisfied first. Further, our *ability to consume* is not equally great for all goods; of some the possible consumption is very much limited, of others almost unlimited. It is interesting that nearly all the goods to the first units of which we attribute an enormous utility (for instance, food) arrive comparatively quickly at the point of satisfaction, after which a further unit would cause disgust, while the goods, which we meet at first with small desire (for instance, trinkets) can on the contrary, often be consumed in large quantities. There is no limit to the number of pictures I may hang on my wall and the number of diamonds I may use. Further, the rate of decrease may vary. The first unit of some goods meets with a violent desire, the second, however, with a very small one; the rate of decrease is thus very fast. Of other goods we are perhaps no more eager to have the first unit than the second; the rate of decrease is then a slow one. This is graphically shown in Diagram IV, which shows the curves for two goods with, (*a*) a fast and (*b*) a slow rate respectively of decrease of utility. It will be seen that the curve of utility is steep in the first, but flat in the latter case.

But the rate of decrease is not the same right through; it

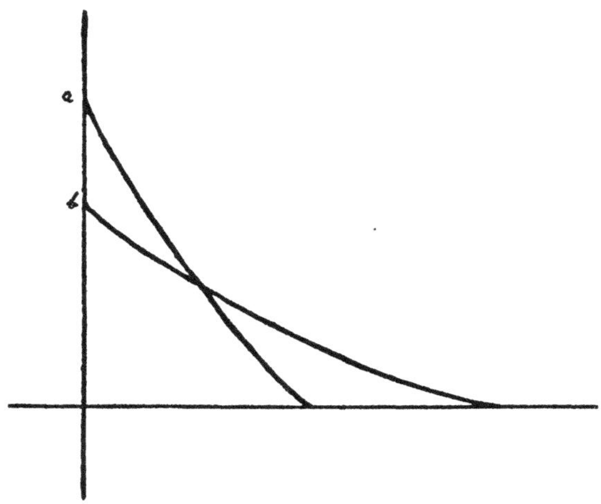


Diagram IV

changes often; perhaps it will be fast at the beginning of our consumption, but slow when the first demand has been satisfied; the curve of utility may then change its form from steep to flat; the change may take place so often that there is no regularity whatever.

Finally a utility curve may change its form as a result of a change in our relation to the thing in question. *Habit* may make an article of luxury a necessity for me (tobacco, coffee); a change in fashion may alter the utility I attribute to a powdered wig, to a crinoline or a corset. Fashion operates even in cases where nourishment is concerned. Advertisement may cause us to overestimate American flour. Every thing has in any case its own individual *curve of utility*, which shows what effect the successive consumption has upon the strength of my desire.

**11. Marginal and Total Utility.**—If a man possesses $n$ units, we term the $n$-th unit the *marginal unit* and its utility the *marginal utility*, $u_n$; the total of the utility of the said $n$ units—$(u_1 + u_2 + u_3 + \ldots u_n)$ written short $u_t$—is the *Total Utility*.

From the law of decreasing utility it appears that the utility derived from a certain quantity of goods depends upon, how much we have beforehand, and how far we are from complete satisfaction. If I have to part with some of my supply, my loss in utility on the same given quantity will depend upon how large the supply is. If I have to part with two units, the sacrifice of utility is greater if I am the owner of 6 than if I am the owner of 10 units.

The term *marginal utility* is really ambiguous, because I can speak of my last unit in my capacity of owner, seller or buyer. If I have 6 units, the 6th is my marginal unit as owner; if I must part with two of the six, the 5th will be the marginal unit of my sale, because I relinquish the 6th and the 5th; if, however, I must buy two more, my marginal unit will be the 8th (because I would then obtain the 7th and 8th unit). From this difference between what is my marginal unit in purchase and sale a Norwegian author Schönheider derives interest on loans. A man who has a daily income of six shillings will, by lending two shillings to-day, be lending his 5th and 6th, and consequently suffer a loss in utility because, by getting the money back to-morrow, he receives a 7th and 8th shilling (of less utility than the 5th and 6th).

Our community is, however, organised in such a manner that the seller is always a merchant who derives no direct utility from his goods, which for him are only *merchandise*, and that the buyer has himself produced nothing of the goods in question. The *seller* a merchant, has money ($m$) and therewith buys goods ($g$) for re-sale, and obtains for them money ($m$); the *buyer* produces services and obtains for these money ($m$) and therewith buys goods ($g$) for consumption, not for re-sale. We will therefore, in the following, pages deal with marginal utility as being only the utility of the last unit, the respective consumer can command *according to his income*.

The marginal utility decreases as the number of units of the goods owned by the individual increases, while the total utility increases: therefore *Marginal and Total Utility* vary in opposite directions. While $(u_1 + u_2) < (u_1 + u_2 + u_3)$, $u_2 > u_3 \ldots$

according to the rule of decreasing utility; this inverted proportion is the reason for what *Smithenner* has termed the demoniac in economics. Value has its origin in marginal utility; the *greater* the number of units the *greater* total utility, and the greater satisfaction, but also the *smaller* marginal utility and the smaller value. *Einarsen* calls this the paradox of value; that the maximum of total utility coincides with worthlessness, while value is determined by the higher marginal utility, which is conditional upon *scarcity*. General *Walker's* conception of progress is that marginal utility, and consequently value, becomes next to nothing, and he shows that this has been the case as far as many goods are concerned This is still the case on some South Sea Islands, where the population is not too crowded, and where land is not occupied and under private ownership; for, as we shall show later, private appropriation of land may also in communities, where land is plentiful, create a scarcity value for land and its produce. (Compare Proudhon's expression: "Autinomie de valeur").

It has become a matter for the subjective school of economics to show that value and human satisfaction do not follow the same lines, because the latter is determined by the total and the former by the marginal utility. The classical school has, like the practical business man, only considered value, and therefore assents to a social order where all efforts of those individuals, through whose hands the goods pass, tend to make the *goods valuable and humanity valueless*; and if it does happen now and again that labour attains high value, because there is an abundance of goods, it seems to be a world calamity, which "fortunately," is redressed by a crisis.

The formula $u_1 + u_2 + u_3 < 3 \cdot u_3$ means that the marginal utility is always less than the average total utility per unit.

If we have such abundance of a thing that the utility of the last unit for us is nil, we no longer desire to increase our stock; the marginal utility of the thing has reached its minimum and the total utility its maximum. We would only now continue to desire this thing, which has no direct, actual utility for us in itself, if by exchanging some of it we could obtain another desirable commodity (for instance, the stock in trade of a merchant).

Air is a clear example of the antagonism between total and marginal utility. We can obtain as much as we need without sacrifice; if we should desire still more, air would have to be exchangeable; we have no use for our superabundance ourselves; its direct utility is thus nil, and air cannot have utility for us as merchandise, as everybody else is in the same happy position of having sufficient of it. If air could be monopolised, it would be rare and *scarce* (Cassel), *i.e.*, its marginal utility would be positive for a larger number of the community; air would then be valuable and the monopoly would represent capital for its owner.

**12. Utility and Scarcity.**—In order to be the subject of exchange, a thing must thus have positive marginal utility for one or more of the community; but to have positive marginal utility it must be *useful* and be present in limited quantity—*i.e.*, be scarce. When *Walras* employs the expression "rarèté" where we employ utility, he is not wrong inasmuch as the *scarcity* and the marginal utility of a thing follow identical rules. By scarcity we understand the shortcoming of a thing compared with an absolute sufficiency. The first unit is scarcer than the second; the second again more scarce than the third. If we express the scarcity in a case where I own one unit, as $w_1$, two units, $w_2$ . . . . and $n$ units $w_n$, we arrive at $w_1 > w_2 > w_3 \ldots\ldots > w_n$.

The scarcity and *marginal value* of the supply—both relative conceptions—run concurrently, and both reach nil at the same time. The marginal utility of a stock of goods is thus a function of its usefulness and its scarcity; but scarcity is a relative, utility an absolute term. We can speak of total utility, but not of total scarcity. But this leads us no further, because we must then ask what determines the limit of scarcity? The reply is: The difficulty in producing the given quantity of the thing in proportion to the limit of demand. Marginal utility is thus associated through scarcity with the difficulty in producing the given quantity of goods.

In scarcity there is a subjective as well as an objective element; the latter depends upon the quantity absolutely in existence, the former on how much our demand amounts to.

Value being dependent upon scarcity (rarity) is in a way a sign of *poverty*—*i.e.*, a sign of difficulty in satisfying the demands of the public. In the sheep-rearing state of Wyoming the pre-war price of a sheep was a dollar. Land is of inconsiderable value, although it may be of fair quality. How poor that State is, measured by value, in comparison to that home of misery, New York, where scarcity of land has given square yards the value of thousands of dollars ! How much value might not be created if we were able to monopolise air ! Malthus may probably be right in his statement that a newly-born child will often be unable to produce what he needs for existence; but his existence will, at any rate, always create more *value* by raising the price of the existing supply of goods and means of production. Value is created by the disproportion between the demand and the supply available to cover it.

As utility without reference to the form and intrinsic qualities is an expression for our desire, every thing can, without regard to its own composition or form, have utility, and, presuming the *marginal utility is positive,* consequently be the subject of exchange.

Further, the thing—or the right to utilise it—must be *transferable* from one person to another, or, in any case, some means must be found to effect such a transfer ; for instance, the indulgence of the Pope can be exchanged for money with the letter of indulgence as vehicle, and the royal favour through the written patent of office.

Any thing the product of labour or service, material or non-material which can be transferred, or for which some means of transfer from one person to another can be found, and which has positive marginal utility for one or more members of the community, may then be the subject of sale or exchange.

The outer form of the thing is thus immaterial to the valuation, the deciding factor is our desire. Indulgences and honours may be the subject of exchange to the same extent as obligatory rights, and these again just as much as physically appropriable things, and consequently are dealt with in the theory of value. Non-material means of satisfaction follow the general economic rules, for instance, the rule of decreasing utility. A titled landowner would, for instance, not care for the office of parish councillor, which would be coveted by a farmer. Further, the distinction between productive and unproductive consumption is immaterial from our point of view. Production of goods is only unproductive if the products are not desired by anybody.

The distillation of spirits and the making of guns are productive, subject to these conditions. Somewhat different are teleological considerations ; into these there enters the social point of view, the profit or loss to society or, in the last resort, ruin to the individual (public welfare); but this does not come within the economic category and in our non-moral theory of value we are concerned only with such economic considerations.

Consequently all goods come under treatment in the theory of value in so far as they have any relation to value, but only in that relation. Free goods—*i.e.*, such as are desired but of which there is no scarcity, and which are not comparatively limited, because everybody can have enough, have no positive marginal utility for anybody and are therefore without value—*i.e.*, do not concern the theory of value. Things which besides being useful are also rare (comparatively limited)—*i.e.*, of which some people desire *more*, have value and are called economic goods. Their usefulness conditions their utility; the disinclination of nature or the world to supply them conditions their scarcity and determines *where* on the scale of utility we are to *stop* and settle their value.

Readers who are familiar with other theorists dealing with marginal value will have noticed that we here speak of marginal value in a sense somewhat different from the current, according to which marginal utility is the marginal utility of an *infinitely small addition* to a given supply of goods. This may be advantageous for some purposes and has been so in the past; but now, when this path of reasoning is well trodden, this abstract thought appears to be of little use, and even harmful by keeping back many students who are not familiar with the differential calculus.

The fact is that we *do not* exchange infinitely small quantities of goods, but tangible quantities; often there is also a difference between the *unit of division and the unit of exchange*. A loaf of bread may be divided into perhaps a hundred pieces, but in spite of this one cannot buy less than a half-pound. The unit of division for pins is one pin, but it is not possible to buy less than a dozen; one cannot buy less than a house; one does not rent less than a flat. The marginal utility, which determines the value will then neither be the utility of an infinitely small increase, nor the utility of the last *unit of division*, but that of the last *unit of exchange*. If, for instance, I buy pins, it would neither be the utility of a fraction of a pin, nor of the last of the pins I buy, but the combined utility of the last twelve pins, which would determine my subjective price. *Jevons*, who points out that Mill's theory of price suffers from exceptions, drops into the same pitfall himself, because he puts forth special rules for the sale of things which cannot be divided. This we avoid by regarding the marginal utility as being the combined utility of the units, one or several, which are comprised in the last *unit of exchange.*

**13. Our Wants.**—It is only in fairy tales that there exists a " general commodity " which, if touched with our wishing-wand, can be put to any use, and may thus satisfy *all* our wants ; the varying human wants must in the real world be satisfied by the consumption of hundreds of different goods.

We may divide our wants into the *primitive,* as, for instance, the demands for food, drink, warmth and air—created by our hunger, thirst, cold, or need to breathe—and the *developed.* While the first are *absolute,* the developed wants are *relative.* To these latter belong wants of a cultural nature—our ear demands harmonies of sound, our eye compositions of colours—our demand for music, art and literature ; and as the highest our desire to understand the link of cause and effect of scientific phenomena. While absolute wants will always be *physical* and determined by our *own nature,* relative wants will not infrequently be *non-material* and *socially determined.*

A number of wants are social—*i.e.,* not created by the nature of the individual, but arising from the intercourse of the individual with others. The human social nature demands power and authority or, for want of better, of *symbols* of esteem and power, the makeshift of the fool, the insignia of power : decorations, titles, pearls, and other shams desired in " Vanity Fair." These desires for the "fool's tool" are more fictitious than real ; we have here the peculiarity that our want and, consequently, the utility of the things may be dependent on conditions, which have nothing to do with the thing itself or our state of mind.

In itself a faked and a genuine pearl may satisfy our desire for beauty to the same extent but nevertheless we do not attribute the same utility to them. The utility of pearls, as is the case with *all* means of social distinction, is dependent upon their scarcity. While a surplus of bread would only alter the marginal utility which determines the value, but leave the total utility unaltered or even increase it, a surplus of pearls would not only alter their marginal utility, but also *detract from* their total utility, because pearls create desire conditional upon their giving social distinction. The power of bread to satisfy is an inherent quality in bread; on the contrary, this is not the case with the power of pearls to satisfy vanity. If pearls were as numerous as pebbles *only few* would adorn themselves with them; bread we must eat, even if it costs nothing.

In another sense we say that part of our wants are socially determined, or rather are determined, by the social *class* to which we belong. An examination of our own consumption will reveal that our requirements as to housing and clothing are practically determined according to our class in the sense that one loses caste if the social claims are not complied with. However small a loss the individual would feel by relinquishing socially imposed requirements, the minority only have the courage to do so.

The wants of the poor are primitive, urgent, limited, uniform, physical and quantitative, while those of the rich are developed, weak, varying, unlimited, qualitative and of more mental nature. The primitive necessities of the rich are combined with developed requirements; their food must satisfy palate as well as appease hunger. It is, however, not quite correct to associate developed requirements with culture; where these requirements are only sensual, little mental development is needed. Clothes, good food and articles of splendour are more to the upstart than to the sage.

By the expression *collective want* we understand a necessity which does not exist for the individual, but only for individuals who co-operate as a community; as, for instance, the demand for a King, Military Establishments, National Honour. We have other wants, which originally were individual, but because they are common to everybody may be satisfied jointly; the *mutual* wants, for instance, for high roads. The want of the individual is not strong enough to compel him to undertake the work of constructing the road; added together the individual wants become strong enough to conquer the difficulties; the mutual requirement in this way assumes the character of a collective want.

We have contended that the wish of maximum satisfaction is the leading motive in all our economic actions. Against this it has been said: It is an egoistic point of view, which fortunately does not hold good; the human being is willing to sacrifice something for moral reasons. Even so the rule is correct: If a man without the prospect of compensation in this life makes a gift to the public, he certainly attributes some satisfaction to his act, and, consequently, gains some "*utility*." He has perhaps a strong feeling of social justice, which does not leave him in peace, or he wishes to atone for some wrong. When *Tetzel* went through Europe with the "Klingbeutel" selling indulgence to repenting sinners, he was not far from doing the right thing; a man's repentance may, to a certain extent, be measured by his willingness to make a sacrifice.

Just as satisfied ambition is for many a generous reward for sacrifice, there is no doubt that a satisfied conscience is likewise a generous reward. In practice, even as an altruist, one acts on the rule of maximum satisfaction. In conferring a benefit the donor, not the receiver, is the gainer.

Often one want carries another with it; salt food creates thirst. There is no want which has so many consequences as that for a large house; if a reduction in the budget is necessary the start should be made by having a room less; the rest will adjust itself in due course. Otherwise our demands are connected according to our requirement, at one time for *harmony*, at another for *variation*.

The existence of our wants brings forth the goods which satisfy the wants. It does happen, however, that new goods appear, and that the demand first arises afterwards (the gifts of the new world—Tobacco and Potatoes). Wants are often for a certain article, but they are so frequently vague that the same want may in whole or in part be satisfied by another article, which is *substituted* for one previously used.

In quality there will always be some difference between goods, which may substitute one another in consumption. Advertisement creates demand to a great extent. Through it not only new goods for old wants are brought to our notice, but also quite new wants. A well advertised and well-established brand of goods may not only stand for a comprehension of certain qualities in an article, but also for the demand of a multitude of customers, created or adapted as a result of successive influences.

The demands of the individual become a habit until he arrives at a schedule of demands, which is the expression for the standard of living of a class, slightly adapted according to the characteristics of the individual in question. We have then not only a *scale of utility* showing the decreasing utility of the various units, but also a *scale of wants* which ranges from the more necessary to the less necessary goods. Supposing my demand comprises three things, A, B and C ; let these have the following schedule of utility:

| A | B | C |
|---|---|---|
| UNITS. | UNITS. | UNITS. |
| 100 | 61 | 53 |
| 80 | 55 | 42 |
| 60 | 50 | 30 |
| 40 | 45 | 20 |
| etc. | etc. | etc. |

According to the rule of maximum satisfaction, I would start my selection with the first unit of A ($A_1$= 100 units of utility—UU), next $A_2$ (80 UU), then $B_1$ (61 UU), then $A_3$ (60 UU), then $B_2$ (55 UU), then $C_1$ (53 UU), then $B_3$ 50 UU), etc., which means that in our consumption we move like a bee, now from one unit to another, now from one kind of goods to another, seeking the maximum satisfaction, now intensively down the schedule of utility for the same thing, now extensively from commodity to commodity along the schedule of demands, starting with the most *urgent* demand.

The first unit of the most necessary commodity, for instance, bread, has a very great utility. *Hobson*, however, warns us against over-estimating this factor, for even if it is correct that in the desert a loaf or a drink of water may mean life, and its utility accordingly be next to infinite, because all the possibilites of life and all the tortures of hunger depend on that piece of bread, normally existence is not at stake ; normally the first piece of bread means only an enjoyment, which may be postponed.

In addition our wants often overlap ; the demand for food is actually distributed over a number of things and it would be absurd to say that the first piece of bread and the first potato each have an infinite utility. In a case where it is a matter of satisfying hunger and I have eaten my first piece of bread, the first potato is not met with hunger, but only by a partly satisfied desire, and corresponds thus to the second potato, if potatoes had been the only nourishment available. This may be expressed in another way : certain goods are valued, not so much according to their positive utility, but more according to the loss their non-existence would cause us. But this loss, which we suffer through not having a piece of bread, is different if we have other vegetable food, from what it would be if we had not. But regarding this a standard work, *Psychologie Economique* (*Tarde*), has been written, to which a good many additions might even be made.

# CHAPTER III

## Direct and Indirect Utility

**14. Utility is Conditional.**—We have up till now presumed that utility was unqualified, simple, immediate, direct, presently evident and certain. It may be the opposite. Our desire is, in a way, always conditional in as much as it is presumed that the thing desired is actually useful. If this presumption fails—as, for instance, if a child reaches for the wax apple believing it to be eatable—the desire, and, with it the utility, disappears. Most articles of social distinction, for instance, articles of fashion, have their utility wholly or partly conditioned by their value and not *vice versa* ; if a man at present wants a fine cigar-case it must be of platinum and not of gold. Platinum does not appeal to our sense of beauty, but to our desire to boast, because platinum was difficult to obtain during the war. It is a well-known publisher's experience that it is easier to clear a fancy-edition of, say, 100 copies at £10 each than 800 at £1.

The usefulness of a good deteriorates and is finally destroyed by use. The period of use may be of *short* duration, as with food, or *lasting*, as with clothes and furniture. By lasting use the thing in question yields utility distributed over a period of longer duration. A coat, which would normally last a year, means a warming utility to be employed in 365 successive acts of consumption ; if the coat has been bought second-hand it may only represent utility for 150 days.

By owning a thing I secure the command of all the utility it is able to yield as long as it is at all useful; by hiring it I secure the utility, which it yields during the period of hire, but no longer. If a coat will last a year I am said to buy it if I acquire its utility for 365 days; but if I acquire its utility for a week only, I am said to hire the coat for this period. The difference between purchase and hire is therefore actually only a *period of use*. The utility of a lasting article of direct consumption is thus a composite of the uniform utility of successive periods of time.

But the utility of the thing may be composite, otherwise than in respect of time, as, for instance, when a lady's gown at the same time yields warmth, adorns and satisfies the demands of decency.

The utility of the thing is here a sum total of three different, but simultaneous utility effects, and each of these may have its own rate of decrease.

If a thing has *several* utility effects, but such that they are *alternative*, we must ask which of the various utilities of use we must attribute to it, and which of these determines the price of demand. According to the rule of maximum satisfaction obviously the largest possible! Let us take a well-known example: The farmer's three sacks of corn, of which the first sack yields him all the bread he desires, the second gin, while the third enables him to keep peafowls and turkeys. As he is enabled by his first two sacks to satisfy his desire for bread and gin, it is obviously not the bread he deprives himself of, as little as the gin, if he has to part with one of the three sacks, but the pleasure of keeping the rare poultry. The marginal utility of the three sacks of corn is therefore the utility he derives from the poultry.

If a thing may be employed in several ways we therefore distribute a given quantity of it over the various uses in such a way that we derive the same marginal utility from each use—*i.e.*, reduce the commodity to the *point of indifference*, the limit, at which every subsequent employment in each of the various uses would yield less utility than the distribution of uses chosen. But that also is the rule for the utility of money: The wealthy man who can buy food and clothes as well as precious stones will have the marginal utility of his income determined by the small utility of the precious stones (because " as well as " means that the smallest utility determines the marginal utility); while the poor man, who can only buy the necessary food, has the marginal utility of his money determined by the very great utility of food-stuffs (because " either-or " means that the greatest utility determines the marginal utility).

**15. Indirect Utility.**—A thing, the utility of which is small, may have its utility increased *when* it can be exchanged with the first units of another thing which we desire, but are not in possession of. In this case I have found that my commodity, even if it yields me only a slight satisfaction, supplies a short cut to another, and I consequently attribute to my less desired thing the utility of the more desired, and will now produce more units of it, even if their original utility was not previously great enough to overcome the marginal disutility of labour. In as far as we discover by the accidental exchange that the thing we produce has a great *indirect* utility, we are tempted to apply ourselves to the production of the article in question, which is produced comparatively easily. Exchange is therefore an essential for division of labour. Not until farmers discovered that ready-made garments could be bought for 30s. did they cease to weave and sew.

The existence of indirect utility increases the total utility of a given quantity of goods and increases its marginal utility. Its effect is the same, as if the same article had got *a greater number* of possibilities of use than before, and the curve of demand is consequently flattened. Indirect utility is always qualified—*i.e.*, can I really, by means of the thing, to which I attribute indirect utility, obtain the article, which has direct utility for me ?

A stock in trade has no direct utility for the merchant. Of a stock of 1,000 coats he only wants a few himself, the remainder he values according to the price he can obtain for them. He anticipates a market price and attributes to the separate parts of his stock the utility of this amount of money. His motive to trade is the same as my motive to work : to gain a daily wage, the marginal utility of his income determining the absolute minimum of his demand. But if the expected market price always fails the stock in trade will revert to its direct utility, which must be nil or negative, because no merchant can use a stock in trade himself *e.g.* the devaluation of food-substitutes when the war was over.

If I cannot obtain the article of direct consumption (consumer's good) I desire, nor acquire it by exchange, I should be willing to accept a raw material or semi-manufactured article, in as far as, by applying my labour to it, I may turn it into an article of direct consumption. Many such consumer's goods, meat, fish, etc., I really do not buy in a state ready for consumption, as my household is presumed to make it eatable by preparation. Habit, however, has caused us to disregard the disutility of conversion, and maintain that anything which is bought for the household has direct and not indirect utility. It is, however, a characteristic sign of our time that households buy all their goods in a state nearly ready for consumption. We no longer buy wool, spin and weave it and make clothes from it, but we buy the garments ready-made. City people do not kill a bull nowadays, but buy steak roasted and in tins, and all the preparation consists in warming. This has also had the result that a household does not need so many servants and, where the number of children is small, does not give the wife opportunity for employing her day productively. It also makes it necessary for the husband to have a larger income now if he has to maintain the same standard of living as 50 years ago; (this is the reason for the insufficiency of the salaries of officials, even if the level of prices had remained unchanged).

If a woman buys cloth for the purpose of making her gown herself, the utility of the cloth is conditional upon a gown being actually made of it—*i.e.*, the raw material derives utility from the finished article.

The sacrifice I must submit to in order to obtain a gown is greater than the sacrifice I would make to obtain the cloth. The latter entails my taking the trouble to transform it and make a gown of it. The net utility of the raw material is therefore the utility of the finished article less the disutility of labour entailed in making the raw material into an article of direct consumption.

The same applies to auxiliary goods as, for instance, coal and oil.

I am also willing to make a sacrifice in order to make another man work for me—*i.e.*, I attribute to the work of the other man a utility equal to the thing produced by him, if the raw material costs nothing. If I have also to pay for the raw material, I must apportion the utility of the finished article between the labour and the raw material. If the sacrifice to be made in return for one factor is known, the utility of the second is equal to the utility of the finished article less the sacrifice required in order to obtain the first factor.

If we do not know the effective utility of the separate factors, because technically they must co-operate in production, as, for instance, an article consisting of several raw materials, or if labour as well as raw material is essential for the production of an article, the case is the same as if we were to examine which has the greater utility, the upper or the lower blade of the scissors. If we have the upper blade and want the lower one, our desire for this is the same as for the complete pair of scissors. To the factor of which we have least in proportion to the other factors we are inclined to apportion the greatest utility. If I have an excellent gun and bullets, but want gunpowder, the gunpowder has for me the same utility as the roebuck I am aiming at.

This question becomes of practical interest inthe theory of prices proper, when we come to determine the price of raw material and labour (goods in complementary relation) by the process of "*imputation.*"

A complementary article—*i.e.*, one which is demanded together with another, as is the case with most raw materials, has as its maximum value the value of the finished article, if all other factors cost nothing; its minimum value must in the long run be estimated according to the trouble in producing the raw material in question in the given quantity; but where to fix the price of demand for a raw material, which is to be employed together with other raw materials or machinery—somewhere between minimum and maximum—cannot be answered before we come to deal with the process of imputation. As the finished article has a decreasing utility and the production of the raw material entails an increasing sacrifice, it is apparent that we also attribute a decreasing (indirect) utility to the amount of labour we purchase by hiring the working power of a man.

The other producer of energy, the *machine*, performs the labour of one or more men, which it *saves* us. To begin with the gross utility of the machine will be equal to the disutility of the amount of labour saved, from which we must deduct the disutility of producing the machine in order to arrive at its net utility. This comparison will, however, often fail—*i.e.*, in cases where the work could not be done at all without the help of the machine; a giant crane, for instance, cannot very well be estimated from the point of view of how many labourers it may replace; we must then be content with the purely technical estimate of its capacity expressed in foot-pounds. An ocean liner cannot be compared to the number of rowing boats required to carry the same freight. We must in such cases compare the utility of the machine with the utility of the goods produced by it. It will only be as an exception—*e.g.*, when *a new machine is introduced*, that the utility of a machine is valued according to the labour saved.

A thing may thus have both direct and indirect utility; the larger of the two will then "cover" the lesser. Philosophy has a similar distinction between intrinsic and effective value, the latter attributed to a thing, not for what it is in itself, but for its effect and the attending circumstances.

**16. Covered Utility.**—The same want may be satisfied by more than one thing; the utility of one thing is then said to cover or overlap that of the other. If I have smoked three pipes, a cigar does not yield me the utility of the first cigar, but of the fourth pipe, presuming that I care equally for each of them. Very few goods will be congruent in their utility-effect, for one thing will have merits preferable to those of another. The most simple case is that of difference in quality, as, for instance, first and second grade margarine; but it is complicated if there is a difference in the nature of the two goods, as between butter and margarine. In most cases it is only in case of need that we discover that a certain article may satisfy a want which has been habitually satisfied by means of another. The Siege of Paris revealed the utility of rat flesh as a food. Some tribes do not know the utility of pork. Habit and prejudice make the diet of the Chinaman abominable to the European. At present mushrooms are in vogue as food.

Sometimes we know the thing which may be used as a substitute in consumption but only make use of it as an exception; such goods are called *substitutes.* If there is no pronounced difference in the effort of producing the two goods, the utility of the substitute is "covered." A great difference in the difficulty of production may cause the principal article to disappear altogether, at times for the entire population, at other times only for some classes. The twentieth century is the era of substitutes; compare only what was eaten of a pig a generation ago, and how every part of the animal is now utilised. There are classes whose only meat is that which used to be thrown away (minced liver and lights, tripe and onions). If we knew the secrets of manufacture we should be surprised.

Utility is often composed of several elements; the first object of a gown is to yield warmth and decency, but there are gowns which furthermore satisfy taste and vanity. The first two are essentials and the utility of the two latter is small in comparison.

Suppose margarine, which satisfies the demand for something to spread on bread, to have a utility schedule as in the first column below, and the additional utility beyond that of margarine yielded by butter because of its taste to be expressed by the figures in the second column:—

100 + 20
70 + 18
60 + 16
40 + 15
30 + 14
15 + 13
10 + 14

The first unit of margarine has a utility of 100, while that of butter would have 120; the second unit, 70, while that of the second unit of butter would be 88. If I have eaten a unit of margarine, and afterwards wish to eat a unit of butter, the utility will be 100 for the margarine and 70 + 20 for the butter, because the butter as far as the demand for fat is concerned is the second unit, but with regard to taste the first.

As for the principal and secondary curves, the former will be steep, while the latter will be flat, because the addition is a less substantial luxury demand, while the principal curve stands for coarse substantial utility.

**17. Deferred Utility.**—If we felt the want of the present only, and acted on the principal that "sufficient unto the day is the evil thereof," the utility of the different goods would soon be exhausted, and the limit of possible consumption be reached after the enjoyment of only a few units.

We might desire plenty of variety, but we cannot consume more than a limited quantity of food in one day, etc.

Human beings have, however, the faculty of being able to anticipat the sufferings of the future. The more quasi-civilised a community is the more developed is this faculty, and the stronger consequently the thrift of man. If we have satisfied the hunger of to-day our thoughts turn to the hunger of to-morrow. All of us anticipate our future wants, some of us only slightly, as in the case of the spendthrift, others, as in the case of the miser, with frightful vividness. In this we do not take into consideration that, in the desire to save, the pathological element, the collecting mania also plays a part.

Our anticipation of the want of the future entails that goods, which are to be used in the future only, attain actual utility. We are however, unable to imagine the needs of the future as intensely as we feel those of the present. By projecting the utility and disutility of the future to the level of the present, it seems smaller to us than it really proves to be on the day of enjoyment or sacrifice. In other words, we view the future in foreshortened perspective.

Suppose $f$ to be the discount on the future article, so that an article which to-morrow will yield an actual utility of $u$, seems to-day to have only an utility of $u(1 - f)$; we will not, then, if we must obtain a thing which is not to be employed until to-morrow, compare $u$ with the sacrifice involved to get it, but with the discounted utility $u(1 - f)$. If the thing is not to be employed till the day after to-morrow, the deduction will be a larger one, for instance, $u(1 - f_2)$, etc. The utility discount is not very regular; some will think of the near future with much vividness, but, on the other hand, not look at all to six months into the future; others will save for a whole year with the same zeal as for one month. Our curious faculty of abstract thought makes us attempt to save beyond our own, and even beyond our children's possible consumption.

For goods, the consumption of which lasts for some time, there is a future element. A coat represents its use to-day, plus its use to-morrow, plus its use the day after to-morrow, etc. These acts of use are not equally vivid in our imagination and for this reason we will not attribute to a coat, which may be used for two years, double the utility of one, which only lasts a season, quite apart from the variation, which gives the short period goods preference over those of long duration. It is not only frivolous superficial individuals who prefer cut to durability.

Let us suppose that we have to-day a schedule of demand for a commodity as in the first column in the table below. Because of the discount on the future the utility schedule of our presumable demand for the second day will correspond to the second column; similarly with that of the third and fourth day:—

| | 1ST DAY. | 2ND DAY | 3RD DAY. | 4TH DAY. |
|---|---|---|---|---|
| 1st unit ... ... | 100 | 80 | 66 | 50 |
| 2 units ... ... | 81 | 65 | 42 | 30 |
| 3 ,, ... ... | 60 | 45 | 21 | — |
| 4 ,, ... ... | 40 | 20 | — | — |
| 5 ,, ... ... | 19 | 15 | — | — |

If I did not think of the future, I would, for instance, procure 4 units of the commodity with a marginal utility of 40, presuming that the minimal utility of the 5th unit (19) *does not* exceed the marginal disutility of labour. With the future in mind, and acting on the rule of maximum satisfaction I discover that the 3rd unit to-day yields me a utility of 60, but saved for to-morrow a utility of 80. I now arrive at another utility schedule for the commodity:—

| | | | | |
|---|---|---|---|---|
| 100 | (1st | day's | 1st | unit) |
| 81 | ( ,, | ,, | 2nd | ,, ) |
| 80 | (2nd | ,, | 1st | ,, ) |
| 66 | (3rd | ,, | 1st | ,, ) |
| 65 | (2nd | ,, | 2nd | ,, ) |
| 60 | (1st | ,, | 3rd | ,, ) |
| 50 | (4th | ,, | 1st | ,, ) |
| 45 | (2nd | ,, | 3rd | ,, ) |
| 42 | (3rd | ,, | 2nd | ,, ) |
| 40 | (1st | ,, | 4th | ,, ), and so on. |

The 5th unit, which previously had a utility of 19, has now, when saved for the next day, a utility of 65. The curve of utility, which has been supposed to be comparatively steep, becomes flatter and the marginal utility for the same quantity higher.

We are consequently willing to submit to the greater disutility of longer working hours, if we think of the future, than if we think of the present only. People with highly developed thrift are shocked at the lazzaroni of Naples and the negro of Haiti, because they do not care a pin for to-morrow.

We distribute our supply in such a way that the average marginal utility for every day at the moment seems to us to be equal. The marginal utility of income will also be larger for the thrifty, for whom a sovereign is the rent of the next week, than for the spendthrift, for whom it yields a merry night.

If I must produce a unit of goods with a disutility-sacrifice of 60, I would not produce the 4th unit if I forgot to think of to-morrow. If, however, I do produce it, the first unit of the next day will yield me a utility of 80 ; in other words, I reap the benefit of my saving in the form of the additional utility of the article to-morrow. This does not agree with the general doctrine, that the future utility of a thing is less than that of the present. The fact is, however, that I save a later unit in the series to-day in order to have an earlier unit to-morrow, the utility of which is great enough to bear the discount. In so far as a fixed period of time, and a definite supply or capital are concerned, a profit in the form of interest need not exist as an incentive to saving. We may also express this in another way : by saving I exchange a present thing for a future one ; where the latter is an earlier unit than the former, its utility will often be greater ; where the present thing is the same or an earlier unit, the subjective value of the future article will always be lower. In any case I reduce the utility of the future unit by a discount if we start with the present, but which proves to be a premium when the present has become the past.

If by postponing my consumption, I store a thing, I run the risks firstly of not living to see the future, and then of its deteriorating. The same risk is involved if I undertake to produce a thing ; in all production there is a possibility of failure and a probability that a certain proportion will come to nothing. Suppose the probability of obtaining a thing is only 50 per cent., I will then reduce my estimate of the utility of the thing desired to one half—and, consequently, only sacrifice half as much disutility of labour to obtain it—or, if the labour is known, I must have an addition in utility to balance the reduction in utility which is made on account of the risk. The utility of raw materials and implements must therefore be found, first by deducting the disutility of conversion, next by taking the element of the future into consideration (it takes time before the raw material becomes a finished article and the implement is worn out and earned), and finally, by recognising that both the process of production and the future itself are attended by elements of risk.

From this chapter it will appear that I attribute utility, not only to goods the enjoyment of which is in the present, but also to those the enjoyment of which is in the future, not only to such the enjoyment of which are secured for me, but also to those in which there is a possibility that I may be disappointed, not only to goods I may consume, but also to goods which by some process may be ready for consumption, or simply exchanged for consumer's goods. While the enjoyment of consumers' goods, of which I make immediate use, is certain, on account of my present want, the utility of goods, the enjoyment of which is future, indirect, conditional or uncertain must be reduced (discounted). But if I attribute to a thing even a reduced utility, I am also willing to make a sacrifice in order to obtain it—*i.e.*, goods the enjoyment of which is future, conditional, indirect, etc., may also have a subjective price as well as consumers' goods, the utility of which is unconditional and present. Such goods, if they come within the rule of scarcity, may also become economic goods and the subject of trade—*i.e.*, come within the scope of the theory of value. But through this we arrive at the fact that I also attribute utility and value to mere promises or letters of title to obtain in the future a number of goods, by estimating the title to be equal to the utility of those quantities of goods, which are successively promised me, reduced in consideration of their futurity and uncertainty. Consequently, the value of such titles and privileges also comes within the scope of our investigations.

# CHAPTER IV

## UTILITY EQUATIONS

**18. The Utility Fraction.**—In our economic actions we have the choice put before us between the greater and the lesser evil, either to do without a desired article of direct consumption or submit to the sacrifice which is necessary to acquire it. This sacrifice may, in the case of *exchange*, be a thing, which we must *renounce*, or, in the case of *production*, the *trouble* involved in producing the article required. Presuming the raw material to be free, the sacrifice will be the energy of the labour performed, expressed in normal working hours. This energy of labour is the *objective expression for the technical cost. The technical cost* is, therefore, the objective resistance, which the world makes against yielding me the thing desired. The word objective implies that this resistance is something which is not dependent on my will, but upon circumstances. If the technical cost is the labour, this as has been previously shown, has also a subjective measurement in the disutility of labour.

In production I therefore discover, by comparison between the utility of the thing and the disutility of the labour required, whether I am acting according to the rule of maximum satisfaction by producing a given quantity.

If we call the utility of the thing desired $u_d$ and the disutility of the sacrifice $u_s$ (whether this is disutility of the labour or utility of the compensatory thing) we must compare $u_d$ and $u_s$ in order to be able to make our choice in such a manner that it yields us the smallest disutility or the greatest surplus of utility. In comparing $u_d$ and $u_s$ we arrive at a fraction $\frac{u_d}{u_s}$, the numerator of which is the utility of the thing desired, and the denominator the utility of the compensatory thing sacrificed (or if we manufacture it ourselves, the disutility of the labour involved).

If $u_d > u_s$ we are willing to submit to the sacrifice in order to obtain the thing desired, because we then gain in utility; if $u_d < u_s$, *i.e.*, the utility fraction is $< 1$, we prefer to do without our fancy and "keep our oranges."

The point of equilibrium is where the utility fraction is $= 1$, when $u_d = u_s$, *i.e.*, the utility of the thing desired and the disutility of the sacrifice are equal.

If our " economic man " must himself produce everything he requires, he will, according to the rule of maximum satisfaction, produce the goods which yield him the greatest utility for a given sacrifice, striving towards the greatest net utility. He is willing to work if only $u_d$ is a trifle greater than $u_s$ ; but he prefers, of course, that $u_d$ is 100 times as great as $u_s$.

If the disutility of the sacrifice is equally great for several goods, he will choose that, which yields the greatest utility for the smallest disutility. If both the disutility of the sacrifice and the utility are different for the various goods, he will choose the one whose utility-fraction is the largest—*i.e.*, the utility of the thing chosen must be at least as much greater than the utility of any other thing, as the disutility in producing the former is greater than the disutility in producing (or acquiring) the latter.

It is, therefore, the man's desire which decides how great a sacrifice he will submit to. The goods may have equally great utility, without regard to the greatness of the sacrifice (for instance, a non-*reproducable* thing) and a thing may be acquired by a very great sacrifice without yielding any utility (a crinoline when the fashion has changed). It is *not the amount of the sacrifice* ; it is the *strength of the desire* which is the governing *principle* in the formation of value. Goods have not utility and consequently value because work is " crystallised " in them, but we are willing to apply labour to them *because* they yield us utility. *Consumption* is the final object and, consequently, the *motive* of our economic actions, production only the *means*. This seems so obvious that only the fact that *Stuart Mill's* theory of the cost of production (for the old school of economics) and *Adam Smith's* theory of labour as the basis of value (for the Marxists) have become dogmas, justifies us in emphasising the fact that labour is only of secondary importance for the creation of value.

We may produce, directly or indirectly—*i.e.*, by producing a compensatory article, which is of no importance to us and exchange it for the thing desired ; this we do if first, the utility of the directly desired thing is greater than the disutility of the labour, and secondly, the disutility of that labour is less than the disutility involved in directly producing the thing desired.

**19. Utility and Disutility.**—Whether we desire a great or a small number of units of a certain thing, the disutility of labour in producing each unit must be less than the utility yielded by the unit in question. But the *utility of goods is decreasing and the disutility of labour increasing*; therefore there must be for any thing, the production of which entails labour, a point where the disutility of producing one more unit is greater than the utility of that unit.

Suppose an article of direct consumption to have the following schedule of utility, and that I have to produce it myself :—

| | | | | | |
|---|---|---|---|---|---|
| The 1st | unit of the article A | yields a utility of | | 64 | units (UU) |
| 2nd | ,, | ,, | ,, | 51 | ,, |
| 3rd | ,, | ,, | ,, | 41 | ,, |
| 4th | ,, | ,, | ,, | 33 | ,, |
| 5th | ,, | ,, | ,, | 26 | ,, |
| 6th | ,, | ,, | ,, | 21 | ,, |

Suppose further that my schedule of disutility for 1 hour's energy to be the following (we presume that the work proceeds at the same rate right through) :—

| | | | | | |
|---|---|---|---|---|---|
| The 1st | hour's work | entails a | disutility of | 4 | units. |
| 2nd | ,, | ,, | ,, | 8 | ,, |
| 3rd | ,, | ,, | ,, | 16 | ,, |
| 4th | ,, | ,, | ,, | 32 | ,, |
| 5th | ,, | ,, | ,, | 64 | ,, |
| 6th | ,, | ,, | ,, | 128 | ,, |

If, now, every unit of the article demands one hour's work, I will in my first hour's work (which causes a disutility of 4 units) produce the first unit of the article, the utility of which is 64; consequently I gain utility on the first unit.

The second unit of the article yields a utility of 51 units, while the labour of the second hour entails a disutility of 8 units. The third unit yields a utility of 41 units to be procured by the work of the third hour, the disutility of which is 16. For the fourth unit the utility (33 units) will still be greater than the disutility involved in the production (32 units). On the contrary, I will not profit by producing the fifth unit, because in this case a utility of 26 units is attended by a disutility of 64 units. In other words, I must stop when I have produced 4 units in order not to lose utility.

This may be stated as follows :—

$$\frac{33}{32} > 1 > \frac{26}{64}$$

in which the numerators represent the utility of the 4th and 5th units and the denominators the disutility entailed by the 4th and 5th working hours.

This fact is shown graphically in Diagram V, by taking the curve from Diagram II. and placing it on top of Diagram III. The line *s n* is the marginal utility = the marginal disutility of the labour, the curves intersecting at *s*; the line *o n* represents the number of units produced, in this case 4. As shown in the instance above the length of *o n* will not be exactly 4 units, but a trifle more; as, however, we cannot produce less than 1 unit, I must be content with the production of 4 units.

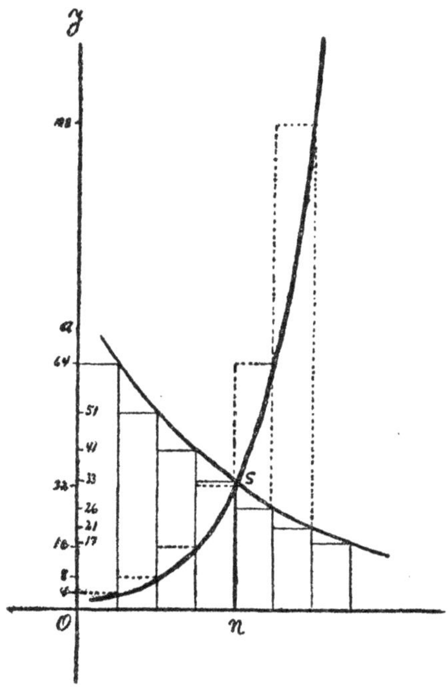
Diagram V

By a sacrifice of 4 working hours I have thus procured 4 units of the article Its marginal utility is therefore 33; the marginal disutility of the labour 32.

If I had been content with one unit less of the article, I would have saved one working hour (the fourth). From this it is seen that the utility of the last unit of the article must be, if only a trifle, greater than the disutility of the last working hour.

If the work required for each unit of the good had been two hours I would, by doing without the last unit of it, have spared myself for the last two working hours. Consequently this condition must hold good: the utility of the last unit of the article must be greater than the combined disutility of the two last working hours, and the utility of a further unit of the article be less than the combined disutility of two additional working hours (the unit of exchange is in this case not one but two hours).

If in my working day, I, produce different goods, the same rule applies to all of them, that each one of them is produced down to the *point of indifference*, where the utility of the last unit of a thing is equal to the combined disutility of so many of the *last working hours of the day as would have been saved by doing without the last unit of the thing in question*, and also that the disutility in increasing the working time would have been greater than the utility of the quantity of goods manufactured in the additional time. If this did not hold good, there would have been a gain by continuing. The same applies if the making of a piece of furniture has required a whole working day ; the utility of the piece of furniture must be greater than, or in any case equal to, the total disutility of the *whole day* (the working day and not the single hour in this case being the unit of exchange).

If, during 10 successive hours, I produce 3 units of the Article A, which each require 2 hours of work, and 4 units of the Article B, which require 1 hour's work each, the 3rd unit of A must have a utility greater than (or equal to) the combined disutility of the 9th and 10th hour, while the 4th unit must yield a utility which is less than the combined disutility of the 11th and 12th hour. Similarly the 4th unit of B must yield a utility greater than the disutility of the 10th working hour, and the 5th unit of B yield a utility which is less than the disutility of the 11th working hour. All goods are produced down to the point of indifference, where in proportion to the labour applied we gain the same utility from the last unit.

Expressed in algebraic symbols our economic man will, in producing $n$ units of the thing D, have the following conditions of work, presuming that the length of the day he works for is $t$ hours (even if they are utilised in various ways :—

$$u_n = u_l \cdot q^t,$$

in which $u_n$ represents the utility of the $n$-th unit and $u_l \cdot q^t$ the disutility entailed by the $t$-th working hour, presuming that each unit of the thing only requires one hour's work ; if two hours had been required the denominators of the utility-fractions would have represented respectively the disutility of the last two working hours.

This formula again states that the *marginal utility of any thing* produced during the day must be greater than or equal to the *marginal disutility of the relative labour*, and also that the utility of a subsequent unit must be less than the disutility of increasing the period of labour.

It will be seen from our example that while the utility of the marginal unit and the disutility of the marginal working hour are equal, the other "production-pairs" (a unit of the thing compared with the working hour required for its production) yield a surplus of utility ; the surplus of the 1st unit is $64 - 4 = 60$. The total utility of the 4 units is $64 + 51 + 41 + 33 = 189$, the disutility of the sacrifice $4 + 8 + 16 + 32 = 60$; the surplus 129.

In Diagram V. the total utility is shown by the area *o-a-s-n*, the total disutility by *o-s-n* and the surplus of utility by *o-a-s*. This surplus is an expression for the value of life and it is this surplus which, however miserable life may seem, in the last instance makes life worth living, if nothing more.

**20. The Subjective Ratio of Exchange.**—If I have a stock of goods I may, instead of consuming it, give it in exchange for a stock of another thing, and I do not then need to procure *this other commodity* by work. In this case I simply substitute for the disutility of labour in the utility fraction the utility of that quantity which I give away, and which therefore is the disutility of my sacrifice. Where no organized trade exists, there would be no *option* of buying a greater or smaller number of units; the subject of the transaction is a collective quantity of goods, which must be bought as a whole or not bought. I am willing to make the exchange as long as $u_d > u_s$; at the point, where it makes no difference to me whether the exchange is effected or not, the *subjective ratio of exchange* is formed, by which I decide what is the most I am willing to give and the least I am willing to accept This subjective exchange equation, $d$ of D $= s$ of S is, however, very much qualified: ($a$) the utility-fraction must for me $= 1$; ($b$) I must only exchange once in the proportion $\frac{d}{s}$ not twice, because if I exchange more than once the following units of D the thing desired will have less utility than the first $d$ units I receive, while the next $s$ units of S, the thing sacrificed, will yield me a greater utility than the $s$ units first sacrificed (as the sacrifice brings me nearer to the strictly necessary quantity, the utility of which is very great, while the contrary is the case with the desired thing); (*c*) I must be seller of S and buyer of D.

But by exchange we are, as a rule, free to choose whether we will buy a greater or smaller quantity. For this reason it will not be the total utility of the quantities exchanged of the two goods, which we substitute in the utility-fraction, but the utility of the last units, which are exchanged, that is the marginal utility of D and S respectively.

Let two goods, D and S, have the following schedule of utility. I own 5 units of S, and desire to obtain from the possessor of D some units of D, which can only be got by barter. Let one unit of S be exchanged for one of D.

| D | S |
|---|---|
| 18 | 20 |
| 15 | 18 |
| 12 | 16 |
| 11 | 14 |
| 10 | 10 |

First of all, I shall sacrifice my 5th unit of S (10 UU) and obtain for this the first unit of D (18 UU). The 2nd unit of D (15 UU) $>$ the 4th of S (14 UU). On the other hand, I will not exchange the third unit of S for the 3rd unit of D because $12 < 16$ UU. These figures show that I must exchange until I have obtained so much of the thing desired and sacrificed so much of my own that the marginal utility of my stocks of the two things are equal.

As a result of exchange, then, there is also a surplus of utility, because the total utility of the two units I offer in the said case is $10 + 14 < 15 + 18$; this surplus of utility is 9, but would have been less if I had acquired the 3rd unit, on which I would have lost 4 UU.

**21. The Social Advantage of Barter.**—To find the profit arising out of barter we may take another example expressed in figures :—

Two persons, Tom and Harry, produce marmalade and sausages. Each of them produces 1 lb. of marmalade in an hour, but of sausages Tom produces 1 lb. in an hour, whilst Harry produces 1 lb. of sausages in half an hour. Let us assume that they have identical utility schedules for the two goods and a schedule of labour as given below :—

| MARMALADE (M) | SAUSAGES (S) | LABOUR. |
|---|---|---|
| 72 | 50 | 10 |
| 60 | 40 | 20 |
| 42 | 30 | 30 |
| 36 | 20 | 40 |
| 30 | 10 | 50 |
| etc. | etc. | etc. |

Their scale of demands is thr same, and they feel the same irksomeness in worknig. The only difference is that they do not take the same time to produce tha same quantity of sausages.

As long as they do not know of one another's existence, they will produce in the following manner :

| | TOM. | HARRY. |
|---|---|---|
| 1 hour | (10 UE $<$ 72 UU) $M_1$ | (10 $<$ 90) $S_1 + S_2$ |
| 2 hours | (20 UE $<$ 60 UU) $M_2$ | (20 $<$ 72) $M_1$ |
| 3 ,, | (30 UE $<$ 50 UU) $S_1$ | (30 $<$ 60) $M_2$ |
| 4 ,, | (40 UE $<$ 42 UU) $M_3$ | (40 $<$ 50) $S_3$ $S_4$ |
| 5 ,, | (50 UE $>$ 40 UU) $S_2$ | (50 $>$ 42) $M_3$ |

Tom produces in 4 hours 3 lbs. of marmalade (M), and 1 lb. of sausages (S).

Harry produces in the 4 hours 2 lbs. of marmalade and 4 lbs. of sausages. The hour being the unit, he produces 2 lbs. of sausages in 1 hour.

| Total Utility | — | Total Disutility | = | Surplus of Utility. |
|---|---|---|---|---|
| 224 | — | 100 | = | 124 |

| Total Utility | — | Total Disutility | = | Surplus of Utility. |
|---|---|---|---|---|
| 272 | — | 100 | = | 172 |

The collective surplus of utility gained by the two men by *Production* is 124 + 172 = 296.

They discover, however, that they can exchange 1 lb. of marmalade for 2 lbs. of sausages. Tom will now only produce marmalade and Harry only sausages. If Tom produces marmalade, he may either consume it or exchange it for 2 lbs. of sausages, while Harry in each hour produces 2 lbs. of sausages, which he may either consume or exchange for 1 lb. of marmalade. The schedules of production will now be :—

TOM :

| | | | |
|---|---|---|---|
| 1st hour | (10 $<$ 90) : $M_1$, | which is exchanged for | $S_1 + S_2$ |
| 2nd ,, | (20 $<$ 72) : $M_2$, | which is consumed as | $M_1$. |
| 3rd ,, | (30 $<$ 60) : $M_3$, | ,, ,, | $M_2$. |
| 4th ,, | (40 $<$ 50) : $M_4$, | which is exchanged for | $S_3 + S_4$. |

5th hour (50 > 42) : $M_5$, which would have been consumed as $M_3$

HARRY :

| | | |
|---|---|---|
| 1st hour | (10 < 90) : | $S_1 + S_2$, which is consumed as $S_1 + S_2$ |
| 2nd ,, | (20 < 72) : | $S_3 + S_4$, which is exchanged for $M_1$ |
| 3rd ,, | (30 < 60) : | $S_5 + S_6$ ,, ,, $M_2$ |
| 4th ,, | (40 < 50) : | $S_7 + S_8$, which is consumed as $S_3 + S_4$ |

5th hour (50 > 42) : $S_9 + S_{10}$, which would have been exchanged for $M_3$

Tom works for 4 hours and produces 4 lbs. of marmalade, of which he keeps 2 and exchanges the other 2 for 4 lbs. of sausages.

| TOTAL UTILITY | LESS TOTAL DISUTILITY | = | SURPLUS OF UTILITY. |
|---|---|---|---|
| 272 — | 100 | = | 172 |

Harry likewise works for 4 hours and produces 8 lbs. of sausages, of which he consumes 4 and exchanges the other 4 for 2 lbs. of marmalade.

| TOTAL UTILITY | LESS TOTAL UTILITY. | = | SURPLUS OF TILITY. |
|---|---|---|---|
| 272 — | 100 | = | 172 |

Their combined surplus of utility is 344 (>296) ; the difference, 48, is the gain in utility by the division of labour and exchange ; it will be seen that in our example Tom has the benefit of all the gain.

If, however, we had chosen another condition of exchange—*e.g.*, where 1 lb. of marmalade is exchanged for 1½ lbs. of sausages, the gain by exchange would be distributed between the two parties ; in this example Harry would further have gained by working 1 hour longer.

From this we deduce first that exchange and division of labour increase our surplus of utility (how this gain is distributed between the parties to the exchange will—as we shall see later—depend upon their commercial ability and their monopoly power in relation to one another) ; secondly, in a community where barter takes place, more is produced than in one, where every household produces its own necessities ; thirdly, exchange *may* make people increase their period of labour ; fourthly, the utility of the quantity of goods, which is produced in one hour, will, as a rule, increase ; the marginal utility of the thing which a man is best able to produce, and of which he will consequently be a seller, will increase, while he will hav a larger quantity and consequently also a lower marginal utility of the thing, of which he becomes a buyer (as he was less able to produce it). If exchange, from being occasional becomes regular, and thus leads to a regular division of labour, there must be a difference in what has been called the *comparative disutility* in the production of the article. If both individuals produced both goods in the same manner, nothing would be gained by exchange, even if they had a different progression of utility.

If, on the other hand, as in the example, both produce marmalade at the same cost, but sausages at a different cost, it will pay Harry to buy marmalade (which both produce at the same cost).

Let us take another example : Tom takes 2 hours to produce sausages and 2 hours to produce marmalade, while Harry takes half-an-hour to produce sausages and 1 hour to produce marmalade. We would now think that an exchange would be *impossible* because Harry is superior in the production of the two commodities. Let us suppose now that Tom produces 3 lbs. of marmalade and 3 lbs. of sausages, while Harry produces 8 lbs. of marmalade and 8 lbs. of sausages, both working for 12 hours. In spite of this it will pay Tom to produce 6 lbs. of marmalade and give up the production of sausages, because Harry will easily be able to exchange 5 lbs. of sausages for 3 lbs. of marmalade ; for in the time Harry saves by not producing 3 lbs. of marmalade he is able to produce 6 lbs. of sausages, of which he then gives up 5 and keeps one as the net gain in utility effected by the exchange.

*It is, therefore, not the absolute, but the comparative technical cost, which determines whether two parties are able to profit by a division of labour*, and by a system of barter which, from being occasional, becomes regular and continuous, *as a consequence of division of labour*.

**22. The International Barter.**—We may quote Ricardo's *Principles*, Chapter VII, with which Mill agrees in his *Principles*, Chapter XVII and XVIII :

"If Portugal had no commercial connection with other countries, instead of employing a great part of her capital and industry in the production of wines, with which she purchases for her own use the cloth and hardware of other countries, she would be obliged to devote a part of that capital to the manufacture of those commodities, which she would thus obtain probably inferior in quality as well as quantity.

" The quantity of wine which she shall give in exchange for the cloth of England is not determined by the respective quantities of labour devoted to the production of each, as it would be if both commodities were manufactured in England, or both in Portugal. England may be so circumstanced that to produce the cloth may require the labour of 100 men for one year; and if she attempted to make the wine, it might require the labour of 120 men for the same time. England would therefore find it to her interest to import wine, and to purchase it by the exportation of cloth.

" To produce the wine in Portugal might require only the labour of 80 men for one year, and to produce the cloth in the same country might require the labour of 90 men for the same time. It would therefore be advantageous for her to export wine in exchange for cloth. This exchange might even take place, notwithstanding that the commodity imported by Portugal could be produced there with less labour than in England. Though she could make the cloth with the labour of 90 men, she would import it from a country where it required the labour of 100 men to produce it, because it would be advantageous to her rather to employ her capital in the production of wine, for which she could obtain more cloth from England than she could produce by diverting a portion of her capital from the cultivation of wines to the manufacture of cloth. Thus England would give the produce of the labour of 100 men, for the produce of the labour of 80. Such an exchange could not take place between the individuals of the same country. The labour of 100 Englishmen cannot be given for that of 80 Englishmen, but the produce of the labour of 100 Englishmen may be given for the produce of the labour of 80 Portugese, 60 Russians or 120 East Indians."

Both Mill and Ricardo then arrive at the following conclusion :—The greater the difference in the relative technical cost of the goods in question between the countries exchanging, the greater obviously will be the advantage of the exchange. If, however, there is no difference in the relative cost in the two countries, the fact that the goods are produced with a great difference in the absolute technical cost will not be an incentive to exchange.

Scharling interprets the correction made in this theory by Mill in a later edition to read "that the effort saved by a country in obtaining the goods desired from abroad instead of producing them at home determines the demand of the country in question." Scharling draws this conclusion in order to arrive at agreement with his theory of value for domestic trade which reads as follows:

"It is the effort which we are *saved* by acquiring a thing or receiving a service that finally determines the offers of the parties concerned. The exchange value is effected at the point where the realisation of their mutual dependence forces them to meet."

The rule of saved effort (originally propounded by *Bastiat*) only holds good as a paraphrase of what I call the *law of substitution*: that I will at the most give as much for a thing as I would give for another which satisfies the same demand, and that behind the market price of everything there is another possible price (which the next buyer would give, or which would be given for a less important use of the thing) below which it will not fall. *Aschehougs'* criticism of Scharling's and Bastiat's theory as being confusing is so far not unjustified.

What the classical school here says above about international trade is, however, the same as we have said about barter between individuals, only that we have introduced the conception "the *technical cost*" which, as we shall see, is *something* different from the *cost of production*. International and domestic trade, consequently, do not follow different, but identical, rules. This is, however, obscured by the fact that Denmark, for instance, does not import as much from England as she exports to that country, the trade being done in a roundabout way. Denmark sells to England and obtains from this means with which to pay her imports from other countries, which in turn obtain goods from England against these means of payment. But the same is the case between individuals. The circle of exchange does not consist of two, but of many persons, each of whom produces his own special commodities.

The intervention of money has the further effect that the rule of "comparative technical cost" does not operate accurately as it takes a long time to discover the difference between the technical costs of two countries from the cost of production as expressed in money. One more source of error is to be found in *custom*, as the individual does not choose his vocation according to his best ability, but according to custom and chance, in which povərty, his father's calling, his own education, etc. play a part. But the same is the case between countries; an advantage in climatic conditions, in the easy access to raw materials, a mere chance technical knowledge, is maintained a long time after the alteration of the conditions, which were the origin of this advantage (compare the industrial supremacy of England). Further, it is not the *countries* which trade with one another It is the individual Jones in England who sends shirts to H. Manuel & Co. n Portugal, and it is another Englishman who imports Spanish oranges. And if England holds the mortgages on the land property in Portugal, which is heavily indebted, it may happen that Portugal exports goods (wine, fruits) to England, and even to all Europe without receiving other goods in exchange. In this sense a " favourable balance of trade " will be an expression for the fact that Portugal is a field of exploitation for foreign capital, and an unfavourable balance of trade would, for England, be a sign of England's financially strong position.

All these sources of error result in international division of labour not being effected according to the rule of highest productivity. It would be the object of a wise tariff-policy to enforce the distribution of production most favourable to the country; but this is not done by granting a protective duty to every trade, for what the Swede, *Dr. Brock*, calls *Solidar-protection* would only mean that the price of all goods would be increased in the same proportion, and would, in effect, only result in a different distribution of incomes to the advantage of the industrial leaders and to the detriment of all those through whose hands goods do not pass; for instance, all salaried individuals. It is expedient to favour those special trades which are presumed to be best suited to the country, by making use in some cases of Import duties, in others of Export duties. Import and Export premiums may be employed just as often in order to favour that industry in which it is supposed that supremacy can be attained, at the cost of other industries. This may be a necessity, where on account of the difference in the wages of labour there is a different level of prices in two countries which has not been equalised. England may, in Ricardo's example above, give a premium on the export of her cloth, which may then be sold cheaper in Portugal, where the level of prices is supposed to be lower. In order to reimburse herself for this premium England may put a duty on wine. Customs duty and export premium act as a kind of lock which supplies the same water-level for incoming and outgoing vessels, although they come from lakes with a different level. Portugal might attain the same end by putting an import premium on cloth and cover this by an export duty on wine. It seems absurd to put an export duty on the article which it is desired to produce and export, but nevertheless it may be correct.

A commercial treaty between two countries ought, consequently, to be based upon investigation of the comparative technical cost of those goods which it is intended to exchange.

All such expedients must obviously not be permanent, but only temporary—*i.e.*, until the right distribution of production is attained, (which is something different from Lizt's " educational customs policy ").

The rule of *comparative technical cost* entails for individuals as well as for the community that goods must be produced under a highly developed system of division of labour.

But at the same moment at which the goods change their nature for the producer they are no longer *goods* which yield utility, but *merchandise*, through the sale of which a *profit* is to be gained. The goods, therefore, are only *yielding utility* to the buyer, but are simply merchandise to the seller. The simple formula is labour and goods which yield utility (L — G); this is changed into the article $G_1$ which is exchanged for the article $G_2$ ($L — G_1 — G_2$), or, where the mercantile element pre-dominates the commodity G has the character of merchandise (W) ($L — W_1 — W_2$). If we arrive at capitalistic production, we have the formula—money, which buys merchandise, which is again sold for more money or *Marx's* formula : $M — W — (M + m)$, in which $m$ is a surplus, the net income of the merchant, who will exchange it for consumer's goods, which yield utility. For the consumer, however, the formula will read : Services, by which they obtain money which is spent in order to obtain goods, or $L — M — (G = W)$.

Modern production is an exchange ; the producer is a merchant who buys raw material, labour and machinery, and brings them together in some product of labour, which he again sells. The rule of the comparative technical cost has, therefore, no *direct* influence on the cost of production, but upon the distribution of labour and trades, partly between individuals, partly between groups within the same state, and partly between the great communities. The influence of this rule upon prices is only indirect and of slow effect.

## CHAPTER V

### SUBJECTIVE PRICE

**23. The "General" Commodity.**—Let us imagine a magic article, a "general commodity," which may be used for every purpose, and can satisfy all requirements in such a way that a unit of this commodity, at our option, can satisfy all those wants which are satisfied by bread, boots, clothes, wine, etc., and let us, for the sake of simplicity, assume that we have only the three wants, A. B and C, the utility series of which are :

| | | A | B | C |
|---|---|---|---|---|
| 1st unit | ... | 100 | 92 | 75 |
| 2nd ,, | ... | 90 | 65 | 61 |
| 3rd ,, | ... | 60 | 48 | 40 |
| | | etc. | etc. | etc. |

If, now, our magic commodity can satisfy all our wants, we shall arrive at the following schedule of utility 100 ($A_1$), 92 ($B_1$), 90 ($A_2$), 75 ($C_1$), 65 ($B_2$), 61 ($C_2$), 60 ($A_3$), 48 ($B_3$), etc., the letters stating the kind of commodity and the indices the number of the unit in question in the series.

I have not three, however, but thousands of wants, which are satisfied by thousands of different goods. In using the magic commodity I commence satisfying those of my wants which are most urgent, and gradually work down to the last units of my least important want. The utility curve of the magic commodity will therefore start very high and extend very far, starting very steep and growing more and more flat as the later units cover less necessary demands (those of luxuries); the utility curve of the general commodity, therefore, agrees with our schedule of wants, intensively as well as extensively. In this general commodity we have practically reduced the differing outward form of the goods to a uniform and common shape, in the same way as our wants, measured through our desire (whatever commodities satisfy our demand) are expressed by this uniform feeling, and in the same way as behind production we find the technical cost measured by the common imaginary and abstract measurement, units of energy. Such a magic commodity does, to a certain extent, exist in the shape of *money*.

**24. The Functions of Money.**—In its historic origin money is :

(*a*) An article of consumption which satisfies a particular demand amongst a *certain* section of the population.

(*b*) The money-commodity acquires indirect utility by being converted into a *representative of goods.*

(*c*) In this capacity the money-commodity becomes a *means of exchange*—*i.e.*, the medium by which barter is broken up into two distinct transactions.

(*d*) As a medium of exchange and representative of goods the money-commodity becomes the *social medium of credit*—*i.e.*, the medium by which the community *postpones the rendering of an equivalent for the loss in utility arising from the sacrifice* made by the individual member. By rendering a service we make a sacrifice ; for this we will not at present receive anything, the direct utility of which counterbalances the disutility of the sacrifice made, but only a *coin*, which is an order (bill) issued by and upon the community and which entitles us, on demand, at any time and place, to obtain a great or small quantity of anything we choose. (As to *quantity*, we are given a *non-binding* acceptance (engagement), but no definite promise).

(*e*) As the social medium of credit, the money-commodity, becomes the *means of payment* by which the individual discharges his liability in respect of a service received. The community, however, is not relieved of its liability in relation to the individual who has received the coin ; only when the individual in question exchanges the coin received for the thing which he desires and for the sake of which he is working, has the community redeemed its pledges.

(*f*) Money is the means of giving goods a *mobile value* in so far as money represents a given stock of goods which is waiting to be bought for this money. How much of a given stock of goods it is desired to make mobile will vary.

(*g*) Money, being a claim (order) on the community's stock of goods becomes the *hoarding agent.* This function of money is only perfectly performed by means of credit, which enables us to buy *future* goods for the equivalent of our labour instead of present ones.

(*h*) In this capacity money becomes the representative of *capital*—*i.e.*, the expression for economic *power*, while money as a representative for income is the expression for *purchasing power* in relation to the goods produced during the year.

(*i*) The last function of money is to be a *measurement of value*, the general denominator by which values are assessed and by which utility and sacrifice are compared. As we shall see later, the measurement of value is very defective inasmuch as it only affords a proper means of comparison for such goods as have their last and price-determining buyers in the same class of similarly situated persons; and actually money is only a reliable measurement for the individual when he compares the utility-fraction for different goods. The protean and conditional nature of value must be a warning against attributing too much to any conceivable measurement of value.

Money, then, is past, present and future; it is work, capital goods and services, productive power and income. Money is the wonderful fairy by whose help the shaking hand of the old man can hold the piece of bread, which the prudent youth denied himself. Money eliminates time and enables us to defy the law of transitoriness; it is the means to evil doing as well as the second-best helper of the charitable.

**25. The Marginal Utility of Income.**—As a representative of goods money has a utility which is identical with the above-mentioned utility of the general commodity on the assumption that one shilling will buy one unit of this. The utility curve of money will then be identical with that of the general commodity, starting high and extending infinitely far because our demand is insatiable; " we have hardly covered one want before another crops up." The utility of money is therefore derived from the utility of goods. It is present and future, because we may save up our claim on the stock of goods of the community, which saving will enable us to make a claim on the future stock. Money is like a thing, which may have a hundred uses (compare the example of the farmer's sacks of grain).

When the individual attributes utility to his money, he does not of course, base this on the amount which he chances to have in his pocket, but either on his capital or his income for a certain period. By money we therefore mean the income of the individual, by which we express his purchasing power during a certain period; his purchasing power is often extended by the mobilisation of the economic power which his capital represents. If we take the figure example in Sec. 23, substituting a man's income for the general commodity, and suppose his daily income to be 3s., the utility of his last shilling is 90; if he has 5s. it will be 65; and if he has 8s. it will be 48. The marginal utility of his money-income is therefore equal to the utility of the unit of goods which he would have had to do without if he had not had the last shilling—*i.e.*, *low* for the rich man because a decrease in his income of 1s. only means that he will do without an unimportant luxury, *high* for the poor man, because his last shilling means an indispensable commodity.

If we have satisfied our indispensable, but primitive needs, we turn to those goods which yield us decent comfort, the last shilling spent continually having the same utility as the last thing bought. If I have an income of, say, £1,500, after having provided for food, drink, clothes, and house, I will, perhaps spend the remainder in pictures or jewellery if I do not buy "future goods"—*i.e.*, save up my income by placing it at the disposal of others against my being able to command a corresponding sum of money in the future.

We value our money according as to *how large* an income we have —*i.e.*, according to the marginal utility of our income. It may, however, happen that the amount of money in a man's possession, and not his income, will be the deciding factor. There are, of course, people who are dependent upon their stock of money—*e.g.*, the reckless student in the early days of the month. The war supplied a curious example; I have known rich people who put aside several pounds in gold in August, 1914; this money was severed from their remaining income and was attributed the anticipated utility which a man who is the owner only of a similar amount, must attribute to this.

**26. Bernoulli's Formula.**—Daniel Bernoulli, one of the famous family of mathematicians, to whom, for instance, we owe the laws of ' large numbers," has conceived the idea of "fortune morale," which is defined as "la valeur relative d'une somme infiniment petite" (quotation from Laplace.)

This rule may be expressed approximately as follows: If the utility of the first shilling is $\frac{C}{1 - a}$, in which $a$ is the minimum of existence and C a constant, the utility of the second shilling will be $\frac{C}{2-a}$, of the third shilling $\frac{C}{3-a}$, etc., and of the $n$-th shilling $\frac{C}{n-a}$. The marginal utility of income, for which we use the designation $u_{pm}$ is, therefore, a *constant* (by which the level of prices is expressed), *divided* by the *absolute amount of the income,* from which is deducted a quantity, which represents the minimum of existence. For larger incomes we can leave the unimportant difference between $\frac{C}{n-a}$ and $\frac{C}{n}$ out of consideration; for the sake of simplicity we therefore employ the formula $u_{pm} = \frac{C}{n}$, which states that the *amount* of our income and its *marginal utility* move in *opposite* directions.

It must be a matter for statisticians, and an extremely difficult one, to verify Bernoulli's hypothesis of the *marginal utility* of income. So far the material is not sufficient, but everywhere throughout the world the work commenced by *Le Play* of collecting and dissecting household accounts has been continued. Most of the Government Statistical Departments have undertaken voluminous and valuable investigations in this direction.

As the individual in most cases actually receives the fruits of his efforts in the form of money, whether this be profit or wages proper, the utility we acquire as an equivalent for the disutility of labour must be the utility of money. The marginal utility of my remuneration is the utility of my last shilling. We may therefore say that the marginal utility of our income is equal to the marginal disutility of our labour, or, perhaps, more correctly, that the marginal utility of our income is equal to the disutility we must submit to by increasing our income one shilling, as the income of everybody is not dependent upon their work.

Let us suppose the falling curve in Diagram V. in Sec. 19 represents money and not a commodity; we then have the proof of what we have maintained above, that the marginal utility of our income is equal to the marginal disutility of our labour. If my wages of labour amount to 4d. an hour, and I am free to fix the length of my working-day, the utility of my 4d. is greater than the disutility of the first working hour, and if the working day is one of

10 hours, the last 4d. I earn of the 3s. 4d. earned during the working day, must have a utility equal to the disutility of the 10th hour, and the following 4d. (an increase of our daily wage from 3s. 4d. to 3s. 8d.) must have less utility than the disutility involved in working an 11th hour.

Expressed in symbols, $p \cdot u_{pm}$ ($p$ representing the pay for one hour and $u_{pm}$ the marginal utility of the daily wage) is equal to $u_l \cdot q_t$, in which $t$ is the number of working hours.

**27. The Utility of the Money Sacrifice.**—When we wish to procure the goods we desire, we do not manufacture them ourselves, but buy them with the money we have earned. Our sacrifice to obtain the utility acquired in buying the goods must then be the same as the utility of the money with which we pay. If a man has spent his money wisely he will, after having spent $m - 1$ shillings, come very near to having acquired the satisfaction which he can expect to obtain according to his income. The utility of the thing acquired with his last shilling will therefore be less than the utility of any thing previously bought. When speaking of the utility of income—whether we are to receive payment for our work or we are to pay for goods—we speak of the utility of the last shilling we own. This is emphasised here in order not to attempt to draw a parallel between money and consumers' goods. The more I sacrifice of the latter the nearer will I come to the limit of the *absolutely necessary consumption* of the goods in question. It is not so with money; the more money I have spent the nearer I will have come to my point of satisfaction, and the expenditure of one further shilling more will therefore cause me a comparatively small loss of utility, because it represents a comparatively late demand.

If I pay 1s. for an article my loss of utility will be approximately $l \cdot u_{pm}$, because $u_{pm}$ in this case is the total utility of the last unit of exchange. If the price of the article is 3s., and we presume my income to be £50, and the utility of the 1000th shilling to be $\frac{C}{1000}$, of the 999th shilling $\frac{C}{999}$, of the 998th $\frac{C}{998}$, etc., the total loss of utility I suffer by sacrificing 3s. must be

$$\frac{C}{1000} + \frac{C}{999} + \frac{C}{998}$$

As the difference between $\frac{C}{1000}$ and $\frac{C}{999}$ and $\frac{C}{998}$ is insignificant we may, without being very far wrong, write the utility of our last 3s. as $3 \cdot u_{pm}$, in which $u_{pm} = \frac{C}{1000}$, and if the price of the article is $p$ shillings, we may write the utility of the last $p$ shillings we are willing to pay as $p \cdot u_{pm}$.

*The symbol* $u_{pm}$ varies partly according to my income and partly according to the purchasing power of my money—*i.e.*, the level of prices. It must, however, be taken into consideration if we presume the population to be divided in classes according to income, firstly, that each class satisfies their wants with different classes of goods, and secondly, that even where they use the same commodity, for instance, bread, the expenditure for the commodity in question is not of the same relative importance for different classes of consumers. While the expenditure for bread in the budget of the poor swallows up a relatively large part of their income, it is a negligible quantity in the budget of a wealthy man.

If, therefore, we speak in this connection of the marginal utility of money as a function of the level of prices, we are thinking of the particular level of prices for that class to which the buyer belongs. The level of prices for a class is, therefore, an average of prices for the goods which the said class is accustomed to buy, computed with special regard to the relative importance of the goods in question in the consumption of that class.

An increase in the price of bread only will then result in an alteration of the level of prices for the poor, but leave that of the rich unaltered.

The question has been raised whether $u_{pm}$ is not altered in proportion as we spend our money. Presuming that we buy economically, *i.e.*, according to the rule of maximum satisfaction, this is not the case, for, as stated above, he who has spent his money sensibly has come very near to the satisfaction he can expect to obtain according to his income. It is otherwise in the case of the man who makes wrong dispositions and who, for instance, on the first of the month permits himself an extra luxury. In his case the marginal utility of money will, of course, alter, viz., grow greater.

The total utility of our income increases as a natural consequence with an increase in our income, but with a continually decreasing addition. Suppose A, B and C to have respectively 2s., 6s., and 10s. income: according to the formulae employed their total utility will be respectively 1·5, 2·45 and 2·93C, or 6·88·C in all. If we divided the income equally between them, so that each had 6s., their collective total utility would be three times 2·45 = 7·35 C. An equal distribution of income would yield the population the maximum of utility (provided such a measure, by destroying the willingness to produce, would not bring about a condition in which there would be nothing to distribute). Supposing that one man earns £50,000, and that 1,000 labourers earn £50 each; if we take £5,000 from the rich man and distribute it between 1,000 labourers, we decrease the total utility of his income by the small utility of the £5,000, which makes the difference between an income of £45,000 and £50,000, and increases the total utility of the income of each of the 1,000 labourers by the comparatively great utility of the £5, which increases their income from £50 to £55. (Dalton, *The Inequality of Incomes in Modern Communities.*)

**28. The Equation of Exchange.**—While goods for the merchant become merchandise, which he buys only to sell again with a profit, they continue, from the point of view of the consumer, to be goods which yield utility, even if he buys them with the money which he has acquired by work, or by the services he has rendered to the community.

In the equation of exchange (Sec. 16) the thing desired is the merchandise we want to buy, while the sacrifice is the money we must expend to obtain the good. We are, as a rule, free to choose if we will buy one or more units, for which reason, if the price is $p$, the utility of each unit must be compared with the utility of those $p$ shillings which we spend; but the utility of this sacrifice is the marginal utility of the money multiplied by the price. If the price is 2s. the sacrifice will be $2 \cdot u_{pm}$; if it is 5s. it will be $5 \cdot u_{pm}$.

Suppose that a man demands the first unit of an article D, which will yield him a utility of $u_1$; if, the article costs $p$ shillings per unit and the utility of the last shilling is $u_{pm}$, the utility of the first unit, $u_1$ must—in order to make him buy at all—be at least equal to the loss of utility involved in giving up $p$ shillings, which loss in utility we write as $p \cdot u_{pm}$.

If he is to buy the second unit as well, the utility of *this* must be greater than or equal to the utility of $p$ shillings, or $u_2 \geqq p \cdot u_{pm}$.

If he is to buy a third unit, the utility of this ($u_3$) must again be greater than or equal to $p \cdot u_{pm}$, etc.

This results in the following schedule :—

$$
\begin{array}{l}
u_1 > p \cdot u_{pm} \\
u_2 > p \cdot u_{pm} \\
u_3 > p \cdot u_{pm} \\
\text{—} \quad \text{—} \\
\text{—} \quad \text{—} \\
\text{—} \quad \text{—} \\
u_n \geqq p \cdot u_{pm} \\
u_n + {}_1 < p \cdot u_{pm}
\end{array}
$$

assuming that $u_1 > u_2 > u_3 \ldots . > u_n > u_{n+1}$, the index not only stating the unit, to which the utility refers, but also an increasing reduction compared to the utility of the first unit.

It will be seen from this that he will keep on buying until the point where the last unit, which he obtains of the article, yields him a utility equal to the utility of the money sacrifice, and that he will cease buying if a subsequent unit would yield him a smaller utility than its price, multiplied by the marginal utility of his income.

In the open market, where the buyers are free to choose whether they will buy a greater or smaller number of units, and therefore have not the option put to them, to buy a certain quantity or not to buy at all, we therefore have the following condition for exchange :—

$$\frac{u_n}{p \cdot u_{pm}} > 1 > \frac{u_{n+1}}{p \cdot u_{pm}}$$

The point of indifference is $u_n = p \cdot u_{pm}$, by which it is expressed that the marginal utility of any article bought must be greater than or equal to the marginal utility of the money-sacrifice, and also that the utility of a further unit of the article which has not been bought, must be less than the marginal utility of the money-sacrifice.

In order to find out what is the most our "economic man" will give for $n$ units of the article, we convert the utility-fraction $\frac{u_n}{p \cdot u_{pm}} = 1$ into the *utility equation* $p \cdot u_{pm} = u_n$ (*i.e.*, the utility of the $n$-th unit must be at least equal to the utility of his last $p$ shillings).

**29. Subjective Price Relations.**—The utilities $(u_1, u_2, \ldots . u_n)$ and $u_{pm}$ (the marginal utility of money) being known, this equation will have *two variable factors,* p *and* n, *the price and the quantity of goods bought; these being functions of one another,* p *can be arrived at if* n *is known, and* vice versa.

From the equation $u_n = p \cdot u_{pm}$ we deduce $p = \frac{u_n}{u_{pm}}$, *i.e.*, a subjective price is equal to *the marginal utility of the article divided by the marginal utility of our income.* From this again we conclude *not only that the price per unit and the quantity we are willing to buy vary in opposite directions,* but also that *subjective price and the marginal utility of income vary inversely*—i.e., *that subjective price varies in the same direction as the absolute amount of income.* The first rule appears from the fact that the greater the index ($n$, which states whether the reduction factor for $u$ is great or small) the smaller is the utility of the unit in question ($u_n$) and that therefore $n$ and $p$ vary in opposite directions.

By substituting in this equation the utility of various goods, or different amounts for $n$ or for $u_{pm}$, we find the subjective price which the buyer at the most will give for *a certain quantity of goods,* for the *different* goods, for *varying quantities* of the same goods, and for persons with *different incomes.*

Substitute first various figures for $n$ (1, 2, 3 units, etc.), and assume the other factors to be known; we then find various figures for $p$, viz., $p_1$, $p_2$, $p_3$, etc. (the price of the 1st, 2nd and 3rd unit, etc.) and through this we arrive at a series of buyers' *subjective prices* for various quantities of the article D.

| For the 1st unit | his subjective price | will be | $p_1$; |
|---|---|---|---|
| 2nd | ,, | ,, | $p_2$; |
| 3rd | ,, | ,, | $p_3$ |
| — | | | — |
| — | | | — |
| $n$-th | ,, | ,, | $p_n$ |

in which $p_1 > p_2 > p_3 \ldots > p_n$; wherein is shown the rule of the *falling schedule* of the individual's subjective prices. The rate of decrease in price appears from the following comparison :—

$$\frac{p_1}{p_2} = \frac{u_1 \div u_{pm}}{u_2 \div u_{pm}} = \frac{u_1}{u_2}$$

i.e., *the demand of the individual decreases at the same relative rate as the utility of the thing.* It would be wrong to state that the utility-curve and the price-curve are parallel. The reason for this is the effect of the factor $u_{pm}$. Let us suppose a thing has the same utility schedule for two persons, say, 1,000, 900, 800, 700, 600 UU for the 1st to the 5th unit, and assume that the final utility of money for one man is 50, while for the other, who is only half as well situated, it is 100. By taking the decreasing utility as nominator and the marginal utility of money as the denominator, we find that the two men have the following schedule of demand :—

| A's | B's |
|---|---|
| $p_1 = \frac{1000}{50} = 20s.$ | $p_1 = \frac{1000}{100} = 10s.$ |
| $p_2 = \frac{900}{50} = 18s.$ | $p_2 = \frac{900}{100} = 9s.$ |
| $p_3 = \frac{800}{50} = 16s.$ | $p_3 = \frac{800}{100} = 8s.$ |
| $p_4 = \frac{700}{50} = 14s.$ | $p_4 = \frac{700}{100} = 7s.$ |

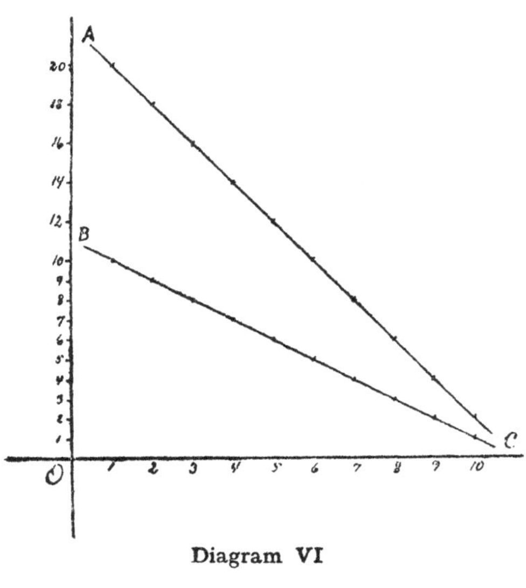


Diagram VI

This is graphically shown in Diagram VI First we plot the price curve for A, and then find the price-curve for B. It will be apparent that the price-curves of different persons for the same thing cannot be parallel, because the curves start at different heights and finish at the same point, presuming that the curve of utility is identical.

Actually the series is somewhat different from this in form, as the marginal utility of our income is altered, if even the price of one article is changed. The marginal utility of my income is affected by the degree of satisfaction I obtain from my consumption, by how near or far from my maximum satisfaction the amount of my income and its relative purchasing power enables me to be.

The Schedule of demand for a thing is formed in the following manner: For the first unit I am willing to give a price equal to $\frac{u_1}{u_{pm}}$, *i.e.*, the utility of the first unit divided by the marginal utility of my income, as it is when I buy my first unit. For the second unit I am willing to give a price equal to $\frac{u_2}{u_{pm2}}$, the utility of the second unit divided by the marginal utility of income subject to the purchase of 2 units of the good. For the third unit my price of demand will be $\frac{u_3}{u_{pm3}}$, etc.

We will, however, leave this out of consideration and operate with the simpler formula for decreasing subjective prices.

**30. Income and Subjective Price.**—We have now found that every unit has its own price, and that this is lower the later a unit is in the series, and we have found that with the same utility schedule for a thing every person has a different price for the same quantity, a price which varies in the same direction as the amount of his income and in the opposite direction to the marginal utility of income.

The subjective *price-curve* is, in the first instance, dependent upon the curve of utility, steep if this is steep, even or flat if this is even or flat; secondly, its form is determined by the marginal utility of income, as shown in Diagram VI. If our income is increased our demand-prices also rise. According to the adapted Bernouille formula, A's subjective prices will be increased 25% if his income is increased at this rate, for instance, his $p_1$ will be increased from 10% to 12½% and $p_3$ from 8s. to 10s.

The same *difference* in utility in the above schedule (100 UU) corresponds to 1s. for the poor man and 2s. for the richer. The same difference in utility results in a difference in price, which varies according as the man is rich or poor. In the same manner as the same utility is expressed by double the price for the rich than for the poorer man, the same difference in utility will obviously express itself in double the difference in price. The price-curve of the rich, which starts higher than that of the poor, will therefore be steeper.

From this the fact arises that although the same quantity of a commodity may yield a rich and a poor man equal utility, and even have the same marginal utility (in any case as far as the more primitive demands are concerned), the rich man can and will give a far higher price for this quantity than the poor man. Or if the price is fixed, and the *individual* must decide *how much he will buy* at this price, his income will lead him to judge accordingly: for the poor man the very high marginal utility of his income will perhaps be equal to the utility of even the first unit of the thing, while for the rich man his very small marginal utility of income will perhaps first be equal to the 17th or 18th unit.

Let us suppose that three persons, A, B and C, have the following series of subjective prices expressed in shillings, and suppose that their schedules of utility are approximately identical, the difference in income being the only cause for the difference in the subjective prices, by which they express their desire.

| A | B | C |
|---|---|---|
| 90 | 75 | 60 |
| 81 | 68 | 54 |
| 72 | 61 | 51 |
| 66 | 55 | 44 |
| 59 | 50 | etc. |
| 53 | etc. | |
| 48 | | |
| etc. | | |

This schedule shows us, for instance, that A does not become a buyer until the price is 90, and that the price must fall to 75 before B applies, while C first comes in when the price falls to 60. At a price of 72 A will buy 3 units, B 1; if the price falls to 59 A will buy 5, B 3, and C 1 unit; but even if the price falls to 56 none of the parties will increase their purchase.

The price may vary from 59 to 54 without A altering his purchase, and from 61 to 56 without B altering his. As we do not buy infinitely small quantities but substantial units of exchange, we are practically unable to buy in such a manner, that A, for instance, at a price of 56 is able to buy a quantity of between 5 and 6 units. For each buyer a *margin of latitude* arises in this way, and the price may vary inside this without changing the amount of the turnover. The richer the man and the steeper his curve of utility, the greater may this latitude be. Supposing that my series of demand for winter overcoats is, for the first, £10 and for the second, £2, the price of winter overcoats may then vary between £2·1 and £10 without altering the amount of my purchase. The existence of this margin therefore results in that in as far as a smaller increase in price comes *within* this, the turnover in the article in question is unchanged, which fact is of importance inasmuch as the possessor of a monopoly may force the price from the lowest to the highest point without losing customers.

If we examine how a *tax* of $p$ shillings is to be distributed, we may employ the formula $p =$ the marginal utility of the thing acquired divided by that of the income. If we assume (what is strictly not permissible) that the services rendered us by Government and Municipality, and for which the tax is payment, yield everybody the same utility $u_x$, the tax can be arrived at in the following manner :—

$$\text{tax} = \frac{u_x}{u_{pm}}$$

If we assume that $u_{pm}$ is equal to a constant divided by the income, *i.e.*, that the subjective price increases in the same proportion as the income, we arrive at the *proportional* but *not* at the progressive tax. The progressive tax presumes a rate of decrease of the utility of income, which only holds good as far as smaller incomes are concerned, and does not particularly affect that part of the curve of income at which the progressive tax is aimed. Compare, however, *Hermann*, who has realized the influence of income on subjective prices. If a labourer has an income of £160 and a merchant one of £3,000, and what Hermann terms the strict necessities of life require £140, the labourer will, after meeting this, have £20 and the merchant £2,860 left for the purchase of other goods, for which their subjective prices will compare as 20 to 2,860. According to this formula we arrive at least at the proportional tax with the minimum of existence deducted from *all* incomes ; compare our formula $\frac{C}{n-a}$. The progressive tax must therefore undoubtedly seek justification in another manner—*i.e.*, by the activity of the community in co-operating in the creation of their incomes.

**31. The Rule of Indifference.**—We have above solved the task of finding how much the individual will give for the various units of a certain thing, to use our figure example in the last paragraph: If A has no choice (option) he will pay for 4 units 90 + 81 + 72 + 66 = 309s., while B will give 75 + 68 + 61 + 55 = 259. As a rule, however, we have an option whether we will buy a greater or smaller number of units; the so-called *rule of substitution* comes into play here, according to which we will not pay more for 1 unit of a thing than we would for another which may substitute it. In the case of general goods, of which the separate units are interchangeable, *i.e.*, are equally useful, I will not give more for the first unit than for the fourth. According to the rule of maximum satisfaction, assuming the price to be 71, it would pay A to buy the first, second and third unit, because his subjective price for each of these is above 71, but he would not buy the fourth unit because his subjective price is less than 71. The price for all units must go down to 66 if he is to buy all 4 units. In all, he pays for 4 units 4 times 66 shillings = 264 shillings only, because he has an option, while without an option he would have paid 309 shillings.

To make a man buy $n$ units (the $n$-th being the marginal unit and the subjective price of this his marginal price of demand), the price he actually has to pay for each of the $n$ units must not be greater than his marginal price. Everybody, therefore, has for every thing a schedule of demand which is determined by desire and by income, and by which he expresses not only how much he at the most will give for 1, 2, 3, etc. units, respectively, but also how many units he will buy if the price is fixed. For the individual buyer the price is actually fixed by others; through his schedule of demand he reacts against this price by extending or decreasing his purchase. If in our example A finds that the price is 66 he will buy 4, if the price is 81 he will only buy 2 units. However, he also exercises a direct influence on the price (and not only on the quantity sold), but this he does together with others as a small fraction of an enormous joint force.

From this chapter we have seen that it would be useless to speak of the *quantity of demand* without mentioning "*at which price*," as well as to speak of the *price of demand* without stating the *quantity demanded* at this price. Price and quantity sold are functions of one another.

We do not buy one but many goods, for them all the equation of the subjective price is valid; the price of demand is equal to the marginal utility of the good divided by the marginal utility of income. We may state this in another way: That in purchasing various goods we buy of everyone of them as far as to the *point of indifference*, at which point it does not matter to which purchase of goods I apply my last shilling.

Assuming that we buy *a* units of the thing A, *b* units of the thing B, *d* units of D at a price of 2s., 3s. and 4s. per unit respectively and describe the utility of the last unit as $u_a$, $u_b$ and $u_c$ respectively, the following equations must hold good:—

$$u_a = 2 \cdot u_{pm}; \quad u_b = 3 \cdot u_{pm}, \text{ and } u_d = 4 \cdot u_{pm}.$$

From this we conclude that

$$\frac{u_a}{u_b} = \frac{2 \cdot u_{pm}}{3 \cdot u_{pm}} = \frac{2}{3}$$

or: the individual distributes his income in such a way that *presuming prices to be fixed, he buys so much of every thing* of which he is a consumer, *that the marginal utility of the goods* (approximately) *are proportional to their prices*, which is actually the same as *Gossen's* rule, that all goods (of which the price is the same) have the same marginal utility.

This rule is valid not only as regards goods which are for immediate use, but also as between future and present consumption. If I save 5s. of my income, the future utility of these 5s., reduced on account of our inability to feel future desire as keenly as present desire, must be equal to the marginal utility of goods, the price of which is 5s.

We have now explained not only how the *demand* of the individual expresses itself, and the rules governing the conception of this demand, but also how a person distributes a given income. We shall now turn to an examination of the confluence of the demands of the individuals which determines the *market price*.

# BOOK II

## VALUE AND MARKET.

## CHAPTER VI

### OBJECTIVE PRICE

**32. The Composite Demand Schedule.**—The demand of the individual, however, does not only act passively in the sense that it reacts against a given market-price by altering the amount purchased, but it has also a price-establishing effect inasmuch as the demand schedule of the individual, in conjunction with those of all other individuals for the same article, forms a composite schedule of demand which directly affects the market-price.

The subjective prices of A, B and C, given in the example Sec. 30, are collected in the common schedule of demand given below—*i.e.*, a schedule of prices for 1, 2, 3, 4, etc., units sold ($p_1, p_2, p_3, p_4$, etc.); the bracketed letter and index, for instance ($A_1$), stating who is the buyer and which unit, because the price in question (for instance, 90 shillings) is equal to A's subjective price for 1 unit.

| | | | | | |
|---|---|---|---|---|---|
| The market price for the | 1st | unit is | $p_1 = 90$s. | ($A_1$) |
| ,, ,, ,, | 2 | ,, | $p_2 = 81$s. | ($A_2$) |
| ,, ,, ,, | 3 | ,, | $p_3 = 75$s. | ($B_1$) |
| ,, ,, ,, | 4 | ,, | $p_4 = 72$s. | ($A_3$) |
| ,, ,, ,, | 5 | ,, | $p_5 = 68$s. | ($B_2$) |
| ,, ,, ,, | 6 | ,, | $p_6 = 66$s. | ($A_4$) |
| ,, ,, ,, | 7 | ,, | $p_7 = 61$s. | ($B_3$) |
| ,, ,, ,, | 8 | ,, | $p_8 = 60$s. | ($C_1$) |
| ,, ,, ,, | 9 | ,, | $p_9 = 59$s. | ($A_5$) |
| ,, ,, ,, | 10 | ,, | $p_{10} = 55$s. | ($B_4$) |
| ,, ,, ,, | 11 | ,, | $p_{11} = 54$s. | ($C_2$) |
| ,, ,, ,, | 12 | ,, | $p_{12} = 53$s. | ($A_6$) |

We may express this graphically in the marked curve of demand (Diagram VII., which also may represent a thing that is used in several ways by the individual—A, B and C in this case not signifying different persons, but different uses).

While the curves for A, B and C fall evenly, this is not the case with the composite curve; the rate of decrease in price changes often. As long as the price is above 75, A is the only buyer, but as soon as it reaches 75 B's demand creates a disturbing influence, and at 60 even that of C; at 61 B buys his 3rd unit, at 60 C his 1st, and at 59 A his 5th. Now the fact is that the lower the price the greater the number of new buyers who make a bid. As further, the number of persons having an income of £100 is greater than that of those having an income of £200, this composite demand curve will often be irregular in its decline, for every time the price diminishes so much that another and more numerous class can afford the article, the curve will become flatter—*i.e.*, the difference between subjective prices becomes less the further we progress.

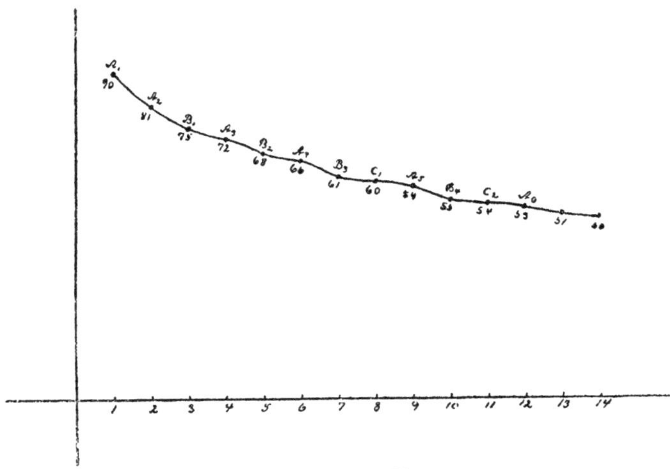

Diagram VII.

We have obviously not the same desire and, therefore, not the same schedule of demand for all goods. Consequently the schedule will also be different, for different goods. Further, the varying purchasing power of the different groups of the community which are able to buy certain goods, causes the figures of the composite schedules to differ for the different goods, or every commodity has its own individually formed curve of demand. A thing for which the subjective prices from the 1st to the 5th unit are, for instance, 20s., 18s., 16s., 15s., and 14s. has a more evenly declining curve than one, the subjective prices of which are 20s., 16s., 12s., 8s., and 5s.—*i.e.*, the curve in this case is more steep. This difference in the form of the curves is of importance for the fluctuations in price, to which the goods are subject.

From the rule of substitution we deduce what Jevons has termed the *rule of Indifference*; in the same market, at the same time and place, the same price will be ruling for any unit of the same thing, presuming that all buyers have the *option* whether they will buy a greater or smaller number of units. From this it is apparent that the subjective price of the marginal buyer for his last unit must be identical with the common market price for all units. Our schedule of demand tells us that at a price of 60s. the sale is 8 units, neither more nor less, and that those units are distributed in such a manner that A takes 4 and B 3 units, but C only 1; at a price of 68s. only 5 units can be sold, 3 for A and 2 for B; at a price of 54s., 11 units, etc.

*The composite schedule of demand, therefore, states the subjective prices which correspond to the given quantities sold*, or, in other words, the co-relation between the market price and the quantity of goods, which can and must be sold at that price. Even the strongest of monopolists must respect this schedule of demand; if he can decide the quantity to be offered, the schedule of demand must decide the price at which the quantity offered can be sold; if he is able to decide the price, the schedule of demand will decide the quantity to be sold; nobody can at the same time command both the price and the quantity sold, because the relation between price and quantity sold is determined by something not within the power of the seller—*i.e.*, the composite schedule of demand. This, consequently, supplies the subjective element, our changing *desire*, which—*through the effect of the distribution of income—is materialised in subjective prices.*

The objective element also is present—in the technical conditions under which we may procure the article desired. *Karl Marx* speaks of the "socially necessary work" as the determinant of value. This is, however, only a catchword, because he does not explain which work is "socially necessary." The schedule of demand, however, shows us this, because it states the possible prices at which the different quantities of the article can be sold. Scarcity (shortage, the technical cost of production, which varies for different quantities) decides *which* of the many possible prices of the schedule of demand will, as marginal price, be equal to the market price.

If the market has settled down to a turnover of 7 units at a price of 61s. the price must be brought below this if more than 7 units have to be sold. The prospective buyers of that quantity by which the stock of the market has been increased must either be people who have already bought a certain quantity, and now are to be induced to increase their purchase, or people whose demand on account of their smaller income has never become effective at the price given. The first mentioned have a lower subjective price for a greater than for a smaller supply, because in the first case a later unit, the utility of which is less, will be their marginal unit, while the less well-situated buyers, who are to be induced to buy a thing of which they have previously not been consumers, must be catered for at lower prices.

The schedule of demand, therefore, contains the subjective prices of the *consumers* to be when they come to their market, which actually consists of retailers whose selling-prices again are often far above even the cost of production. Obviously we do not know the whole of the schedule for any thing, but we know it from experience in the neighbourhood of that quantity, which remains unsold, if the price is increased (the marginal unit).

Knowing the prices of demand for variations in the turnover of about 20% on either side, we also know the probable fluctuations in price. Consequently we only operate with part of the schedule; this part contains the last units of some rich buyers, but also the first units which are demanded by that class of buyers who are the least well-situated of those who consume the thing. By a *class of buyers* we understand a group of economically and socially, approximately equally situated individuals, whose appraisement and schedules of demand are fairly uniform. If the consumption is fairly regular amongst the poorest class of buyers in question, their subjective schedule of prices (corresponding to the schedule of utility) must govern the fluctuations in the price of the thing; but when a change in price makes a class of buyers come in or leave off buying, the curve of utility is no guide to the estimate of possible fluctuations in price.

**33. Demand as Will and Power to Buy.**—As we have seen, it is desire which makes us attribute utility to goods and—conditionally upon scarcity—also value; desire which is "*primus motor*" in all our economic actions, is expressed by the demand and determines the strength and compass of that demand.

But demand is determined also by another factor, the element of income. We must examine the desire in order to find out what the individual is *willing to sacrifice*; we must examine the distribution of income to find out what he *can sacrifice*. Consequently an alteration in the demand must be owing to the fact that either the *desire* or the *income* of some buyers has been altered. While desire is something latent in the individual himself, which, however, may be influenced by something from without—as, for instance, fashion and social habits—the distribution of income is completely outside his influence. Even the subjective price will therefore be determined by subjective and objective influences. The *composite demand*, which is composed of the schedules of demand of all individuals, will therefore be an *expression for the distribution of income* in the community in question.

Demand does not state the desire of the community measured according to the claim that the community, as a whole, must derive the maximum utility from the goods; but it states the desire of the individuals, expressed and limited by their income, by their paying ability or purchasing power, as this happens to be distributed. Only converted in this manner does our desire determine which goods can be sold and at what price: And expressing the *will* and *power* to buy, demand is the magnet which attracts production. It is according to the proportion between schedules of demand for the different goods, that all productive forces must be distributed and the goods produced if they are to be saleable. Production is the effect, demand the cause.

Every time the distribution of income is altered all curves of demand are altered, and in the second instance production is reorganised; for *only goods in demand are saleable*. Demand becomes at the same time the cause of production and a regulator governing possible alterations in price.

*Adam Smith* adds the correcting adjective "effective" to the word "demand," and acknowledges hereby that the word demand requires an explanation; but "effective" does not supply this, because the phrase that effective demand affects prices, only states that those who become buyers have actually been able to pay the market price—which is tautological.

Demand is, however, existent and is of importance, even if no transactions are effected. A labourer is a prospective buyer of champagne, but his price of demand is perhaps only 1s. a bottle; whether his demand becomes effective—*i.e.*, whether he becomes a buyer, depends upon the objective element, the conditions under which the wine is produced. As soon as the technical conditions are altered his demand may become effective, as when, for instance, the introduction of mass-production has made certain goods so cheap that what used to be the luxury of the rich has now become the beggar's necessity.

**34. The Modern and Aristotelian Theory of Value.**—For us the conception "demand" is not an empty phrase, because we know how it is composed, how its intensity is determined, and how it acts as an economic reason. To use Westergaard's modest expression: "We have really come one dig of the spade deeper." This we owe to the subjective theorists, who by giving us the expression "marginal utility," have taught us to manipulate the conception "marginal value" and thereby opened a rich field for our investigations, and last, but not least, have supplied the means to prove that also in economics that unity which we seek in all phases of existence may be found.

By going back to desire as the economic motive we have been able to produce a theory of consumption, a rule of the final object of goods—enjoyment—which was so much forgotten in classical theory that *John Stuart Mill*, in his great *Principles* of 1,200 pages, can spare no more than a couple of pages for the conception "demand," and that only through a quotation from *de Quincey*.

Even Aristotle conceived that our needs are our economic motive: "Every possession," he states, "permits a double utilisation, of which one—*consumption*—is related to the quality of the thing, the other, viz., *exchange*, is not." From an ethical point of view he examines what is a *just* price. "In all contracts, the result of which is an exchange, justice does *not* consist in perfect outward *equality*, but in a *proportion* between what is given and what is received. Anything to be exchanged must, to a certain extent, be comparable and commensurable. Co-operation would be impossible without exchange, exchange without equality, and equality without a common measure. Some such measure must exist, something by which everything can be measured. This measure is certainly the *desire,* for if nobody had desires or the needs of several did not meet, exchange would be impossible. Exertion of art and handicraft would be impossible if the activity of one part did not correspond to the receptivity (demand) of the other part in amount as well as in kind."

Now justice demands that anybody who exchanges receives proper payment. " Now values (the measure of which is our needs) are *equal* if one of those who exchange feels as great a desire for the thing belonging to the other as *vice versa.* A proper and proportional remuneration for both exists when such equality in desire is present ; for instance, if the desire of the farmer for shoes has the same proportion to the shoemaker's desire for grain, as the value of the work of the shoemaker to that of the farmer." Here already we find the objective element protruding, and later the scholastics became absorbed in this and lost sight of the subjective element, our desire.

**35. The Schedule of Supply.**—But demand does not onesidedly determine the market-conditions ; the schedule of demand only fixes a price at which a given supply of goods *may* find buyers. The supply actually determines how great this quantity of goods is. The *supply expresses the scarcity,* whether scarcity is evident through a limitation of the supply, which results in some individuals not having as much of the thing as they are able to consume, or through the fact that an increase in the existing stock is dependent on some effort. This cost of *increasing a given stock of goods* finds its expression in the *minimum price* of the seller, which varies from next to nothing if he is unable to use or store the good which he cannot sell, to infinity if he is unwilling or unable to sell.

Just as the buyer has a series of maximum prices, which state the most he will give, the seller of goods also has his minimum prices, prices at which it is *indifferent* to him, whether he sells or not. For some sellers the price is subjective in the proper sense of the word, because it is conditioned by desire—*i.e.,* he estimates the thing as a consumer's commodity, as is the case with most of those goods which, from private stock, again come into the market as second-hand goods and with original barter. Some individuals must have money or have no room for the article in question, or fear that it will deteriorate; the minimum price of such individuals is very low—*i.e.*, their offer acts through the quantity offered, but not through a fixed sale price.

Next come a multitude of producers and merchants, whose relation to their goods is not determined by their desire (a baker cannot use his stock-in-trade himself) but—with the exception of Edgar Poe's artist-smith, who grieved to part with his work—only by the wish for profit; they are certainly sellers, but only on the condition that they obtain a certain price. We shall see later how this is determined, and here only maintain that this minimum price is different for different merchants (or producers). In this way we arrive at a series of sale-prices, which we may arrange, starting with the lowest minimum price and ending with the highest, concerning which we may state *a priori*, that the higher the price offered by the buyers the greater the number of effective sellers who will appear; yes, even the individual seller has often a different selling price according as he has to sell (produce) a greater or smaller quantity. As is the case with demand, the *price* at which sale is intended, and the *quantity* sold are functions of one another, but while the price of demand and the quantity vary in opposite directions, the selling price and quantity vary in the same direction (at least in the short period market). Supply, therefore, does not mean a certain quantity, nor a certain price, but varying quantities, each with its own price. Just as there are hundreds of different demand-prices for the same thing, there are also hundreds of different selling-prices.

Each market must, therefore, have a composite *schedule of supply* with increasing prices, corresponding to the decreasing prices of the schedule of demand; supposing $s_1, s_2, s_3, \ldots s_n$ is the price, at which 1, 2, 3 .... $n$ units are offered for sale, $s_1 < s_2 < s_3 < \ldots s_n$.

As an example, take the following schedules:—

| | | | D (DEMAND) | | S (SUPPLY). |
|---|---|---|---|---|---|
| 1st | unit is | demanded at | 10s. ($p_1$) | and offered at | 4s. ($s_1$) |
| 2nd | ,, | ,, | 9s. ($p_2$) | ,, | 5s. ($s_2$) |
| 3rd | ,, | ,, | 8s. ($p_3$) | ,, | 6s. ($s_3$) |
| 4th | ,, | ,, | 7s. ($p_4$) | ,, | 7s. ($s_4$) |
| 5th | ,, | ,, | 6s. ($p_5$) | ,, | 8s. ($s_5$) |
| 6th | ,, | ,, | 5s. ($p_6$) | ,, | 9s. ($s_6$) |

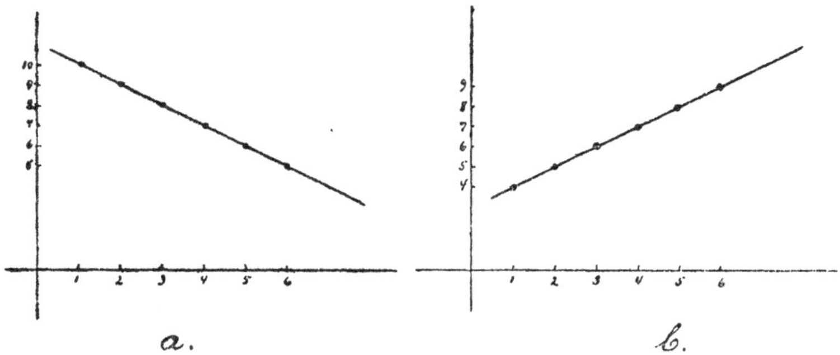


Diagram VIII

Graphically we may show these two schedules in the above diagram in which *a* represents the curve of demand and *b* the curve of supply.

**36. The Meeting of the Schedules.**—We find the market price by placing the two schedules beside one another. We start with the buyer, whose maximum price is the highest, and the seller, whose minimum-price is the lowest,. for if any transaction is effected at all, the one who will sell cheapest and the one who will pay the most are in any case certain to be parties to the transaction.

In the ideal market, where the effect of the rule of indifference is unhampered, the market price is fixed by that competition between the individual buyers and sellers respectively, which *Adam Smith* terms the " higgling of the market " ; by this process the market arrives at an equilibrium, so that there is an equal number of effectively demanded and effectively offered units.

Supposing now that the highest bidder is in the market willing to pay 10s. ; at that price all 6 units of our series will be offered. The market is, therefore, not in equilibrium, as there are six sellers against one buyer. Some of the sellers must, therefore, be forced out of the market or more buyers attracted, or both things must happen by the market-price being forced down, for instance, to 8s. Now, there will be three units effectively demanded and five offered but only when the price is lowered to 7s. will there be an *equal number*, viz., 4 each of buyers and sellers, 4 being the marginal unit. This point of equilibrium, at the price of 7s.,—both for sellers and buyers the marginal price—is permanent and stable. For if the price rises to 8s. there will be a greater number of sellers than of buyers, and if the price falls to 6s. there will be more buyers than sellers. In the short period market there is obviously only one possible market condition for price and turnover.

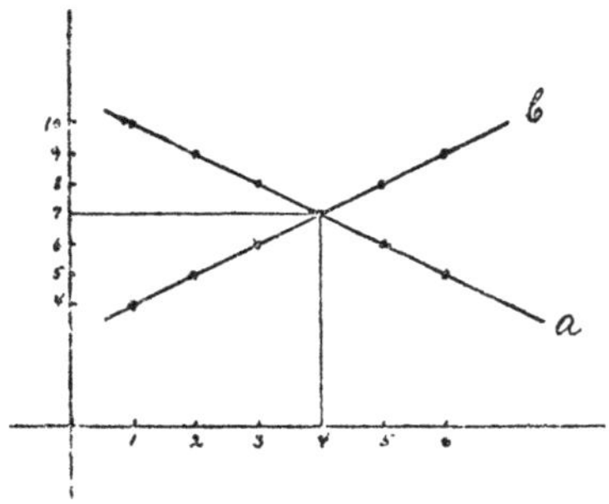


Diagram IX

To explain graphically, we can superimpose the two curves in Diagram VIII. on one another, as shown in Diagram IX., in which we have lifted the curve of the schedule of demand (Diagram VIIIA) and superimposed it on that of the schedule of supply (Diagram VIII*b*) making the bases of the two figures cover one another exactly, the two measures stating the prices of demand and supply respectively for the corresponding quantities of goods. The point of equilibrium is where the two curves (straight lines in the diagram) intersect; the price of the lowest accepted bidder ($p_n$), and of the highest accepted seller ($s_n$) are both identical with the market-price ($p = 7$s.).

If the subjective price of demand for the 4th unit had been 7s. 6d. and the 4th unit could have been sold for 6s., this would not have altered the quantity sold. The price might have been anywhere between 6s. and 7s. 6d., although it must have been somewhat above 6s.; otherwise the 5th buyer would have joined in and disturbed the equilibrium. As the seller will go as high as he can without reducing his sale, the price would be able to reach 7s. 6d.; in the long run it would not, because the greater profit, which the seller derives from the fact that the marginal price of the buyer is higher than the marginal cost would attract other producers and thereby press the market-price right down to the marginal cost. The market-condition is only that $p_n \geqq p \geqq s_n$; this condition makes it possible that there may be a margin between $p_n$ and $s_n$ within which the price may fluctuate, *without* affecting the turnover.

The arrival of two more men cannot have any influence on the market-price and the quantity sold if their price is not *above* 7 if they are buyers or *below* 7 if they are sellers.

The comparison between our schedules has further confirmed that the rule which governs supply and demand respectively, also holds good for the market-condition that *price and quantity sold are inseparably connected.* On the stock-exchange we experience this every day: Because an industrial security has been dealt in at 21s. to-day, I dare not conclude that to-morrow it will cost the same; neither can I if, for instance, I want to sell £5,000 shares expect to get 21s. for them because I have sold £250 of these shares at this price. If, during a panic, the Savings Banks sell their securities in order to obtain cash, even Government Bonds may fall perhaps as much as 20%.

The rule of indifference is, however, not absolute. The seller may at will single out part of his customers, perhaps the richer ones ("on large quantities we allow a discount"), but just as often he will secure a larger turnover by keeping two prices: one for a well-situated and one for a poorer *clientele* (children and soldiers half price). Of the latter we have an example in the American Tobacco Company, which for a long time sold the same tobacco in two different packages at a different price, and in the case of soap, which is sold in a different make-up in order to give an incorrect impression of difference in quality.

The individual buyers and sellers are sometimes not posted as to the actual condition of the market, and therefore offer their subjective price, as, for instance, in our example, if the sixth seller whose price is 9s. outside the market, finds the second buyer, whose price is also 9s. If the goods are not generic, but every unit has its own small peculiarities, transactions may therefore take place at prices above as well as below the natural market-price, as is the case with houses: two cottages, which are alike in all essentials and situated in the same part, may therefore be sold simultaneously at widely differing prices.

When treating the theory of wages, we shall see that, where wages are not fixed by agreement or law, the wages in the same trade may vary much, especially when the individual labourer must go round himself to find an employer; compare the demand for a legalised minimum wage for home-workers, just because the workers have difficulty in learning from the various intermediaries what conditions other employers are offering. We may mention further that retailers do not keep the same prices; the prices in the suburbs often appear to be lower than those of the shopping centre.

**37. Alterations in Demand or Supply.**—By alteration in demand or supply we understand alteration in quantity, (demanded or offered) in price or in both. The alteration in price may be due to a change in only a few of the subjective prices or to the alteration of all of them. The alteration of a given subjective price changes its place in the schedule; sometimes the prices of those units, which are not far from the marginal unit, are altered, and this will affect the quantity sold and the market price; at other times there is a change in prices of units somewhat higher or lower in the schedule than the marginal one; then the change is irrelevant. It may happen that a former buyer, whose price before was sufficiently high, now comes below the market price, and the opposite may happen according as his taste or means are altered.

There may be many reasons for the alterations in the demand price for an article; a change in our desire or taste, the introduction of a new commodity which draws consumption away from another, the better utilisation of a given supply of goods, a change in the distribution of income, the increased price of a thing which satisfies the *same* demand, the cheapening of an article which is in *supplementary relation* to the commodity in question (which consequently increases the demand for this article), and the cheapening of a number of other goods, which stand in no supplementary relation whatever to our commodity, but leave the consumer more money to buy it with. Alteration in the *supply* may be due to internal or external causes; altered technique, either in respect of method or machinery, the utilisation of a by-product, an alteration in the cost of extracting raw materials, the introduction of new raw materials, higher efficiency of working, an alteration in the price of the factors which co-operate in the production of the thing in question, and, finally, taxes or excise duties imposed on the production, which may be either a tax per unit—uniform *without* taking the price into consideration, or *proportional* or *progressive* on the price—or a license duty imposed once and for all, or variable, levied on all or on some trades. The quantity offered alone may be altered, for instance, by an intended monopoly, or as a consequence of scarcity of goods on account of a breakdown in the means of transport, on account of war, or on account of a failure of the credit system.

Let us suppose that in our price schedules in Sec. 35 the buyers of the commodity get a greater desire for the article (fashion), or as a result of the failure of the supply of another commodity, to which they have been accustomed, they detect the hitherto hidden qualities of the thing in question—[the war has shown us many instances of this]—and so cause the prices in the schedule of demand to rise in that part of the scale, which has the deciding influence. Suppose all prices to be increased by 2s. while the supply prices are unaltered, the comparison of the schedules will then appear as follows :—

| | D | | S |
|---|---|---|---|
| Demanded at | $10 + 2$ ($q_1$) | Offered at | 4 |
| | $9 + 2$ ($q_2$) | | 5 |
| | $8 + 2$ ($q_3$) | | 6 |
| | $7 + 2$ ($q_4$) | | 7 |
| | $6 + 2$ ($q_5$) | | 8 |
| | $5 + 2$ ($q_6$) | | 9 |

Instead of equilibrium being at 4 units, sold at 7s., it is now at 5 units sold at 8s. An increase in the demand must increase the price and increase the turnover. The price will, however, not increase as much as the increase in the intensity of the demand, because an increased turnover will entail a later buyer coming in, who had previously a price which was below the old market price, and which, with the increase added (in the above case, 2s.) will be less than the price of the last buyer previously accepted with the same addition. If we assume that the quantity offered is unaltered, *i.e.*, that only 4 units are in the market, the price would not continue to be 7, but would be increased to $7 + 2 = 9$s. In other words, *when* an increased demand does not meet with a quantitatively strengthened supply, the price will rise very considerably, and more than when the supply can be increased, even if at a higher price. (The opposite is, of course, the case with a decrease in prices in the demand schedules.)

In any case, in the *individual daily market* the old rule holds good, that increased demand raises the prices and entices more indifferent sellers to appear. We shall later see that in the long run this rule does not generally apply.

If, now, the *supply* prices are increased as a result of increased expenses or a tax—without the demand being altered—for instance, by 2s., we arrive at the following schedules :—

| D | S |
|---|---|
| 10 | $4 + 2$ |
| 9 | $5 + 2$ |
| 8 | $6 + 2$ |
| — | ——— |
| 7 | $7 + 2$ |
| 6 | $8 + 2$ |
| 5 | $9 + 2$ |

The price must, in this case, also rise from 7 to 8, but the turnover decline from 4 to 3 units.

The expenses or the tax need not be equal for all units. Suppose it to be proportional to the price, whatever this happens to be, for instance, 25% of the effective price (to be found in the schedule of demand), we may then add to the original supply price for each unit 25% of the corresponding demand price. We then arrive at the following schedule : —

| D | S |
|---|---|
| 10 | $4 + 2\frac{1}{2}$ (= 4 + 25% of 10). |
| 9 | $5 + 2\frac{1}{4}$ (= 5 + 25% of 9). |
| 8 | $6 + 2$ etc. |
| 7 | $7 + 1\frac{3}{4}$ |
| 6 | $8 + 1\frac{1}{2}$ |
| 5 | $9 + 1\frac{1}{4}$ |

We may also deduct the 25% from the demand price, as this price, from the point of view of the seller, *appears* to be reduced by the amount of the tax.

Finally, we have the frequent case where the supply fails (is reduced), without its minimum prices being altered ; for instance, where only 3 instead of 4 units are brought to the market. The price will then rise from 7s. to 8s., *i.e.*, a buyer, earlier in the schedule, then becomes the marginal buyer, whose price decides the market price.

If the supply fails, the price is increased with a decreased turnover, by how much will, of course, depend on the schedule of demand, which is the only protection of the buyer.

If the amount of supply is increased in such a way that the units then on offer are offered at lower prices than before, the price will decline with an increased turnover. The rule that *increased supply forces the price down*, therefore, only holds good (*a*) in the individual market, and (*b*) on the condition that the prices of the additional sellers are below the previous price. Without this condition the turnover will be unchanged.

In Diagrams X, $E_1$ is the original and $E_2$ is the curve of increased demand, $U_1$ and $U_2$ the curves of original and increased supply, $n_1$ and $n_2$ the amount of turnover, and $p_1$ and $p_2$ the market price before and after the increase. What is necessary in all cases is to find what are the effects on price and turnover, on $p$ and $n$, of alterations in the curves.

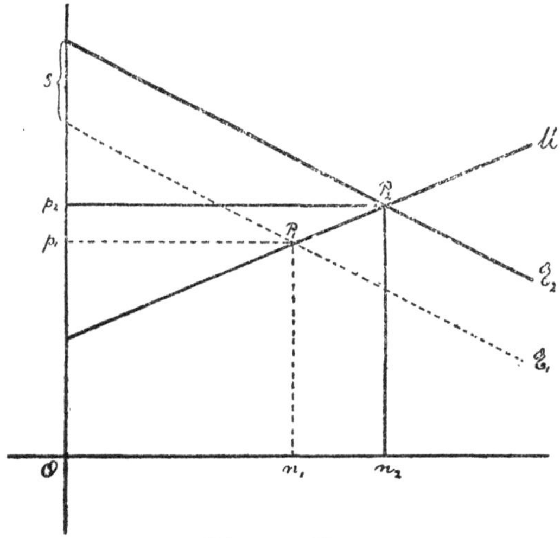


Diagram Xa

In Diagram X*a* the demand has been increased, the curve of supply is unaltered, the supply being increased, but at increased prices, making $n_2 > n_1$ and $p_2 > p_1$.

In Diagram X*b* the supply price has been increased by an equal amount per unit, but the demand prices are unaltered, making $n_2 < n_1$ and $p_2 > p_1$.

In Diagram X*c* the amount of supply has been decreased from $n_1$ to $n_2$; the demand is unaltered, making $n_2 < n_1$ and $p_2 > p_1$.

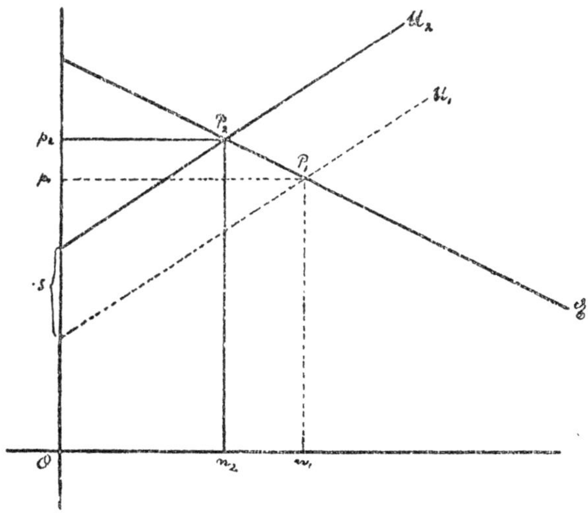

Diagram Xb

A tax varying proportionately with the market price (which moves along the curve of demand, compare page 82) will cause the demand price, from the sellers' point of view, to be reduced by the same percentage as the tax; for instance 50%. In

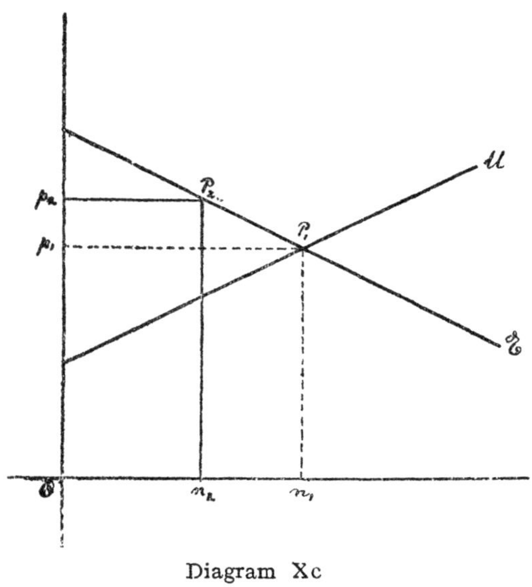

Diagram Xc

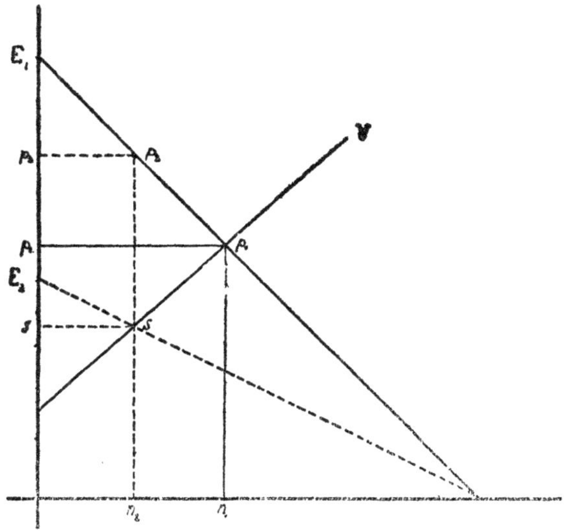

Diagram Xd

Diagram X*d* U is the curve of supply, $E_1$ the curve of demand, $E_2$ this curve reduced by 50 %, starting far from the original curve, but gradually, as this falls, approaching it (because, for instance, 50% of 10s. > 50% of 5s.). The turnover is *decreased* from $n_1$ to $n_2$, the price is *increased* from $p_1$ to $p_2$; of this the seller obtains the moiety *s*, and the remainder $p_2 - s$ reverts to the Government. In this way the Government may confiscate one half of the addition in price a holder of supply may gain on account of a shortage of the supplies of a country (compare the war taxes on wine and spirits in Denmark).

Obviously supply and demand may be altered at the same time. If they are altered in opposite directions, for instance, by an increase in the demand and a fall in the supply price, it may happen that the turnover is immensely increased at *unchanged* prices; if they are altered in the same direction, the price will be altered, but *not* the amount of turnover. The student is advised to attempt to draw the curves for various cases, and in each one to find $p$ and $n$.

If in Diagram X*a* the demand is increased, but the supply cannot be augmented, then the price will rise considerably; with an unchanged turnover we would have to prolong the line $n_1 p_1$ to the point, where it intersects the new curve of demand, and from this point to draw the parallel to the base line towards the ordinate.

The expression *increased supply* means that a greater amount of goods are offered; the expression, "a higher schedule of supply," is something different, and corresponds to a decreased supply, while a lower schedule of supply corresponds to an increased supply offered.

We can already see that the contentions that *increased demand means higher price and increased turnover*, and that *increased supply means lower price*, are only correct with a qualification, and only hold good for the *individual market*. We shall later see that in the long run an increased demand may lead to lower prices, while a decrease in the demand, which necessitates a decrease in production, may even lead to higher prices.

We now also understand a peculiarity of the policy of war-time *maximum prices*. Supposing the demand schedule to be 10s., 9s., 8s., 7s., 6s., 5s., and 4s., and the cost 5s. per unit, the turnover is 6 units at 5s.; the supply is now reduced by shortage to 4 units, which corresponds to a price of 7s., which on the 4 units yields an extra profit of $4 \times 2 = 8$s. This is not considered permissible, and the price of 5s. is fixed as a maximum price. But to this price there corresponds a turnover of 6 units and the supply is only 4, *i.e.*, the supply is consumed too quickly; only 4 may be supplied—not according to the buying power of the public, but according to their patience in waiting in front of the shop and other chance causes. The right thing in this case is not to fix a maximum price, but to impose a monopoly duty of 2s. per unit; in this case there would be equilibrium between the quantity demanded and offered. The Government and not the seller would reap the profit of the increase in price.

If, however, the thing in question is a necessity of life, this means cannot be employed. In this case it is necessary that the thing must not only be cheap, but must also be sufficient, which entails its *rationing*, so that nobody can have more than, for instance, two-thirds of his ordinary consumption. Then we have $6 \times \frac{2}{3}$ (= 4 units) at $\frac{2}{3} \times 5 =$ 3s. 4d. per portion, which corresponds to 5s. per unit.

Where the demand price is capricious, prices may fluctuate very much, and the seller must therefore take into consideration a special element of risk—that his stock is not sold—and, consequently, calculate his selling price so much higher. It is curious to notice how the market for works of art and the objects of the collecting mania may fluctuate ; the price at which the merchant acquires a stock of this description is therefore far below the price at which he normally disposes of it again—not only because merchants in the said line of business are often shrewd and crafty persons. Something similar is the case where the supply is capricious ; during the war, with uncertain supplies, we have had this confirmed ; a high profit is taken on a stock bought at abnormal prices in order to cover the loss bv a later fall in price caused by abundance.

# CHAPTER VII

## CONCERNING MARKETS

**88. Short and Long Markets.**—If the transactions were to take place in a number of successive markets, independent of one another, the fluctuations from one day to another would be very violent; the *uncertainty* as to the number of buyers appearing or the seller's varying need for cash would decide the market condition. There is, however, a *regulator*, a kind of ideal market, intangible, and yet behind all the separate markets, connecting them and making them stable. The simplest market consists of the barter between two persons, in which A sells his commodity and buys B's, while B sells his commodity and buys A's; but, passing from exchange between a few individuals to regular and organised trade, where the same transactions are repeated every day, the seller of the commodity is a *merchant*—*i.e.*, a person who produces or procures the commodity, *not* because he intends to make direct use of it, but because it is a means for him to gain a daily wage from the difference between his selling-price and his cost-price. Where merchants are established, the *market* proper is formed, comprising a number of buyers and sellers, who can know of one another's presence and can form an opinion about the transactions which take place, and thereby judge if the rise or fall of the market is temporary, and act according to this judgment, each eager to obtain the same advantage as any other has got.

Even if I might be willing to pay £10 for a coat, the ordinary price of which is £5, a rise in price to £10, or an accidental scarcity in coats will, if I consider it to be temporary, cause me to postpone my purchase, provided I am able to do without the article for some time; accidental circumstances are not allowed to have effect, because seller as well as buyer may withdraw from the market. In the same way as markets through this circumstance are connected in respect of *time*, they are also connected in respect of *place*. Geographically the market has certain boundaries, but it may be national, and even international, provided that the means of transport permit the seller to move his goods from the market which is the worst for him to that which is the most advantageous, and the buyer to transfer his demand to that which is the cheapest for him. The buyer is, as a rule, less mobile than the seller, who is a merchant (although the buyer may be a merchant, travelling buyers, employers of labour, etc.). The fact that the market may be either national or international does only benefit or prejudice the consumer through the retailers, or through a wholesale merchant, who is able to change his place of purchase. The local market, where the consumers appear, will therefore be relatively comprehensive, and both in respect of time and place be connected with other markets. This connection between the local and daily market and other places and the markets of the future creates what may be termed the long market, where also the *static* price is ruling. The connection takes place in this way: There may, of course, be something which we will want immediately, and which must therefore be accepted at the chance condition of the daily market; but our ability to *postpone* or *substitute* our consumption causes the demand schedule for the goods to remain comparatively unchanged from day to day, independent of the fact that a greater or smaller number of buyers are present. If the price for the day appears to me to be accidental and low, I will consequently, as a matter of course, press my purchase, and by this force the price upwards. But if I discover that a change in price is not a passing phenomenon, I give in and accept the new price as a fact, according to which I must adjust my purchase. Anybody who has come from a country with a low level of prices to one with a high level will have noticed how at the beginning he reacts against the high price level, but finally gives in, adapting his consumption to the level of prices.

As with the buyer, so with the seller. Even if his minimum price is next to nothing, the expectation of being able to obtain a higher price will cause him to postpone his sale. A merchant *must* have his cost price and expenses covered; whether he can obtain that on the daily market or not is quite uncertain. Once there he will, however, reason as follows:—Can I expect to be covered in the near future? To discover this he asks if the fashion, the distribution of income or other elements of demand will alter, and, on the other hand, he ascertains the price at which he can *replace* his stock when sold. In the case of supply it is *not* the cost of production, but the cost of *re-production* (first pointed out by *Carey*) which will counteract the uncertainty of the individual market.

**39. The Cost of Re-production.**—The rule that the cost of reproduction is price-determining is derived from the rule of substitution; that a thing cannot cost more than another which may substitute it. If I—and others—am able to supplement my stock at a lower cost than my cost of production, competition will cause the lower cost to be determining; *vice versa* the fact that the cost of production of my stock is, say, £5, will not save me from loss if I sell it at £5 and must re-purchase it at £6 in order to exist as a merchant. The observation, that *work once applied is without influence on the value, is indisputable.* We do not ask what a thing has cost, but what it will cost. Its cost of reproduction will have more potential than direct regulating effect (Scharling). The knowledge that this cost may become the actual cost of production will make the sellers unable to take an unfair advantage if the period of production is shorter than the time for which a sensible buyer can postpone his consumption. If, however, the period of production is long and, consequently, it takes a longer time before the output of the commodity can be increased, the buyer is unable to wait; in this case the continuance of the long market will be interrupted, and the local market, which is time-determined, is affected by the demand in proportion to the *actual* (small) output. This we have experienced during the war.

We know that all producers are not able to re-produce the thing at the same price; consequently there will also in the ideal market be different costs of production for the different quantities offered.

While temporarily there may be a very great difference between the technique of the different producers, in the long run a group of producers will be formed, working with a certain amount of capital and with a certain technique which is natural or habitual to the country in question. These *representative firms* (Marshall) will, without actually being marginal producers, come very close to the margin. A number of producers will be working under poor conditions (often strong in numbers, but weak in importance) representing an inferior technique (perhaps the normal method of the past) and less ability, and there will also be some *few*, but in capacity *important*, producers, who come above the normal and represent a higher technique—perhaps that technique which in future *will* become the normal. Every country, every period and every trade has its type of representative concern, which, with a fair profit, is actually leading, and whose *cost of reproduction* is the regulator of the price of the output ; the marginal producers earn nothing and may even work at a loss. Those above the normal often earn a large " *differential rent*,"—*i.e.*, the difference between the market price and the actual cost of production, which becomes the marginal price.

**40. The Market Regulator.**—When conditions have settled, the long and the short market will be identical in the static community. In the dynamic community this coincidence of the two markets is *not* permitted to be completed, because the long market is altered by technical and other causes. In the long market also the rule holds good that the marginal buyer meets the (profitless) marginal producer, whose expenses are higher than those of the representative firm. There will even be producers, who in their fight against dissolution will produce at a loss simply to save some of their capital or prolong a doomed existence by all means. This type of man will, however, not determine the marginal cost (for then the price would be higher) ; they only cause the other and more able producers to have a smaller turnover in proportion to their capacity, and are otherwise more of importance in respect of numbers than in respect of their share in the production.

There will then be a difference between the ready market of the day and the natural market backing it, which cannot be said to coincide with this or that daily market, but which still is always present as an active force, stabilising and connecting the separate markets.

Apart from this we may at once point out a peculiarity which distinguishes the long market from the daily market, viz. : that while there is only *one* point of intersection and equilibrium for the formation of price in the latter, there may in the former be several points of equilibrium, because there may be several prices at which an equal number of units are demanded and offered. It may, for instance, happen that a small quantity of a certain thing, which has been produced with some trouble, will find buyers whose income is sufficiently high ; by a great increase in production it often happens in industry that the cost of production is reduced so much that it corresponds to a low price, at which even the poor—*i.e.*, a great number may become buyers.

In the price of the day therefore is included the effect of the market conditions and prices of the following days. Likewise we may say that in the local market which is in touch with other markets, the conditions of these other markets are taken into consideration. This tendency towards equality, caused by the connection between markets, which are separated in respect of time and place, arises in a way naturally, inasmuch as the individual buyers and sellers take into consideration future conditions and conditions elsewhere ; it is in this way that the world market arises, expressed through a number of local markets, by the connection of which the former has been established ; this equalisation is purposely effected through the *Arbitrage,* which estimates the differences between the various markets, present and future, and by retaining goods, removing and distributing them, and by creating by artificial means demand and output in the different markets, alters the price of the day or the local price in the direction indicated for the future. A dealer in futures, whose judgment is correct, yields a service to the community, inasmuch as he brings the output of the present into accordance with that of the future and by this hinders great variations in price. If, in his judgment, the output in the near future will be small, his high price for future supply will cause the price of the day even during a momentary abundance to be relatively high, and, through this, consumption is restricted and, consequently, better distributed over the period. The speculator has, by forcing us to store, forced us to create a *time*-utility, in the same way as by carrying the commodity from a market with a low price to one with a high .price he assists in creating *place*-utility ; to add another expression we may state that the producer who re-forms the goods, creates *form*-utility.

A correct distribution of a given supply of goods in *time, place* and *use* yields the maximum utility to the community and at the same time an equalising of prices in respect of time, place and form. In a community in which the productive powers or the stocks of goods are slow to move from place to place in accordance with the rule of maximum advantage, the speculator who " manipulates the machinery " will be able to further the tendency to move—but certainly also to counteract movement, leaving out of consideration that he always causes some expense in the turnover.

**41. Distress and Monopoly Price.**—For goods which are not reproduceable, the cost of reproduction is infinite; for air it is nil. According to the rule, that price cannot be outside the schedule of demand, the *market-condition* for air as well as for non-reproduceable goods will be determined by the *prices of the schedule of demand compared with the amount of output,* but *not* with definite selling prices. If there is only one Rembrandt in a country, the price for this must be what the richest connoisseur will give; but the sum will be dependent upon the income of the buyer; if the income of the rich collector of pictures is £5,000 annually, the same picture will fetch just as many shillings as it would fetch pounds if his income were £500,000 or more. (This is, however, the maximum as the next price below is determined by the income of the second richest collector.) The price of all such non-reproduceable goods will be dependent on the amount of output and also on the number and strength of the rich men of the country.

The rule for non-reproduceable goods, in fact, also holds good for goods which cannot be stored: only in this case the prices of the schedule of demand will not only be exclusively determining, as the output only acts *quantitatively,* but the regulator of the long market, which will have some effect in the case of non-reproduceable goods that may be stored, fails where non-storable goods are concerned; in this case we speak of the *distress*-price which means that so much has been offered on the market that the sellers are forced to sell below the cost of re-production, and that it is impossible by awaiting a better opportunity to avoid the vagaries of the daily market. The buyer may, in a sense, be said to be in distress when he absolutely must have the commodity; if the buyer is in distress, and cannot postpone his consumption, we say that the seller can dictate a monopoly price. Buyer and seller will never be equally strong; one will always be in a relative position of monopoly to the other, who on the other hand will be in distress. We may express this by saying that among a number of persons who trade or act together, the one who stands in a position of monopoly in his relation to the others will reap the greatest advantage. Capital is nearly always in a position of monopoly in relation to labour, but this position may be more or less strong.

If the stocks of a commodity are limited in quantity, we may say that the curve of supply, when the last unit has been reached, rises steeply ; if only 6 units exist, the selling price of the seventh will be infinitely high. The rule governing non-reproduceable goods which have been brought to the market and goods which have to be sold *a toutprix*, is the same as that for other goods. The curve of demand supplies the limit, but the quantity of goods offered in proportion to the selling price determines which of the prices of the curve of demand will become effective. For perishable goods the selling price is simply infinitely small, unless the owner himself, to a large extent, is a consumer of his own commodity. In the case of non-reproduceable goods, which the owner will not part with, the cost of reproduction is infinitely high and, consequently, does not meet with a buyer, whose subjective demand covers an offered price. As will be seen, there is *no* difference in the fundamental rule in the two cases.

We may also say that the cost of reproduction affects the minimum-price of the seller, but only in proportion as to how quickly reproduction is possible before the stock is cleared. If there is a possibility of quick reproduction, the cost of reproduction is the minimum and in most cases also the maximum price, but the longer the time which is required for reproduction, the less will be the price-determining influence of this cost in relation to the daily market.

For goods which have no selling price, there may still be a kind of increase in the cost, if an excise duty on the sale is imposed. If three units have to be sold, and more cannot be procured, the tax will only have the effect of an impost, which has been paid and borne by the seller, and which cannot be shifted on to the buyer ; in other words, the buyer's price will from the seller's point of view have been reduced by the amount of the tax. The case is different if the non-reproduceable commodity may be withheld, in which case a high tax will prevent it from being sold, or assuming that more than one specimen of the thing exists, it may cause one seller to withdraw from the market and thereby make a bidder who was before more willing to pay, the actual buyer—*i.e.*, increase the price. In this case there is some shifting of the tax in the form of a higher price with a decreased turnover (compare taxes on the sale of real estate.)

What has been explained in the foregoing paragraph may also be expressed in another way. The seller's minimum price is determined in four ways: (*a*) according to the direct utility which the thing yields the seller himself, as in the case of barter or sale of private supplies or in the case of non-reproduceable goods, which have sentimental value (the elf-lock of a lover, Napoleon's sword or other objects of the collecting mania) ; (*b*) the seller's minimum price is nil if he must sell at any price and cannot store the thing; (*c*) the seller may *one-sidedly* fix a price, which, however, is not based on an estimate of utility, but on a calculation of the possibility of a maximum profit. This is done in the case of *monopolies*—whether *natural* (everybody who wishes to produce is not able to do so) or *legal* (no others are *allowed* to produce) or *intentional* (others are prevented from selling by the monopolist's command of raw materials or of the markets). The seller's price is in this case only fixed one-sidedly to the extent of the seller's command, because he arrives at the price by a tentative estimate of the curve of demand in comparison to the cost, in order to find which turnover will yield him the maximum profit. Monopoly price is above the natural market price (where the prices of the marginal buyer and the marginal seller are equivalent) and at the same time the monopoly turnover must obviously be less than the natural market turnover. Finally, (*d*) in the case of reproduceable goods when the seller does not command the amount of production, the cost of reproduction will take effect if the commodity can be stored and the consumption postponed; otherwise either the buyer or the seller will be in distress. Without going further into the question of cost, we may state here that this is based upon the *technical cost, the sacrifice of energy* involved in the production of the thing. The technical cost must be paid, and the payment is the cost of production or the cost of reproduction respectively. There is a subjective element in the technical cost, viz., the disutility of labour, and also where it is necessary to save in order to procure implements, the sacrifice of doing without the consumption of the day ; but in the developed commercial community this is of so small importance that we may regard the technical cost as a purely objective phenomenon. The *demand price* is based on the psychological element, our *desire,* which must materialise by passing through themedium of the distribution of income and thus becomeing the subjective price. Behind the selling price—the cost of production, we find something objective—the technical cost. Desire for utility creates the demand price, which in the market price must meet and cover a selling price, which is arrived at by a valuation of the technical *cost* of reproduction of the commodity. This valuation is again affected by the curve of demand of the finished article.

**42. Statics and Dynamics.**—We may treat our problem *statically* or *dynamically*, and by both methods of treatment we may review the economic phenomena as a snap shot or as a series of cinematograph pictures. By means of the snap-shot we have a description of the state of things at a given moment ; but in order to find the rules of cause and effect connecting the separate phenomena, we must see the economic life in working and note how the cogwheels move simultaneously with the fly-wheel, and the movement of all the wheels and axles which transmit the power to the former. " We take a collective view of the economical phenomena, considered as existing simultaneously " (Mill). The difference between the dynamic and the static examination consists in the fact that in the latter case we certainly start from a movement, but one which continually repeats itself because the forces affecting it are unchanged. Static theory assumes that the demand is always the same—*i.e.*, that the income is always distributed in the same manner ; that the amount of circulating money, fashion and taste, and the population as well as its distribution in respect of sex and age are always the same. We assume consumption to be like a river, with the same level and volume, even if the particles are continually changing. With regard to the output we assume that there is no alteration in technique, that exactly the same amount of capital is present ; that the distribution between the effective and poor producers is the same, so that if a beginner is working up, a representative firm will go down ; there is a continuous movement, but the movement repeats itself uniformly. The productive powers—in themselves unchanged—incessantly travel in the habitual way towards their destination. *Dynamics*, on the contrary, take life as it is, with *varying* motive powers and consequently varying movements, which do not repeat themselves exactly. The distribution of income, habits and population—and, consequently, the schedules of demand—vary from day to day ; capital is increased or diminished ; technique is altered, the number of labourers available varies and, consequently, the conditions of production, while the amount of means of currency changes ; the requisite technical cost as well as the value of the same—the schedules of supply, are continually changing.

Many incorrect statements in economics are due to the fact that a distinction has not been drawn between Dynamics and Statics, the rules for which are not identical.

In the static community there will be no difference between the short and the long market price ; in the dynamic community there will be different rules affecting these two prices. In the short market an increase in demand will always cause prices to rise correspondingly. In the long market an augmented demand may even cause lower prices by creating a possibility for mass-production. In the long market we not only see the action, the cause, of a certain effect, but also the reaction ; the effect as the cause of its own cause, altering this cause and rendering ineffective the forces affecting itself. As the prices of the output as well as of the demand are continually altered in actual life, the equilibrium, expressed by the quantity *actually sold* and the *objective* price obtained, is altered ; and the latter fluctuates continually. In the static community price and turnover are as cut in stone. This difference will, for instance, also result in different rules for the net-profit in the static and the dynamic community—rich, varying and continually returning in the latter, but in the former tending to be eliminated, as the representative firm, when the static condition has been arrived at, will finally fill all of the schedule of demand, and as the unchanging demand will leave room for neither profit nor loss from market fluctuations. In theory we often operate with statics ; strictly speaking, it would be right, as done by *Clark*, first to find the rules of statics and then those of dynamics. I prefer, however, to operate with an unchangeable community, not stagnant, but repeating its movements, and to deduce the rules of cause and effect by altering one or other of the active factors at will and leave other conditions unchanged ; " ceteris paribus " (as *Schumpeter* says) is the motto of the isolating process ; but then we must at the same time point out that the rules arrived at are not valid in the community in which we happen to live.

Also in dynamics it is the long market of the *statics* which regulates and connects the separate markets. The long market of dynamics is something different—*i.e.*, a market in which the effects of alterations in the active forces, through readjustment of the factors in their tendency towards equilibrium, *have had* time to take effect, but where new influences are already felt.

**43. The Prices of Supply in the Long Market.**—The selling prices, with which we operate in the *long* market under static conditions, should be arranged in a single schedule, where at the bottom we find the cost of some profitless marginal producers, above those the cost of the representative firms, and at the top the smaller costs of the prominent, successful producers.

Without entering upon an exposition of the difference between *the technically necessary cost* and the *expenses necessitated by social powers only*, or upon a distinction between expenses, *determining* the price and *determined* by the price, and leaving the rules of the conversion of technical cost into cost of production to a separate book, we will only point out that the employers' expenses should be divided between the fixed expenses, which do not vary, or in any case not for a definite amount produced—*i.e.*, General Expenses, which are composed of the Amortisation and Interest on Plant and the general annual expenses, and those which vary according to the quantity produced, the Expenses per unit, prime cost. Partly for this reason, and partly because it is a natural rule (as shall later be proved), the rule holds good for all concerns—industrial as well as agricultural—that until the plant is utilised to its full capacity, the expenses per unit will be falling.

In the following we make a distinction between the technical schedule and the schedule of supply proper. From the technical schedule it will appear, that the cost, if I make 1 unit, is, for instance, $e_1$; if I make 2 units, consequently, $e_2$, and if I make $n$ units $e_n$. What does $e$ stand for? Either the average cost or the cost of the last unit. *A priori*, we must understand that if I produce 6 units and continue to do so, the total expenditure in doing so must be covered; otherwise, I would go out of business. The price must then be equal to or above the average cost. But we also know that if it costs more to produce the 6th unit than the

5th, the expense entailed in increasing the production from 5 to 6 units must be covered, for otherwise I would stop at 5 units. As both costs must be covered, the price I demand must be large enough to cover the larger of the two costs. We may here state that where the cost increases from one unit to the next (increasing expenses), or, what comes to the same thing, each shilling we apply yielding a decreasing return, the cost of the last unit, the marginal cost, must be included in the schedule of supply of the individual seller. If, on the contrary, the profit increases for each shilling I apply (increasing return) or, in other words, the cost of each new unit decreases (decreasing expenses) the *average cost* must be covered by the price, as nobody will be satisfied with a price, which certainly covers the cost of the last unit, but does not cover the total cost divided by the total production.

If we leave out of consideration the general expenses and suppose that the cost per unit of the extraction of raw material amounts to 6s. for the 1st, 7s. for the 2nd and 8s. for the 3rd unit, the average expenditure will be $21 \div 3 = 7$s.; the marginal cost is 8s. A schedule would then read: $e_1 = 6$, $e_2 = 7$, $e_3 = 8$. Suppose an industry in similar conditions to have the cost of 8s., 7s. and 6s. for the 1st, 2nd, and 3rd unit respectively,. In the production of 1 unit in this case the average will be equal to the marginal cost (8s.); if 2 are produced the average will be $(8 + 7) \div 2 = 7\frac{1}{2}$; but the marginal cost is 7s.; at 3 units the average cost is $(8 + 7 + 6) \div 3 = 7$s., while the marginal cost is 6s. In this schedule there must therefore be included: $e_1 = 8$, $e_2 = 7\frac{1}{2}$ and $e_3 = 7$. In the case of decreasing return we use the marginal cost of the several producers, in the case of increasing return the average cost as the amount, which the price must reach in order to make a producer go on producing.

The case is never a simple one, but *provisionally* we may make the following statement: The Artisan works with a constant, Industry with an increasing, and Agriculture with a decreasing return.

When all work under the same conditions—as in the case of artisans or, in the smaller industries, where all firms come close to the representative firm, as will be the case in a static community—the schedule of supply will contain prices which come close to one another. This selling price, which is to be included in the market-schedule, might be written as $s$, and, consequently,

$s_1 = s_2 = s_3 = s_n$. The differences which may actually arise in the cost of production will *not* take effect as a *difference in the selling price*, but only leave a different profit. (It is, for instance, often the case with artisans that the worst situated producer will offer at the lowest prices, and certainly works at the verge of starvation, while the artisan with the larger circle of customers and sufficient implements can command higher prices and a comfortable standard of living.)

In the trades producing raw materials we may provisionally take for granted, that the expenses of the technical schedule will increase for each unit, the same technical cost, the same number of units of energy employed in the various forms required in the given case, as, for instance, labour, manure, auxiliary, or raw material, machinery, etc.—yielding a constantly decreasing additional quantity of goods, when additional units of energy are applied. But in this case the final production of each producer will not be entered in the joint schedule of supply—but a price for each separate unit he may or may not produce; only a higher price will make him extend production, because the cost of a subsequent unit is higher than that of those previously produced, for which reason the 6th unit may be, for instance, the second producer's 3rd unit and the 7th the 3rd producer's 1st unit, and the 8th the 2nd producer's 4th unit. We therefore compose the schedule of supply as follows :—$s_1 < s_2 < s_3 < \ldots\ldots s_n, s_1, s_2, s_3$, etc., not stating the total production and minimum price of the individual producers, but the price of each of the separate units, which are to be produced.

With regard to *industry*, which is said to work according to the rule of increasing return, the $s_1$, $s_2$, $s_3$, etc., which are included, will be the average cost of the different concerns for the production, which they actually have or are designed to have.

Now one might think that $s_1 > s_2 \ldots > s_n$. The average cost is, however, *not* entered in the schedule in such a manner that the smallest concern and its prices are put first, and the second smallest next and the largest and cheapest producer last; even in this case the concerns rank in the schedule according as to how cheaply they are abl to sell, because even here the rule holds good that the cheapest producers are always certain to find customers. The concerns, therefore, rank according to cost, starting with the best and cheapest producer, and finishing with a poorly and expensively producing *marginal producer*, and having that similarity to the schedule of supply for raw materials, that $s_1 < s_n$, only that in this case a multitude of units will have the same price. If, for instance, A produces 4, B 3, and C 2 units (with an increasing return) the schedule will read: $s_1 = s_2 = s_3 = s_4 < s_5 = s_6 = s_7 < s_8 = s_9$.

In a static community this schedule will remain unchanged once equilibirum is attained; but in dynamic state, in an ever changing world of reality, there will be the difference between the two schedules, that while the schedule for raw materials tends to remain unchanged, or in any case, will change only in such a way that the producers retain their place in the composite schedule of supply; the schedule for industrialproduce will constantly change, because each separate concern has the possibility of *extending*, and thereby *decreasing its expenses of production*, and consequently *changing its place* in the schedule. An effect of the alterations in the schedule, and through this of the alterations in price, and even in market conditions will therefore be different, according as the *technical schedule* is governed by the rule of *increasing* or *decreasing* return, even if the market schedule of supply in both cases starts low and rises, if a greater number of producers must be called in in order to supply the market. The other difference between the schedules under decreasing and increasing return is, as stated, that in the former each separate unit is entered with its (marginal) cost, whilst in the schedule of the latter the production of each individual *producer* is entered with its (average) cost.

In the schedule of demand in Sec. 35, in which the market condition is 4 units at 7s., the monetary expression for the total utility for the buyer, *i.e.*, the *total of subjective prices*, is $10 + 9 + 8 + 7 = 34$s. The difference between $t_d$ (the total of subjective prices, here 34s.) and $n \cdot p_n$ (4·7s.) is called the consumer's rent ($r_d$), and is in this case $34 - 28 = 6$s. The difference between the price actually obtained ($n \cdot p_n$) and the total cost ($t_s$) is the producer's *differential rent* ($r_s$), the basis for his profits.

## CHAPTER VIII

### Value

**44. Valuation.**—To estimate value is to compare one thing with another as a fixed measure. The valuation may be ethical; the measurement may be what is expedient, it may be quantitative, whether this be in one of the three dimensions or by weight. In other words, we may take any of the qualities of the thing and estimate its value in comparison with the corresponding quality of another thing in relation to ethics, to power, to public welfare, and so on. By examining the utility of the thing we also make a valuation; this has caused some authors (Aschehoug and Westergaard) to speak of subjective value where they mean utility. As, however, the accepted definition of economic value is a proportion of exchange between the goods, we cannot apply the word value to something which is actually a state of mind without creating confusion. By subjective value we mean the buyer's highest valuation of a given quantity, expressed in another commodity, while utility expresess a given strength of feeling; the former is the expression for acknowledgment; the latter for agreement.

(Concerning valuation, the Swede, Dr. Liljequist, has written an interesting treatise about Meinong's basic theory of valuation, in ch. iii., secs. **3** and **4**, of which the author proves to have great knowledge of modern economic theory; compare also the Dane, Wilkens: *Fundamental Values of Life*.)

The proportion in which I may exchange two commodities without loss of utility is my subjective ratio of exchange; I am willing to exchange *d* units of the thing D for *s* units of the thing S, provided, for one thing, that I am a seller of S and a buyer of D. If I am to trade, the second party must be situated in the same way as I, only that he is a buyer of S and a seller of D. While each of us have respectively a maximum and a minimum price, I would like to obtain for my *s* units of S more than my minimum *d* units of D, while the other party would rather give less of that commodity. The condition for the exchange being effected will therefore be that the parties who desire one another's commodity are willing to sacrifice their respective goods, and can meet in a common ratio of exchange, where $\frac{d}{s_a} \leqq \frac{d}{s} \leqq \frac{d}{s_b}$; $d$ is the quantity of goods which A desires and B is willing to sell, while $s$ is the quantity of goods, which A would sell and B would buy. The indices state the subjective proportion of exchange between the two goods D and S for the parties A and B. From this we deduce the third condition of exchange $s_a \geqq s \geqq s_b$. If now the seller demands money and not goods, $s_a$, $s_b$ and $s$ will stand respectively as the buyer's highest, the seller's lowest, and the price actually obtained for the commodity D.

**45. The Idea of Value.**—By saying that $d$ units of D are exchanged for $s$ units of S we state that the economic value of $d$ units of D is $s$ units of S, which we express by $d.\mathrm{D} = s.\mathrm{S}$, from which we deduce: $\frac{\mathrm{D}}{\mathrm{S}} = \frac{s}{d}$, or the value of the two goods is inversely proportional to their ratio of exchange. If the proportion between D and S is 3 to 2, the ratio of their value will be 2 to 3.

Value, which in itself is a ratio,—*i.e.* the inverted ratio of exchange—is consequently relative, a quality attributed to the commodity which expresses the ratio, in which the individual is willing to exchange for another commodity (subjective value) or in which proportion the two things have actually been exchanged (objective value, which becomes market-value, when the objective proportion of exchange has been ascertained through several purchases and sales.) The exchange value of a commodity is neither another good nor the ratio between them. It may be described as a sort of power inherent in one commodity which can only be exercised in connection with a similar power in another commodity, and which can only be estimated by the ratio between the quantities exchanged. This ratio states how much one thing is desired more than the other, compared with the question whether one is more easily obtainable than the other, or: Value is a relation between the human desire to have a commodity and the difficulty in obtaining this, compared with our desire to have another commodity and the difficulty of obtaining that thing. (Compare Aristotle's definition).

**46. The Scale of Value.**—We may compare one commodity with another ($d$ units of D = $s$ units of S), or with all goods, making, for instance, the value of $d$ units of D = the value of $s$

units of S = the value of $p$ units of P = the value of $q$ units of Q, etc.; a set of such equations will state the respective places of the goods in the scale of value. The relative place of the goods is largely conditioned by the distribution of income, by the demand schedule, by technical conditions and still more by the number of persons trading. We shall see later that, for instance, the value of a stock of merchandise at a given time is conditional upon the fact that say only 5% at a time is offered in the market; should greater amount than the usual come into the market, a *depreciation of the value* will take place. A given *scale of value* is conditional upon the non-alteration of the distribution of income, the relative demand and the relative scarcity of the goods.

From the fact that value is a ratio follows the fact that the value of one commodity alone cannot be altered without the value of all other goods at the same time being altered in the opposite direction.

Suppose the following to be the *scale of values* (= to read as "equal in value to the value of"):

(*a*) 20 loaves = 10s. = 3·6 grammes gold = 16 kilogrammes bacon = 5 hens = 3 cwt. coal = 100 cigars.

We may convert this as follows:—

(*b*) 1 cwt. coal = $6\frac{2}{3}$ loaves = $\frac{3}{4}$s. = 1·2 gr. gold = $5\frac{1}{3}$ kg. bacon = $1\frac{2}{3}$ hen = 33 cigars.

(*c*) 1 kg. bacon = $1\frac{1}{4}$ loaf = 0·5s. = 0·21 gr. gold = $\frac{5}{16}$ hen, etc.

(*d*) 1 hen = 4 loaves = 2s. = 0·72 gr. gold = $3\frac{1}{5}$ kg. bacon.

(*e*) 1s. = 2 loaves = 0·36 gr. gold = $1\frac{3}{5}$ kg. bacon = $\frac{1}{2}$ hen = 10 cigars, from which we find the following *current prices*:

1 loaf = $\frac{1}{2}$s., 1 gr. gold = 2·78s., 1 hen = 2s. 1 cigar 0·10s., etc.

In this we have not only placed the goods in comparison to one another, but also measured them with a given thing, stating how much we can get of any commodity for 1 cwt. coal, 1 kg. bacon, 1 hen and 1 shilling—*i.e.*, we have found the *purchasing power* of the thing *assuming* that we were able to use it to purchase with.

It will be seen that if we make an alteration in (*a*) the value of hens, so that 20 loaves (= 10s., etc.) is not equal to 5 hens but to 4 hens, the (*d*) scale, expressed in hens will read:

1 hen = 5 loaves = $2\frac{1}{2}$s. = 0·9 gr. gold = 4 kg. bacon etc.

If we express the value of all goods in hens, an alteration in the exchange ratio of hens would lead to the alteration of the whole of the scale of value; the level of value has in our case been lowered—*i.e.*, for the same quantity of other goods fewer hens than before will have to be paid, while a hen on the other hand will command more of other goods than before. Previously the price of a loaf was $\frac{1}{4}$ hen, now it is only $\frac{1}{8}$ of a hen; hens have become relatively scarcer than other goods. If we do not take the hen, but a gramme of gold or the shilling as the general denominator, the same rule will apply.

If in our scale (*a*) 10s. = 3·6 gr. gold is altered to 10s. = 7·2 gr. gold (*i.e.*, the amount of gold in the shilling is doubled), then

(*c*) 1s. = 2 loaves = 0·36 gr. gold = $1\frac{3}{5}$ kg. bacon = $\frac{1}{2}$ hen = 10 cigars

will be altered to

1s. = 4 loaves = 0·72 gr. gold = $3\frac{1}{5}$ kg. bacon = 1 hen = 20 cigars, or 1s. will buy more than before (its purchasing power is said to be *greater*), and all other goods have become cheaper, expressed in terms of shillings. Previously a loaf cost $\frac{1}{2}$s. now it costs only $\frac{1}{4}$s.; previously the price of a hen was 2s. now only 1s.

As far as money is concerned, we may actually speak of *purchasing power*, because the purpose of the shilling—and its *only* direct purpose—is to buy goods; with regard to other goods, *purchasing power* is a misnomer, because other goods are *not* intended to buy, but to be bought.

Karl Marx has really the same exposition, only that he attributes to it an almost supernatural importance and equips its obviousness with Pallas Athene's most fearful war-paint.

The formula, *a* units of A = *b* units of B, he terms the *simple formula of value*, in which A is in the *relative value-form*—*i.e.*, its value is expressed by a certain quantity of another commodity; the commodity B is in the *equivalent form*, as through a certain quantity of its *natural form* it expresses the value of the commodity A. The next development is: *a* units of A = *b* units of B = *c* units of C = *d* units of D—*i.e.*, the scale of value, which Marx terms the *complete formula of value*, where each individual commodity is in the relative valueform, but the countless others in the equivalent form. If we compose the scale thus:

$$\left.\begin{array}{l} b \text{ units of B} \\ c \text{ units of C} \\ d \text{ units of D} \end{array}\right\} = a \text{ units of A.}$$

we have the *general formula of value,* in which all goods are in relative value-form with the exception of the one, A, for which this is determined, and which is in the equivalent form. If now we suppose the thing A to be gold, the general formula of value will be the *money-formula* proper, in which the general equivalent form is coalescent with the specific natural form of gold.

**47. The Level of Prices.**—The scale of value, in which the shilling is the unit, expressing the ratio of exchange of goods, is converted into the *price-list* from which we deduce the level of prices, telling us the value of the goods in proportion to the unit of coin. The level of prices varies inversely to the value of money—*i.e.*, the greater the value of a shilling (the greater its purchasing power) the *lower* will be the level of prices (and, consequently, the prices of goods) ; the smaller the purchasing power and the lower the value of a shilling, the higher will be the *level of prices.* A rise in the level of prices means that the shilling loses in *purchasing power,* and that the goods increase in value—*i.e.*, are scarcer than the money. While *all* values *cannot* rise (or fall) at the same time as they are altered in proportion to one another or in opposite directions, *all prices* may be altered in the *same* direction, and the price of the separate goods may be altered, without the prices of other goods being altered as a logical consequence.

As money is a representative of goods, and as such a right on the supplies of goods existing at any time, it is certainly a fact that money at the will of the holder may buy any kind of thing, but it is not certain *how much* he may obtain of that thing. If I receive money, for instance, an official's salary, I have a sort of expectation as to how great a quantity of goods I may procure, but it is not certain that this expectation will hold good ; the level of prices may alter. The correct level of prices for the individual is found by a comparison, either between how much he obtains for a given income at two different points of time, or between how much he must pay for his usual consumption ; the level of prices will, as previously shown, depend upon the consumption of that *class* to which the individual belongs.

A very rough expression for the difference in the purchasing power of money (income) is found by taking certain standard goods (often raw materials) adding up their prices, and comparing the sums at two points of time. Without entering into the technique of the method of calculation (it is a matter for the statistician) we must maintain that only by using the absolute figures of the family budget, and through this finding the relative importance of a thing for the individual budget, will we find a true level of prices. As the importance of a given thing, for instance, bread, is different in the budget of the rich and the poor man, we must, as shown before, calculate the level of prices for each class separately, if we wish to find its "aisance relative" (Guyot). A common level of prices for all gives no true picture of what we want to know, the proportion between income and purchasing power. An absolute calculation of the level of prices is difficult, because an altered level of prices always results in an altered scale of consumption, as the consumption of different persons is not affected to the same extent—because the income of the individual does not increase proportionally with the level of prices—and finally because a doubling of this does not take place by all prices rising in the same proportion.

As an example, we may quote from *The New Statesman*, the weekly food budget for a large English working class family (*a*) before the war; (*b*) what it would have been in 1916 with unchanged consumption and (*c*) as it actually was with an altered consumption. The quantity is given in lbs. and milk is, for obvious reasons, only entered at half of its weight.

| | *a* 1913 Quantity | *a* 1913 Total Expenditure | *b* 1916 Total Expenditure with unchanged consumption | *c* 1916 Actual Consumption Quantity | *c* 1916 Actual Consumption Total Expenditure |
|---|---|---|---|---|---|
| | lbs. | s. | s. | lbs. | s. |
| Meat ... | 7 | 1/8 | 10/6 | 2 | 3/– |
| Sugar ... | 4 | 1/– | 2/– | 2 | 1/– |
| Bacon ... | 3½ | 2/4 | 4/1 | 2 | 2/4 |
| Cheese ... | 3½ | 2/2 | 1/8 | 1 | 1/2 |
| Potatoes ... | 50 | 4/10½ | 6/10½ | 20 | 2/9 |
| Flour (?) ... | 3½ | 5 | 10 | 1¾ | 5/5 |
| Milk ... | 12 | 3/– | 3/6 | 7 | 2/0½ |
| Pudding material | ½ | 4½ | 6½ | ab. ¼ | 3½ |
| Total ... | 84 lbs. | 16/– | 30/– | 36 lbs. | 13/– |
| Bread ... | 48 ,, | 5/– | 8/– | 84 ,, | 14/– |
| Total ... | 132 lbs. | 21/– | 38/– | 120 lbs. | 27/– |

If the consumption had been unaltered, the expenditure of the family would have increased from 21s. to 38s., or 81%; being forced to alter the consumption and increase its consumption of bread at the expense of other goods, the family was able to keep its additional expenditure for food as low as 6s., or 28½%, although the weight of the total consumption was decreased by nearly one-tenth. This budget is not exhaustive; several goods, butter, groats, marmalade, tea, etc., are missing. If the breadwinner has not increased his income, the 6s. must have been taken from other parts of his budget, for instance, clothes, amusements, etc. *H. Westergaard* is of the opinion that it would have been more correct—instead of calculating the consumption for 1913 and taking the prices for 1916—to take the actual consumption in 1916, and then calculate the total expenditure according to the prices of 1913, in which case we would have had a lower percentage of increase.

Which of the two figures, 81 or 28½, is now to be taken as the percentage of increase in the level of prices? The question is justified when we deny the expediency of speaking of a common level of prices for the community as a whole, but demand that a special level of prices for each class of buyers should be compiled. By the level of prices we express to some extent the price of the *general commodity* mentioned in section 23.

The value of money is the said ratio of exchange between the money and the *general commodity*, a proportion which expresses the purchasing power of money. The income of a person is the purchasing power placed at his disposal for a certain period through the distribution of the money value of the goods produced.

**48. The Substance of Value.**—The price of goods is the inverted proportion of exchange between the good in question and the representative of goods, money, and, through this, to some extent, all other goods, and consequently the "general" commodity. This, however, does not allow us to state that the price of a thing is its purchasing power. Firstly, the thing is not intended to buy, but to be bought; secondly, the price is something very relative; and thirdly, the fact that many goods have a quite different class of buyers will not allow us, for instance, to dare to say, that Millet's Angelus would buy 6,000 tons of wheat, even if the price of both was £50,000.

If the goods cost, A 5s., B 10s., and C 20s., the proportion between their prices is 1 : 2 : 4. This proportion states the relative element of value, inasmuch as it gives the respective place of the goods in the scale of prices. Why has the thing, for instance, exactly this position and no other in proportion to other goods? Some authors would here make use of the definition *absolute* in contra-distinction to *relative* value.

We must, however, maintain that value is a ratio and as such not absolute; but still the question is repeatedly advanced. Does no value-substance exist by which to measure the actual wealth of the world? *Marx* finds this in the "working hours expended," which are incorporated in the commodity; the value of two commodities is proportional to the "working hours expended" which have been applied to the goods. Adherents of the theory of the cost of production make the expense of production the substance, but forget that the expenses themselves are prices, and they would also have to make special rules for cases where the goods have another value than the cost of production. If Marx's theory of "working hours expended" is extended to apply to all factors in *the technical cost*, measured in units of energy, we would find in any commodity this substance, this *cost*, reduced to *units of energy*. But here also the fact applies that these units of energy appear in different forms, now as a raw material, now as labour, now as a machine, etc., and that without the help of the price—*i.e.*, of value, it is impossible to add them up to make an entity. Further, these prices of the elements in the finished goods are not decided according to their inherent energy, but according to some *outside* influence—their *position of power* (*Oppenheimer*), the relative position of monopoly.

From an abstract point of view we might perhaps say that for reproduceable goods these amounts of energy as a rule indicate a substance—something concrete and absolute—which in the long run and for the individual determine the place of a commodity in the scale of value, and which decides if a pound of tobacco shall be equal to three loaves or a loaf equal to three pounds of tobacco. The sum of the units of energy thus incorporated in goods and means of production should be the actual wealth of the world.

There is also something in the idea of fair price, by which is meant that the price of a commodity in proportion to that of other goods must not only adjust itself according to the amount of energy incorporated, but must also be in a *customary* proportion to the price of labour-wages. But for one thing it is impossible to compare the different forms, in which the energy of production is applied; secondly, there are some goods, where we have no idea at all of the energy applied (a picture); thirdly, in the individual market the goods will be placed quite otherwise than in proportion to the energy applied, and the price of the factors of production will finally neither be in proportion to the (uncertain) amount of energy, which produces them, nor to that energy which they themselves are able to yield. But even if these difficulties could be surmounted, the goods would then only exchange according to the energy incorporated in their *marginal units*, which is something different from the *actual* energy applied to a definite quantity of goods.

Behind the prices we will accordingly often feel a *substance* which in a static community will in many cases be in conformity with the number of units of energy applied to the *marginal unit* of the commodity, but this substance cannot be measured, nor even ascertained. The demand for a fair price is then only the demand for the maintenance of the customary price, even if an economically powerful position for a time, for instance, during war, may allow the producer or the holder of goods to raise the price, and perhaps also that these prices of goods at current wages must yield the labourer a living wage. Further we cannot advance, for the rules of price will repeatedly teach us that value is not anything absolute, but a ratio; every time we try to reach Juno we embrace the cloud.

**49. Value and Values.**—However, our investigation in the last section has not been altogether futile; we have learned to distinguish between human wealth and energy, incorporated in goods and means of production, the sum of which may at least theoretically be ascertained by adding the number of units of energy incorporated in these goods, and which is increased the greater the amount of work and talent we apply to the matter, and (2) the *economic value* of these concrete goods, which is *not* increased by the units of energy applied, and which we more probably *reduce* by our industry because our production reduces the marginal utility of the commodity. We have previously spoken of "*values*" as something originally applying to the concrete goods—*i.e.*, the sum total of their prices, but disconnected from that substance of concrete things to which they belonged. If we were to estimate the world's wealth in " values," we would arrive at a quite different result from what we would find if we make the estimate in units of energy. We might imagine that there were enough of all goods; in such conditions there would not exist any *economic value.* Values could not very well exist without a substratum of concrete substance of goods, of incorporated units of energy; but this substance may be very small: the maximum substance of goods keeps " values " at a minimum, while a deficit in the substance of goods keeps " values " at a maximum.

If we employ the expressions " a value " and " values " in this sense we wish to express the *economic strength* of the goods *in proportion to human capacity and need.* But this strength is not dependent upon the physical quantity of the goods, but on their *marginal desirability*, which again is a function of the number and demand of the population.

Now we also understand the contention previously advanced, that each additional child, without needing to increase the concrete supplies of goods proportionally, will *more than proportionally* increase " the values "—*i.e., the strength of goods in proportion to humanity—i.e.*, to those human beings who do *not* own the goods. The expression " values " comes to be in opposition to human labour, if this becomes cheap, values will be increased. Now we can see that " values " are nearly the same as property, in which we do not measure the productive power and stock of goods of a community (which is wealth), but only the command of the capitalists over the non-capitalists, their power to gain income without work. We here speak of " a value " and " values "; this is something different from the conception " value " with which we have worked in this chapter, and which is not absolute, but only the inverted ratio of exchange between two or more goods. This value has no plural and we cannot add up the value of goods, strictly speaking, it cannot be increased, because when one thing increases in value all others must fall.

But nevertheless we talk of adding up the value (we mean really prices) of all boots (total price) to that of all pipes and all other goods, forgetting that value in this sense is nothing concrete, no substance but merely a ratio; and ratios cannot be added to one another.

I return to this repeatedly, because not only merchants and politicians, but also economists and particularly statisticians are so much at fault in their conclusions about the *real* wealth of nations.

# BOOK III

## RELATIONS OF SUBJECTIVE PRICES

## CHAPTER IX

### THE DISTRIBUTION OF INCOME AND PRICES

**50. The Effect of Altered Income.**—The subjective prices of the individual are approximately proportional to the amount of his income. Simultaneously with a fall in the income of a buyer, a consequent reduction of his prices of demand must take place; these prices would all be reduced *by the same percentage* if the marginal utility of his income remained unchanged. This fact is not directly apparent, and seems to be contradicted by experience. Supposing the schedule of demand for a necessary and a luxury to be respectively N and L:

| | | | N | L |
|---|---|---|---|---|
| 6th unit | ... | ... | 240 | 133 |
| ——— | ... | ... | — | — |
| : : : : : | ... | ... | — | — |
| 11th unit | ... | ... | 133 | 108 |
| 12th ,, | ... | ... | 100 | 100 |

At a price of 100 for each of the goods I will buy 12 units of each and spend 1,200 + 1,200 = 2,400. Suppose now, that my income is reduced by 25% my schedule will now be

| | | | N | L |
|---|---|---|---|---|
| 6th unit | ... | ... | 180 | 100 |
| ——— | ... | ... | — | — |
| ——— | ... | ... | — | — |
| 11th unit | ... | ... | 100 | 81 |
| 12th ,, | ... | ... | 75 | 75 |

If the price is unchanged at 100, I will buy 11 units of the thing N and 6 units of L, with a total expenditure of 1,100 + 600 = 1,700—*i.e.*, my subjective prices being reduced by 25% has a different effect for the two goods. Apparently the decrease in my income has not made a very great alteration in my effective demand for bread, but then an examination of the schedule will show something different.

It is, however, not quite correct to maintain that the prices of demand in our case have been reduced by 25%. The circumstance that I will have to renounce on my usual consumption to a varying extent, by clinging to the necessary and resigning the luxury causes an alteration in the marginal utility of my income with the result that my prices of demand are not altered in quite the same *proportion*, even though in most cases in the same *direction* as the income. This can be proved if we examine the influence of the level of prices on the prices of demand.

**51. The Level of Prices and Subjective Price.**—Take our "*general commodity*," which we presume able to satisfy any demand; suppose the curve of utility to be the figures of the first column of the table below. Let us further presume that each unit of the commodity costs 1s. The marginal utility of income will then be equal to that of the "general commodity." Let the price fall to one half; the marginal utility of income will then be equal to the figures of the second column as the first shilling will give me the 1st and 2nd units; the second shilling the 3rd, and 4th units of the general commodity, etc.

| I. UNIT. | | | II. UNIT. | UU |
|---|---|---|---|---|
| 1st | ... | 330 | 1st | 580 |
| 2nd | ... | 280 | | |
| 3rd | ... | 261 | 2nd | 504 |
| 4th | ... | 243 | | |
| 5th | ... | 225 | 3rd | 435 |
| 6th | ... | 210 | | |
| 7th | ... | 196 | 4th | 378 |
| 8th | ... | 182 | | |
| 9th | ... | 168 | 5th | 325 |
| 10th | ... | 157 | | |
| — | | | | |
| 15th | ... | 105 | | |
| — | | | | |
| 17th | ... | 89 | 9th | 169 |
| 18th | ... | 80 | | |
| 19th | ... | 75 | 10th | 144 |
| 20th | ... | 69 | | |
| — | | | | |

| I. UNIT. | | | II. UNIT. | UU |
|---|---|---|---|---|
| 35th | ... | 25 | | |
| 39th | ... | 20 | 20th | 39 |
| 40th | ... | 19 | | |
| — | | | | |
| 49th | ... | 15 | 25th | 30 |
| 50th | ... | 15 | | |
| — | | | | |
| 59th | ... | 13 | 30th | 26 |
| 60th | ... | 13 | | |
| — | | | | |
| 69th | ... | 12 | 35th | 24 |
| 70th | ... | 12 | | |
| — | | | | |
| 79th | ... | 11 | 40th | 22 |
| 80th | ... | 11 | | |
| 81st | ... | 10 | | |
| — | | | | |

| I. | | II. | | I | II. | |
|---|---|---|---|---|---|---|
| UNIT. | UNIT. | | UU | UNIT. | UNIT. | UU |
| 25th ... | 45 | | | — | | |
| — | | | | — | | |
| 29th ... | 35 | 15th | 68 | — | | |
| 30th ... | 33 | | | etc. | | |
| — | | | | | | |

First we will deduce from this the marginal utility of an income varying from 2s. to 40s., if the price of the general commodity is respectively 1s. and 6d.

| | 1s. PER UNIT. | 6d. PER UNIT. |
|---|---|---|
| S. | UU | UU |
| 2 | 280 | 504 |
| 5 | 225 | 325 |
| 9 | 168 | 169 |
| 10 | 157 | 144 |
| 15 | 105 | 68 |
| 20 | 69 | 39 |
| 25 | 45 | 30 |
| 30 | 33 | 26 |
| 35 | 25 | 24 |
| 40 | 19 | 22 |

By a fall in the price (or in the level of prices) or what comes to the same thing, an increase in the purchasing power of money, we find that the marginal utility of income, the moral value of the shilling, for small incomes, is very much increased, because the shilling comes to stand for a greater number of units. For large incomes, on the contrary, the marginal utility of money will fall, for even if a shilling will buy double the quantity it did before, the two very late units do not yield as much utility as did previously the single one. It is probable that when we come to the very rich, whose money curve beforehand is flat, the falling prices will cause the marginal utility of money to again increase, because the 120th picture does not yield much less utility than the 60th (the utility of both being minimal); the 120th, plus the 121st, picture therefore yield greater satisfaction than the 60th. *Sir Sydney Chapman* has proved that the income-curve does not decline the whole way, but may even rise for a short interval. If the 10th shilling gives me the rise of $x$ (utility $u_x$), then an 11th shilling may yield $y$ ($u_y$); but it may happen that the pleasure of $x$ and $y$ together is greater than the sum of pleasures they yield us separately. It may be, concludes Chapman, that obtaining a larger income, we learn some new enjoyments of a higher value than that of those we appréciated with the smaller income. An art collector may in this way derive great pleasure from the 10,000th pound sterling quite beyond that which so late an amount should be able to give him. This is another reason why the money-curve may end as a straight line.

For *middle class incomes* it is probable that the marginal utility of money remains unchanged ; what is gained by having 2 units instead of 1 is just balanced by the fact that the 2 units are very late ones. We may express this thus : $u_x \lesseqgtr u_{2x} + u_{2x-1}$ in which $u$ states the utility and the index the unit referred to. At those stages of the curve of income, where the rate of fall in utility *is greatest* and smallest, the marginal utility of income decreases with an increase in prices ; at those stages, where the rate of fall is even, an increase in the level of prices may increase the marginal utility of income.

For the poor an increase in prices appears to entail a diminution in the moral value of the shilling, for the middle incomes rather an augmentation and for the well-to-do no change and for the richest again a diminution. The reservation must however be made regarding the statements in Sec. 51 that the tables are only examples, showing a tendency, but not proofs.

Alterations in price due to conditions affecting the supply, as a rule, affect the comparatively necessary goods ; an increase in the price of a necessary thing is most often due to an increasing scarcity in proportion to earlier supplies, while an increase in the price of a luxury will be due to greater purchasing power of the well-to-do, or to the fact that their number has been increased, which produces a relative scarcity and must entail either that some luxury-consumers are pushed out to the advantage of others—as war-economics have shewn—or that the luxury-industry must be extended at the cost of other industries. With this reservation concerning the conception "level of prices" we may make the following resumé : A general increase in prices, by decreasing the moral value of the shilling for the poor and the richest, will entail that they will pay a larger number of shillings than before, in any case, for those goods which comprise their minimum standard, while for other persons it will decrease their subjective prices by increasing their marginal utility of money; compare, however, the following:—

In the formula for marginal utility of income, $u_{pm} = \frac{C}{n - a}$, (Sec. 26) the Constant, C, will for the majority be increased with the purchasing power of money—*i.e.*, the higher the level of prices the lower the numerator C; also the denominator $(n - a)$ is increased by an increase in the purchasing power of money—*i.e.*, when the level of prices falls, because *a*, the minimum of existence, in that case can be bought so much cheaper; but through this the alteration in the constant is counteracted, as stated, most for the poor, for whom *a* is large in proportion to *n* (their total income).

The symbol *a*, then, is only an amount, which varies according to the level of prices—*i.e.*, the quantity of goods, of which *a* is the total price—the minimum of existence—is constant; *a* is, therefore, the same factor which is employed by *v. Thünen*, when he expresses the just wage of labour as $\sqrt{a \cdot p}$, in which *p* is the productivity of labour and *a* is the necessary consumption of the worker.

For a thing, the price of which *follows* the level of prices, an increase in this level makes a person, whose income is *unaltered*, *reduce* his purchase, but increase it for a thing, the price of which has remained unaltered in spite of the alteration in the level of prices. In other words, the alteration in the level of prices has forced him to change his consumption. The amount of our income, together with its purchasing power—expressed in the level of prices—determines the moral value of our income, and thereby our subjective prices and the quantity and nature of our purchase.

But as the subjective prices are included in the composite demand-schedule, any alteration in the income of the individual must, by altering his subjective prices, alter the composite schedule. If the schedules of demand are, respectively, A: 6s. 5s. and 4s., B: 8s., 6s. and 5s., and C: 10s. 8s., and 6s., the composite schedule will read: 10, 8, 8, 6, 6, 6, 5, 5, 4. If now C's income is decreased, making his schedule 5s., 4s. and 3s., this must alter the composite schedule to 8, 6, 6, 5, 5, 5, 4, 4, 3. C has become the last buyer, while B has become the first; if, now there are 6 units in the market, the market price, before the alteration being 6s., would, after the reduction in C's income, alter to 5s.

The schedule made up by compounding all the individual schedules will therefore be formed and altered according to the distribution of the "national dividend," whether "few have too much and fewer too little" (Grundtvig), or whether a large class of rich men exists whose economy is conditioned upon a lower class living under the conditions of a proletariat.

**52. Groups of Buyers.**—As the price-determining demand comes close to the marginal pair, it is sufficient to know *that* part of the schedule of demand, the centre of which is the actual price. The units last sold may be the 10th unit for the rich, the 4th for the middle classes, but the 1st for the labourer.

It may, however, be observed that in the case of a commodity, seeking consumers within several groups of buyers, and not as is especially the case with goods, which are produced in several qualities, being taken up completely by a single class of buyers, there will still be a single group of buyers whose demand becomes price-determining, because they form a *class of marginal buyers*, whose reaction on the turnover becomes decisive owing to the relatively great number in this class. What the well-situated will pay for bread is of no account whatever; even if a 4-lb. loaf costs 4s., the well situated would still eat sufficient; if on a market 100 lbs. of tea are sold, of which the rich buy 75 lbs., while the poor buy 25 lbs., the price will not be more than 2s., even if the price of demand for the first 75 lbs. is 3s., because the buyers of the last 25 lbs. cannot pay more; and even if the well-to-do increased their price of demand to 4s., this would be quite without influence upon the market price. What the poor man will pay for diamonds is, on the other hand, of no consequence, because the poor man's demand lies so far below the possibility of effectiveness. As we have non-competing groups of workers, so we have non-competing groups of buyers, groups which are consumers each of their own special goods.

The form of the curve of demand for a commodity is then, on the determining part, as pointed out by *Professor Cassel*, dependent upon the class of buyer which is the last with regard to the commodity in question. Now the income classes are arranged pyramidically; on a broad basis of incomes of, say, £50, rests a somewhat smaller number of incomes of £75, and above these again a still smaller number of incomes of £100, etc. Supposing 100 rich (R), 500 of the middle class (M) and 1,000 labourers (L), and that their purchase of a given commodity at the different prices runs as follows:

| | R | M | L |
|---|---|---|---|
| £5 ... ... | 1 | — | — |
| £2 10s. ... | 1 | 1 | — |
| £1 5s. ... | 4 | 2 | 1 |
| £1 ... ... | 6 | 4 | 2 |

this results in the following price-schedule :—

| At a price of | | TURNOVER |
|---|---|---|
| £5 | 100 R will buy 1 unit ... ... ... | = 100 units |
| £2 10s. | 100 R ,, 2 units, and 500 M 1 unit, each | = 700 ,, |
| £1 5s. | 100 R ,, 4 units, 500 M 2 units, and 1,000 L 1 unit ... ... ... each | = 2,400 ,, |
| £1 | 100 R ,, 6 units, 500 M 4 units, 1,000 L 2 units ... ... ... each | = 4,600 ,, |

The composite curve would appear as in Diagram XI.

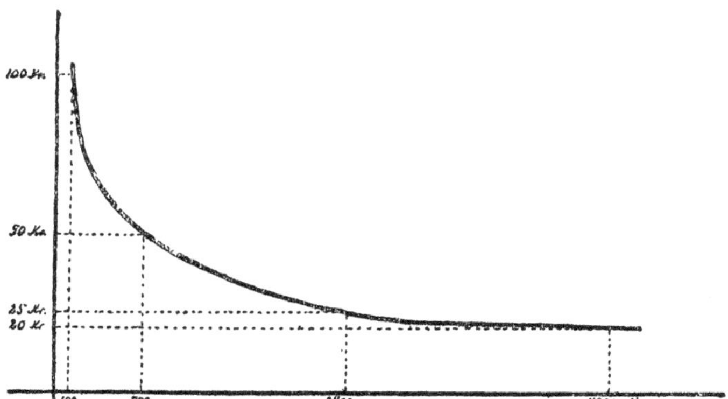


Diagram XI

While a decrease in the price from 100s. to 50s. increases the number of buyers by 600, the small decrease of 5s. (from 25s. to 20s.) will call forth an additional demand for 2,200 units, because a very numerous class of labourers double their consumption.

Goods, the last buyers of which come between two classes, and the consumption of which therefore is *not* regular, need not fall very much in price because the output is considerably increased. If the price of a commodity, which is one of the luxuries of the working class should fall in price, the numerous class of labourers may become effective buyers ; if the price is increased the whole class may probably discontinue buying the commodity.

In 1854 the price of coffee had fallen to 70% of the price in 1850 ; but the import into Denmark suddenly grew to 2½ times as much as in 1850, while the consumption of coffee from one year to another before as well as after 1854 was normally proportional to the movements in price ; this seems to be explicable only by the fact that the price in 1854 had come so far down that a quite new class only then became buyers of coffee and remained so.

If a new class of buyers starts buying a thing, this will sometimes have the character of a luxury for them. Habit may make it a necessity, and we will therefore see, as with coffee, that an increase in price equal to the fall which made the class in question consumers, will not make them again stop consumption. The reduction in 1891 of the Danish sugar duty gradually made sugar a necessity for everybody, and one which only a rather large increase in price will make even the poor give up again. After the fall in price of petroleum, which made the farm-labourers consumers, a very great increase in price is required to make them return to tallow candles.

**53. Some Price-Paradoxes.**—The distribution of income amongst the various classes of the community, through its influence on the schedules of demand, is the determining factor for the prices of goods. A well-situated working class raises the prices of those food-articles which lie above the minimum of existence ; a poor upper class, on the other hand, makes the art of painting a poor vocation. A redistribution of the yield of production, which makes the richest class disappear, must make diamonds very cheap ; but by this the production of diamonds will be stopped, as the cost is not covered by the low price which the best situated are *now* able to offer, and which is the price the actual stock will fetch.

The existence of a class of rich men whose marginal utility of income is sufficiently small, produces a strong demand for goods of infinitely small utility in comparison with the trouble their production causes the community—*i.e.*, other individuals. £1,000 means next to nothing in utility for the millionaire—*i.e.*, he will sacrifice them for a small satisfaction ; but the same £1,000 means for ten miners the consumption of the whole year and the great utility thereof ; they would therefore undertake a year's labour in order to produce an unnecessary luxury. An unequal distribution is, therefore, the condition for the production of unnecessary luxuries.

The fact that the marginal buyers of different goods come within different classes of buyers explains a difference in price between a commodity and its substitute of more than 100%, even if the difference in utility is infinitely small. If the substitute or the second quality article yields a utility of 100, and the first quality only adds 10 units of utility, but the substitute is being bought by a very poor class and the original article by a very rich class, it may happen that the 100 UU of the former are expressed by a price of 2s., while the additional 10 UU of the original article add 20s making the price of the best quality 22s. Many luxuries satisfy a necessary demand, which might also be satisfied by a substitute, but have the same rather unimportant additional utility, which, for instance, distinguishes a genuine Rubens from the work of a great living artist.

It is the same rule which becomes apparent in estimating the value of non-reproduceable goods, the rarity of which reduces their buyers to a very small number of very rich persons ; old masters, genuine Buddha figures, first prints, relics, etc. We must not be misled by the fact that a high price, which has thus been established by a limited circle of buyers, is apparently accepted by others, inasmuch as everybody who is able to procure the money at all, would be willing to pay £2,500 for a Rubens and £25,000 for the "Koh-i-noor." We would only buy them as sorts of intermediaries in the safe expectation of being covered by a later re-sale to one of those few, or as a temporary storage and investment of our capital. Even ordinary Galician Jews hold diamonds out of proportion to their capital, a habit from a past, where the lack of acknowledged representatives of capital as well as frequent confiscation of the property of Jews made it necessary for them to have easily transportable values on their person ; but through this there has arisen besides the final buyers a number of other buyers, whose subjective prices are indirect, and therefore come close to those of the proper buyers.

The rule of the influence of the classes of buyers on the price is again confirmed by the wages given for services. Body-servants, jugglers, astrologers, artistic hairdressers and cooks receive a very high wage in proportion to their education, on account of the large income of the marginal buyers of that class of work, while a great philosopher will perhaps starve to death because his *clientèle*, on the average, is poor. The great teacher of singing, Madame Marchesi, received 150 francs for an hour's lesson, while her Danish pupil received 10 francs ; living at Reykjavik before the war her remuneration would have been only 2 francs. There is also another reason for this to be found in the fact that we are more liberal to those who have part in our pleasures than to those who take part in our work, without considering the fact that, as a rule, we pay for personal services through the consumption of our net income, while the wages of our workers is an expense of production and an item on the expenditure side of our business ; there is, therefore, nothing surprising in the fact that the same calculating business man pays a seamstress 1s. a day and tips a waiter 1s. for serving a glass of beer.

If we wish to divide the income of a rich man, say £5,000, between 100 labourers, we would find that the £5,000 income is not identical with 100 times £50, which the 100 labourers have in total income. The rich man consumes the greater part of his income in the form of paintings, silk clothes, boxes at the theatre, the price of which increases with the number and income of the rich class, fashionable houses in Park Lane, in other words, goods the utility of which is small ; he uses only a very small part for bread and beer. But the £5,000, which the 100 labourers have together, means 100 times as much bread as the rich man consumes, perhaps 50 times as much butter, 30 times as much meat, 20 times as much wool, etc.

In the consumers goods of the general public there is more capital and less work incorporated than in luxuries, and in proportion to the value considerably more raw material is employed in necessaries than in luxuries. A re-distribution of income would therefore lead to a certain scarcity of raw materials, which are produced under the law of decreasing return. The war, for instance, by securing sufficient food and clothes for the soldiers—*i.e.*, more than they receive in ordinary conditions, has increased the great steam-trawling of the world-stock of raw materials.

If the workers had the rich man's money, the marginal utility of their money would decrease; through this the prices of their schedule of demand for ordinary necessaries would rise—*i.e.*, the increased income would then be spent in buying goods, which they previously bought for less money. The higher prices of ordinary articles of consumption would certainly call capital and labour, which had been spent in the production of luxuries, to produce the former articles, although at a higher cost, because more raw material would be required. An equal division, which, for instance, trebles the income of the labourers, would at the most double the quantity of goods, which they would receive for their real income; a trebled nominal wage would scarcely be equal to a doubled real wage, even in normal times.

**54. Adaptation of Demand and Supply.**—As the actual consumption is determined by the demand, and this again by the distribution of income, it will be the latter which decides which goods are demanded and are saleable, and which consequently must be produced. *The distribution of income determines the direction and amount of production as well as the prices of goods.*

But the distribution of income in our community changes. Every time consumption and production of goods have arrived at an equilibrium, this is again disturbed, because the demand is altered together with the distribution of income; but the corresponding reorganisation of production takes time—*i.e.*, we will have a *shortage in the production* of some goods and an *over-production* of other goods, which the new recipients of income will decline, and which the old ones can no longer afford. If the upper classes are impoverished, the demand for luxuries will decrease; if the lower classes are impoverished it is the dispensable consumers' goods of the labourer which fall in price, while the indispensable goods—which, further, may be substituted in consumption by other goods (which previously had not been bought)—may even arise.

This augmented demand for a certain commodity—owing to the altered distribution of income—will entail a rise in price to cut off some of the demand, as the amount of the output cannot be altered at an hour's notice. This rise in price will be stopped by the *undertaking of new production* until equilibrium has been attained. But this takes time, and if the alteration in the distribution of income is sufficiently violent and sudden, there must be a crisis. For we must produce according to the demands of the purchasing power—*i.e.*, according to the distribution of income; we may regard the latter as being absurd and unjust, but in any case we must take its consequences and produce goods which correspond to it. Just as absurd as it is to produce motor cars where there is no rich class to buy them, so absurd is it to produce boots for a population whose income only runs to wooden shoes. In the criticism of luxury consumption the *socially desirable* is confused with the *economically necessary.* If there is to be equilibrium between demand and supply, so that all the goods produced can be bought, those goods which the recipients of income *will* have, must be produced. It is another matter that it is a duty of an economic upper class to save—*i.e.*, employ part of their income for the purchase and production of means of production, but carried beyond certain limits too much "saving" is unhealthy. For it is no more rational to employ part of the income of the nation for the erection of factories to produce boots for the labourers than to produce leather footwear direct, when the consumers for whose demand we wish to produce cannot buy the article. This will, as Marx maintains, only lead to a crisis.

This defence of the luxury consumption of the rich is *conditioned* by the liberal acknowledgment of the inequality in the distribution of income. The defence is naturally not identical with the statement, that luxury consumption gives work (or that window panes should be smashed when the glass-works are idle). And still there is in the last mad argument a truth; a fall of snow is really a good thing for the unemployed, because it creates for them a possibility of existence which they would otherwise not have (by clearing the snow), and forces the rich to spend their money in "idle" services which do not require raw materials. The necessity for agreement between paying ability and production is often overlooked; the textile industry and the landlords of houses are really interested in the fact that the working class, as consumers, have high wages; as isolated employers it is their interest to pay their own staff a low wage. In other words by making wages high each individual acts against his own interest as an employer of labour; by making wages low he acts against his interests as a seller of goods.

Another example of the lack of adaptation of production to demand can be found in the history of protection. The Austrian sugar duty was, before 1902, so enormous that the home price was bound to attract new producers, but poor consumers were scared away. The consequence was an absurd policy of export bounties. After 1902 the reduction of the protection in the countries of the convention caused the price to fall, in reaction against which production was reduced and consumption increased, until equilibrium between supply and demand was again attained.

We have used the expression *partial* over-production—*i.e.*, that too many units of a thing have been produced in proportion to the demand—*i.e.*, *the will to buy of the recipient of income*. This happens when all the units in the market can only be sold at prices which are below the seller's purchase price. In the economic sense there may be an over-production of boots, even though the majority of a population with small purchasing power must go barefoot; there may be an over-production of houses, although the labourers live in hovels.

Every time taste and fashion alter, every time the distribution of income is altered, there will immediately be an over-production of certain goods, and, as a rule, also a shortage in the production of other goods the price of which is rising. In 1916 the price of motor cars went up, because the many new rich men wanted them, and there consequently was a *shortage of production* in proportion to the will to buy.

A period of speculation which coincides with new tastes, or a chance demand that is particularly apparent, exaggerates the amount of this demand and therefore ends in over-production of the goods which satisfy such a demand; in this case over-production is due to the output being forced, while it is otherwise due to the fact that the demand for goods is reduced.

If the upper class starts saving, there will be a shortage in the production of means of production, but over-production of those luxuries which the upper classes have given up. If the saving by the upper classes takes place at the cost of the wage-earners, whose real wage, for instance, has been forced down, and not by any self-denial on the part of the capitalists, there will be an over-production of the more dispensable consumers' goods of the labourers.

In periods of crises the purchasing power also fails for reasons of a monetary nature, which creates an *over-production* of most goods, a general glut, which ends in a collapse of the level of prices. The expression for purchasing power, ready money or credit, temporarily disappears; but if credit has again ventured forth, purchasing power will again have its means of expression and the over-production will cease.

*J. B. Say* states in his "*loi des debouchés*" that every product will find as many more possibilities of sale as there is variety and abundance of other products. The best means to further the sale of one thing is the production of another. If by this he only means that the product in question thereby comes into a position of scarcity, he would be right, but in this case he proves nothing, for the other goods, of which there is an abundance, would then be in distress; but if he means that if the growth of production and demand take place simultaneously and in the same proportion, over-production would be impossible, then he indirectly alleges that it is possible—*i.e.*, when this condition is not present.

The argument of Say's in the above theory that there cannot be a general over-production, because goods are exchanged for goods, is tempting, but not correct; firstly, he does not take into consideration the regular breaking down of the credit system; and secondly goods are not exchanged for goods, but for money acquired as *remuneration* for services. The formula is Services—Money—Goods, not Goods—Goods, nor Goods—Money—Goods. There need not be equilibrium between the services rendered and the goods produced; obviously, neither more nor less money is paid for goods than what is paid out to labourers, recipients of interest and other partakers in the profits of production; but production will often have taken place in such a way that it does not correspond to the distribution of income, quite apart from the disturbing elements, that the employer must first sell the final product, before his share of the profits is at his disposal for the purchase of goods, and also that the means of circulation for a time may partially disappear and thereby cause general shortage of consumption.

**55. The Ambiguity of Value.**—In 1898 the *Blue Diamond* of the *Hope* collection was sold for £50,000. For this sum at the same time there could be bought 50,000 quarters of rye. As the price was alike it would be tempting to say that the Blue Diamond could tempt farmers to produce 50,000 quarters of grain, and the consumers to do without that quantity.

This apparently equal price obscures a great difference; this fiction that the Blue Diamond is of the same value as 50,000 quarters of grain is caused by the existence of a measurement of value. The fact is that the sale of the two goods in question has taken place in two different classes of the community; the Blue Diamond has passed from one rich man to another, both of whom have a very small marginal utility of money; the 50,000 quarters of grain, however, have been grown by a quite different class of men, who have suffered a great disutility of sacrifice, and have been bought by people whose marginal utility of money is very high.

The importance of money as a measurement of value is *smaller* than would be presumed; that 50,000 quarters of grain and the Blue Diamond, two such incommensurable quantities, can be measured by the same measurement of value is really the veriest fiction. The same price covers a totally different substance of value. Nobody will maintain that because two children in play exchange brass buttons to an imaginary value of £50,000, these buttons have that value; but in the above transaction the Hope Diamond played the part of the brass buttons and the two rich men those of the children.

Similar cases have appeared during the war; when, for instance, Germany is stated to have used more than 300 milliard marks (three-quarters of the national property) for the purposes of war, Germany will actually have used scarcely one-third of the national property. All prices have gradually been trebled, wherefore the same technical energy is expressed by thrice as much money; the soldiers are apparently taken away from the production of valuable goods, but more than one third of the soldiers did *not* previously perform such production; a number of men who previously rendered personal services (servants, tenor singers, etc.) now earn a wage at the front. If, out of seven retailers in the same street, six are called up for military service, the retail turnover will still go on as usual. Five thousand million pounds sterling neither means food for 100 million workers nor 5 milliard quarters of grain, nor 2 milliard tons of coal, nor could there have been built for the said milliards a double-tracked railway tunnel between Cape Finisterre and

Vladivistock and some distance out into the Pacific. Certainly, the tunnels through the Alps cost £220,000 per kilometre, but if 30,000 kilometres had to be built the cost per kilometre would have been, not £220,000, but more than £1,000,000 on account of the rise in price of all the elements of cost, regardless of the technical impossibility of procuring sufficient productive power. Neither would we for 5000 million pounds sterling be able to build three-roomed flats for the entire town population of Europe—even if that could be done, calculated according to normal prices.

The fact is that a *price* only holds good for a corresponding turnover between given classes of the community, and that other classes as the parties to the exchange and other quantities produced would give quite different price relations.

This is still more glaring, as pointed out often before, for instance, in Sec. 49, where an estimate of the national property is concerned, if we take the separate items and compare their value, we will come to a wrong result for the above reasons ; if we take capital in a private sense as a means of income free of labour, we would arrive at such anomalies as, for instance, that the national property (statistically) is increased if an increase in the population or a monopoly increases the ground rent (house rent) and thereby the property of individuals.

Value and price is an infinitely relative proportion, conditional upon a *limited* turnover. A great number of goods, to which we attribute great value when we estimate our property, can only maintain that value under the presumption that they *do not have to be* sold, or are only to be sold provided that an eager buyer appears of his own accord. If the few blue diamonds in existence only change hands quite accidentally, but otherwise remain in the ownership of certain families, we may say that their value is £50,000 each; but as there is a deal perhaps only every 50 years, this valuation is really of no consequence.

A price does not, strictly speaking, give any definite indication of the purchasing power of a thing, nor are the prices of goods generally any guide to the economic conditions of the place or the year. The fact that the price of a thing is the same two years in succession does not entitle us to draw any conclusion with regard to the state of the market (because the turnover may at the same price be greater in one year than in another), nor can we compare local differences. A price of grain which would be an expression for famine in India would in Denmark mean abundance. Only a comparison between price and the wages of labour and degree of employment would give us a basis for estimating the conditions of a community.

"Good and bad times" are therefore disputable expressions; if "good times" mean large profit and high prices, the workman who finds that his nominal wage (in money) does not follow the price of goods and that consequently the real wage (*i.e.*—expressed in goods) is falling, may find "times hard." Malice has framed the maxim: "In good times the labourer starves because his wage has no purchasing power; in bad times because he has no work." Money is certainly a measurement of value, but we must not trust the comparison for more than it is worth; because the price of one thing is ten times the price of another, we cannot conclude that it will buy ten units of the other, or is able to yield us more utility; neither needs the difference in the price of a thing at different times and stages be the expression for any difference. This is also my reason for rejecting "purchasing power" as a definition of the term value. The term "price" says neither more nor less than that, under certain strictly defined conditions and between certain individuals, a given thing has been exchanged for money in the ratio stated by the price.

# CHAPTER X

## THE ELASTICITY OF CONSUMPTION

**56. Elasticity and Sensitiveness.**—The merchant, the producer or a taxing authority has to make a survey of the form of the curve of demand—*i.e.*, ascertain if there is a great or a small difference between the subjective prices of successive units. Otherwise the merchant will not be able to solve the problem, the correct solution of which is the basis of his economic existence;

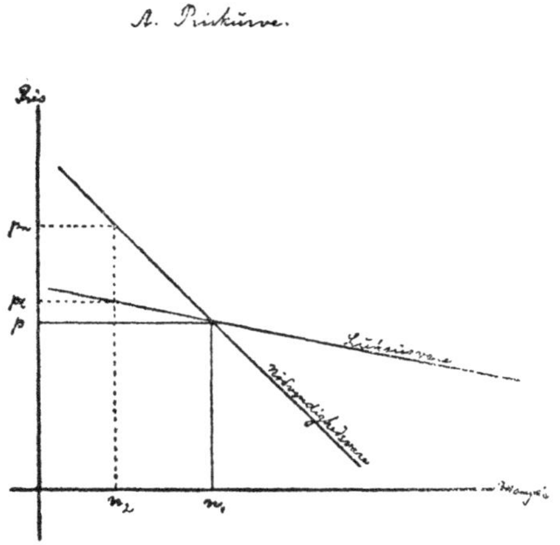


Diagram XIIa

neither would it be possible for the science of finance to find out the effect of taxation on production or consumption. The problem, which is a double one, reads: (*a*) *Will an alteration in the selling price of a thing produce a large or small alteration in the number of effective buyers ? and (b) Will an altered output affect the market price perceptibly or not ?*

Diagram XII gives the customary *curve of demand* for two commodities, one steep—*i.e.*, the utility of the thing decreases at a quick rate, the other one flat—*i.e.*, the utility has a very slow rate of decrease. Experience has taught us that the first curve is that of a necessity, the second one that of a luxury.

In Diagram XII*b* we have reversed the curve and entered the price along the abcissa and the quantity along the ordinate. The curves thereby become *curves of quantity*, stating the quantities in proportion to varying prices. It will be seen that the quantity-curve of the necessary good becomes rather flat, while that of the luxury is steep.

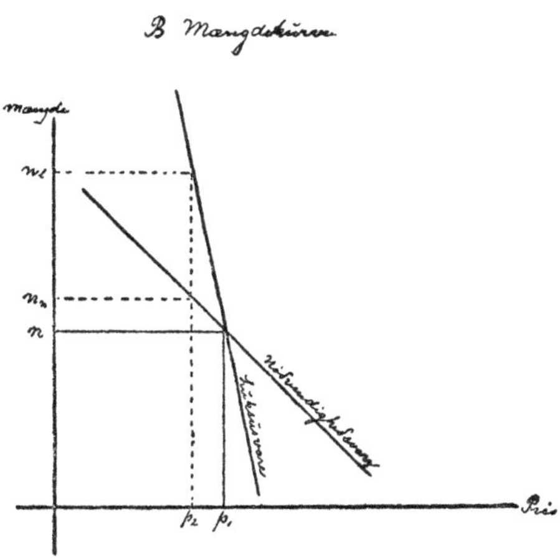

Diagram XIIb

From the two diagrams we may immediately read the effect of altered price and altered output respectively. If the output (diagram XII*a*) for both goods is reduced from $n_1$ to $n_2$ the price will increase from $p$ to $p_l$ for the luxury, but the far larger distance from $p$ to $p_n$ for the necessary good. With the steep price curve an alteration in the output causes a very great alteration of the price (in the opposite direction), while an alteration in the output with the flat price-curve only causes a small alteration.

If a given price for both goods of $p_1$ falls to $p_2$, the quantity sold will be increased from $n$ to $n_n$ for the necessary good, but from $n$ to the far greater quantity $n_l$ for the luxury. In the steep price-curve and, consequently, flat quantity curve, an alteration in price only causes little alteration in the output, while an alteration in the flat price-curve (and steep quantity curve) will cause great alteration in the turnover.

We say that a thing, which has a *steep price-curve* and, consequently, an even quantity-curve, is *sensitive in price*, but *inelastic in consumption*, and a thing which has an *even price-curve* and consequently a steep *quantity curve*, is *insensitive* in price, but *elastic* in consumption.

**57. The Conditions for Elasticity.**—(1) The price curve of the *necessity* is steep, while that of the *luxury* is flat. *Gregory King* advanced the rule for grain, that an increasing deficit in the crop caused prices to increase in a geometrical proportion. For salt we have *Neckers'* estimates, and also a comparison between consumption and price from 1848.

We may construct the following two price-schedules :—

| | GRAIN. | SALT. |
|---|---|---|
| QUANTITY. | PRICE. | PRICE. |
| 33 units ... ... ... | 1,000 | 270 |
| 50 ,, ... ... ... | 550 | — |
| 60 ,, ... ... ... | 380 | — |
| 70 ,, ... ... ... | 260 | 200 |
| 80 ,, ... ... ... | 180 | — |
| 90 ,, ... ... ... | 130 | 150 |
| 100 ,, ... ... ... | 100 | 100 |

The same fall in price from 270 to 100 triples the consumption of salt, but only increases the consumption of grain by 50%.

Supposing, for instance, the curve of the necessary good to be 10, 7 and 4, while that of the luxury is 8, 7, 6, 5, 4, our result will be that an increase in price from 4 to 7 will only reduce the consumption of the necessity by 1 unit, but of the luxury by 3 units.

(2) The price curve of the *rich* man is steeper than that of the *poor* man, because the same difference in utility for the former may be expressed by 10s. for the latter by 2s. ; an increase in price of 10s. will only make the rich man give up 1 unit, but make the poor man stop consumption completely.

(3) If a well-to-do class comprises 200 persons, who each use 5 units of a thing, the price of which is 6s., and if a price of 5s. would make a *new class of the community* of 1,000 members buy 1 unit each, a fall in price from 6s. to 5s. would double consumption, and a corresponding increase in price make it one half—*i.e.*, when the price falls from 6s. to 5s. the curve will become flat instead of steep; if the consumption had *rested permanently with one of the two classes of buyers* the curve would have retained its relatively steep form throughout.

(4) If there are *no substitutes* for a thing, I am bound to buy it or resign completely the satisfaction of my desire; a monopoly may force me to reduce my consumption and to pay a much higher price for the remainder; if, however, I am able to find a substitute I am independent of the monopoly, because I am only dependent on the main thing for the difference in utility, but my principal demand can be satisfied by the substitute. Substitution is the most effective remedy against a monopoly, a remedy which fortunately exists for most goods and for everybody. If there were no substitute for butter, my want of something to put on my bread would cause me to submit to an increase from 1s. to 2s. per lb., and only react by using less butter; but if there be a substitute, which has only been increased from 8d. to 10d., my principal want can be satisfied by the margarine, and I will not pay 1s. 2d. for the small difference in satisfaction which butter would yield me. But this reacts on the curve of butter according to the general rule, that the price of demand for the first quality is a function of the price obtained for the second quality. A thing which has no substitute may often be a substitute itself; in this case it will be affected by an alteration of the distribution of income or the level of prices making its schedule of demand rise. A period of high prices forces people to give up many composite goods and turn to bread (see the comparison showing the bread-consumption of an English labourer before and during the war.) A dearth will therefore often increase the price, as well as the quantities sold, of such goods as are substitutes for others; the cheaper kinds of food are, considered as a group, substitutes for all other kinds of food.

(5) A thing is said to be of great *relative importance for the budget* if a comparatively great part of our income is spent in the purchase of it. The greater the relative importance of a thing,

the more will I react against an increase in price. If, however, I only want one nutmeg a year, its price may be trebled without making an alteration in my purchase. There is almost no limit to how much the goods which are relatively unimportant in consumption, may rise in price without altering consumption, if they are necessities. The amount of profits earned during the war on buttons, elastic, thread and sewing cotton is surprising.

It is for the same reason that the retailer may make such enormous profits on goods, which are either of comparatively small importance, or are bought in small quantities. Chicory used to yield the retailer a large profit; at the moment of sale it seems unimportant to the customer if $\frac{1}{4}$ lb. of sugar costs $\frac{3}{4}$d. or 1d.; for coal and salt in small quantities the poor pay a very high price. (Sale in small quantities also causes much trouble.)

The retailer often takes his profit where the public cannot see the difference; at one time the same thing is offered for sale under different marks, at another a different thing under the same mark; if the customer *knows* a certain article, he is able to guard against this. Although a great profit can be made on knives and shovels on account of their relatively small importance, a special brand, which has been advertised and is known, can only be sold at a small profit for the retailer (as proved by *Lindberg*). The retailers' prices are otherwise difficult to determine; they are partly dependent upon a local monopoly, partly upon the customary price, and, finally, upon necessity. Where there are many small retailers the turnover will be costly. The Maypole Dairy Company has shown that a large turnover and a uniform system of working makes possible smaller profits per unit and yet larger (net) total profits. The price of demand decides the limit of retail-profits; competition between retailers is mostly apparent through the conveniences and facilities offered the public and by advertising, and not very often through lower prices. Also the competition of the manufacturers is rarely apparent to the public in respect of price; manufacturers compete through the discount, which they allow the retailer.

Sometimes very costly goods come within the category of relatively small importance, that is, when the thing has to be *acquired once* only, and is either bought on instalments, or is bought by a concern in order to be used for the purposes of trade; a typewriter which is sold for £25 in Denmark can be imported for £15. The cost of acquiring one is large compared with one year's income, but of small importance in proportion to the total capital sunk in furnishing the office.

(6) If a thing can only be *employed for one purpose* its curve will be short and rather steep ; if it can be employed in several ways the number of useable units is increased. A reduction of the output will then not mean that an important use has to be given up, but that a secondary use must be discontinued.

We may now make the following tabular resumé :—

| A | B |
|---|---|
| (*a*) Steep price-curve = sensitive in price. | (*a*) Even price-curve = not sensitive in price. |
| (*b*) Even quantity-curve = inelastic in consumption. | (*b*) Steep quantity-curve = elastic in consumption. |

Nature of the article :

| A | B |
|---|---|
| I. Necessity. | I. Luxury. |
| II. Consumed by rich buyers. | II. Poor circle of consumers. |
| III. Bought permanently by one class. | III. Unsteady in the class of buyers. |
| IV. No substitute. | IV. Has a substitute. |
| V. Small relative importance. | V. Great relative importance. |
| VI. Can only be employed in one way. | VI. Can be employed in many ways. |

The qualities mentioned under A make a thing inelastic in consumption ; people will not willingly give it up in spite of an increase in price ; those qualities mentioned under B make it elastic in consumption—*i.e.*, people are willing to give up consuming it. For goods belonging to Group A the producer is the stronger, for goods belonging to Group B the consumer has the upper hand provided everything is otherwise equal.

Actually we cannot divide goods into these categories, because the six deciding qualities may not all be on the same side of our table. A thing consumed by rich buyers may be a necessity or a luxury ; it may have some of the qualities of Class A and others of Class B. Suppose that a poor man's article is a necessity, is consumed permanently by that class, has a substitute, but is of relatively small importance in his budget of expenditure, some of the qualities of the article give it a steep, others an even price-curve. By a combination, in which the effect of the different qualities are of unequal importance there will arise a price-curve, the form of which the *merchant must* anticipate. Still more complicated is the case if the same thing is actually a luxury for the poor, but a decided necessity for the rich, or when the thing for the same class of buyers through habit changes its character from that of a luxury to that of a necessity (for instance, tobacco) or if a class gives up the consumption of a thing on account of dearth, and the determining part of the curve of this article therefore now shows itself steep instead of even (as was the case with meat during the war). The limits are the *poor man's luxury*, the curve of which is flat like a Dutch high road, and the *necessities of the rich*, the curve of which is as steep as a rock side. The rich man's luxury curve starts higher than the poor man's necessity curve, but as the latter reaches nil quicker, it is steeper, just as the side of a hillock may be steeper than a mountain side.

The curve of the substitute is steep, and that of the commodity, which it substitutes, is flat; but as the consumers of the former article are mostly poor, and those of the latter are rich, it may happen that the curve of the substitute seems flatter than that of the main article.

**58. The Curves of Various Goods.**—Below we will examine the factors, which are of importance for the form of the curve of demand for certain goods.

*Rye.*—In normal conditions the determining marginal consumption will be the use of Rye as a *feeding stuff*. For this purpose there are, however, a number of substitutes, and the price-curve will be *even* on that part, which stands for the demand for this purpose: an increase in price would decrease the demand to a very great extent. For *bread* rye is in Denmark a necessity and may be regarded as a substitute for some other foods (elements in the *steep* price-curve) but it has (1) a substitute in the potato; (2) the class of the marginal buyers is the poorest and the commodity is (3) of relatively great importance in their budget; further (4) the marginal class of buyers is unsteady, being as stated sometimes "cattle" and sometimes human beings; and (5) rye, besides being a cereal and feeding stuft, may be used, for instance, for the manufacture of liquor. These five elements which tend to make the price-curve *even*, are counteracted by the two first-mentioned which will make it steep. The result is then a price-curve for rye, which on the *first part* (as a cereal) *is steep, but later* (as feeding stuff, etc.) more *even*.

*Wheat.*—For those countries where wheat is the cereal, something similar to what is said above of rye will apply. In

Denmark, however, wheat bread is a luxury, which may be given up if necessary, so that the class of buyers is not altogether steady, but may be forced to use the substitute, rye bread. In contrast to these three elements in an even price-curve there is only the fact that wheat bread and coffee in a way form a substitute for hot food. On the whole, in Scandinavia, the price-curve of wheat will be considerably more even than that of rye.

Cereals as well as other *crops* are subject to special rules because the price of grain is not only a derived price (based on that of bread, meat, etc.), but also a wholesale price, decided on a market where speculation operates, and *must* do so, because our knowledge of the last crop is unreliable, and because the crop of the coming season can only be estimated with great uncertainty. Otherwise there are special price-rules for goods, the quantity of which is fixed for a certain period (for instance, the crop of a year) and cannot within that time be increased at will. The market price oscillates round a kind of *season-price*, determined after considera tion of the crop, the amount of which again decides, which part of the curve of demand becomes price-determining, whether this be a later part, where the producers of meat, or an earlier part where the consumers of bread are the marginal buyers.

*Bread.*—This is naturally subject to exactly the same conditions as set forth above with regard to cereals. The curve of demand will be very *steep*. The poorer a family is the greater will be its expenditure for coarse bread, not only relatively, but even absolutely (bread and potatoes substitute other food). This increase of consumption may even be noticed with rising bread-prices, which have the same effect as a decrease in the income. For our poor class at least 10% of the income is paid for bread (coarse and fine), and this yields $\frac{1}{3}$ of its food; during the war the same families were using more than $\frac{1}{4}$ of their income for this purpose and bread yielded more than one half of the necessary calories

*Meat.*—The great population of Europe has learned during the war that meat is not a necessity. It is somewhat different in normal conditions where the fairly well situated (especially in the towns—in the country meat is not of nearly as much account) actually regarded meat as a necessity and therefore had a rather steep curve of demand. The poor part of the population must, on the contrary, be content to regard meat as a desirable variation in the weekly bill of fare, and for this unsteady class of buyers even a moderate consumption will mean a considerable amount in the household budget, and be regarded as a luxury, because there are thousands of substitutes (all other foods).

While thus the meat-curve on the first part is rather steep, it will, later on, be more and more even, making a comparatively small increase in price cause a considerable decrease of consumption. It should also be remembered that the term "meat" covers many different sorts and qualities down to what is merely offal, so that within these changes in price and consumption may take place. A rise in price for one quality will entail an increased demand for a poorer quality, which will also rise in price, etc. The great steepness of the upper part of the meat curve affects the prices of grain and fodder, if there is a scarcity of these, so that the rich meat consumers must be prevented by rationing from demanding grain, which should be used for bread.

*Spirits* may perhaps for a certain part of the population be regarded as a necessity, and the class of buyers is fairly steady; further, there is no substitute (for furniture-polish, methylated spirits, etc., would only be used by completely degenerate individuals). These elements cause a steep price-curve. On the other hand, the marginal buyers are poor and the expense is of relatively great importance in their budget. The first two facts mentioned will, however, have the deciding influence, making the curve of spirits (gin, whisky) rather steep. The reduction, which, since 1900, has taken place in the consumption, is more due to the agitation of abstainers and to the fact that the labourers are now drinking beer, than to the increase in taxation. (Since 1917 taxation has been so heavy as to have the deciding effect.)

*Coffee, Chicory.*—According to the statistics compiled by a Danish District Judge, the consumption of chicory by seamstresses is the same regardless of the income, but the addition of coffee varies according to the amount of income.

A greater income in a class does not mean that the coffee-substitute is exchanged for coffee, but only that more is consumed of the brown fluid, and that the increased expense is arrived at by increasing, not the amount of chicory, but the proportion of coffee in the mixture. Inquiries made by the author have given similar results for labourers' families. It is only when we come to the class of expert workers, that coffee replaces chicory, even if very rarely altogether, and that the consumption of chicory decreases absolutely as well as proportionally ; the fact that certain classes drink coffee instead of eating cooked food, however, obscures the question. Chicory, then, has a very steep curve, while that of coffee is much more even, in any case, on the lower part ; on the upper part, it is probably quite as steep as that of chicory. Coffee is an example of the number of goods, the curve of demand for which *changes form* (and consequently rate of decrease) if they extend from the consumption of one class to that of another.

*Groceries.*—A price-curve cannot be outlined, as there are great differences within this group of goods. Some must be regarded as necessities, others as luxuries, some are of great, others of small importance in the budget ; for some the marginal buyers are well-to-do, for others they are the very poorest. In some cases there are substitutes, in others not. Of a number of spices the consumption of the individual is exceedingly small, for which reason they are of no importance in the budget even of the poor : the curve of demand may therefore be very *steep*.

A number of groceries have passed through the development from originally being a luxury to becoming a necessity even for the poor (sugar, coffee, etc.). The steepness may also be due to the fact that a physiologically *fixed* point of satisfaction stops the demand for the thing—*i.e.*, consumption can neither very well be decreased nor increased. It has been observed that increase in prices owing to pre-war taxes has not altered the number of *tobacco* consumers, the smoker having only turned to a cheaper quality (smoking-mixture substituted for cigars, Virginia for Turkish).

*Sewing Articles.*—These goods are necessities even for the poorest ; substitutes do not exist, and the relative importance for the budget being only small, the class of buyers will be very steady. The price-curve will therefore be very steep, and it may be added that the sale takes place in small lots, which permit still larger profits.

*Teachers of Singing.*—These must presumably be regarded as a luxury, but the class of buyers is steady and rather well-to-do ; (a reduction in the price for a lesson for instance from 5s. to 4s. will not result in any increase worth mentioning in the number of pupils). The price of demand, in other words, is dependent on the marginal utility of money to the well-to-do. A large class of rich people interested in Music will make the remuneration of teachers singing very high, while it will only be moderate in a country where the number of well-to-do is small and not much interested in the art of Apollo. In addition, the demand for lessons is a kind of joint demand, as to this there must be added appliances and the pupil's own sacrifice of time.

*Literature.*—As far as books are concerned, we must distinguish between expensive and cheap editions. As an instance we may take English novels at 6s. and at 7d. For the first the price is so high that the marginal consumers are the upper middle class and the intelligent section down through all classes of the population, who sacrifice other necessities in order to acquire books and therefore—in spite of the high marginal value of their money—may have a high subjective price. The class of buyers will therefore be fairly steady and the curve of demand be rather steep—a moderate increase or decrease in price means no alteration of importance in the consumption. To cause such an alteration the price must be considerably reduced. At a price of 7d. a book will find buyers far down in the scale; a completely new class of buyers is attracted, for whom the 6s. edition is far too expensive. The great English publishing houses employ the principle to issue a book at 6s., and when it has had the sale which can be expected at this figure, they reduce it first to 2s. 6d., and then finish with a popular edition at 1s. or 6d. or 7d.

For newspapers something similar is the case. If large papers are practically exclusively subscribed for by the well-to-do bourgeoisie, their price of subscription may be very high. The small papers which appeal to the lower middle class and the labourers are, on the contrary, obliged to keep low prices.

*Milk.*—As is the case with corn the curve of demand has several sections, as milk cannot only be employed for food, but also for feeding purposes and in industry (casein). Further, it must be remembered that milk is the raw material of other foods, cream, cheese and butter, for which reason the price of one will affect the others (competition in the production). That part of the price-curve which represents the use of milk for *food* will be steep; children cannot in any case do without milk, however poor the class to which they belong, for which reason the class of buyers is relatively steady. Milk-prices will therefore be able to stand a rather heavy increase. On the other hand, a greatly *increased production* will meet a demand from agriculture itself as well as from industry, so that the fall in price will far from correspond to the form of the curve of demand on the upper part.

*Butter* is a luxury, as we have a substitute in margarine which is almcst as nourishing. In normal conditions the class of buyers will reach very far down, with the interruption however, of a middle-class struggling to keep up its standard, and which consume margarine—the higher working class resuming, after the interruption, because, as conditions are, they are not content with the artificial butter. If butter, as during the war, goes up in price to 3s. and 4s. per lb., the upper class will be the only effective buyers.

Students may with advantage practise the combination of rules for the mutual relations of butter, cheese and milk.

At the present stage of human development some "buttering" of bread must be regarded as an absolute necessity As it is itself a substitute, margarine has none, lard being more expensive. The class of buyers is therefore steady, and even if it reaches to the very poorest, the curve of margarine will be rather steep. Margarine forms one of the most apparent examples of the fact that the population of a country is itself content with a secondary article, the substitute, in order to liberate the main article, which is exported to another country, where such consumption can be afforded. If the profit gained by this for the country is employed for imports of luxuries by a well-to-do class of the population, the export is socially detrimental.

Margarine, like all goods of a secondary quality, has, however, on one point a fate in common with the article of the higher quality, that an increase in price may be guarded against by turning to the other commodity, which fact causes the curve of margarine not to start so high.

(Compare my book *Prices and Taxation of Real Estate*, concerning, for instance, the relation of two and three-roomed flats, and flats in different parts of the town. I would recommend students to use the different prices of goods during the changing stages of the war for testing the rules advanced above ; they will then find many interesting facts concerning substitution of consumption as a defence against increase in prices of goods.)

**59. Expenditure and Prices.**—Having found the effect of

the alteration in price on the quantity sold and the effects of an altered output on the market, we shall now examine *the effect of alterations in prices on the purchase of goods—i.e.*, how much we spend out of our total income for the purchase of the good in question.

For a thing of which, at a price of 10s., I would buy $x$ units, I spend $10 . x$s. If the price is increased to 12s. I would use a smaller number of units, say $x - a$.

Now there are three possibilities, that I pay the *same* amount, or a *larger* or *smaller* amount for the thing—*i.e.*,

$$10 \cdot x \gtreqless 12 \cdot (x - a).$$

Suppose that the curves of demand for two goods, one a necessary and the other a luxury, are as follows :—

| | | | NECESSARY. | | LUXURY. |
|---|---|---|---|---|---|
| 10 | units are | demanded at | 20s. | ... | 13s. |
| — | ,, | ,, | | | |
| — | ,, | ,, | | | |
| — | ,, | ,, | | | |
| 14 | ,, | ,, | 13s. | ... | $12\frac{1}{4}$s. |
| 15 | ,, | ,, | 12s. | ... | 12s. |

At a price of 12s. 15 units of the necessary would be sold, and the total expenditure would consequently be £9. If the price were increased to 13s. only 14 units would be sold, the total expenditure being £9 2s., which is more than before.

Of the luxury 15 units would be sold at a price of 12s., total expenditure, £9 ; if the price were increased to 13s. the turnover

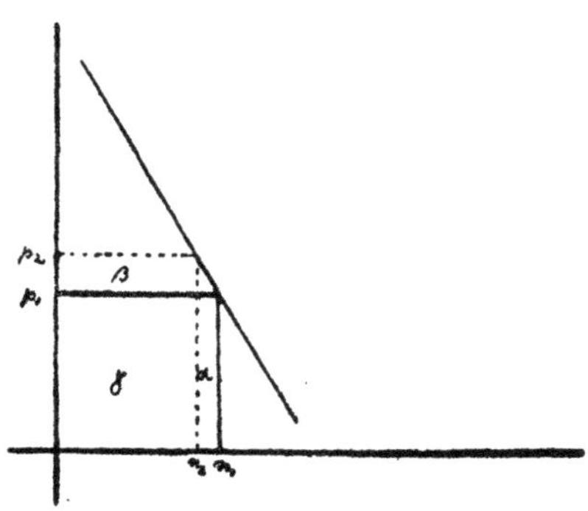

Diagram XIIIa

would decrease to 10 units, making the total expenditure only £6 10s.

The same facts are apparent from Diagrams XIII*a* and *b*, where the same increase (from $p_1$ to $p_2$) for the necessary and the luxury decreases the turnover from $n_1$ to $n_2$, but in such a way that the distance between $n_1$ and $n_2$ is greater with the flat curve.

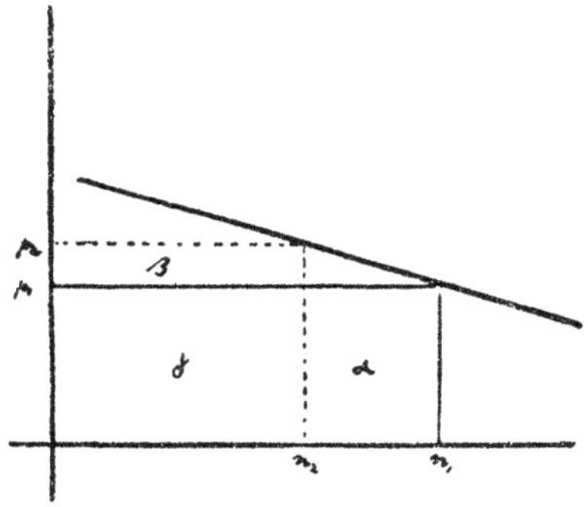

Diagram XIIIb

The amount spent in buying $n_1$ units is the rectangles $\alpha + \gamma$, the amount spent in buying $n_2$ units is $\gamma + \beta$; a survey of the diagrams shows that the proportion between the sizes of the rectangles $\alpha$ and $\beta$ decides whether we will pay more money for the thing than before; $\beta$ will be larger than $\alpha$ for the necessary, but smaller for the luxury. The rule will therefore read as follows :—

The steeper the price-curve at the point where consumption and output are balanced—the more *inelastic* the consumption of a thing—the smaller is the extent to which the increase in price reduces the turnover, so that the total expenditure for the thing must be increased, while a fall in price entails a *smaller* expenditure for the article in question. The flatter the curve—*i.e.*, the more *elastic* the consumption of the thing, the more an increase in price decreases the consumption, and the more the total expenditure is decreased ($\beta < \alpha$). A fall in price will here, on the contrary, increase the total expenditure. For a thing which has poor as well as rich buyers, the rich will, by a fall in price, reduce their total expenditure, but increase it when prices rise, while the poor will increase their total expenditure when prices fall and reduce it when prices rise. In this case it should be remembered that the rich man's price-curves are so high that even at a very high price he will use down to the last unit he is able to consume of necessaries, and that alterations in price do not affect the rich man's consumption of these goods, but only his consumption of other goods. During the war the rich have been willing to pay fancy prices for meat and butter rather than do without.

We may also express the above rules in the following manner :— A reduction of the price to one half will double my consumption ($x \cdot p = 2x \cdot \frac{1}{2}p$) if $2u_{2x} = u_x = p \cdot u_{pm}$—*i.e.*, if the utility of the two last units of a doubled consumption are equal to the last unit of the original consumption, which in both cases must be equal to the marginal utility of the money ($p$) spent. If $2u_{2x} < u_x$ (*i.e.*, for necessaries or the rich man's consumption) I will not double my consumption by a fall in price and therefore will spend *less* than before ; if $2 \cdot u_{2x} > u$ (*i.e.*, for luxuries and the poor man's consumption) my consumption will be more than doubled, and I will consequently spend more money than before on the said commodity.

Consequently for goods with a steep price-curve $12 (x - a) > 10 \cdot x$ (increase in price increases the total expenditure) but for goods with a flat curve $12 (x - a) < 10 \cdot x$ (the total expenditure decreases).

An increase in the price of seats at the theatre will make me reduce my total expenditure for theatre tickets, unless I am much interested in the theatre ; a decrease would increase my expenditure.

An increase in the price of bread will increase my expenditure for bread ; within the different kinds of bread an increase in the price of bread may increase my expenditure for coarse bread and decrease it for fancy bread. Here also the law of substitution operates.

**60. The Curve of the Shilling.**—In Sec. 51 it has been explained how a general alteration in price reacts on the utility curve of the general commodity, and through this on the marginal utility of money. Should the price fall to one half, we may obtain for the first shilling as many units as we previously had to pay with the first and the second shilling. The first part of the utility curve will rise ; but simultaneously a fall will take place in the later part of the curve, because at the lower price we become satisfied at a smaller expense.

The same method may be employed with regard to an alteration in price of the individual article. In this case we operate with what may be termed the *curve of the shilling*, in which the unit is the utility of the quantity of goods, which may be obtained for a shilling (in contradistinction to the usual curve of utility, where we speak of the utility of each unit of the thing). If, for instance, a thing yields a utility per unit of 100, 90, 80, 70, 60, and 50, and its price is 1s. per unit, the shilling curve will look like the general utility curve, but if it only costs 6d. per unit, the curve of the shilling will be 190 (the utility of the 1st and 2nd unit), 150 (the utility of the 3rd and 4th unit) and 110, etc. A fall in price will raise the first part of the shilling curve compiled in this way, and consequently increase my total expenditure for purchase if the consumption before the fall in price was small, but lower a later part of the curve and consequently decrease the total expenditure if the consumption was large before the fall in price.

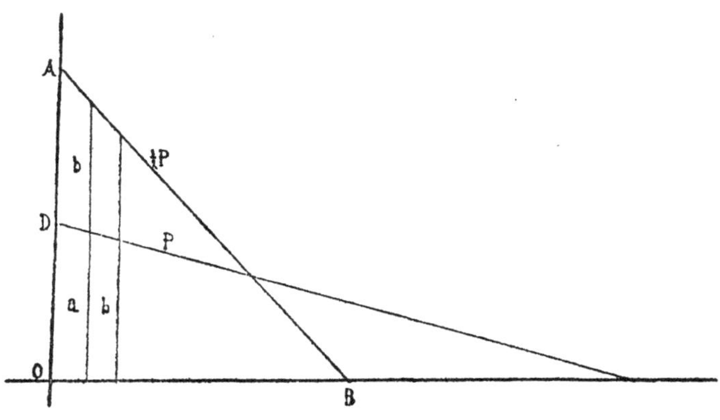


Diagram XIV

In Diagram XIV the steep curve ($\frac{1}{2}p$) will state the new shilling curve, the flat curve ($p$) the old one. If the utility of the 1st unit is $a$ and that of the 2nd unit $b$, and the price 1s., the utility of the first shilling will be $a$ and that of the 2nd will be $b$; but if the price is 6d. the first shilling will buy the 1st and 2nd unit, the total utility of which, $a + b$, will consequently now be the utility of the first shilling. Now the size of the areas AOB and DOC is equal, because the total utility of a thing at complete satisfaction is the same, without regard to the price.

**61. Prices and Distribution of Expenditure.**—The next question is what effect an alteration in the price of a thing will have on the price and quantity sold of other goods. A fall in price may, as stated, increase or decrease the expenditure for a commodity, but this will in both cases result in an alteration of the amount which we spend for other goods, and through this in an alteration in the marginal utility of money. If a fall or an increase in price leads to an increase of the expenditure for a certain article (for instance, meat) we must do without the least necessary part of our consumption of other goods, and the marginal utility of money will thereby be increased. If, on the contrary, the alteration in the price of a thing results in a saving—either because we give up the article, which has become too expensive, or because consumption is not increased in proportion to a possible fall in price—we will be able to afford buying more, and less needed, units of other goods.

This is illustrated in Diagrams XV*a* and *b*, in which an isolated commodity is compared with all other goods—or with the "general commodity." The curve N expresses the utility which a man with an annual income of £50 would derive from the last part of his income—*i.e.*, the shilling curve of the general commodity.

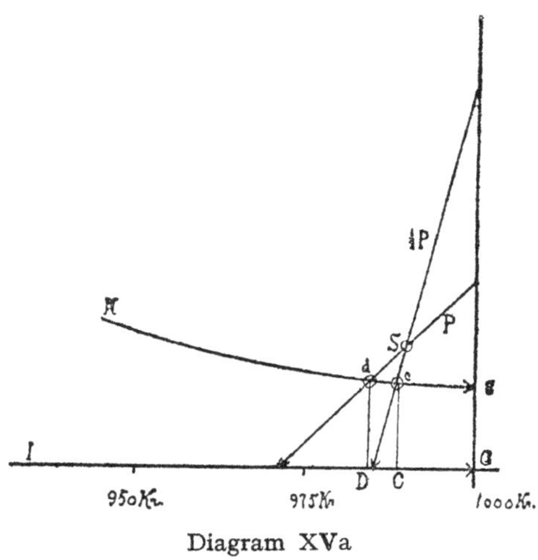


Diagram XVa

Now we must remember that we distribute our purchase over all goods, buying so much of each (in this case the general commodity and the isolated commodity) that the quantity we obtain of each for

1s. will have equivalent utility—*i.e.*, the marginal utility of the general commodity, of income and of the isolated thing must be equal. In Diagram XV*a* the curve N is the shilling curve of the general commodity, P is the curve of the isolated thing at a price of *p*. We must compare the curves as in the case of barter, because we have the choice between buying 1s. more of the "general commodity" and less of the isolated, or of adding this shilling to our purchase of the isolated thing. The point of intersection is *d*, and the marginal utility of the shilling, of the general commodity and of the isolated thing is *d*D. If now the price falls to one half, the shilling curve for the article will, as described above, become the steeper incline ½P. The demand for the article is now satisfied more quickly, the expenditure is decreased to OC and the point of intersection is changed to *c*, the marginal utility of the last shilling of the general commodity and of the isolated thing at the same time being reduced from *d*D to *c*C.

In Diagram XV*b* the thing B has been substituted for A, the utility curve, P, of the former being flatter. In this case the fall in price stimulates consumption, so that the expenditure for the thing, when the price is halved, will be increased from OD to OC, by which the marginal utility of the general commodity, of the isolated thing and of the income increases from *d*D to *c*C.

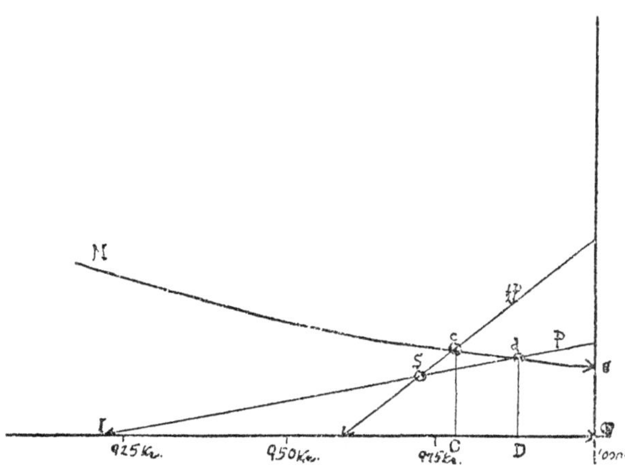


Diagram XVb

The difference between the two examples is that the article A—for instance, a necessary—has a higher and steeper curve of utility, so that the demand at the lower price has come below the demand at the higher price before the curves intersect the utility curve of income, while the two utility curves for B (luxury) are so low and flat that the curve of utility of money intersects them before this point, *s*, *i.e.*, on the first part, while we are still willing to spend more money when the price falls. (Sec. 60 and Sec. 61 have been worked out by one of my pupils, F. Zeuthen, M.A.)

**62. Three Possibilities.**—Suppose that my income is distributed in such a way that I (income) $= 10x + 20y$, in which $x$ and $y$ represent the quantities bought of the article and the " general commodity " respectively and the figures state the prices.

If now the price of $x$ is increased to 12 and I reduce my purchase to $x - a$, the following cases might be thought possible.

(1) If $12\,(x - a) = 10\,.\,x$, my expenditure for the article $x$ is unaltered, and I have the same amount at my disposal for other goods. The marginal utility of money ought neither to rise nor fall with regard to other goods ; but as I have obtained a smaller number of units of the thing in question, I have had less general satisfaction, which must now be balanced by the consumption of such goods as may substitute the article and the utility of which substitutes has previously been covered ; my demand for these goods will increase ; I will obviously have a little less left for the purchase of goods, which do not substitute the article $x$, and my subjective prices for these goods must therefore fall.

(2) If, however, $12\,(x - a) < 10\,.\,x$, I have decreased my expenditure for the thing in question and have therefore more money left for other goods. This will benefit substitutes, even if other goods will also gain thereby. An increase in the price of luxuries will benefit general goods. An increase in the price of the luxuries of the poor will leave them more money for goods which are a little beyond necessaries ; if it is a detrimental luxury (for instance, spirits) a tax may increase the demand of poor people for clothes, habitation, etc., but of course most for other stimulants such as coffee, etc.

(3) If $12\,(x - a) > 10\,.\,x$, and I spend more money on the thing in spite of my decreased consumption, the marginal value of my money increases with regard to all other goods, and my subjective prices for these will consequently fall. This is confirmed by the dearth of food during the war. The cause of the rise in price of luxuries, in spite of this, is the fact that it is a new class who

have become buyers; the persons, whose income is practically unchanged, have given up their accustomed luxury consumption.

I will increase my consumption of a certain community: (1) When my desire is increased (*i.e.*, the thing changes place in my scale of demands); (2) when my income is increased—*i.e.*, its marginal utility falls; (3) when the price of the thing falls; (4) when other goods, which stand in substitutionary relation to the thing, *go up in price*; (5) when other goods, which *do not* stand in substitutionary relation to it, *fall in price*—*i.e.*, I will either considerably increase my demand for the thing, which has fallen in price, and have in this case less to spare for other goods, or I will not increase my consumption so much, that I use the same amount of money as before to buy the increased consumption, in which case I am consequently able to buy *more* of other goods, or, in other words: by the alteration in price of other goods (which do not stand in substitutionary relation to the goods in question) I will increase my consumption of another thing if the reduction in price causes a decrease in my total expenditure for that thing, which has been altered in price.

This rule is not generally applicable to the derived prices.

*Examples*:—We will now outline the effect an increase in price for a few of the goods previously mentioned will have on the prices of *other goods*.

An increase in the price of *bread* can not, as stated above, be reacted against by a decrease in consumption; the total expenditure will therefore be increased, for which reason less will be left for the purchase of other goods. The subjective prices of other commodities will therefore be reduced, and if the market price of the commodity of which the poor are the marginal buyers is not correspondingly reduced, consumption must be decreased. On the contrary the goods, the price of which is determined by the consumption of the rich, will of course be independent of alterations in the price of bread.

If *meat* is much increased in price, this will cut off a great number of the marginal consumers; during the war even part of the middle class has been almost prevented from consuming meat. We then turn to other foods such as fish, and perhaps also increase the consumption of vegetables. If now the prices of these goods remain fairly unchanged, this redistribution of the consumption would even cause a saving in expenditure. The increased demand for other foods will, however, obviously force these prices up, so that the total expenditure will actually become quite as large and probaby in most cases larger than for the original consumption of meat, which again alters the prices of demand for all other goods in a downward direction.

An increase in *house rent* must in any case in the first instance, have the same effect as a decrease in income ; it depends upon personal judgment in which direction we will now reduce the satisfaction of our other requirements. In the second instance, we will meet the increase in rent by a reduction of the *area of the rooms*, or the *situation* or the *equipment* of the flat.

If we take " *luxury articles* " generally, we know that an increase in the price of these will entail a comparatively great decrease in consumption, making the total expenditure less. This will again mean an increase in the prices of demand for necessaries. For the producers of these a heavy taxation of the luxury consumption is therefore an advantage, while on the contrary the producers of luxuries are interested in low prices for all necessaries.

Every producer is interested in high prices of other goods if these are luxuries or substitutes, but in lower prices if they are necessaries.

# CHAPTER XI

## INTERDEPENDENT SCHEDULES

**63. The Inter-Dependency of Prices.**—Only few goods depend on themselves in respect of demand or supply; most of them are interdependent.

(*a*) In the *level of prices* the price of any commodity is a determining factor, but the level of prices decides the marginal utility of our income, which again determines our demand for consumers' goods.

(*b*) The price of all goods which have *indirect* utility, is a function of the price of another thing. This applies to raw materials, machinery, labour, and capital. For such goods the price of demand and, consequently, the market price of the *finished* article will affect the schedule of demand for the raw material. The subjective prices for the raw material are inversely proportional to the other expenses which are necessary to convert the raw material, and, consequently, also with other raw materials employed to make the finished article.

(*c*) On the other hand, the *price of all finished articles* is dependent upon the cost of producing the *raw materials* and the machinery required, these factors determining the quantity of finished articles, which can be produced at the sale price obtainable.

Another connection between goods arises from competition between them.

(*d*) *Through Competing Demand.*—Strictly speaking, a composite schedule of demand is always formed by the competition of demands; in this case, however, we refer to the fact that, for instance, saddlers and shoemakers have a competing demand for the same thing (leather). Then the price will be determined by the fact that the demand of two or more employments are competing for the article (raw material), so that alterations in one employment will affect not only the conditions for sale of the raw material, but also that of the other employment.

(*e*) *Competition in Production,* the same raw material

through a continued process of production may be transformed into different finished articles, so that one application excludes the other, for instance, egg and chicken, or cream, butter and cheese ; in this case substitutionary relations also come in.

(*f*) *Competing Supply* is present between a commodity and its substitute or between different qualities of the same commodity. In this case the schedule of demand for the first quality will be determined according to the price obtained for lower qualities.

(*g*) *Joint Demand* is present when the demand for one thing necessitates demand for the other (pipe and tobacco, lamps and petroleum)—*i.e.*, jointly they satisfy one demand. Joint demand is also present between several raw materials, which are used in the production of the same finished article. In this case the market conditions for one commodity will determine the price of demand of the other. Such goods are said to be in complementary relation to one another.

(*h*) *Joint Supply* is present where different goods are produced in the same process of production (main product and by-product). From coal there is, for instance, produced gas, coke and tar, from the cotton plant fibre and seed, from a slaughtered animal nearly 50 products, from raw petroleum, refined petroleum (paraffin) and benzine. The interdependency becomes more complicated if the process can be varied—if, for instance, it is possible at will to extract more or less petroleum or more or less benzine from the raw oil, than it would if the proportion were given by the technical process itself. It is particularly in manufacture on a large scale that the utilisation of the by-products is made possible —*i.e.*, that it pays to employ and collect waste material and convert it into by-products. Further, we will often meet with an intermediate case in which several goods are produced by the same process, but each of them further requires its own special process—*e.g.*, petroleum and vaseline, or tar, benzol and dyes, etc. In a way, it is a case of joint supply if many different goods are produced at joint general expenses, and even when several otherwise independent goods are offered for sale from the same store.

If the schedules of demand are formed in the usual manner, *joint demand* arises when one want can only be satisfied by consumption of several goods, while joint supply arises out of a *joint process of production*. In joint demand there is only one *original schedule of demand* for the goods to be consumed together, each of which has its own schedule of supply; in joint supply there is only one *original schedule of supply*, but each thing has its own schedule of demand. A separate schedule of demand for each thing in the case of joint demand, and a separate schedule of supply for each thing in the case of joint supply, must be constructed artificially through the process of imputation.

*Goods related in production* are such as have something or other in common in their production—*e.g.*, have raw materials in common.

This relation between the prices of various goods—whether this be *inherence* (that one price includes the other) *causality* (that there is a causal relation between the prices) or *correlation* (reciprocal action) (*Kant's* division) makes price problems so intricate, that it takes much analytical work to find the simple and distinct rules, the co-operation of which apparently creates the special rules for the forming of price in the cases mentioned in this chapter. It does not tend to simplify the problems that several forms of relation between the goods may exist simultaneously (for raw materials practically *all* forms of relation may be present—joint demand and supply, competing demand and supply); as furthermore monopolistic price-manipulation at some point or other can nearly always be traced, we have postponed the treatment of the question of price-related goods to Book V., the subject of which is the manipulated market.

**64. Joint and Competing Demand.**—While the separate schedules of demand remain unchanged in joint supply—or joint production—independent of one another as well as of the respective schedules of supply, two schedules of demand will arise by division or imputation in the case of joint demand. Suppose that I have a want, only to be satisfied by the simultaneous consumption of A and B, and that my joint schedule of demand is 10, 9, 8, 7, 6s., for from 1 to 5 pairs of A and B. If both the mutually supplementary goods are produced by the same manufacturer (*e.g.*, cups and saucers), the matter is clear. The unit of exchange is then the pair of goods. But if the two goods are produced by different processes and by different producers, we have a joint schedule of demand against two mutually independent schedules of supply. If the expenditure for the article

A is 4s., there will arise from the prices of the joint schedule of demand, less the 4s. a schedule of demand for B—*in casu* 6, 5, 4, 3, 2s. for from 1 to 5 units of B. Should the price of A rise, the prices in the schedule for B will drop.

We now turn to *competing demand* —*i.e.*, demand for a thing from various sides in such a way that it is mutually independent employments of the same goods which cause the double set of demands. The thing may be an article of consumption, as the housewife's demand for pork for consumption, and the exporting packers' demand for raw material for canned goods.

In this case we have two mutually independent schedules of demand against a common schedule of supply ; these two (or more) schedules of demand are united in the same manner as the demands of the individuals are amalgamated in composite schedule of demand.

Competing demand is seen in the case of most raw materials, the price relations of which are complicated, not only because their value is indirect, but also because they are the subject of a *joint demand*, as several raw materials are required to make the one finished article.

**65. The Derived Schedule of Demand.**—Indirect utility will cause the subjective price to be indirect and to be lower than that of the finished article. The indirect utility will then be a difference—*i.e.*, the utility of the thing, which I desire, less the disutility of the sacrifice, which is required to make, for instance, raw materials, semi-manufactured articles, auxiliary materials, machinery, etc., into finished articles. As it is a merchant—the manufacturer—who requires all these materials in order to produce consumers' goods, the price of demand for these will not be derived from the indirect utility, but from the price of the finished article ; the schedule of demand fcr the raw material is derived from that of the finished article.

Suppose that the schedule of demand for the finished article A is 22, 20, 18, 16 and 15s. for a purchase of 1, 2, 3, 4, and 5 units, respectively and suppose the expense of converting a raw material into the finished article to be 9s. per unit, which has to be deducted from the price of the finished article in order to find the schedule of demand for the raw material, viz. :

For the 1st unit a price of 22 — 9 = 13s. can be paid.

| | | | |
|---|---|---|---|
| For 2 | units a price of | 20 — 9 = 11s. each | can be paid. |
| For 3 | ,, | 18 — 9 = 9s. each | ,, |
| For 4 | ,, | 16 — 9 = 7s. each | ,, |
| For 5 | ,, | 15 — 9 = 6s. each | ,, |

But the same raw material may enter into several goods. Suppose that the schedule of demand for another thing, B, is 20, 19, 18, 14, 13, 11s. for 1, 2, 3, 4, 5 and 6 units, respectively and that this thing can be made from the raw material at an expense of 4s. per unit, the producer of the thing B will then have the following schedule of demand for the raw material :

| | | | |
|---|---|---|---|
| For 1 unit | he can | at most pay | 20 — 4 = 16s. |
| 2 units | ,, | ,, | 19 — 4 = 15s. each |
| 3 ,, | ,, | ,, | 18 — 4 = 14s. ,, |
| 4 ,, | ,, | ,, | 14 — 4 = 10s. ,, |
| 5 ,, | ,, | ,, | 13 — 4 = 9s. ,, |
| 6 ,, | ,, | ,, | 11 — 4 = 7s. ,, |

By comparing the two schedules of demand we arrive at the following schedule of demand for the raw material :—

| | | | | | |
|---|---|---|---|---|---|
| 1st | unit is | demanded by | $B_1$ | at a price of | 16s. |
| 2nd | ,, | ,, | $B_2$ | ,, | 15s. |
| 3rd | ,, | ,, | $B_3$ | ,, | 14s. |
| 4th | ,, | ,, | $A_1$ | ,, | 13s. |
| 5th | ,, | ,, | $A_2$ | ,, | 11s. |
| 6th | ,, | ,, | $B_4$ | ,, | 10s. |
| 7th | ,, | ,, | $A_3$ | ,, | 9s. |
| 8th | ,, | ,, | $B_5$ | ,, | 9s. |
| 9th | ,, | ,, | $A_4$ | ,, | 7s. |
| 10th | ,, | ,, | $B_6$ | ,, | 7s. |
| 11th | ,, | ,, | $A_5$ | ,, | 6s. |

If only 5 units of the raw material can be produced, the price will be the price of demand for the 5th unit—*i.e.*, 11s., while if only one employment had been possible, say A's, the price would have been 6s. The actual price of the raw material will further correspond to the last accepted buyer's price for any thing, for which our raw material is the basis of production, less the expense of its conversion into a finished article, the reason being that in any employment we will produce down to the point of indifference, at which we are just covered by employing the raw material at the given price. As will be seen, this rule is on analogy with that governing consumers' goods, that the subjective price of the marginal buyer for the unit last bought covers the market price, and that each consumer buys *so much* that *his* individual marginal price covers the market price.

Raw materials have also the rule in common with finished articles of consumption, that it is the objective element, the difficulty of production, which decides which of the prospective buyers will be the marginal buyer, and which of the subjective prices will be the marginal and, therefore, the market price. If the *usefulness* of a raw material is increased, the schedule of demand for it will be increased, as shown by the above examples; as long as the thing was useful only to A, the schedule was 13, 11, 9, 7 and 6s.; when B became a buyer the schedule was altered to 16, 15, 14, 13, 11, 10, 9, 9, 7, 7, and 6s. If only one employment is possible, a price of 7s. would mean that 4 units were sold ($A_4$), if two are possible, 10 units would have been sold.

**66. Price of Substitutes.**—Goods which are related in quality and can substitute each other will, as a rule, be used by different classes of the community and find their marginal buyers within these classes. Consequently, the price of the main article may be more than double that of the substitute, in spite of a very small difference in utility between the two goods. Suppose the utility of the substitute to be 100 and that of the finer article to be 100 + 20, for A, who is rich, as well as for B, who is poor. Suppose, further, that the marginal utility of money for A is so low that 20 units of utility correspond to 8s., while 100 UU for B correspond to 5s. and 20 UU to 1s. B will consequently be able to pay 5s. for the substitute, which yields 100 UU; as the subjective price of the last buyer is the market price, the price of the substitute will be 5s.

Now A has the choice between being content with the substitute and paying 5s., or buying the finer article, which would yield him 20 UU more than the cheaper article; but these 20 UU will for him correspond to 8s. As long as the price of the finer article is below 8 + 5 = 13s., he will therefore choose this, and if the supply of the finer article is so limited that A becomes the marginal buyer, the price for this will consequently be 13s., while the price of the substitute is 5s, although there is only 20% difference between the utility yielded by the two goods. This example confirms that the difference in price between substitute and main article may be far more than 100%, even if the difference in utility is minimal.

Suppose the prices of demand for a thing to be 10, 9, 8, 8, 7, 7, 6, 6, 5, 4, 4, and 3s. for the 1st to the 12th unit and it can be produced for 5s ; in the present instance 9 units would be sold at this price; but—$x$ a finer quality now comes into the market, and for this we would, according to the above, pay the price for the inferior article ($x$ = 5s.) with an addition, by which the consumer expresses the difference in utility between the two goods. If our first prospective buyer is willing to pay an additional 6s. in order to obtain the finer article, the second 5s., the third 4s., the fourth, fifth, sixth and seventh respectively 3, 3, 2 and 1s., the schedule of demand for the finer quality would be as follows, presuming $x$ = 5s. :—

| | | |
|---|---|---|
| 1st unit | | $x + 6 =$ 11s. |
| 2nd | ,, | $x + 5 =$ 10s. |
| 3rd | ,, | $x + 4 =$ 9s. |
| 4th | ,, | $x + 3 =$ 8s. |
| 5th | ,, | $x + 3 =$ 8s. |
| 6th | ,, | $x + 2 =$ 7s. |
| 7th | ,, | $x + 1 =$ 6s. |

How many units can be sold depends on the cost of the first quality, and also, indirectly, on the number of units which must be sold of the second quality, as in this case only 9 units in all can be sold of the two qualities. If we presume that the cost of the first quality is 10s., 2 units of this will be sold, and, consequently, 7 units of the second quality at 5s. (presuming that the cost of production of the second quality is still 5s., even if not 9, but only 7 units are sold.)

# CHAPTER XII

## THE SUBJECTIVE PRICE OF LABOUR AND OF THE SACRIFICE OF WAITING

**67. The Subjective Price of Labour.**—From Sec. 26 we know that a person who is able to decide for himself whether he will work short or long hours will work down to the $t$-th hour, presuming that his comparison between the utility of his wages per hour ($p.u_{pm}$) and the disutility of labour is as follows :—

$$\begin{aligned} p \,.\, u_{pm} &> u \,.\, q \\ p \,.\, u_{pm} &> u^l \,.\, q^2 \\ p \,.\, u_{pm} &> u^l \,.\, q^3 \\ p \,.\, u_{pm} &= u^t \,.\, q^t \\ \hline p \,.\, u_{pm} &< u_l\, q^{t+1} \end{aligned}$$

From the formula found in this manner, $p \,.\, u_{pm} = u_l \,.\, q^t$, it will appear that the wages I demand per hour are $p = \dfrac{u_l \,.\, q^t}{u_{pm}}$ or equal to the marginal disutility of labour divided by the marginal utility of my income ; $p$ and $t$ will increase in the same direction—*i.e.*, the longer the working hours required, the greater the increase in the *hourly wage*—in other words, the hourly wage must increase more than the working hours. How much more cannot be decided by the mere comparison between $p$ and $t$, because there is also a factor $u_{pm}$ which in this case is variable, and is *directly dependent upon the hourly wage* ; by ten hours work my daily wage will, at an hourly wage of 4d., be 3s. 4d ; at an hourly wage of 6d. it will be 5s. ; now $u_{pm}$ and the daily wage vary in *opposite* directions : an increased hourly wage may make me work more hours, but this is balanced by the fact that perhaps I do not now estimate the utility of my last 6d. to be more than I previously attributed to my last 4d. An increase in pay of 1d. for an additional hour's work might tempt me if the daily wage is 3s. 4d., but might not do so if the daily wage is 5s. It is proved repeatedly in the annals of labour that low wages may make people work 14 and 15 hours, because even the disutility of the 15th hour is smaller than the utility of that shilling, which yields me indispensable food. On the contrary, it is apparent that people with large incomes will not go to any trouble, and not even run a risk, if the remuneration is not great, because their $u_{pm} = \frac{C}{n - a}$ (in which $n$ is the income) is far too low.

If $u_{pm}$ is very low the other factor—$p$—the remuneration must be very great to make me move.

A young, able and poor engineer would for less than £350 a year and for the honour be pleased to become the General Manager of the Danish State Railways ; an engineer who is the manager of a big concern, would decline to accept the honour even if it were accompanied by a salary of £1,000. Millionaires are expensive labourers, and yet I have known ex-millionaires who, in their hey-day, found it disgusting to have to move for £50, and who have afterwards had to do clerical work at 6d. an hour. The demand for profits—as we shall see later—will therefore not be dependent on the labour required of the merchant, but on his capital and income ; these are the factors which decide if anything is worth while. But for the unmoneyed the choice is an easy one ; after all, it is more interesting to be a Bank manager than a teacher ; even if the wages were equal, our Bank managers would chose the Bank in preference to the school.

This consideration—that the disutility of the marginal hour must be equal to the utility of its remuneration—is only valid provided we are free to choose whether we will work longer or shorter hours—*i.e.*, for artisans and home workers. For most wage labourers the choice is between working the hours of the establishment or not working at all. Their equation will therefore read : the total disutility of labour = the total utility of the daily wage ; but the total disutility of labour is $< t$ times its marginal disutility and the total utility of wages is $> t$ times its marginal utility ; consequently, we demand considerably less per hour if we have no option, but must take the working hours as something decided by outside influences. When the worker sells his labour, he has not therefore the advantage of the law of indifference ; his units of exchange are not the last hour and the wages of the last hour, but the *whole* working day and the *total* daily wage.

Labour is often in distress, also because the labour offered cannot be saved up ; this is not quite true, because we may store energy by resting from labour ; but if the rest is enforced—not *leisure* but *idleness*—and is accompanied by underfeeding, it is more apt to consume energy.

It therefore appears that the individual labourer, if he has no capital to back him, has no minimum-price, below which he will not work except the *individual minimum of existence, i.e.*, the smallest quantity of nourishment which is necessary to be *able* to perform the work—*i.e.*, that factor *a*, which we have mentioned in the formulas $u_{pm} = C \div (n - a)$ and $\sqrt{a \, . \, p}$.

**68. The Substitution Price of Labour.**—There is, however, something which alters this—*i.e.*, the *Law of Substitution*. My wages in one trade cannot sink below what I can earn in *another*. Now there is, first of all, the substitute to be a *vagabond* or a thief, "*trades*" which, although poor and risky, will yet yield a man the individual minimum of existence—not to mention the insurance against unemployment. In Denmark the State provision for the unemployed labour-reserve has in 1918–20 backed the working men's demand for a rise in wages. However, most of it has a possibility of substitution and a *substitution price* in another trade ; if our wages should sink below a certain limit, we may leave the trade. But many of us have not a substitution price, especially the defenceless, the quite young, the old, the weak, and the women who have to be self-supporting, and for those there is only this limit to how little they may be paid, that in any case they must have the strength required to perform the work imposed upon them. An excellent monograph, published in 1917 in the official statistics of Sweden, and treating the home industry of that country, proves how little a woman needs in order to exist and how much work she will perform for this minimum.

On the other hand, the price of substitution will often be evident in the manager's salary a merchant demands, even if he has no capital. If his special ability is to sell a thing or create a position of monopoly for it, to force the customer or press the seller, the existence of several concerns, which would give him possibilities to utilise these abilities, would make him strong enough to command a high pay for *management*.

Here in Denmark we have an instance of a manager of a little private railway, who drew a high salary, and who refused the office of General Manager of the State Railways. When young, Tietgen (Managing Director of the Privatbanken, Copenhagen, and for many years the leader and organiser of Danish trade) might at a salary of £700 have accepted the office of Postmaster General, but the great Bank manager might not have been had for ten times that amount. It was not ability, but the existence of a substitution price, which gave to the successful man a value which the young man dared not hope to attain.

The fact that the individual has a price of substitution will decide the minimum he will accept. The possession of capital should, strictly speaking, have the same effect, but for the individual only, not for the class. For the individual the possession of, for instance a half year's salary would mean the possibility of weathering a storm without " sinking and losing caste," and without the necessity of falling back upon his substitution price. Further, it permits the industrious to qualify for a better salaried position, to establish himself as a master or—as the only possibility for the factory hand and unskilled labourer to escape from wage labour—to start a small business. But if the capital is no more than the wages of a couple of months, the economic strength of the labourer will most likely be his insurance through the Trade Union. £5,000 in the hands of the Trade Union are actually more support for 1,000 labourers than £5 each in the hands of the individuals. Possession of some capital is of most importance for those persons who, in their connections and education, belong to the middle classes.

But if the possession of a small capital, particularly in a *certain form* becomes usual for a certain class of workers it is more likely to have a negative effect on the demand for wages, because, for instance, tools, which the worker himself must supply, are bought on the hire-purchase system, which contract presses as hard on its man as the consideration of the immediate state of need of his family. A Danish optician before the war was not paid more than 6s. a day, although he had to keep instruments to the value of £25. The *sewing machine* has not improved the position of the home worker, in many cases even aggravated it. We find a similar instance in the case of " small holdings " in the " rack rent " which is higher than the ground rent proper ; the latter is therefore supplemented with an amount which the small holder earns by working as a labourer on the farms. Certain master artisans earn less than a fair wage—also for the same reason—they are bound down by machinery that has not been paid for.

One would believe that staying in the home of parents or husband resulted in economic power of endurance, expressed by a demand for higher wages. The records of women's work show that just the fact that the inferior employments in the sewing, shop and office trades are held by the subventioned women—whether this subvention be legitimate or not—keeps the wages *below* the minimum of existence. When middle-class ladies make crochet work for knitted shawls for a pay of about 2d. an hour in order to have pin-money, they do not realise that their low pay has the same cause as the wages, which sewing shops offer the occasional prostitutes—that they are subventioned.

Poor relief given in addition to wages earned to persons who are able to work has a similar effect—the effect of a subvention of the bad employers and demoralisation of the recipients. (Compare Malthus' criticism of the English " allowance system," and, contrarywise, Pigou's opposite view in *Wealth and Welfare.*)

**69. The Minimum of Existence.**—Somewhat different from the minimum of existence of the *individual* is that of the *family*. This does not affect the individual labourer, but the class. The class must live and reproduce itself, and for this something more than the mere individual minimum of existence is needed. This is not quite correct, for we will often find that the wife and children may be wholly or partly self-supporting; (where this is the rule of the country the income of the family does not suffice much better than where the husband is the principal breadwinner). Finally, a man can be worked to death in various ways; he may be educated until his 14th year, and then be given a chance for supplementary education as " half-timer " besides which short working hours, sufficient wages and healthy working conditions may give him a chance to keep his working power unimpaired from his 18th to his 65th year. But he may also be employed from his 8th year, and under unfavourable conditions be finished before his 35th; by early marriage reproduction will still be possible in spite of a great mortality of children. In the long run the exhaustion of man-power will have a destructive effect on the race, but it may probably take place for a hundred years without the danger being detected by the employers, and the wages may always be kept low, when the labourer is supported by poor relief. The Swedish monograph previously mentioned quotes examples of home-workers, who work 60 to 70 hours every week, and even then are forced to apply for poor relief.

Finally, we have the " Standard of Life " as a social minimum ; this may support *custom*, which is a powerful factor, and the violation of which may make a peaceable workman take to the barricades ; but while a standard of life once attained will make the class willing to venture a revolution rather than submit to a reduction, the individual will *gradually* lose it without much opposition, and if the individuals are sufficient in numbers, the standard of life of the class is altered so slowly that it will not easily come to a reaction in the form of revolts.

Trade Unions maintain the standard and attempt to force it upwards ; their means is the *reduction of the number of persons willing to work* or of the working hours offered. By reducing the number, a later and more experienced worker will become the marginal worker, for reasons which we shall later learn—a more " productive " worker, whose product is of greater value than that of a later worker ; through a monopoly action—restraining the output—the Trade Union may protect a certain standard—*but* only temporarily ; a strong combination of employers may defeat the workers, because very few strike funds can be calculated to last more than three months. The strike has, however, nowadays become a strong weapon—*i.e.*, in all trades where the wages of labour form a small part and the machine power an important part of the expenses of production. In such cases the wages of labour are of so small importance, that the employers would rather pay substantially increased wages than fight a strike, which would leave their machines to rust for three months.

If we divide the labourers into trades, there will in most trades be some who would be content with the individual minimum of existence and others, who have a substitution price ; it *is the latter who, by threatening to leave keep up the wages of the trade* (Simon Patten). Within the poorest-paid trades are all those who have no substitution price, and, as a rule, are not even in an organisation which enables them to wait for a time ; in such trades the individual minimum of existence is the only limit to the workers' subjective price. If all workers did the same work, the small demands of these (final) workers would determine the wages for the entire class ; but they are divided into separate trades, the worst paid comprising 10 to 16% of the entire population—which saves the remainder of the workers from misery. *Charles Booth* estimates that 8% of the population are *very* poor ; 22% are poor, 51% live in comfortable lower-class conditions ; 18% are middle, and 1% upper class. Consequently, the wages of labour will actually not be as low as the subjective price of the individual ; they may be higher. Only in the poorest trades—which become reservoirs partly for the defenceless and partly for the least able, and particularly for the unwisest persons—will the minimal subjective price be equal to the individual minimum—*i.e.*, even lower than that minimum of existence, of which *Ricardo* speaks.

In some trades, the wages of which are above the individual minimum, the workman will attain the family minimum, more or less, according to the strength of his position—*i.e.*, strength not as much in organisation as in scarcity in proportion to the demand for this special class of working power, and in some trades he will attain a standard of wages and living which is established for each group of workers, and which is equal to that of the middle class ; then he has actually a position of relative monopoly ; his wages contain a " differential rent."

Even the best-situated manual workers (including clerks) will not attain very much, and the brain-workers are really only paid reasonably when the public is their employer ; somewhat different is the position of the workers, when they can sell their services *direct* to the public and are not obliged to use the intermediary of an employer, or if they are protected by custom and position of monopoly, which may even change their role from that of the anvil to that of the hammer (lawyers, brokers and waiters).

The reason for the fact that it is not the individual minimum of existence, but the minimum of the family, which has attracted Ricardo's attention, is that he examines the position of labour in the long run. And here the demands of the labourer consist of two elements : (1) What is necessary for him in order to produce the special qualities desired, and (2) what he himself will work for. With regard to point 2, this may vary from that of the individual minimum to the standard of life and the individual substitution price. In the first respect, the wages must in the long run be sufficient to reproduce the labour—*i.e.*, more than the individual minimum. And if we want labourers of a certain power—able to yield work of a greater number of foot-pounds or of more intelligence, able to tend expensive machines—we must give them better food and shorter hours and more healthy workshop conditions. According to the theory of the " economy of high wages " we must pay an hour's work better in order to obtain a relatively cheaper product, attained by the greater productivity of the hour. It will be noticed from this that the minimum of existence even in Ricardo's sense will be rather high. The standard of wages necessary for continual reproduction of the working power desired will consequently state the *cost of production* of this working power for the community. But the labourer may obtain a wage which may be above or below this. There will be many trades in which the wages through generations remain at the individual minimum or at the minimum of reproduction, which yields poorer workers and lower human beings. The *social* and *physical process of elimination* will cause such trades not easily to fall short of labourers, and in periods where the increase in population takes place at a quicker rate than the formation of capital and technical development, nearly all the labourers' trades, where the workers are not in a position of relative monopoly, will sink below the minimum of existence of the race. This condition is considered by *Lasalle* to be natural for the capitalistic state of the community, viz.: his deduction of the iron rule of wages from Ricardo's theory that wages oscillate round a low minimum of reproduction, where a *decrease* is reduced by a higher death-rate and an *addition* by a higher rate of births and length of life. *Ricardo's* theory rests on the postulate that " there is a correlation between the standard of life and the birth rate and (in the long run) between the increase in the number of labourers and the wages " (Taussig). In the poorest trades the supply of labour does *not act through* a *subjective* price, but through quantity only, and in other trades the substitution price or the possession of capital in connection with the ability to joint action create a demand for minimum prices, which must be honoured.

But in its principle the subjective price of labour is—in contradistinction to our subjective price for the good—*not a price of demand, but a price of supply.*

In this volume we will not examine if *Malthus* perhaps was right in the very long run when he stated that as long as we do not command our ability to reproduce ourselves, the population will grow to the limit of misery, which technique and the occupation of new worlds may postpone. If he is right, then the iron rule of wages will apply for the long periods, while the theory that the wages of labour vary from technical and social causes will apply for the separate generation only, the minimum of existence being a continuous threat, *always* effective in the outcast trades and the industrial reserve army; and as *Smith* says: "The demand for men, like that for any other commodity, necessarily regulates the production of men."

**70. Discount of Deferred Utility.**—In Sec. 17 we have shown that by being saved up a thing may have an earlier place in the utility schedule and therefore attain a utility, which, even discounted in consideration of the fact that the future is not as keenly appreciated as the present, is greater than it would be if we consumed the good at once. The same is, of course, the case with the representative of all goods—money; 1s. saved from my surplus for a day when I may have nothing may mean so much that the utility thereof, even discounted, is greater than the indulgence of which I deprive myself to-day by omitting to consume that shilling. This means that, within certain limits and within a certain capital, I am rewarded for omitting to consume all of my income by the fact that the shilling saved means sustenance of life, while if consumed to-day it would only mean a luxury. Many people have, however, an expectation of having the same income every day, and for those a luxury shilling saved to-day does not mean a necessary shilling to-morrow, but only a postponed luxury. If it is probable that every day I will have an income of 4s. I will, provided that I save my fourth shilling to-day, not count this the first shilling to-morrow (of which I believe myself certain) but the fifth.

Actually the calculation is wrong, but most people, and especially those who expect a larger income in the future, take it for granted that their income is secured them.

But if the $u_4$ of to-day becomes the $u_1$ of to-morrow, $u_1$ will, even if reduced in my estimate on account of its being future, often be greater than the postponed $u_4$. Where this is not the case, and, for instance, the unit saved takes the same place in the series to-morrow as to-day, the case is different: $u_4$ to-day is always $>$ $u_4$ to-morrow—*i.e.*, the postponement of consumption results in a loss of utility for me, for which reason $u_4$ to-morrow must have an additional utility of, say, $u_x$, which will perhaps correspond to $\frac{1}{4}$

of a unit, making the utility of 1¼ unit to-morrow equal to that of 1 unit to-day. This additional quantity we term *interest*, which is therefore the positive expression for the deduction, which we make in the value of the future thing as compared with the present.

The loss of utility arises in two ways : because an early shilling by being repaid, may become a *later* shilling, and because a shilling to-morrow appears to me to have *less* utility than the corresponding shilling to-day. This is the nucleus of *Schoenheyder's* theory of interest, which is better than that of *Boehm Bawerk*, who advances the strictly speaking incorrect contention that the future good is judged to have less utility than the present one ; this rule applies *only* to units with the same place in the series. The advantage of the present demand in respect of utility, if the income is fairly equal, appears from the fact that most people are more willing to repay a loan of 90s. in ten monthly instalments of 10s. each than, for instance, in two monthly payments of 45s. each. On the day when the future becomes the present, and the to-morrow to-day, it proves that the shilling or good saved has not only the anticipated reduced utility, but its full utility. Through this I obtain additional utility for nothing ; if this is expressed by a tangible addition to my income, the interest, we may, with *Marx*, speak of unearned increment. But we must remember that this does not appear on the day when I charged my interest, on which day it appeared to me to be a necessity, a "*conditio sine qua non*." The unearned is the *maturing* ; that the "future good" some day will be present, and the "present good" will then be of the past, *by which the discount (the deduction in the the value of the future good) becomes interest (an addition to the value of the present good)*. This change from discount to interest is expressed by the ordinary formula of interest $C = \frac{C_n}{(1 + r)^n}$ converted into $C_n = C \cdot (1 + r)^n$, in which $C_n$ is the value of the present capital $n$ years hence with accumulated interest, while C is the present value of the future capital.

**71. The Demand for Interest.**—At a time when money and representatives of capital (as shares or obligations) are not available, I must save goods—*i.e.*, supplies which are difficult to store. My saving will then often take place only with the necessity of storing supplies in view, and my recompense is the fact that the last sack of flour of to-day becomes the first to-morrow, or that the supply is necessary in order to maintain my position and continue my trade ; in this case I will even pay a negative interest in the form of the waste and trouble of storage.

Raw materials and implements have not only indirect, but also future utility, inasmuch as they only become goods ready for consumption through a process, which takes time ; also the presence of a certain quantity of them is an absolute condition for existence and continuation of the trade, or for satisfying the desire, which all people with economic tendencies have for extending and consolidating their business.

Part of the implement capital in one's own business is produced at the expense of the good for immediate consumption, without thought of gain of interest, simply because for the continuation of the business not only maintenance, but also extension is required, and because our economic sense, and even our sense of order, causes us to wish to keep our business in working order and even extend it. The recompense in this case is the joy of seeing things thrive under our hands, a joy which is not known to the merely accumulating passive capitalist, and which, in his case, is not at all compensated by the satisfaction of the collecting mania or greed.

Implements are worn out and stores saved are consumed ; they must, consequently, be repaired and substituted. But at that very moment we again meet with the question of immediate and future use. Our *will to save is not only required to make* implements and stores, but *also to maintain them* and to compensate wear and tear, in other words, to *re-invest liquidated* capital. But here again the economic instinct comes in ; even without gain of interest many *concerns owned* by single persons will be maintained and the necessary savings for this purpose will be made ; for even without interest many people would think twice before converting liquidated capital into articles of consumption.

**72. The Theory of Abstinence.**—It has been made easier to save if, instead of implements or stores, I may accumulate money which does not take up room ; it becomes easiest of all when I postpone my consumption by lending money to others—*i.e.*, transfer my purchasing power from one time to another *with or without the intermediary of a bank or a savings bank*, or, in other words, if for my purchasing power I do not buy consumer's goods or means of production which I may use myself, but only a claim for *future* purchasing power. In this case there is technically no limit as to how much I may "save."

In the pre-industrial community saving would recommend itself on account of the general uncertainty of life, in order to secure the great utility which the necessities of a future were bound to have, even in foreshortened perspective. This motive applies to-day for those who own comparatively little: the horror of the workhouse is a motive beyond the present. Persons who have to face this possibility do not think of interest at all; they think of rainy days. The labourers may even often have a *negative interest* in their saving—the sewing machine of the seamstress—and yet they save; their savings are often made through insurance companies, the costly administration of which and expensive system of collecting weekly premiums result in there being no proper proportion between premiums and risk, so that the insured loses more than the interest. How little interest means for the quite unmoneyed appears from the small measure of success of voluntary old age insurance, *even* if the Government contributes large amounts (which correspond to a very high rate of interest). *Irving Fisher* calls attention to the now topical risk run by the savings being accumulated in money that this as well as goods may deteriorate—in the present case lose purchasing power by an increased level of prices (negative interest).

Among the many (mostly) negative virtues of the middle classes is also the saving instinct; in this the increase of the rate of interest will certainly cause increased saving, but only to the limit of the social standard of respectability of the class. On the other hand, there are in this class persons who dream of retiring from business or buying a house in the suburb; a high rate of interest will in such cases permit them to reach more quickly that standard of capital or income, which for them is the key of liberty—*i.e.*, the higher rate of interest will allow them to stop saving earlier.

While the poor man, in order to save, must sacrifice the necessities of the moment, and the poorest part of the middle classes must resign decent and natural comfort, the rich will sacrifice the most unnecessary luxuries of the moment in order to secure the continuation of their standard of life and position of power. The sacrifice is not great, because the sacrifice as well as the compensation are consumers' goods of relatively small utility; the utility of the compensation is very much weakened by the fact that rich people presume that their incomes will be continuous. We cannot speak of abstinence in this case, and *Lasalle's* irony over the "abstinence" of the Rothschilds is justified; the consumption of a rich man is fairly even from year to year; he saves his real surplus.

In all of us there is a tendency to maintain an accustomed standard of life (to use more than usual because for a couple of years we earn more is considered vulgar); but if for a succession of years we gain a larger income, we will finally live up to it—in any case, if a leisured class should arise in the second generation—and we will thus have another standard of life. Somewhat different is the case with the *very* large capitals, the yield of which even a spendthrift cannot get through; the 20th Century starts with an actually hereditary aristocracy of millionaires, whose enormous incomes, in spite of laudable efforts, force them to increase their capital. Confiscation and State bankruptcies are the only things which may prevent these avalanches of giant capitals from crushing the entire earth. It is in a way correct that the existence of a class of wealthy people will give a community greater possibility for saving and accumulating capital *without* government restrictions for the individuals; a rich man with an income of £100,000 will save £25,000 with less sacrifice than 500 citizens who each must save £50 out of their £200; the savings of the poor call for a self-denial, which is greater than the importance of their savings for the formation of the national wealth.

This observation has been formulated by an American mathematician and economist, *Newcomb*, into the apparently brutal, but not incorrect contention, that of two countries with an *equal national dividend*, the country which has a small class of wealthy men and no middle class will save up more than the country which has a numerous middle class and no wealthy class.

But as the quantity of existing wealth in itself cannot be the final goal of our activity, especially if it is intended to be employed in the satisfaction of the whims of a plutocracy, which in its power is dangerous to the liberty of other citizens, other means might be found to compel the population to make the necessary savings, for instance, taxes, the proceeds of which are invested in public utilities.

But there is something correct in the view that it is the rich man's task to save—*i.e.*, not consume what he forces others to produce. This contention will be hard to swallow for those who do not understand that money which is not used for useless luxuries will be employed, either by the wealthy man himself or by a borrower for purchasing machinery or for paying labourers—*i.e.*, buying means of subsistence.

If it were not a fact that a continual accumulation and investment of capital might strangle the entire economic life of a community, the majority of which are unable to purchase the goods produced, we might maintain that *Shylock*, who is certainly not productive, but who indirectly forces others to save, is more valuable to his community than *Timon of Athens*, who, however, under a too unequal distribution, attains his right of existence as a set-off to the Venetian Jew, and without whose extravagance purchasing power and production would be unable to adjust themselves.

Facts, therefore, to some extent, weakened the theory of abstinence maintained by *Senior* and *Cairnes*, which for a long period was the ruling theory of interest of the liberals. This theory does not only seek a defence, but also a cause of interest in the *sacrifice of abstinence* made by the person saving (his will to postpone the enjoyment), which is at present open to him. Any investment of capital, it reads, any employment of productive power—also personal work—to make implements and stores are to the same extent as the lending of money or goods, a sacrifice of the present enjoyment, which must be conditioned by a compensation, *the interest*; this may arise in the form of a product, which is of greater value than the productive factors which have produced it, or, more correctly than the technical components of which it is composed, or as in the case of lending, in the form of a tangible yield apart from the capital lent, whether this be money or goods.

**73. The Ratio of Saving.**—In a number of cases the *rate of interest* determines the ratio of saving; in others the motive is partly that the future is the necessity, while the present sacrifice is the relatively superfluous; in others, again, we save because we cannot help it. In some cases 1% is sufficient, in others 4 or 5 and in others again 10 and even 20% are needed in order to make people sacrifice the enjoyment of the moment. While the more passive natures often have as a motive for saving only the thought of future consumption—old age, the marriage of a daughter, acquisition of some piece of furniture, or, at the utmost, the wish to have a house, the more active, on the other hand, will certainly react against the cessation of a yield of interest by increasing their annual consumption, but their principal motive for saving is not that the interest is 3, 4, or 5% ; they are attracted by the possibility of *social* power and extra profits, which are promised by an accumulated capital. An increase of the rate of interest within the narrow limits of 3 and 6% will therefore induce some, but not many, to increase their savings. While it is probable that the complete cessation of a yield of interest will considerably restrain saving and re-investment, the actual amount of interest will be of less importance than is attributed to it. There are, of course, intermediate cases where the motives are combined, and where the actual market rate of interest will decide the amount of savings, and these cases are determining when they are at the *margin*—*i.e.*, where the saver becomes a marginal saver.

The *interest demanded*, which expresses how much higher we value the present thing in proportion to the future one is, therefore, for the individual dependent upon (*a*) the amount of his annual income ; (*b*) how much he owns ; (*c*) how he judges his prospects for having a similar annual income in the future ; (*d*) what are the goals he sets himself for the future : if this is the modest savings of the poor in order to avoid the workhouse, if it is the middle-class wish for a cottage and an income from interest, or the active man's hope for social and economic power ; (*e*) if his standard of consumption has reached his accustomed income, and (*f*) his habit of mind, if miserly or extravagant, generous or egoistic. For the community the *rate of saving* is influenced partly by the distribution of income, partly by the habits of mind of the population (the population of France in contrast to that of Russia), partly and perhaps most by the national dividend (*i.e.*, the total income of the population), and by these rather more than by the causes which for the individual decide the strength of the demand for interest. There must, of course, be something to save from, but as a qualification it must be added, something in proportion to the standard of life of the population, particularly the standard of that class which have such incomes as permit saving. In the Savings Banks the small savers make the number of accounts, but the few large savers cause the total amount of savings to increase. It is only on the battlefield, at the ballot, and in the churchyard that the unmoneyed have weight—otherwise they are only ciphers. (A number of the large accounts in Danish savings Banks, however, belong to workmen's societies.)

Other relevant factors are the risk of the objects of investment in proportion to their probable dividend as well as the probability of keeping what is saved up. Excessive taxation will stop the willingness to risk very much, to earn much, as well as the will to accumulate. The taxes must therefore be directed principally against such incomes on the creation of which the taxpayer has little or no influence. Another thing is that the will to earn money would hardly be less if all inheritance for instance reverted to the Government against payment of interest to the legal heirs for a period of 50 years. The motive—family considerations—would be more likely to increase the accumulation. (*cf.* Dalton, *Inequality of Incomes.*)

**74. The Schedule of Interest.**—The deciding factor is that the demand for interest as the reward for saving and non-consumption of property, or, to quote *Marshall*, for the *sacrifice of waiting*, is different for different individuals, and further varies according to how much they have beforehand, their income, etc. We therefore arrive at a schedule in which is stated how much is demanded for the accumulation of various amounts. As the person who saves practically *buys future goods—in an abstract form—and pays with present goods* which he sacrifices, we may construct the following example of a schedule of demand for future goods :

| | | | | | |
|---|---|---|---|---|---|
| For the | 1st | £100 in future values | | £100 cash are offered. | |
| ,, | 2nd | ,, | ,, | £99 18s. | ,, |
| ,, | 3rd | ,, | ,, | £99 16s. | ,, |
| ,, | —— | ,, | ,, | —— | |
| ,, | —— | ,, | ,, | —— | |
| ,, | *n*th | ,, | ,, | £95 | ,, |
| ,, | $n+1$ | ,, | ,, | £94 18s. | ,, |

Instead of constructing a schedule of demand for future goods (in an abstract form) we may construct it as a schedule of supply : the first millions will be saved without any interest compensation, the next against 1 per mille, the next again for 2 per mille ; for each per mille the interest is increased, some millions will be added. It is possible that the greatest increases in saving take place at 2 to 3%, and again after 10%, when the rich begin to find it worth while to make a real saving sacrifice ; much compensation is demanded, because it is difficult for anybody to reduce even the most extravagant standard of life. This may be compiled as a series or drawn as a rising curve, on which we read how much the capital saved may be increased by an increase in the rate of interest. The demand for interest has *no direct* influence on the actual rate of interest—as this is determined by the proportion between uninvested capital and unexploited fields of investment—the rate of interest has on the other hand, influence on the rate of saving. If the demand for interest, for instance, at £200,000,000 is 3½% and £205,000,000, 4%, this would mean that in order to increase the capital by additional savings to the amount of £5,000,000 the rate of interest must be increased ½%, if other conditions are equal. In a *static* community the market rate of interest will be identical with the interest demanded by the last saver, because saving and possibility of investment would there follow immediately upon one another. In our dynamic community the two rates of interest—the demand of the marginal saver and the actual market rate—may be very widely different, even if they will tend to approach one another through an alteration in the rate of saving. In any case there will always be a marginal saver, who ceases to save when the rate of interest and the standard of security is reduced, and instead converts some of his property into articles of immediate consumption.

The capitals of the present day, however, have only to a small extent been formed by saving out of annual income, but as far as a large part is concerned created by capitalisation, for instance, when property increases in value because for every year it yields a larger dividend. In this case no *sacrifice of waiting* is involved in the formation of capital (for one reason because from a social point of view no formation of real capital has taken place). But in order not to exchange the profit arising from increase in value into consumers' goods, a sacrifice of waiting is certainly required, which is *not* only required when forming a capital but also in order not to spend what we have.

Saving must, therefore, not be understood literally, but as

comprising the formation of capital *as well as* the non-consumption of what has already been saved. The latter (passive) saving will probably need less encouragement in the form of interest than the former. In a community where saving is immediately converted into the right of interest, which deprives the owner of the right to the capital—as would be the case in a community where production had been socialised, but which still allowed individuals to have capital and incomes free of labour—the amount of interest would have no influence on consumption or non-consumption of what had already been saved, but certainly on the formation of new capital; only the government, which prohibited all private ownership of capital, and which itself accumulated out of the annual profits of production, could afford to do away with interest, if interest was not necessary in order to distribute capital between production of present and future goods.

**75. Loans for Consumption.**—The schedule of the sacrifice of waiting is not an actual one, which by the *lenders* is placed against the schedule of interest of the *borrowers*; it simply states how the community reacts against a rate of interest actually in force, which has been decided by other elements. The *actual* demand for interest only arises from an estimate of utility, inasmuch as the rate of interest actually obtainable decides, if I will consume uninvested capital or reinvest it. But most people will be content with the rate of interest obtainable for the capital, which they already own, and only react against it by the nature and riskiness of their investments.

With loans, which are only sought for the purpose of consumption, the interest offered will also be determined by our estimate of the utility of future goods compared with that of the enjoyment of the present. Some will be more reckless than others, or in such a state of need that they put a very small value on the future good and offer 100%, others might allow themselves the consumption of to-day to be paid by future sacrifices, but only if the rate of interest is 2%. But also the financial status and prospects of the borrower come in. The heir to a fortune may be justified in offering a high rate of interest in order to enjoy the goods of life at once in golden youth; those who in the future expect only the same or a smaller income must be reckless if they borrow money in order to obtain *dispensable* goods to-day, which they have to pay for by sacrificing earlier and more important goods in the future. The motives of the person borrowing for consumption to *avoid* borrowing are the same as those of the saver to save : the individual discount of the future, and the need of the present compared with that of the future—*i.e.*, his financial status.

The borrowers for consumption, therefore, form a schedule of demand for present goods to be paid for with future goods, and some will pay an exceedingly high interest, others next to none. Nowadays consumption loans do not often come within the capital market proper ; some loans are given very cheaply (by relatives or friends) others are offered by the professional "moneylenders" who must themselves be paid for risk and trouble of collection. A lending business of this class is, therefore, a business in the proper sense of the word, the "undertaker" procuring means either from his own capital or by borrowing. His subjective price—*i.e.*, the rate of interest, which he himself at most is *able* to offer, is like in any other business determined by the profits of the business. If he takes more than the customary rate of interest it will be a case of *usury* ; whether a lending contract comes within the term usury or not, does not depend on the absolute rate of interest demanded, but must be decided by the question whether the lender, taking advantage of the borrower's need or lack of knowledge, takes a higher rate of interest than that which corresponds to the borrower's status—*i.e.*, his ability to fulfil the contract.

Naturally some people borrowing for consumption will also apply at the capital market direct.

Only the borrower for consumption will let his offer of interest be dependent upon an estimate of utility. All other borrowers who demand capital for the sake of profit will have their maximum offer determined by the probable amount of this profit, even if they naturally wish to pay less if possible.

**76. Present Goods in Comparison with Future Goods.**—The demand which the individual makes for saving—also the demand of the marginal saver—which practically amounts to the conditions of the community for *maintaining a given rate of saving*, is the expression for an individual comparison of the estimated value of the present and the future goods ; by the first is meant in the present case the existing supply of goods, by the latter what is expected to come into existence at some future time. The *actual* rate of interest, which is otherwise determined by the marginal profit promised to the last capital unit of the prospective investor (£1,000,000, £1,000 or whichever unit we may choose), will, on the contrary, be an expression for a social objective estimate of the *actual* proportion between present and future goods.

(*a*) A high rate of interest tells us that there is a *scarcity of present goods* (*stocks are small, prices high*) ; only a high rate of interest will entice us to give up the *highly-valued* present goods, which only suffice for the immediate demand, in order to obtain consequently *relatively more plentiful future goods, the value of which is estimated lower.* Scarcity and abundance are, of course, relative terms, dependent upon to what extent the classes earning income press their demand.

*Labour* is always *cheap in proportion to the present goods, by* which it is *paid,* and *costly in proportion to the future goods, which it produces*—the perpetual tragedy of labour. But its conditions are most unfavourable when the rate of interest is high, because its produce is estimated at a very low value and its payment at a very high one—*i.e.*, the actual wages are low.

(*b*) A low rate of interest tells us that present goods are plentiful (warehouses filled and prices low) ; a *low* rate of interest will then be sufficient to tempt us to give up the present goods, which are estimated at a low value, and which are sufficient for more than the present, and to prefer the relatively scarce and therefore highly valued future goods. In this case the payment of labour is relatively cheap, and its produce highly valued, etc. The actual wage is high. In the case (*a*) much capital is sunk in permanent erections (factories, farms, etc.) ; in the case (*b*) only little capital is sunk in this way. This is in agreement with the fact that a low rate of interest stimulates, and a high rate of interest stops the starting of new enterprises.

It is well to bear this in mind, because (*a*) the level of prices, and (*b*) the lending policy of the banks obscure actual conditions.

For a period it is possible for the bank to keep the rate of interest low by inflating the currency and thereby the level of prices, which the scarcity of goods had already caused to advance.

**77. Capitalisation.**—If there were no difference between the present and the future, the value of any periodical income might be found by multiplying the amount by the number of years, for which the amount had been secured—not however, beyond the 150 years which were once stated by a writer to be the limit of our *personal* interests. But as those goods, which the coming year promises to place at our disposal, are reduced in utility and often in value in proportion to the goods of the present year, and the goods of a subsequent year still more, we arrive at a schedule consisting of at most 125 to 150 figures, of which each figure is smaller than the preceding one. The lower we value the future, and the greater our discount thereon, the quicker will be the rate at which the series will decrease, and the smaller will be the total amount of the figures. The right to a " perpetual " interest, a dividend not limited in respect of time, to be acquired without personal effort simply by virtue of legal title, will then have a *present price of exchange*, which is a product of two factors : the *amount of dividend* and a *multiplier*, which in the business world will be dependent upon the rate of interest by which the community, under the existing distribution of capital through its marginal saver, expresses its lack of respect for the economy of the future. If the annual interest ($r$) of £100 is £5, we compare any title to a perpetual income of £5 with the sum which yields £5 in interest, and have then no reason for estimating its value at more than £100—*i.e.*, the multiplier is 20 ; if the rate of interest is 4%, the multiplier will be 25 and the capitalisation of a perpetual interest of £5 will be £125, because £125 invested at 4% would otherwise yield me £5 interest ; if the rate of interest is 3% the capitalisation factor will be $33\frac{1}{3}$, if the rate of interest is 10% then only 10. The multipl er ($m$) is consequently $= 100/r$, and the capitalisation, the private capital $= m \cdot A$ (in which A is the amount of annual interest).

The right to a perpetual annual dividend will consequently in the long market have as its present price a value which is inversely proportional to the rate of interest, and directly proportional to the annual dividend. Its value may therefore change when the rate of interest fluctuates. The multiplier is consequently dependent upon the permanency of the dividend, but also the security thereof, or probability of permanency, comes in and reduces $m$, if this probability is not $= 1$.

We have here introduced the term " *private capital*," by which we understand a right, guaranteed by the community, of a returning income, not connected with personal labour, and which is transferable when statutes or custom do not directly prohibit transfer. By " *guaranteed* " by the community we do not mean a positive guarantee, but only a certain expectation secured by the nature of the matter or by the character of the social institutions. The right may be an adjunct to the possession of certain tangible goods—for instance, stocks of goods or factories—and may be of a merely obligatory nature. The dividends may come from a productive plant, taken from the net profits thereof, or may be taken from the general income of another person, the debtor, or it may—as is the case with the interest on the National Debt—be taken from taxation, and therefore have nothing to do with production. For me, as the recipient of an income, it is immaterial how the income free of toil has arisen, if only I have the right to keep and employ it and there are no social or moral " drawbacks " to the acquisition and possession of it ; these drawbacks may, however, only too often be counter-balanced.

*Private capital*—as a *capitalisation of future dividends*, the basis of a *right of interest*, as a *medium of income*—may also, by emphasising its peculiarity that it is a legal-historical category, be termed *legal* capital (*Gide*), as distinguished from *economic* capital, *capital goods*, or, in order to use an established expression, *social* capital, which includes our productive power (outside our own labour force) with the addition of stocks and supplies necessary for the maintenance and exercise thereof. This is again different from *technical capital* (means of production).

When the right of dividend is limited in respect of time, in other words, a *terminable annuity*, its value will obviously be less than if it were perpetual ; on account of the phenomenon of compound interest the difference between the value of an annuity with a currency of 99 years and a perpetual interest will, however, be only a couple of per cent. The value of an annuity increases with an increase in its durability, but with a continually decreasing addition ; if we go beyond 125 years, the value of the terminable annuity and the perpetual interest will be nearly equal.

The amount of annual dividend, permanency, security and comparative freedom from work in conjunction with the multiplier, which varies inversely with the rate of interest, will therefore determine the value of a right of interest in the long market. In the short daily market it may fluctuate with varying supply and demand according to the special form of the private capital in question.

**78. Risk.**—If we *postpone our consumption* this is done either by producing or causing to be produced instead of consumers' goods, implements, which only by a second process are converted into consumers' goods—or by storing part of the results of production ; in most cases the saving takes place by the transfer of purchasing power to another person, who then undertakes the process of production.

But in all postponed consumption there is, besides the trouble of storage, also an element of risk : first of all, we may not live to see the future (optimism and family feeling, however, counterbalance that element) ; secondly, what we store may deteriorate, production may be a failure, and, finally—what is of commercial importance—the goods stored or the yield of production, the goods bought may become of less value than was expected when the purchase or production was planned. The merchant does not produce the commodity for its utility, but for its *value* ; but prices do fluctuate.

As is the case on account of futurity, we must also make a reduction in value if the enjoyment is uncertain. If the probability of gaining a result from our labour is 50%, we will only sacrifice half the amount of work compared with what we would sacrifice if the probability were 100%, or if the chances for obtaining the enjoyment are 1 to 2, we will with the same sacrifice demand twice as much as we otherwise would.

This additional utility finds an expression in the premium of risk, which therefore as well as the interest, forms part of the production expenses proper, the covering of which we demand if we are to continue production. If in the manufacture of porcelain one in every two particularly high-priced vases are spoiled in the baking, the price of these must be so high that it not only covers the finished article, but also the second, which has been spoiled.

The developed insurance technique of the present day has specified plainly enough the premium (for the technical as well as the economical risk) as part of the expenses of production, in the form of insurance premium. This is, in a way, a good thing, but also unsatisfactory, because insurance business creates such large expenses for administration and agents that the cost of production of all goods is considerably increased thereby, and because full cover for accidental damage results in our not making our utmost efforts to avoid it. "Interest-insurance," however useful it may be to the individual, is from a social point of view more likely to be detrimental. Another class of risks is connected with capital management, as far as capital is in the hands of an undertaker, but risk of this class is set off by an equal chance of gain and cannot be dealt with in connection with interest proper (*cf.* Hobson's violent attack on treating this kind of risk as a cost of production: "This is a misuse of averages.")

In the wages of labour in all dangerous trades ought also to be included a premium for the personal risk; it was in a way perfectly correct that the Danish socialistic newspapers reported accidents under the heading "The Risks of Labour," But in the wages of labour no such risk-premium will actually be included (unless compelled by law), because the most dangerous labour often comes within the group "unskilled labour," where the number of persons seeking employment will keep wages low. In wages the very great risk of unemployment ought to be, but is not, included, as those trades in which the insecurity of employment is largest often see the lowest figures in the wages-account.

The utility of raw materials and implements must, therefore, be found with the reservation of futurity and uncertainty, the fact that it takes time before raw material and implement become a finished article, and that futurity, the process of production and the sale, contain an element of uncertainty, which naturally must affect the price which we can offer for goods of the "second order." Also in *interest* is included an element of risk; no investment is *quite* without risk; in the *gross interest* is therefore included cover for a risk, which must be deducted in order to find (the *net interest*, the reward for the sacrifice of waiting.) Some authors exaggerate this element; others accumulate several risky elements that are only different aspects of the same risk, because they would rather defend the existence of interest than explain it. Some people, as, for instance, *Courcelle-Seneuils*, go so far that they regard the process of saving up and owning (*i.e.*, keep safe and manage, *Schaeffle*) capital as causing *labour*, which must also be remunerated. If we add abstinence to a great variety of risks, and to this the labour of safe keeping, it appears that a capitalist is a very hard-used individual, for whom no remuneration could be high enough, and even then the Manchester men and the French school have forgotten that also the capitalist's fear of losing his money ought to be rewarded. Of course management of the savings may come into consideration, and this would increase the demand for interest and may account for the difference between the interest a bank accords its depositor and the rate at which it discounts bills; management of savings can for the individual only be spoken of when saving takes place in the form of a stock of goods which requires space and labour, hardly if we speak of money. On the other hand, the demand for interest will be increased if the creation of the interest itself presumes labour on the part of the recipient of interest; but in this case we speak of profits as the reward for employers' work. We can only say that *when* we can have net interest practically free of work and risk (the interest on deposits) then an investment which requires labour and involves risk must yield some per cent. more than the net interest. The lower the rate of deposit interest the smaller is the profit with which we are satisfied, partly because the market interest is part of the profits, and partly because the facility for obtaining income free of work and risk will affect our entire judgment and the conditions we make for working with our capital *ourselves.*

The easier it is to obtain a high rate of interest without trouble the more fantastic must the profits be in order to entice a rich man to undertake labour and risk, provided that the gambling instinct is not the motive, but in this case the gambling instinct will require at least the possibility of large profits.

Actually I ought to have more than two to one when the chance is half. If I have a ticket in the lottery for twelve months with a chance of one in twelve and the premium is only 60s., I will only be willing to pay 5s. for my chance every month if I neither take into consideration the decreasing utility nor the discount of the future. But those 5s., which I sacrifice every month, are the last of 60s.—*i.e.*, my sacrifice of utility is great, because the 5s. represent almost indispensable articles of consumption. One of the twelve months brings me a gain of 60s. in that month; I have a total income of 120s., but the last 60s. thereof will mean for me less necessary goods than the twelve times 5s. which I sacrifice by purchasing the chance. Consequently I ought to have an extra premium. (*Laplace* already treated this problem in the introduction to his *Theorie analytique de la Probabilité.*)

The business man will perhaps reason in this manner, and the professional usurer is not in doubt of the fact that the utility of the sacrifice is greater than the reward ; but most people overlook this fact. Literary laurels tempt many, although very few authors have other pleasure from their works than the joy of producing them.

This is, for instance, also the case in popular insurance where, as stated before, premium and compensation are not in the proper proportion to one another ; here the fact comes in, that the labourer is not an " economic man," as he is quite unable to calculate. Another fact is that in our struggle for obtaining the best places at the table of life as well as in our gambles, we do not, as the business man, coolly calculate the chances, but plunge, in spite of the chances.

Through the ticket in the lottery or the stake in the game of cards, or in our labour to reach the great goal, we offer practically a possibility for intervention to that providence which we all hope will intervene especially on our behalf. Even the clearest thinker has something of the fatalist in him ; we all expect what *Henrik Ibsen* called " the wonder " to fall to our lot.

To the purely economic consideration must be added the value of the big capital as a means to create and exercise power. One Million £ has a moral value which in any case will be more than that of the separate sums of which it is composed. We may consequently be willing to venture in spite of the discount of the future, and of the fact that the profit is a later sum than the many small daily sacrifices. Without this optimism and without this gambling instinct many large enterprises would never have come into existence.

When the Italian labourer suffers a week's hunger in order to try the lottery, what he buys is not the miserable chance, but the right to forget his poverty for a week in dreams of what he would do if a lucky star (a " dice ") made him " a rich and fine Signor," and maybe that dream is worth the stake.

On the other hand, the passive small capitalist's fear of losing his money is very great, so great, that only his credulity and greed will make him invest.

In this chapter we have given a complete theory of the *sacrifice of waiting* and of the *demand for interest* as a condition for saving and also pointed out the demand for an additional remuneration for working with the amount saved oneself instead of lending it. But we must immediately defend ourselves against having advanced a theory of interest through the theory of the sacrifice of waiting; up till now we have only given the theory of the *conditions* for saving and investment.

# CHAPTER XIII

## DIFFERENTIAL RENT

**79. Consumers' Surplus.**—Presuming the curve of utility of the "General good" to be 60, 50, 40, 32, 28, 20, 17, etc., and the curve of disutility of labour to be 4, 8, 16, 32, 64, etc., I will produce 4 units with a marginal utility which is equivalent to a marginal disutility of 32, and with a total utility of 60 + 50 + 40 + 32 = 182 UU, acquired for a total sacrifice of 60 UU. The difference 182 — 60 = 122 UU is my surplus of utility by producing. This surplus will be neither more nor less because money intervenes, and the process by which I personally manufacture the desired commodity is dissolved into two: (*a*) one by which I sacrifice the disutility of labour and for this obtain a money wage, and (*b*) a second, by which I sacrifice my money wage and obtain the desired object.

Diagram XVI*a* gives the case, where I directly produce the direct good by my labour; in Diagram XVI$b_1$ and $b_2$ the process has been dissolved; $b_1$ shows my sacrifice of labour for wages, and $b_2$ my sacrifice of wages for the commodity.

*a.*

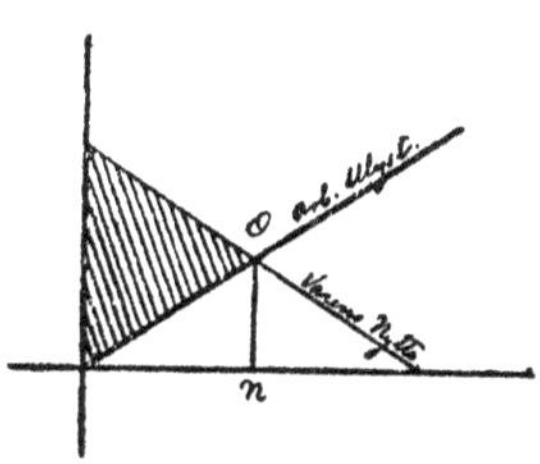


Diagram XVI

Presuming that NO is the marginal utility of the thing, the marginal disutility of labour and the marginal utility of the income, we may say that the surplus in the engraved triangle *a* is dissolved into the two triangles X and Y, of which *x* is credited with the profit derived from the disutility of labour being greater in the last hour than in any previous hour, and *y* is credited with the greater utility of the earlier units of the commodity.

To count the surplus of utility as $x + y$, when I work for my wage as well as when I pay this wage for the purchase of goods, would be counting the same thing twice. The utility of money

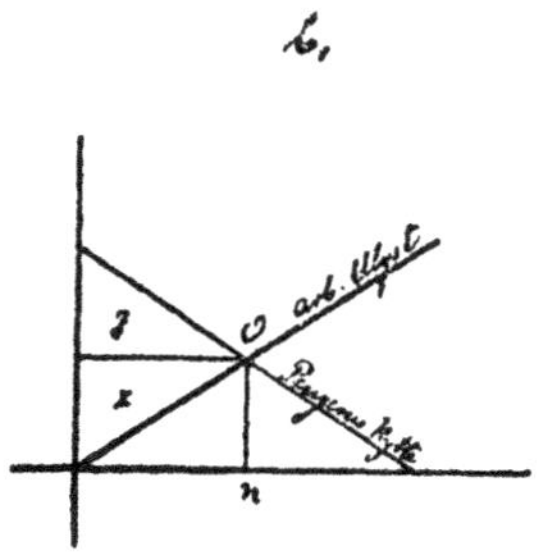

Diagram XVI $b_1$

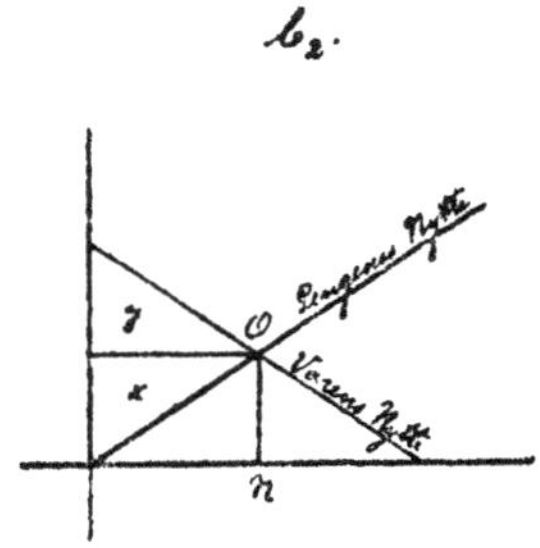

Diagram XVI $b_2$

is derived from that of the commodity and substitutes its utility ; when I have sacrificed my total income on the purchase of the commodity, and this is, say £50, I have not sacrificed 1,000 times the marginal utility of my income, but the very great utility of my first shilling, plus the slightly smaller utility of my second shilling, etc., up to the 1,000th—*i.e.*, I have sacrificed the total utility of my income, not 1,000 times its marginal utility. There is no surplus of utility in the process of spending the money.

Only if I count the utility of money, not as derived from the utility of the commodity, but from the labour I have sacrificed, and when I maintain that the marginal utility of income equals the marginal disutility of the effort in acquiring it, and that the earlier shillings have been earned with a smaller sacrifice of labour than the last shilling, may I count the marginal disutility of money as my sacrifice. But in this case the surplus of utility has again arisen from the double process ; (*a*) sacrifice of effort, balanced by the utility of the money earned, and (*b*) the utility of the money earned sacrificed for the utility of the commodity.

**80. Expressed in Money.**—If the demand curve is 10, 9, 8, 7, and the curve of cost is, for instance, 4, 5, 6, 7, 8s., the price will be 7s. for 4 units sold. *Marshall* now maintains that the *consumer's* differential rent may be expressed in shillings—*i.e.*, as the sum of his subjective prices less what he has actually paid for the 4 units, or $(10 + 9 + 8 + 7) - 4 \times 7 = 6$s. This is the consumer's rent, rent of demand, $r_d$, the differential rent of the consumer, the difference between the sum of the subjective prices $t_d$ (total of demand) and the actual expenditure $(n.p_n)$(compare Sec. 43).

For the first unit the consumer pays 7s and derives a utility which he values at $7 + 3 = 10$s., etc. Am I really entitled to say that the 28s. I have paid for the thing have a value of 34s. ? This is the question which *Nicholson* puts to *Marshall*, and which the latter sweeps aside without replying.

" Suppose that a person has £100 a year. Rather than go without a minimum of subsistence, he would give the whole £100 for this purpose. But—as the vegetarians tell us—he can live on 6d. a day, or, roughly, £10 a year. Therefore, his consumer's rent on this part of his expenditure is £90, which he has left after satisfying his hunger. Suppose, now, to clothe himself decently, he would be willing to spend £60 out of this £90, but that he can get all he requires for £10. Here again there emerges on the commodity of clothing a consumer's rent of £50. And he has still £80 left. Of this he may be willing to pay £30 for furnished rooms rather than do without shelter, but, again, let the actual cost only be £10, and he obtains a consumer's rent of £20. Thus taking only three branches of expenditure, a person with £100 a year has gained a consumer's rent of £160, and has still £70 left to spend. . . . But such a method of measurement seems to me purely hypothetical and illusory. Of what avail is it to say that the utility of an income of £100 a year is worth, say, £1,000 a year." (*Principles*, Vol. I., Chap. iii.)

As previously stated, the subjective schedule of demand varies every time we alter the quantity of our purchase on account of a decrease in prices, because the marginal utility of money is a function of the quantity of goods I may buy. This causes further *deviation* in the consumers' rent expressed in money; the rent is not as large as it appears if we compose a schedule of subjective prices, where these are proportional to the utility of the corresponding units of the commodity. Just as safely as we may state the *consumer's rent* expressed in *utility*, just as lacking in exactitude is the statement in shillings of the advantage of only paying the marginal price for each unit.

We do not reject the consumer's differential rent as expressed in money, but we recognize the deviations to which it is subject, so that we at most are entitled to use it for the calculation of *differences*, but not at all if we operate with its total amount.

But this becomes still worse if we do not restrict ourselves to measure $r_d$ for the individual, but attempt to measure it for the entire community.

A difference in price of 1s. will perhaps for Tom mean a utility of 1,000 units, but for Harry only 100 units. If we calculate that all consumers by a fall in price of a given article would gain a total of, say, £50, we still know *nothing* as long as we do not know which consumers are concerned—*i.e.*, what a shilling means for them. It is, for instance, possible that the consumers may gain only £50 by a fall in price, which yields the producers £75 less income. Which utility must then be attributed to the £50 (great or small for poor and rich) respectively compared with the loss in utility of the producer (what is the importance of the £75 to the producer ?).

*Simon Patten* makes an interesting objection : The first unit of a necessity has in a way next to immeasurable utility, because it stands between us and death, and must consequently be attributed the total value of existence. But may we actually attribute to the first units of our most indispensable consumption such utility, which must be much greater than the combined utility of all other things ?

*Patten* distinguishes in this between " pain economy " and " pleasure economy," the *former* a state where man lives at the margin of his existence (for instance, a starved people of hunters) the *latter* a state where we are above this limit and where in the consumption, even of the necessities for the maintenance of life, we do not think of hunger and cold, but of the more positive wants satisfaction and warmth, because we simply are not and have not at all been at the very margin where bread and fuel mean the difference between life and death. In this case we may consequently only attribute to the first piece of bread of the day a utility which, even if absolutely great, is still very insignificant in proportion to the value of existence, which the traveller in the desert must attribute to his supply of water. (Compare the quotation from *Hobson.*)

Even if we really knew all the *prices* of the schedule of demand, *Taussig* observes, that the difference in income, etc., and the doubtful satisfaction of pain economy would co-operate in making impossible a calculation (based on the consumer's rent in money) of the surplus of utility actually attained.

**81. The Producer's Rent.**—Besides $r_d$ we have $r_s$ or the *Rent of Supply*, the producers differential rent (a Norwegian, *Mr. Keilhau*, terms it correctly rent difference). It arises from the difference between $n \cdot p_n$ and the total expenditure of production ($t_s$).

$$t_d - n \cdot p_n = r_d \text{ (consumer's rent)}$$
$$n \cdot p_n - t_s = r_s \text{ (producer's differential rent)}$$

$$t_d - t_s = r_d + r_s = \text{R, the profits of the community expressed in money.}$$

$r_s$ arises, as we shall later see, in two ways : (*a*) by the producer producing each unit cheaper than the market price, and, consequently, cheaper than the last seller accepted, and (*b*) by his producing his earlier units at a smaller cost than the last one. In both cases the differential rent is consequently a difference between what he obtains (*i.e.*, the market price) and his average expenditure for each unit produced. In so far as the difference between the market price and the average expense arises from an artificial limitation of the production, the differential rent becomes a monopoly rent.

Supposing the price of production per unit to be 7s. and the schedule of demand to be 10, 9, 8s., etc., we will then arrive at the following specification :—

| Quantity | Price | $t_d - n \cdot p_n = r_d$ | $n \cdot p_n - t_s = r_s$ | $r_d + r_s$ |
|---|---|---|---|---|
| 1st unit | 10s. | 10 — 10s. = 0s. | 10 — 7s. = 3s. | 3s. |
| 2nd ,, | 9s. | 19 — 18s. = 1s. | 18 — 14s. = 4s. | 5s. |
| 3rd ,, | 8s. | 27 — 24s. = 3s. | 24 — 21s. = 3s. | 6s. |
| 4th ,, | 7s. | 34 — 28s. = 6s. | 28 — 28s. = 0s. | 6s. |
| 5th ,, | 6s. | 40 — 30s. = 10s. | 30 — 35s. = — 5s. | 5s. |
| 6th ,, | 5s. | 45 — 30s. = 15s. | 30 — 42s. = — 12s. | 3s. |
| 7th ,, | 4s. | 49 — 28s. = 21s. | 28 — 49s. = — 21s. | 0s. |

Expressed in money the maximum of the consumer's rent is at 7 units at a price of 4s.—*i.e.*, full satisfaction at a minimum price, while the producer's maximum is at 2 units—*i.e.*, minimal satisfaction at a maximum price. A turnover of 2 units at a price of 9s. is called monopoly terms, because a monopolist commanding the market and seeking the maximum advantage (*i.e.*, the maximum of $r_s$) will stop there. The maximum of *the sum of the two differential rents is at 4 units at the price of production* (the natural market condition).

From this the liberal school will conclude that the maximum advantage for the community from the exchange is attained at the natural market price, where the marginal prices of buyer and seller are identical. This rule would be correct if the consumer's rent calculated in shillings stated the profit of the community. But this is not the case. The 21s. which represent $r_d$ at a price of 4s. may contain much more utility than the 21s. lost by the producer. The question arises by determining prices for public services; is it best to have a deficit to be covered by taxes, or should we make use of a possible monopoly—in the present case, should the price be 9 or 4 or 7s.?

Here a Danish author advances the theory of the *ideal price*, the price at which the community gains the maximum utility.

When treating the question of monopoly in connection with increasing return, and when we have accounted for the relations between general expenses and variable expenses, we shall show how an ideal price may be found, different from the price of production, even if we have only the consumer's rent expressed in money, and not the utility as a guide.

Supposing that a circus arrives at a town and that the citizens have the same desire (100 UU) to attend the performance, but that their income gives them a different price of demand, say the schedule above (here we have a case where each unit means a new buyer). In our example 4 persons would come at a price of 7s.; the consumer's rent expressed in money will be 6s. Now the owner of the circus reduces the price to 6s. and 5 persons appear, the consumer's rent will total 10s. Here is the peculiarity, that the richest, who would pay 10s., earns 4s. in consumer's rent; number 2 earns 3s., etc; number 4, who previously did not earn a differential rent will now earn 1s. Obviously it is the more *well-to-do who earn most of the consumer's differential rent, in any case, expressed in money*; and a reduction in price yields the consumer advantage in proportion to the quantity which they buy, consequently, most to the richest.

The last arrival, number 5, does not earn a differential rent expressed in money, because the 6s. which he sacrifices correspond to the 100 UU which he attributes to his ticket—otherwise, he would have bought at a higher price. It might be concluded from this that we do not benefit the consumers, which we attract by a reduced price, but only benefit the previous consumers.

The fact is, however, that when number 5 now buys a ticket for 6s. he changes his consumption from something different, for which he previously paid 6s. But this change presumes that he gains utility. The cause is that the reduction in price in the present case alters his level of prices and the marginal utility of his income, and thereby causes him to alter his consumption. But as far as the new marginal buyer is concerned it must be maintained that the differential rent in money is nil, and that the additional utility which he gains cannot be great and is attained by the alteration of the marginal utility of his income.

For goods of which several units may be bought, the same will hold good for that unit, by which we—that is the group of marginal buyers—increase our consumption; but the probable minimal amount which the marginal buyer earns on his previously last and now second last unit may, measured in utility, mean as much as those shillings which the rich man earns on the many units he buys.

# BOOK IV

## THE NORMAL MARKET

## CHAPTER XIV

### With Constant Return

**82. Schedules of Supply.**—Behind the immediate, short market is the *long market,* not necessarily corresponding to any separate daily or local market, but still actually existing, because it is a regulator continually acting on the concrete markets. The long market in a dynamic community is never in equilibrium ; in other words, we must show how a given equilibrium is disturbed in the short market—the immediate effect of the disturbance—and then we must examine how supply as well as demand are again altered, until a permanent equilibrium is once more attained. At the same time we must remember that new disturbing causes in turn become effective, and that these may prevent the state of equilibrium from being completed, and may give the market a totally different line of development by strengthening or weakening forces already existing.

In Sec. 49 we divided goods into three groups according as they were produced under the rule of constant, decreasing or increasing return ; we distinguished at the same time between a technical and an economic schedule, as only the latter will become the schedule of supply.

By the first mentioned we mean a (potential) series of prices, stating what the cost of production will be for a *separate* concern according to the larger or smaller number of units produced. Until the *combination or group of technical components,* from the co-operation of which the finished article results has been fully utilised, an increase in the production will take place under the rule of decreasing expenses—*i.e.,* with decreasing average expenditure, because until this limit has been reached, the general expenses need no increase. An increase beyond this may take place by doubling the group of components, in which case the production from one combination to another comes under the rule of *constant expenses.* But the increase of production may not be brought about simply by doubling the productive components, but by putting them together in a different proportion—*e.g.*, by employing more machine power, more complicated working machinery, which may only be used with advantage by larger plants, or other combinations of raw materials ; in other words, by the employment of other technical methods ; in this case an increase in production by turning to another combination, embodying higher technique, comes under the rule of *decreasing* expenses.

When output may only be increased in such a way that the production takes place under more unfavourable conditions, or one component of the group is a fixed quantity, the working takes place under the rule of increasing expenses.

In the technical schedule is included as the cost of production the larger of the two amounts—the *average* and the *marginal expenditure*—*i.e.*, where the expenses are decreasing, the former, where the expenses are increasing from one unit to another, the latter (compare Sec. 43.).

The economic schedule states at what prices the existing actual and possible producers may offer the changing quantities of goods ; it must be compiled in such a way that the sellers working under the best conditions, consequently the cheapest, are placed first with their quantity of goods, and the poorest producers last ; the better equipped firms, who have the greater capacity, come earlier in the series and have lower prices of output than many typical representative concerns, while many poor firms of small capacity come after the latter. In this schedule of supply of the long run a firm may take several places, according as it produces a larger or smaller number of units. A concern will, in the case of decreasing return, have its output placed earlier in the series with a small production than with a large one, while with increasing return its output will be placed later in the series with a smaller production than with a larger one. In the next volume we will find the rules according to which production takes place, but here we will only ascertain the difference between the technical and the economic schedule, and the fact that production may obey the rules of constant, increasing and decreasing return. We have already pointed out that there is no clear case in any kind of production, but provisionally we presume uncomplicated cases, in order to find the abstract rules.

**83. The Tendency towards Equilibrium.**—Now we are going to consider the movements of the market and find how the schedules of demand and supply affect one another in the long run, and find their interaction. If in any trade the given output yields an extraordinary profit, even the *marginal producer* making profits, we presume that this will entice him or the other producers to extend, or attract entirely new people, who would then increase the demand for labour, raw materials and machinery, and under the incentive of the high price of the finished article, by offering over-price, attract these technical components to the exceptionally profitable concerns, from those concerns where the profit is (relatively) too low; this takes time. We would not, of course, be able to follow the fluctuations in one direction or the other while the forces seek equilibrium, seek new profitable trades, leave the too unprofitable *marginal trades* whose possibilities, even if unchanged, seem too small for the employer. But when the process has been completed and the equilibrium attained we will consider the result, not in order to leave it entirely, *but* tentatively, to learn if by its further effect on other goods, the result may after all only be temporary, and the vibrations be continued. We do not presume that the forces are completely mobile, and by extending the production over a sufficiently long period we are further able to take snapshots of certain of its phases. The rules, according to which the productive factors move under the guidance of profits, will be shown in the next volume; here only this much, that not the *absolute*, but the *relative*, profit determines the distribution of the economic forces in the production of goods. It is quite irrelevant whether the profits are 7% or 5%; an offered profit of 3% is an incentive and a motive, if the usual profit is only 2%. The profits in a certain trade, therefore, are the indicator showing the economic need of producing the article in question—whether the production is to be forced or restricted, and, consequently, also the direction which the productive forces should take: first, in order to gain the maximum recompense, and secondly, in order to be paid *alike* everywhere.

But we must keep in mind that equilibrium is never completely attained, and that in a dynamic community new influences take effect and alter a direction once taken. This should make the economist careful in his predictions, and in any case make him emphasise the need of a reservation for the influence of forces which may arise. The great war has not on *a single point* invalidated the economic laws; but for laymen it has often appeared so, because economic predictions have not been given with the requisite limitation, "*ceteris paribus*."

In this section we will not go as far as to show the effects of an alteration of the market condition on the prices of the components—provisionally we take these prices as being fixed; neither on the distribution of the gross profits, which again reacts on the distribution of income and the prices of demand. But we dare not forget that these effects exist: the classics are therefore not right in their contention that the demand for labour determines the increase in population, unless they remember that the consumption of this increase itself will again increase the demand for labour. Between demand and supply there is always, not only the connection by the former directly affecting the latter, but also the connection that the supply indirectly creates new demand, inasmuch as the persons taking part in the production of a thing, and, consequently, in its money value, may themselves consume some of the commodity produced, and by buying other goods may be in a position to enable the producers of these goods to increase the consumption of the thing first mentioned. In the theory of the wages of labour this reciprocal action is often overlooked. A lower standard of wages will in many trades mean a decrease in the purchasing power of the customers, and, on the other hand, a higher standard of wages may be partly balanced by the fact that the labourers, who have now more purchasing power, force the demand and thereby the prices of goods upwards against themselves.

**84. The Market Conditions.**—Generally speaking, the handicrafts will come under the rule of constant return; here the technical schedule is such as to show the same expenditure for each unit produced; this is not quite true, however, for the plant must be of a certain size, and presumes utilisation to its full capacity.

The economic schedule also is constant; there are large and small artisans, and there is certainly a difference between their conditions of production, but this difference only causes a larger or smaller profit to be left for the well-situated seller. In the handicrafts custom is further so strong that a price attained shows a tendency to create a rather lasting normal for all.

If the cost of production is $s$, the accepted price of demand must—as no producer will lose—be equal to $s$ in order to correspond to the (constant) expenses of the free long market. *The price will then be a given and fixed amount* ($s$), for which reason it will depend on the *schedule of demand how much* will be sold, but *not* at which price. If the *subjective price of the n-th buyer,* $p_n$, *is equal to the constant cost of production,* $s$, *then n units will be sold* at this price, $s$; if a *larger* number of units than $n$ are produced, a later prospective buyer will come in; but his subjective price will be lower than $p_n$; if a smaller number of units than $n$ are produced, an earlier prospective buyer will be the last buyer, and his subjective price be greater than $p_n$ and consequently than $s$, whereby an extra profit would be created for the producers, attracting the productive forces to this trade, until equilibrium was again attained with a total production of $n$ units at a price of $p_n$.

As all units are produced with the same expense, which corresponds to the market price—*i.e.*, $n \cdot p_n = n \cdot s$, the seller will obtain *no* differential rent, the buyers of course retaining their consumer's rent.

**85. Alterations in Demand or Supply.**—An increase in the prices of the schedule of demand must immediately produce an increase in prices, which, however, because it creates an extra profit in the trade in question, will attract new producers and thereby after a while neutralise itself; as an increase in the prices of the schedule of demand will cause a later prospective buyer to have a subjective price, which is equal to $s$, a larger number of units can be sold at an *unchanged* market price; *vice versa*, if the schedule of demand declines. If the turnover is increased much by an increased demand it may cause the raw materials of an article to rise in price, again swelling the price of the finished good, even in the long run—not because it has grown more difficult to produce the article, but because its technical components have grown more expensive.

The cost of production may increase from various causes—on account of a *tax*, or on account of an increase in price of the productive forces, the technical components, which contribute to the production of the good. The increase in expense may be uniform for each unit, and in this case either a *certain amount* or an amount varying according to the price—proportionally or progressively; it may take the form of a proportional increase in the price of the plant, or it may be equal for all concerns without consideration of their size.

Supposing, first, that the cost of production is increased from $s$ to $s + t$; the producer must, in order to continue working, have covered the increase in his cost of production, because there *does not exist a differential rent* from which the increased expenses may be taken; his minimum price will therefore be $s + t$. Consequently the $n$-th buyer will leave the market, and an earlier buyer, whose subjective price is more than $p_n$, *i.e.*, $p_n + t$, will now become the marginal buyer. There will, however, be one *exception*: when $p_n > s > p_{n+1}$, the increase will be borne by the seller, provided that the increase in the cost of production ($t$) is not larger than the difference between $p_n$ and $s$.

A tax on all trade concerns, of an equal amount, would handicap the smaller ones, and therefore offers an excellent remedy in case it is wished to restrict the number of industrial businesses, because when the amount of turnover is fixed an increase in the number of concerns would only mean an increase in the cost of distribution.

Suppose that A, B and C produce respectively 50, 100 and 150 units; an impost on the trade of £5 would then increase the cost of each unit by 2s., 1s. and 8d. respectively. Presuming that the price of the last buyer corresponds to the cost of production, the 300th buyer's price would not be able to cover the previous prices of production with the addition of 2s. Consequently, the production must be restricted, and the last producer (with the smaller turnover) may leave the market. The price of the ware will then be increased with an amount per unit, of £5 divided by the total turnover of the producer who is *now the last*, that is by less than 2s.; other producers will make an extra profit (a differential rent), because the tax of £5 is distributed by them over a larger quantity of goods, and, consequently, is less per unit.

A tax on, or an increase in the price of, the raw material will as a rule have the same effect as an equal tax per unit; it will, however, give those factories which are able to utilise the raw material better a premium, and cut away the poorest producers.

Suppose we—under the assumption that normally 10 kilogrammes of sugar are extracted from 100 kg. beets—place an impost of 1s. on each 100 kg. beets delivered to the factory. Suppose further that the factories A, B, C and D extract 8, 10, 12 and 16 kg. sugar respectively from 100 kg beets. The tax on each kg. sugar will then be 1½d., 1⅕d., 1d. and ¾d., respectively for these factories. A will probably be obliged to leave the market, and the price will be increased by 1⅕d., and not by 1½d., while C and D will gain a differential rent, amounting to the difference between 1⅕d and the tax per unit, which they are actually paying. B is now the marginal producer, who does not earn a differential rent, but is merely covered. If, however, a duty had excluded foreign competition, so that the consumption of home-made sugar need not be restricted, and A is not obliged to leave the market, the price may be increased by 1½d., when the three other producers will all earn a differential rent.

We may express this graphically as follows :—

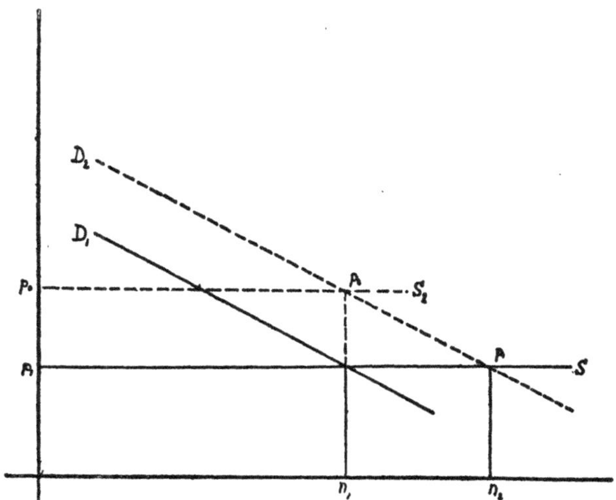


Diagram XVIIa

The curves $D_1$ and $S_1$ are the curves of demand and supply (with constant return the latter is parallel to the base) and $D_2$ represents the curve of demand, when the demand for the good in question has grown stronger.

Before this has happened $n_1$ units are sold at a price of $p_1$. The increase of the demand to $D_2$ will immediately cause the price to be increased to $p_2$ (where the two dotted lines intersect); the extra profit arising therefrom ($p_2 < p_1$) attracts the productive forces and the production is increased to $n_2$, after which the price will again be reduced to $p_1$.

In Diagram XVII*b* the line $p_1S$ represents the constant expenses; the line $p_2S_2$ states the expenses, increased by the

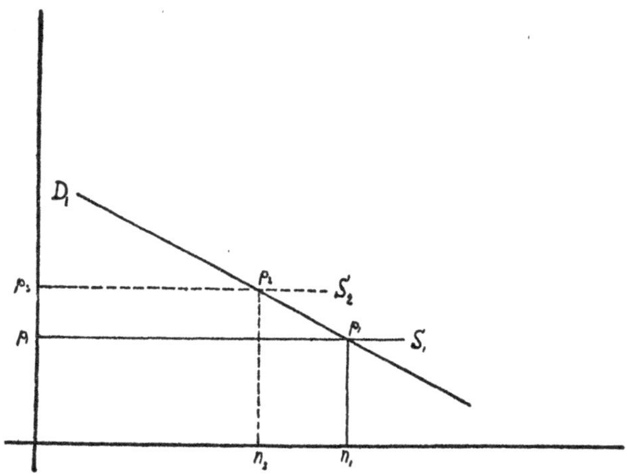


Diagram XVIIb

amounts $p_1p_2$. The increased expense is shifted on to the buyer by its full amount, while the turnover is *reduced* from $n_1$ to $n_2$. It will be seen that with constant return there is still only one point of intersection, and for each given condition only one state of equilibrium.

In Diagram XVII*c* the market condition is stated, with a tax, *proportional* to the price; $p_1$ are the constant expenses, $D_1$ is the curve of demand. If we impose a proportional tax, the effect, from *the point of view of the seller*, is to reduce the price of demand by an amount corresponding to the tax; but the tax, and, consequently, also the reduction, varies with the price; 8½% of 1s. is 1d., while of 6d. it will only be ½d. The reduction is, consequently largest, when the turnover is only small, and the price of the marginal buyer is high. The curve, reduced by the tax, $D_2$, will consequently be flatter than the curve of demand proper. The turnover is reduced from $n_1$ to $n_2$. The price will be $p_2$, but of this the seller will only get $p_1$; the difference

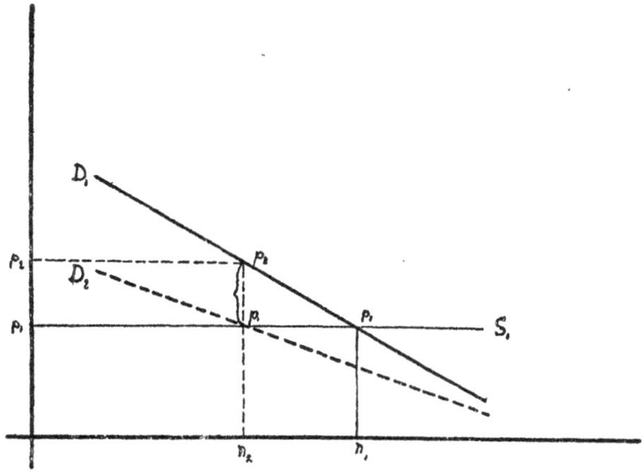


XVIIc

$p_1 < p_2$ is appropriated by the Government, if it is a tax; as there is no differential rent in this case either, from which the seller can spare anything, the tax must be shifted completely on to the buyer.

This diagram is justified because a tax—without taking into consideration the fact that the resistance of *friction* gives it a tendency to rest where it is imposed—has similar effects whether it is collected from the seller or the buyer. Whether I have to pay a rent of £40 and thereafter £5 in taxes on rent, or I pay £45 free of taxes, does not matter to me; whether a house-owner is to receive £40 free of taxes, or £45, of which £5 are paid in taxes, makes no difference *to him.* We may therefore include a tax in a diagram, either as an *addition to the curve of supply or as a reduction in the curve of demand*; but in the latter case we must remember that the price must be found in the original curve of supply, and *not in the reduced one,* which only states the part of the sale price, which is received by the seller.

We may express the same in a figure example, placing the schedules of demand (D) and supply (S) against one another:

| D | S |
|---|---|
| 10 | 7 |
| 9 | 7 |
| 8 | 7 |
| 7 | 7 |
| — | — |
| 6 | 7 |
| 5 | 7 |

If *s* is 7s., the market condition will be 4 units, sold at a price of 7s. If the expenses are increased to 8s., the market condition will be 3 units at a price of 8s. If the price of demand is increased by 1s. and the cost of production remains unchanged at 7s., the schedule of demand will be 11, 10, 9, 8, 7, 6s.—*i.e.*, the state of the market will be 5 units at 7s., as it is now no longer the 4th but the 5th buyer, whose subjective price is 7s. The strengthening of the schedule of demand will only be effective if it concerns the units in the vicinity of the marginal unit; but this is also *sufficient*. The effect would, for instance, have been the same whether the subjective price of all units had been increased or only the subjective prices for the 4th and the 5th unit.

Under constant return a tax will consequently be shifted on to the buyer; with the exception however, that if the producer is *not* able to leave the trade, and his income is more than the individual minimum of existence, the tax will rest with the producer. Home industry has supplied many examples of an increase in the price of raw materials, or a decline in the price of demand, or competition with factory-made articles, which have been met with the misery of the workers in the trade, the trade becoming "parasitical." In this case the recruiting of the trade will certainly be reduced, but it may take a generation to re-establish equilibrium and enable the home-workers to gain once more something above the minimum of existence. Otherwise the home-industry in question would be superseded; it may, however, as was the case with the hand-made boot industry of America, be turned into a highly-paid luxury production with few workers.

## CHAPTER XV

### WITH DECREASING RETURN

**86. Decreasing Return.**—In a concern which works with increasing expenses the technical and economical schedule will take the same form, as an increase of the production will more than proportionally increase the expenses.

Generally speaking all raw materials are produced with a *decreasing return*, and actually also such manufactured goods in which the raw material is the principal component; Mining, Forestry and Agriculture (the cultivation of plants as well as the breeding of cattle) obey the rule of decreasing return. This rule states that the greater the quantity of energy in its various forms (labour, manure, machinery, etc.)—*i.e.*, the greater the number of *units of energy*—which we employ on the same plot of ground, the smaller will be the increase in production for each unit, when a certain optimum has been reached; from this we again deduce that each unit will yield a different return, and that the last one will yield the least. Suppose that the first, second, third, fourth and fifth units produce 10, 9, 8, 7 and 6 quarters of grain; if now 4 units of energy are available, the last unit will return 7 quarters; according to the rule of indifference the price of a unit of energy will therefore be 7 quarters of grain; but the 4 units of energy will produce $10 + 9 + 8 + 7 = 34$ quarters of grain, but only get as reward $4 \times 7 = 28$ quarters; the 4 units have produced more than they get—*i.e.*, 6 quarters, which are *accredited, apportioned or imputed* to the land or, correctly speaking, its owner. How the 7 quarters which are the wages or payment for each unit, will be distributed between the various forms, labour, machinery, etc., is immaterial in this connection.

Here only this much: if the unit of energy had one form only, for instance, labour, its reward would be the marginal return of the units, provided that the land had no special position of monopoly, that is, the wages would be a function of the quantity of labour-seeking employment, and the scale of yield of the land.

But the energy is applied in various forms: Labour, machinery, management, manure; economically we convert these different guises of energy to one unity, collecting the various forms, in which energy must be applied, in the comprehensive conception, doses of capital; by this we understand a certain uniform sum of money, say £50, employed to buy the energy which is to be applied to the land, or, in other words, employed to buy the technical components which besides the land are required to produce the grain.

But we do not need to apply our doses to the same land; we may spread or extend them over several plots of land (increase the cultivation *extensively*, while previously we increased it *intensively*). But these plots will often yield less than the first, either because they are less capable of yield, or because they are more distant.

Suppose there are four fields: X, Y, Z and Q, and suppose that the doses of energy when applied to them yield:

| | ON X | ON Y | ON Z | ON Q |
|---|---|---|---|---|
| | QUARTERS. | QUARTERS. | QUARTERS. | QUARTERS. |
| 1st dose ... ... | 6 | 5 | 4 | 3 |
| 2nd „ ... ... | 5 | 4 | 3 | 2 |
| 3rd „ ... ... | 4 | 3 | 2 | 1 |
| 4th „ ... ... | 3 | 2 | 1 | — |
| 5th „ ... ... | 2 | 1 | — | — |

If only the field X existed, the 5th dose would produce 2 qrs.; if both the fields X and Y existed, the 1st dose would be applied to X, the 2nd to Y, the 3rd and 4th to X, and the 5th to Y. If all four fields are in use and 10 doses of capital are seeking employment, or if 40 quarters of grain are wanted, 4 doses will be applied to X, 3 to Y, 2 to Z, and 1 to Q; on X will be raised 18 quarters, on Y 12, on Z, 7 and on Q 3 quarters. Each dose gets as a reward its marginal yield of 3 quarters, which it earns whether they are applied to the extensive or the intensive *margin of cultivation*, where the yield of the dose must always be equal; for if a dose did yield more on the extensive than on the intensive margin, a dose would be taken from the field X and employed in the cultivation of new land; if a dose yielded less, the field Q would be abandoned and the dose transferred to the field X. We will return to this in a later volume, and will only point out here that each new dose, whether employed extensively or intensively, will have a smaller yield than the previous one; we will not then need to treat the problem of bringing more land under cultivation at present; but we may construct a schedule in which we compare the difference in the yield of the doses when applied to one or more fields.

Let us presume that the first 7 doses yield a decreasing return of 10, 9, 8, 7, 6, 5 and 4 quarters of grain. In order to find the expenses for each, we start with the price of "the dose of capital"—a comprehensive term—say 105s., and we now find that the first 10 quarters are produced with an expense of 105s. $\div$ 10 = 10s. 6d., the following 9 at 105 $\div$ 9 = 11s. 8d., the following 8 at 13s. 1½d., the following 7 at 15s., etc. In other words, we have converted the *decreasing return* for each dose of capital into the *increasing expenses per unit*, compiled as a schedule of supply. This schedule is opposed to a schedule of demand, which, consequently, moves in the opposite direction to the schedule of supply, and the equilibrium is attained, as $p_n$ (the marginal price of the last buyer) $= s_n$ (the price of the marginal seller); presuming that $p_1 > p_2 \ldots > p_{n1}$ but $s_n > s_n < {}_1 > \ldots s_3 > s_2 > s_1$; the buyers will as usual gain their $r_d$, their consumer's rent, and the seller will gain a differential rent, $r_s = n \,.\, p_n - (s_1 + s_2 + s_3 \ldots + s_n)$.

**87. Alterations in Demand and Supply.**—In Diagram XVIII*a* the curves $D_1$ and $S_1$ state the demand and the increasing cost of production, respectively. There is only one point of intersection, and, consequently, only one possible equilibrium—*i.e.*, at the price $p_1$ with a turnover of $n_1$ units. If the prices of demand are increased, the curve being raised from $D_1$ to $D_2$, the price will, in the first instance, rise from $p_1$ to $p_0$; owing to this, the producers, who already earn a differential rent (the triangle S $p_1$ $p_1$) will find this increased by the square $p_1$ $p_1$ $p_{0-0}$. The previous marginal producer, whose cost of production had covered the price of the marginal buyer, will now earn a differential rent; this price and this differential rent, which have been increased owing to the increased demand, will make the producers extend up to $n_2$ units, sold at a price of $p_2$; this price represents a fall against the price temporarily obtained $p_0$, but an increase in comparison with the previous normal price of $p_1$. So far we may follow the representation put forward by a Norwegian, Dr. *Keilhaur*, and, consequently, we do *not* say that the corn-prices are determined by the marginal expenses; but we say that the increased demand in conjunction with the existing supplies determines the corn-prices, and that, if this price is higher than the marginal expenses, then the production will be extended and reduce this price by an increased supply, which must be taken up by a later buyer. The high price thus causes increased cultivation

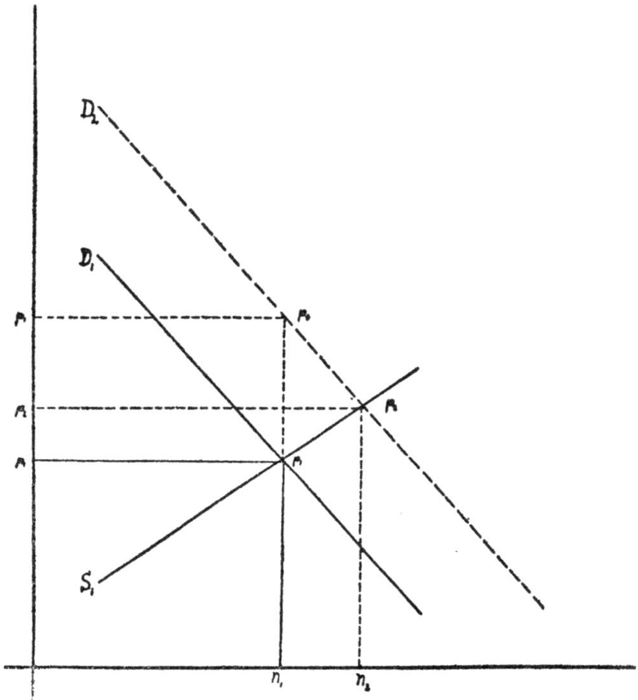


Diagram XVIIIa

which again causes a lower price—*but nevertheless a high one in relation to the price before the increase of demand*; this increase may be due to the pressure of population or to a new employment of the grain, for instance, as fodder or for industrial use, in which it loses in nourishment in order to gain in value, (7 or 8 kilos grain produce 1 kilo pork). The producers' differential rent will have been increased by $p_1\, p_1\, p_2\, p_2$.

In Diagram XVIII*b* $S_1$ is the original curve of supply. If we increase the expenses for each unit with the tax $t$, we arrive at $S_2$ as the new curve of supply; the turnover is decreased from $n_1$ to $n_2$; the price is increased from $p_1$ to $p_2$; the increase is less than $t$. The marginal expenses with a turnover of $n_2$ are smaller than with a turnover of $n_1$, and consequently the smaller expense with the addition of the tax must be less than the larger expense with the addition of the same tax, or additional expense $t$, which is thus not entirely shifted on to the buyer, part of it being taken

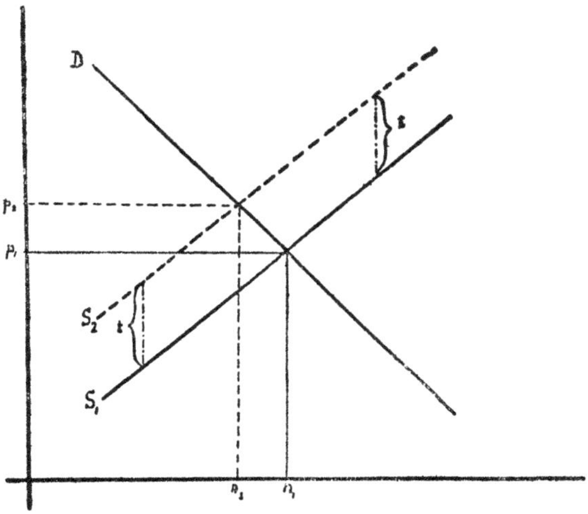


Diagram XVIIIb

from the differential rent of earlier units. The tax will thus force some producers to discontinue ; those continuing can only produce at a higher price, which, however, is lower than the former price with the tax added.

If we start with $S_2$ as the *original* curve and let $S_1$ represent the decreased expenses due to technical improvements, we may provisionally advance the rule, that the turnover is increased and the price reduced, but not with the whole amount saved by the improvement, because the later unit in itself is produced at a higher expense.

From Diagram XVIII*a* it will appear that the increased demand will increase the seller's as well as the buyer's differential rent, from Diagram XVIII*b* that an increase in the expenses will reduce the buyer's as well as the sellers' differential rent ; *vice versa* a decrease in expenses, caused by an improved technique, will not only to a great extent increase the buyer's differential rent (because the price will be reduced), but may even increase the seller's.

**88. The Effect of Taxes.**—We now turn to the above example, that the 1st, 2nd, 3rd to 7th doses of capital produce 10, 9, 8, 7, 6, 5, 4 quarters of grain, respectively ; suppose that to this corresponds a price of demand of 19, 16, $13\frac{1}{2}$, $11\frac{1}{4}$, 10, 9 and 7s.

We now convert the decreasing return into the rising price of supply—*i.e.*, compile a schedule of supply, and then we try to find the market price with the original schedules and with schedules which state alterations in demand and supply.

| | 1 | 2 | 3 | 4 | 5 |
|---|---|---|---|---|---|
| | PRICE OF DEMAND. | | EXPENSE OF PRODUCTION. | | PLUS TAX. |
| | A | B | DOSE. 105S. | DOSE. 77S. | 4S. PER QR. |
| 1st 10 qrs. | 19 | 19 | 10½ | 7 7/10 | 14½ |
| Next 9 ,, | 16 | 17 | 11⅔ | 8 5/9 | 15⅔ |
| ,, 8 ,, | 13½ | 16 | 13⅛ | 9⅝ | 17⅛ |
| ,, 7 ,, | 11¼ | 15 | 15 | 11 | 19 |
| ,, 6 ,, | 10 | 12 | 17½ | 15⅝ | 21½ |
| ,, 5 ,, | 9 | 11 | 21 | 12⅖ | 25 |
| ,, 4 ,, | 7 | 10 | 26¼ | 19¼ | 30¼ |

In this table the first column represents a normal schedule of demand, the second column a schedule of demand when its prices have been increased, for instance, by pressure of population. We have not made the earliest buyers' prices rise, because generally the pressure of population takes place only *further down* the scale. In the third column is calculated the expense of producing one-quarter of grain, when the dose of capital employed is one of 105s.; in the fourth column we have made a better technique cause, that the price of the dose is only 77s., and thereafter found the lower expense per unit; in column 5 the expense from column 3 with the addition of a tax of 4s. has been calculated. We may now compare column 1 with column 3—an ordinary schedule of demand with the corresponding schedule of supply, computed under the given decreasing productivity, and presuming that the price of a dose of energy is 105s.

Strictly speaking, the price of the dose ought to be increased with the increased production, because the increasing demand for the doses of energy—for instance, in the form of labour—must increase their price. We find then that the price will fall to somewhere between 13½ and 13⅛s., that 3 doses will be employed, which produce 27 quarters of corn with a differential rent in kind of 2 + 1 = 3 quarters, the last doses, applied at the margin of cultivation, yielding 8 quarters.

The student is invited, simply for the sake of practice as well as for the results, to compare *a*, column 2 with column 3, in order to find the effect of an increasing demand (larger production, higher price, smaller marginal return in kind, larger differential rent), or *b*, column 1 with column 4 in order to find the effect of a cheapening of the doses of energy applied; for instance, through a fall in the wages of labour (lower price, larger production, higher differential rent in kind, etc.), or *c*, column 1 with column 5 in order to find the effects of a tax.

Finally a table is wanted, through which we may examine the effect of a technical improvement, which enables the same doses of energy—the price of which we presume is unchanged—to produce a larger number of quarters than before. The effect is not the same as that of the cheapening of the dose, as the cause is a different one. The cheapening of the dose will mean that one or more of its components falls in price (for instance, labour) or that there has been a technical progress in industry by which the machines and auxiliary materials of agriculture may be produced cheaper, while the larger return of the dose is due to a technical progress in agriculture itself. This is emphasised here, because it affects the ground rent. Another interesting question is, what is the effect of a uniform tax on area with regard to forcing to more intensive cultivation and to the abandonment of the poorer soil? But this as well as all the questions mentioned in Sec. 88 must be further analysed under the section concerning ground rents in the second volume of this book.

Here I will only quote a couple of observations from my book, *Land Taxes and Land Prices.*

**89. Tithes.**—In Diagram XIX. NA represents the expenditure when N doses of capital are applied, and $N_1A_1$, when $N_1$ doses of capital are applied; the curve A $A_1$ therefore states the expenses by a cultivation of small and great intensity, respectively; NB states the gross return in the first case; the curve $BB_1$ would state the income, if the net income was the *same* without regard to the amount of

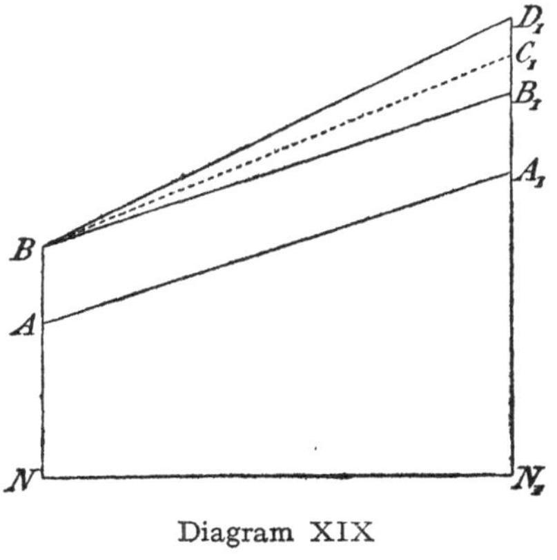


Diagram XIX

capital expended. In cases where the gross return can be stated by the curve B $B_1$ (and the expenditure by A $A_1$), there will be no incentive for the cultivators to employ more capital on the land. If the capital employed is to earn the *same* interest, the gross return would have to be B $D_1$, as $\frac{A\,B}{A\,N} = \frac{A_1\,D_1}{A_1\,N_1}$. This is, however, not the case, in any case after a certain production has been attained. The gross return will certainly increase somewhat more than the expenditure, but at a decreasing rate, and we then arrive at the curve B $C_1$, as stating the actual gross return. *It will be seen that the percentage of net income is decreasing,* for $\frac{A\,B}{A\,N} > \frac{A_1\,C_1}{A_1\,N_1}$.

Suppose, for instance, A N $=$ A B $= 5$, $A_1\,N_1 = 20$, $A_1\,C_1 = 7$, and suppose that we impose a gross tax of 20%. Although the difference in the net return is only $7 - 5 = 2$, the tax will in the first case be 20% of $15 = 3$, in the second case 20% of $27 = 5\frac{4}{10}$ths—*i.e.*, the tax increases more than the net return, and therefore counteracts a desirable, more intensive, cultivation of the land.

A tax of 20% *on the gross return will entail that the seller will not obtain what the buyer will pay,* because the seller of each unit which he produces only has $\frac{4}{5}$ths at disposal for sale, while the tax takes $\frac{1}{5}$th; for the seller it would, therefore, look as if the price of demand has *everywhere* been reduced by 20%. We may also

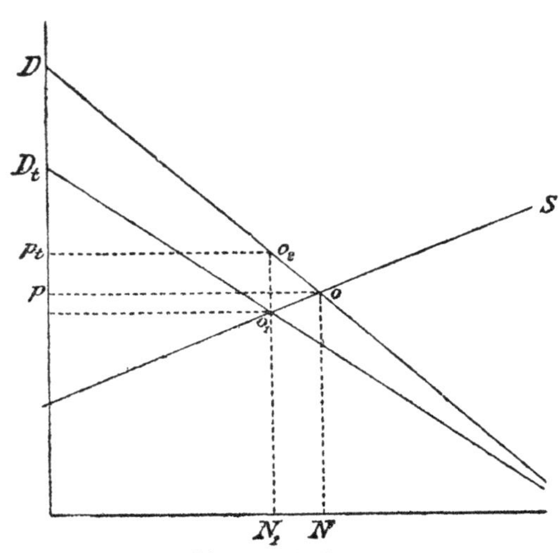

Diagram XX

express this graphically, remembering that agriculture obeys the rule of decreasing return.

In Diagram XX S is the curve of supply and D the curve of demand; the eller only obtains four-fifths of the prices of this schedule, and the Government takes the last fifth. The lower curve, $D_t$ then expresses what the seller obtains with the varying turnovers. The turnover will be decreased from N to $N_1$ and the price raised from $p$ to $p_t$. Of the price ($p_t$). $o_2 - o_1$ represents the tax; in this $o_1 o_2 = p\,p_t + o_1 o$; *the tax is greater than the increase in price.*

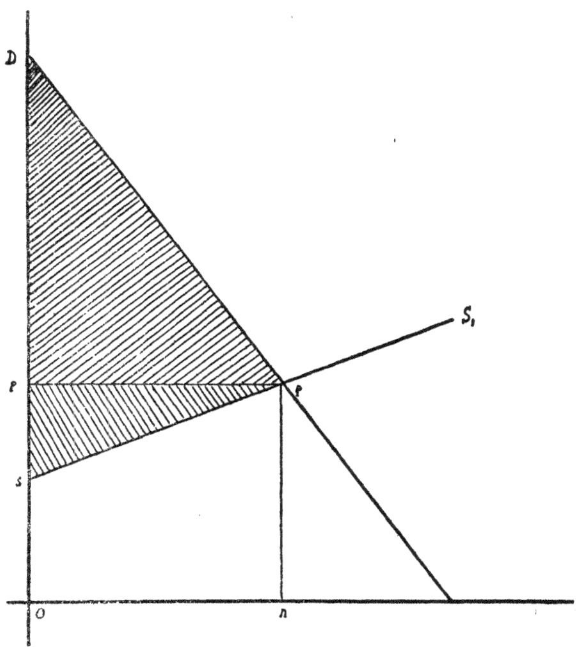


Diagram XXI

**90. The Differential Rent.**—In Diagram XXI we give the simple meeting between a rising schedule of supply and a rather steep curve of demand. The quadrangle, $s\,p\,o\,n$, states the cost of production for $n$ units; the quadrangle, $p\,p\,o\,n$, states what the buyer pays; the difference between the two areas, $s\,p\,p$, is the producer's differential rent, while the buyer's differential rent is the triangle, D $p\,p$. With decreasing return all producers (with the exception of the marginal one) will earn a differential rent, which further has a tendency to be *continual*, because it arises from natural causes ; it is *only* altered by changes in the demand, by taxes, by alteration of the technique of agriculture or altered transport conditions, and is therefore independent of the will of the owner. The case is different under increasing return—*i.e.*, in industry where the differential rent may be altered, if another of the *many* possible forms of production is chosen by one of the producers, instead of the one previously employed by him. In the case of decreasing return the place of the individual seller in the series, and thereby the amount of his differential rent, is certain.

**91. Transport and Market.**—The limit of cultivation may be widened *extensively* in two ways, firstly by employing the same energy on *more* and *often* inferior soil, and secondly, by employing it on *more distant* fields, less suitable economically, *not* on account of *inferior technical* qualities of the soil but on account of the *distance from the centre of consumption.* Land on which grain may be produced at 7s. has not the same value as land of the same quality in the centre of consumption, when the grain from the former has to be carried to the centre, at an expense of, say, 4s. ; but the more distant land is, in respect of money-yield, on a par with the nearer land on which the cost of production is 11s. The necessity for transport is a kind of *negative* quality in the more distant land. If the expense of transport can be reduced, this has the same effect as certain improvements in the soil, as, for instance, draining and marling, which principally benefit the previously inferior soil and change the place of the fields in the schedule of supply. The same is the case with a reduction in the transport charges.

Suppose that the centre of consumption, I. which for a time is self-supporting, will gradually draw the zones II. and III. into its area of supply. We know at once that the marginal price in I. must be equal to the marginal price in II., with the addition of the freight from zone II. to I., and also equal to the marginal price in III., with the addition of the freight from zone III to I.,—*i.e.*, $p_{I} = p_{II} + f_{II} = p_{III} + f_{III}$ ; in order that these equations may be correct $p_{I} > p_{II} > p_{III}$ and $f_{III} > f_{II} > o$ ($p$ is the cost of production, $f$ is freight, the foot number states the zone). Let us now take land of the three qualities, *a*, *b* and *c* on which grain is produced at an expense of 7, 9 and 11s. respectively; suppose that $f_{II} = 3s.$ and $f_{III} = 6s.$

We then arrive at the following specification of the cost, at which the produce of the zone in question may be supplied at the centre of consumption case A:

| | 1st zone. | 2nd zone. | 3rd zone. |
|---|---|---|---|
| *a* ... ... ... ... | 7 | 7 + 3 | 7 + 6 |
| *b* ... ... ... ... | 9 | 9 + 3 | 9 + 6 |
| *c* ... ... ... ... | 11 | 11 + 3 | 11 + 6 |

If the expense of transport is lowered and $f_{II} = 1\frac{1}{2}$ and $f_{III} =$ 3s., we arrive at the following scale, B:

| | 1st zone. | 2nd zone. | 3rd zone. |
|---|---|---|---|
| *a* ... ... ... | 7 | $7 + 1\frac{1}{2}$ | 7 + 3 |
| *b* ... ... ... ... | 9 | $9 + 1\frac{1}{2}$ | 9 + 3 |
| *c* ... ... ... ... | 11 | $11 + 1\frac{1}{2}$ | 11 + 3 |

In the case A we deduce the series given below (the letter stating the quality, the index the zone and the figure in brackets the expense with the addition of freight):

A: $a_1$ (7), $b_1$ (9), $a_2$ (10), $c_1$ (11), $b_2$ (12), $a_3$ (13), $c_2$ (14), $b_3$ (15), $c_3$ (17).

In the case B the series will be altered to:

$a_1$ (7), $a_2$ ($9\frac{1}{2}$), $b_1$ (9), $a_3$ (10), $b_2$ ($10\frac{1}{2}$), $c_1$ (11), $b_3$ (12), $c_2$ ($12\frac{1}{2}$) $c_3$ (14).

A comparison between the two series will show us that in the case B (reduced freight) the land will be employed to a higher extent, according to *its quality—i.e.*, the best soil is preferred, while in the case A (higher freight expenses) it will essentially be employed according to its *vicinity* to the place of consumption. If 4 quarters of grain are to be procured, the price must in the case A be 11s.; two fields of the first quality (*a*) are employed, 1 of the second (*b*) and 1 of the third (*c*), and 3 fields are employed in the 1st zone and 1 in the 2nd. In the case B the price will be 10s.; 3 fields of the first quality (*a*) are employed, and one of the second (*b*), while the third quality field (*c*) is abandoned, or 2 fields are employed in zone I., 1 in zone II., and 1 in zone III.

The cheapening of the transport has *reduced* the price and forced the abandonment of the poorer fields in the vicinity in favour of the better, distant fields; at the same time the saving in freight has taken ground rent from the land of zone I. and added it to the more distant land.

The total ground rent will often have fallen, because the price falls, but the ground rent declines more in the 1st zone, because part of it is removed to the distant zone, where the land now attains value. Often the total ground rent will not need to fall on account of the fall in price, if the consumption can be increased at the same time. In our example the ground rent of the 1st zone will fall from 6 to 4, and of this $1\frac{1}{2}$ is removed to the 2nd zone.

It is this removal of the ground rent (from Europe to America) which took place during the agricultural crisis 1875 to 1898, simultaneously with the fall of the corn-prices ; almost at the same time the opposite movement took place—viz., the removal of the ground rent of the West Indian Sugar Plantations to the beet areas of Central Europe.

By considering the expense of transport in proportion to the value of the good we have come to a better understanding of the conception *world market*, which we advanced in Chapter VII., and to which we will return in the chapter about customs duties.

We may say at once that no *world-market* exists, but only a number of market groups, sometimes entirely without connection. Where there is a lack of means of transport, we may, as in the Russian Empire, have one district with a corn-price of 4s., and another with a hunger price of 28s. But even where transport is possible, there is a boundary to the market group.

A — B — C — D — . . . F —

Suppose that A is the centre of consumption, B, C and D the outer zones and D the temporary marginal zone. We know from the above that : $p_a = p_b + f_b = p_c + f_c = p_d + f_d$. The direction is given : *towards* the centre of consumption, not *vice versa.*

A reduction in freight will cause that less land is cultivated in the nearer and more in the more distant zones, while the marginal expenditure will fall in the former and rise in the latter. Now it often happens that the marginal zone (D) comes under the influence of two centres of consumption—in this case there must be a connection between the two centres, A and F : the price in D must be such that $p_a - f_d = p_d = p_f - f_f$, in which $f_d$ is the freight from D to A and $f_f$ the freight from D to F, and $p_a$, $p_d$ and $p_f$ the price, corresponding to the marginal cost of production in A, D and F respectively. The world price, consequently, does not mean a given price outside the National Domain, but the prices in a number of centres connected through the cost of transport. The different market groups are connected with one another through the prices in the marginal zones, which they have in common. For each centre of consumption the rule holds good, that loco-price = loco-marginal expense = marginal expense with the addition of transport from the *most distant* suppliers. It is the latter which decides the price, against which, however, the centre of consumption itself as well as the intermediate places of supply react by shifting their margin of cultivation.

## CHAPTER XVI

### WITH INCREASING RETURN.

**92. Technical and Market Schedule.**—When production takes place under conditions where either the cost of plant plays a relatively important part, or where an increased production is accompanied by an improved technique, a smaller production will have larger expenses per unit than a larger one—*i.e.*, that an increase of the doses of capital will yield an increase of return, which is more than proportional to the increase of capital.

Consequently, in the technical schedule, the expense of increasing the production from $n$ to $n + 1$ units is less than $\frac{t_s}{n}$, in which $t_s$ is the total expenditure involved in the production of $n$ units. Wherever the production stops, the average expense must therefore be larger than the marginal expenditure; it is therefore the first-mentioned price with which the concern in question comes into the market. Naturally we will arrive at a limit, where further increase in the production does not pay, at least not *technically*, and where the motive for a further increase in production, is either to be able to command the market also economically, or to secure a stronger position towards the suppliers of technical components.

Now the several producers have varying *capacity for production*, and, consequently, unequal expenses, some average—*i.e.*, the normal producers, others low—*i.e.*, those who are particularly strong in capacity, and again others high expenses—among those the marginal producers. The high expenses correspond to the price of the marginal buyer, and do not leave a profit, and interest is often only gained at the cost of the remuneration of the employer himself.

Let us suppose that the technical schedule, which states at which price the different quantities can be produced in the same establishment, has the following appearance :—

| | | |
|---|---|---|
| 1st unit is produced at | | $s_1$ |
| . . . . . | | |
| . . . . . | | |
| $g$ units | ,, | $s_g$ |
| . . . | | |
| $n$ —— | ,, | $s_n$ |
| . . . . . | | |
| . . . . . | | |
| $n + r$ | ,, | $s_{n+r}$ |

in which $g < n$ and $s_1 > s_g > s_n > s_{n+r}$.

Suppose further than there are two producers, G and N, of which G produces $g$ units at an expense of $s_g$ per unit, while N produces some more ($n$) units with the smaller expenditure of $s_n$ per unit. If G and N are the only producers, there will be brought to the market $g + n$ units. To make the production remunerative for G, the market price for $n + g$ units must at least be equal to G's expenses, $s_g$; as $s_n < s_g$, N will earn a differential rent, the difference between the market price, which corresponds to G's expense, and N's smaller cost of production.

Let N increase his production by $r$ units, having discovered he can produce $n + r$ units cheaper than he can produce $n$ units. There will then—presuming that G keeps his production unchanged—be $g + (n + r)$ units in the market, and a later buyer must therefore be attracted as the marginal buyer, if all $g + (n + r)$ units are to be sold.

Presuming the expenses in producing $g$ units equal to the price at which $n + g$ units may find buyers, the price at which the larger number $(g + n + r)$ units are sold, must be lower than G's cost of production. G must then *either extend his production, or if he is not strong enough in capital, leave the market* and cease production; N, who has the larger plant, is able to continue production with a profit.

Competition has a tendency to force the provident manufacturers, and those capable of extension to increase their production (in order to reduce their expenses), and also to force the more immobile producers, or those who are weak in capital, to discontinue production. We may at the same time observe that those who produce *below* the marginal expenses are excluded from competition—*i.e.*, below those expenses which, with the actual industrial organisation, and the actual distribution of the production between the concerns, are those at which the poorest of all the producers work, whose activity is *necessary* for supplying the market under the equilibrium attained.

Let us take a numerical example and still suppose that G and N represent respectively the producers who are weak and strong in capital in their mutual competition.

| | | | Schedule of Demand. | | Technical Schedule of Production. |
|---|---|---|---|---|---|
| . . . | | | | | |
| . . . | | | | | |
| 4 | units are | demanded at | 12s. | and produced at | 9s. |
| . . . | | | | | |
| . . . | | | | | |
| 7 | ,, | ,, | 10s. | ,, | 8s. |
| . . . | | | | | |
| . . . | | | | | |
| 11 | ,, | ,, | 9s. | ,, | 7s. |
| . . . | | | | | |
| . . . | | | | | |
| 15 | ,, | ,, | 8½s. | ,, | 6¾s. |
| . . . | | | | | |
| . . . | | | | | |
| 18 | ,, | ,, | 8s. | ,, | 6¼s. |
| . . . | | | | | |
| . . . | | | | | |
| 20 | ,, | ,, | 6s. | ,, | 6s. |
| 21 | ,, | ,, | 5½s. | ,, | 6s. |

We must here call attention to the fact that the technical *schedule of production is not* to be understood as a *schedule of supply*, but states that if, for instance, 11 units are produced in the same concern, the price of production will be 7s. for each unit, while the price of supply will be 9s. and 8s. respectively per unit, if the 11 units are distributed between two concerns which produce 4 and 7 units respectively.

If now G produces 4 units and N 7 units, N's price of production will be 8s. and G.'s will be 9s.; for the 11 units in the market the price of demand will be 9s., a price which just covers the expenses of the worst situated producer, but which leaves the best situated a differential rent of 1s. per unit—*i.e.*, the difference between 9 and 8. Practically the market is in equilibrium, but this equilibrium is not stable, because N may increase his production with advantage.

If N *increases* his production to 11 units, while G keeps *his unchanged*, there will be 15 units in all, which, according to the schedule of demand, can only be sold at a price of 8½s., a price which is below G's cost of production, but which leaves N, who is now producing at 7s., a differential rent of 1½s., in all 11 × 1½ = 16½s.

G may now *either* cease producing—in this case there will only be the 11 units (produced by N) which may be sold at 9s.—*or* G may increase his production, for instance, to 7 units; in this case there will be 18 units on the market, and these can be sold at 8s.; there will then be another *temporary* point of *equilibrium*, at 18 units sold at 8s., of which G produces 7 at an expense per unit of 8s., and N produces 11 units at an expense of 7s., by which he gains a differential rent of 1s. for each unit produced.

If now N continually increases his production and G is not strong enough to keep up with him, the price will fall below G's cost of production. G must then leave the market to N. N may now either keep his production unchanged, and on account of decrease in the total supply caused by G leaving, obtain a higher price for his article, or he may continue increasing his production up to 20 units, the price of production of which is 6s.—equal to the subjective price of the 20th buyer.

As the equilibrium, which at a given moment exists in the market, as stated, is *provisional* and not stable, heavy fluctuations in price should be possible for goods which are produced under the law of increasing return, because one or other of the producers will continually attempt to increase his production, in order to increase his differential rent; he will often only cause a lower market price, which swallows the gain.

**93. The Course of Competition.**—We may re-arrange the schedules in such a way that against the schedules of demand we place a schedule of supply by starting with the *actually* best producer, and state his cost of production for the quantity produced by him, and let the competitors, who produce at a higher cost, follow:—

SCHEDULE OF SUPPLY.

1st to 7th unit (N) at 8s.
7th to 11th ,, (G) at 9s.

It must be remembered however that it is a schedule, which is *not at rest*, but the form and figures of which are immediately altered, if even one of the producers alters the amount of his production. G is at present, when the 11th unit is demanded at 9s., the marginal producer, but by extending largely he may attain an earlier place in the schedule of supply ; if his competitors extend he may, on the other hand, be forced to leave the market.

What we have explained by small figures—the fight between the large and the small producer—is a miniature of the 19th Century's gigantic fight between handicraft and machine industry, and of that in the 20th Century between the actually concentrated and the individual, machinery employing, middle-sized concerns. The picture is somewhat altered by the fact that at times it is good policy for the large industry to let a number of small concerns exist, when they are numerically strong, but weak in capacity. The large manufacturers may have low expenses, but in order to be able to meet the objections of the Government to high prices, or a tendency to reduce protection, they find it advantageous to guard themselves behind some insignificant concerns whose expenses are very high. They are so much the better able to do this, because when a factory has reached a certain size the technical cost is not reduced by further extension ; if the large industry has been concentrated as much as is expedient, in order to utilise its full capacity, a barrier of small concerns will only be an advantage for the larger ones.

Hard words have often been spoken about free competition, inasmuch as this often entails appalling expenses and waste of power ; but we must not forget that without free competition as the goad, the modern large industry would not have been able to solve its task, to cheapen the *converting* production as much as has been the case. It is *not the free competition* which ruins the craftsman to the advantage of the large industry, *it is the technical progress*, the expedient division and concentration of labour which demand the discontinuation of the small mixed concern—*or rather calls for its specialising.* Competition has been the hard means in the service of a necessary development. Nowadays, however, competition has settled down ; either the sellers have—as in the retail trade—come to a silent agreement, which permits even the poorest to live, and which stops competition between the producers at the doorstep of the retailer, or else industry has reached the stage of positive cartels which reduce production equally for all, and through this prevent the rule of increasing return from working unhampered, or industry has been concentrated in the hands of one combine. Those people who, under such conditions, speak of free competition and maintain that the government must not interfere, forget that we are actually not dealing with free competition, but with a monopoly. And even the trust, which has developed far enough to acknowledge the rule of increasing return and realise technical progress will, once it has secured power, finally become technically conservative and antagonistic towards inventions which may force it to scrap still useable machinery; this is of importance, because where production on a large scale is possible the logical result is a one-man monopoly or a cartel.

We shall later show how the monopolist in most cases does not gain as much by increasing his price as by *omitting* to reduce it, although concentration and economic command over suppliers of raw materials and other components of the article make possible a much lower price; in other words, the monopoly appropriates the advantages of the technical progress, and capitalises these for the creation of income-yielding rights, the private capital. This is the development of the economic life of our age.

The difference between the expenses of the larger producer and those of the small one (the latter being identical with the market price) creates a differential rent for the former. But as the equilibrium is only temporary, the *differential rent of the large producer will also be only temporary*; as long as competition is effective, it will force the large producers continually to increase their production and, incidentally, lower the price; but by this the differential rent of the larger concerns will be decreased, even if they may regain something by the smaller expenses of this increased production. When competition is at an end, too large profits will often entice a concern, which is strong in capital, to attempt competition, as may, for instance, be seen from the history of the American sugar trust, or, what is more often the case, the milder variation of blackmail, of getting the trust to buy up the concern. Also where the main factor in the differential rent is monopoly profits, it is therefore temporary even if it is less evanescent.

Contrary to the differential rent of agriculture, which, even if subject to alterations, is relatively steady, the differential rent of the large industry has a tendency to disappear in the course of a short time. New methods of production arise, larger concerns are established; the differential rent of some producers may decrease, being shifted on to other hands.

**94. Demand Fluctuates.**—If a temporary equilibrium is attained at 11 units sold at a price of 9, G producing 4 units (at an expense of 9) and N 7 units (at an expense of 8), an increase in the prices of the schedule of demand will cause the market price to rise *for the present*, yielding both our producers an extra profit, probably one or both producers may increase their production through this.

They are able to produce cheaper, consequently may bear the reduction in price resulting from the increased supply. A new temporary equilibrium is then reached at a larger production and at a market price *lower* than before the increase of demand.

*An increase in the prices of the schedule of demand will therefore in most cases*—leaving out of consideration the momentary rise in price—*in the long run entail increased production and a lower market price.* An increase of the prices in the schedule of demand caused, in the case of constant return, a larger turnover at an *unchanged* price, in the case of decreasing return, a larger turnover at a *higher* price; but in the case of increasing return, a larger turnover at a *lower* price.

*Vice versa*, in the case of a reduction in the prices of the schedule of demand, for instance, by $\frac{1}{9}$; the price of demand for 11 units will then be 8s., not 9s. As G's expenses for the 4 units which he produces are 9s., G must leave the market if he is not able to increase his production. N, however, may continue to produce, but *his differential rent has decreased.* A reduction in the prices of the schedule of demand will therefore in many cases *not alter the market price, but reduce the production*, as one or more of the worst situated producers must leave the market. The depression may, however, entail that the remaining producers reduce their production; in this case an *increase of the market price* may even be thought possible. This would especially be reasonable if the article finds its last consumers in the margin between two classes; if, for instance, the working classes on account of hard times completely leave off the consumption of a thing, which can only be produced cheaply when a very large quantity can be sold, the other classes must pay the price, at which the reduced quantity of goods can be produced.

1,000 units are demanded at 10s., can be produced at 10s.

. . . .

. . . .

3,000 ,, ,, 5s. ,, ,, 5s.

Suppose now that the last buyers, whose subjective price is 5s., have their income decreased in such a way that their subjective price falls from 5s. to 4s., but 3,000 units cannot be produced below 5s. per unit ; the first buyers are, however, willing to pay 10s., the price which the thing costs to produce, when only 1,000 units are produced ; a reduction in the prices of the schedule of demand in this case causes a very large reduction in the production and a large increase of the market price.

*A permanent alteration in the schedule of demand will, therefore, in the case of increasing return, cause an alteration in the production in the same direction, and often an alteration in the market price in the opposite direction.*

Here we have a case where the rule accepted for the short market, *that a decrease in the demand entails a fall in price, does not hold good in the long run.*

**95. Alterations in Supply Price.**—If the cost of production is increased by, for instance, a tax of $t$ per unit, the production will *most often be decreased, the small producers leaving the market.*

(1) If G's cost of production, $s_g$, is equal to the price at which $n + g$ units may be sold, a tax of $t$ would make G's cost of production $s_g + t$, which is more than the market price at which $n + g$ units are sold ; G must then leave the market. There will then only remain the $n$ units produced by N ; but the demand-price for $n$ units is greater than that for $n + g$ units. If now the price of demand for the $n$ units is at least equal to N's expenses in producing $n$ units, *with the addition of the amount of the tax,* N will, when G has left the market, continue his production of $n$ units, and sell his article at a price of $s_n + t$, *i.e., his cost of production with the addition of the tax.* As the market price before the tax was equal to $s_g$, and $s_g > s_n$, $s_n + t$ will be *less* than $s_g + t$, *i.e.,* less than the original market price with the addition of the tax.

The effect of an increase in the expenses, in *casu* a tax, was therefore, in this case, that *a producer had to leave the market, that consequently the production was reduced, and that the market price was increased.* The price was, however, *not increased by the total amount of the tax,* as part of the tax was *taken from the more fortunate producer's differential rent.*

If the breweries in Denmark had not made a price-agreement, and if the last pre-war beer tax in Denmark had become effective at once by its full amount, the effect would probably have been that the small breweries would have been ruined, and the price of beer only increased by part of the tax.

(2) It is also possible that the price at which $n$ units could be sold after G had left the market was *less* than N's expenses in producing the $n$ units, with the addition of the tax; the equilibrium would then be effected by N decreasing his production, and thereby his output so much, that the price at which the now further reduced quantity of goods could be sold was high enough to cover, not only the tax, but also the increase in the cost of production caused by the decrease in N's production.

In this case the *tax will increase the market price*—by reducing N's production and throw G entirely out of the market—*eventually by more than the amount of the tax,* that is also by an amount sufficient to cover the increased expenses. Further N would have *lost* part of *his differential rent.* A tax would therefore in this case have been *positively harmful*; producer and consumer would have lost *more* than the Government would have gained.

(3) Finally the price at which units could be sold might be *more* than $s_n + t$. N might then be tempted to increase his production, perhaps to $n + g$ units. The cost of production of the $n + g$ units might be so low that these, with the addition of the tax, would not be higher, and perhaps even lower, than the previous market price, when N's output was $n$ units and G's $g$ units. In this case the *tax would have been useful* by spurring on the more fortunate producer to a still further increase of his production, and thereby decrease the expenses. The tax would in this case be *partly taken from the differential rent of the best situated producer, and partly covered through a decrease in the cost of production.* If N had increased his production, but not enough to take up the entire production abandoned by G, the price would have been increased (with a somewhat decreased production), but not by

the full amount of the tax. N would then have regained part of the tax by the higher price—*i.e.*, at the expense of the buyer, and part by the expenses saved; the rest he would have paid out of his differential rent.

Which of these theoretically possible cases will actually arise is difficult to say; probably the first case—presuming entirely free competition—will most often happen—*i.e.*, that with reduced production *the price will be increased, but not by the full amount of the tax.*

A reduction in the cost of production may, with increasing return, take place in two ways; from *internal* causes, when a higher technique or extension of the production reduces the expenses per unit, or from *external* causes, which do not arise from the production—*e.g.*, the cheapening of the productive factors (the technical components); in both cases the production will be increased and the market price lowered.

The decrease in expenses will often act as a stimulus, and make the more able producers increase their production; in this case the price will be reduced by more than the reduction in the cost of production; if a home tax on the consumption of a thing is abolished, the price of this thing will probably fall, not only by the amount of the tax saved, but also by the saving in expenses gained through the increased production, leaving out of consideration the possibility of a cartel or a monopoly.

If the equilibrium in the above figure example has arisen by N producing 7 units at a price of 8s. and G 4 units at the price of 9s., and the market price for the 11 units has become 9s., a tax of 2s. would force G to leave the market: his price would be 9 + 2 = 11s., which is more than the market price for 11 units sold. N may keep his production unchanged, but only 7 units would then come into the market, the price of which would be 10s., a price which will cover N's expenses in producing 7 units, viz., 8s., with the addition of the 2s. tax; in this case the market price would have been increased by 1s. (from 9s. to 10s.) and the second shilling of the tax would have been taken from N's differential rent.

N might also have increased his production to 11 units, which he can produce for 7s. with the addition of 2s. tax, or 9s., a price at which 11 units are demanded. In this case the tax would have caused no increase in the price; 1s. would have been gained by

N in expenses saved, on account of the increase of his production from 7 to 11 units, the second shilling would have been taken from his differential rent.

If the price of demand for 7 units had not been 10, but 9½s., it would not have paid N to produce 7 units, while they cost him 8s. with the addition of the 2s. tax, in all 10s. per unit. It might therefore be very probable that he would reduce his production to, say, 4 units, which he would not be able to supply for less than $9 + 2 = 11$s.; the tax would in this case have swallowed N's differential rent without benefiting the public, because N produces 4 units at higher expenses than 7.

**96. Various Taxes.**—A *uniform* tax for each concern will rest heavily on the small concern and lightly on the large one, because in the conversion to a tax per unit, it must be divided by a smaller number in the case of the small concern. A *tax of* 12*s. on each concern* in the above example would make the schedule read as follows :—

TECHNICAL SCHEDULE.

| SCHEDULE OF DEMAND. | | EXPENSE AND TAX DIVIDED BY THE NUMBER OF UNITS PRODUCED. |
|---|---|---|
| 4 units ... | ... 12 | ... $9 + 3 = 12$s. |
| ... | | |
| ... | | |
| 7 ,, ... | ... 10 | ... $8 + 1\frac{5}{7} = 9\frac{5}{7}$s. |
| ... | | |
| ... | | |
| 11 ,, ... | ... 9 | ... $7 + 1 = 8\frac{1}{11}$s. |
| ... | | |
| ... | | |
| 15 ,, ... | ... 8½ | ... $6\frac{1}{4} + \frac{4}{5} =$ ab. $7\frac{1}{2}$s. |
| ... | | |
| ... | | |
| 18 ,, ... | ... 8 | ... $6\frac{1}{2} + \frac{2}{3} = 7\frac{1}{6}$ |

If G and N produce respectively 4 and 7 units, the tax will immediately cause a deficit to them both, as the market price for 11 units cannot be above 9s., while the expenses of the best producer are now $9\frac{5}{7}$s.; G anyhow will immediately leave the market. N, who is now able to exist, will probably continue, because an increase of his production will not increase the tax;

if he alone produces all 11 units, his cost of production will, in spite of the tax on the concern, still be below 9s.; in order further to ameliorate the tax, he is tempted to increase the production—*i.e.*, the uniform tax on each concern will more quickly drive the small producer out of the market and make the large producer extend, strengthening a tendency already existing in industry.

A tax, *proportional* to or progressive on the price, acts in a similar manner; it grows smaller with a lower price, and therefore invites extension of production and forcing down of expenses. If a manufacturer wishes to exercise his monopoly by reducing his production, he is punished, not only by his expenses growing higher, but the advantage he gains through the higher prices is largely eliminated by a higher tax.

A home tax on consumption, which *varies proportionally* with the price or *is increased more than proportionally* to the price, will, because the expenses are increased by a reduction in the production, be the best means to make a monopolised industry do its duty; to cheapen its production and sell at ordinary profits.

If we imagine that we have reached the final development, that there is only one producer, and he is actually not guided by any desire to utilise his monopoly the technical curve and the curve of supply will correspond.

Diagram XXII. represents the market condition with the decreasing technical schedule, when this corresponds to the

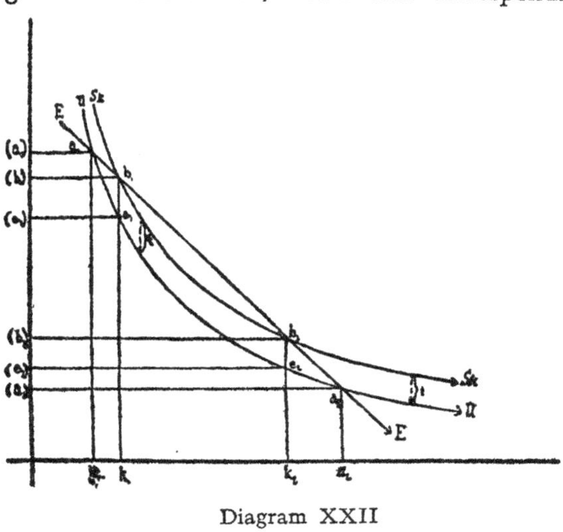

Diagram XXII

schedule of supply, because there is only one producer. We will in this find the market condition before and after a uniform tax per unit has been imposed.

The straight slanting line represents the curve of demand, the lower curve $a_1$ $a_2$ states the prices of supply. There are two points of intersection $a_1$ and $a_2$ ; the prices of demand, however, are, on the part from $a_1$ to $a_2$, higher than the corresponding prices of supply, for which reason production may stop on any intermediate point.

Suppose that the production—which is not very probable—has stopped at a price of $a_1$ and a turnover of $n_1$ units ; the point of intersection between the curve of demand and the curve of supply will then be $a_1$. We now impose a tax of $t$ shillings ($t = bc$) on each unit ; the new curve of supply will be the curve SK which includes the tax. There will now be no point of intersection before $b_1$—*i.e.*, the production must be *extended* from $n_1$ to $k_1$ units, or else be discontinued.

The price has not been increased in spite of the tax imposed ; before the tax it was $a_1$ ; as the expenses per unit in producing the larger number of units are smaller ($c_1$) than in producing the smaller number of units ($n_1$), the price may fall in spite of the imposition of the tax. As we have drawn our curves, the market price will fall by an amount expressed by the line $a_1$ $b_1$. If, however, the production, before the tax was imposed, had reached the last possible point of equilibrium, the quantity sold would have been $n_2$ and the price $a_2$ ; the tax would in this case entail a reduction of the production, as the last possible point of intersection is moved backwards and upwards to $b_2$, which means an increase in price. The quantity sold would then be decreased to $k_2$.

A glance at Diagram XXII. will show us that $b_2$ is greater than $a_2 + b_2 c_2$, *i.e.*, more than the previous price with the addition of the tax. The smaller number of units are produced at higher expenses than the greater number ; the price has then not only been increased by the amount of the tax ($b_2$ $c_2$) but also by $a_2$ $c_2$, an amount which corresponds to the difference in expenditure per unit in producing $n_2$ and $k_2$ units. The tax has in this case caused increased expenses of production, and through this a higher market price and a smaller turnover.

The present case is, in a way, only theoretical, because a producer, who commands the market, will not act as if he had competitors, but would fix the market conditions according to the rules of monopoly.

# CHAPTER XVII

## The Value of the Precious Metal

**97. Value of a Coin.**—If gold were not money, its utility would only be its utility as a good, generally direct, unconditional and present ; if it were money only its utility would be indirect, conditional and future, the latter inasmuch as the utility of money cannot be realised until it is spent. Now gold—like silver— is not only an article of consumption, desired for its own sake, but also money, desired for its property as a representative of goods ; gold, therefore, unites the properties of the good and the properties of money as regards utility.

We must at once point out that gold only forms a very small part of the means of circulation, even if that total be a function of the quantity of gold : money may also be token money, or notes, issued by a Government, by an authorised Bank or by municipalities, and in Denmark the Merchants' Guild, during the Napoleonic wars, issued notes, which for all practical purposes served as money. But the larger part of the turnover takes place through means of credit, sometimes in the form of credit in account, where the money changing hands is only in settlement of the balance of the statement of account, sometimes by cheques, drafts, transfers of credit balances from the payer's account to that of the payee and, at times, even representatives of capital such as shares and bonds, and even unaccepted claims may take the place of the currency.

For all kinds of coin, whether their substance be precious metal, bits of leather or paper, we have the distinction between (1) *nominal* value (expressed by the face amount) ; (2) *exchange* value, the value at which the coin is accepted, which may be more or less than its face value, and (3) *intrinsic* value, the value of the substance of the coin leaving out of consideration small change ; (this has a commercial importance when a heavier coin has disappeared from circulation, and a coin the intrinsic value of which is less than the face value has been authorised for payments abroad). Before the war the face value and the intrinsic value of a standard coin as a rule were equivalent.

The distinction between the nominal and the intrinsic value of money must *not* be confused with the distinction between the *natural value of the money substance* and its *current* value.

The natural value of gold is the value determined by its direct utility (the value of the gold if it were not money, but only a raw material in luxury industries and others—*e.g.*, chemical industries), while its current value is the actual market value of this material, which is *conditional* upon how *large* a part of the supply is employed as money.

**98. The Market Value of Gold.**—In its origin gold was only an article of consumption, a goal for our endeavours, and as such subject to the general economic rules—*e.g.*, the rule that the *price* and the *quantity sold* are functions of one another, varying in opposite directions. At a given price only a certain quantity of gold, *determined by the price*, can be sold. If—at a time when gold has not yet become the means of circulation—the market has reached equilibrium at, say, 100 units, sold at a price of 1 quarter of corn per unit, and the quantity of gold is increased by, say, 100 units, the price must fall below 1 quarter of corn.

But now gold, in its employment for trinkets, is absolutely a luxury article, which is far less demanded than many other goods; it will therefore be a minority only, who after having provided for necessaries, have means to spare for the acquisition of the relatively useless gold, unless gold value declines heavily.

When gold is *not* money a relatively small, well situated class of buyers will determine the *price* of gold; the price of demand of the poor will, on account of their small income, be so low that they are unsuitable as buyers. But if now the poor discover that they may actually obtain necessaries from the rich man for gold in a certain proportion of exchange, they will be willing to accept the gold in the *same* proportion of exchange. That the poor will accept gold as payment for services rendered will now again cause the rich on their part to be willing to accept *more* gold than they would otherwise in the same proportion of exchange, because besides using it for trinkets they may also purchase the labour of others for it.

Gold will, therefore, for all the members of the community,

rich as well as poor, attain an *indirect* utility, which is *not* due to the usefulness of the gold *itself* as a trinket, but solely to the fact that *all other goods* may be obtained for the gold in a certain ratio of exchange. But by *this* gold has become the representative of goods, the means of credit of the community, with the intermediary of which the actual utility compensation is postponed to a later date than the exchange—*i.e.*, gold has become *money*, and, in this capacity, not only able to satisfy a *certain* demand (for the precious metal), but *all* demands.

The quantity of gold must, however, be increased—beyond the 100 units—in order to make gold prevail as money, because the existing quantity, at the given price, can be fully employed for trinkets. If, now, on account of the indirect utility of the gold, the increased willingness to accept gold in the unaltered proportion of exchange should increase the production to 200 units, the the price will not need to fall : the 100 units will, at the previous price (1 quarter of grain), be employed for trinkets, while the additional 100 units will circulate as money, and consequently be of value, not for their glitter, but *exclusively*, because they mean so many other goods— *i.e.*, *are* purchasing power.

The 200 units of gold—the 100 employed as trinkets as well as the 100 circulating as money—will then have the same value per unit as the 100 units which existed before. But if all 200 units were to be employed as trinkets, their price would have to fall from 1 quarter of corn to perhaps $\frac{3}{4}$ of a quarter ; the *natural* value of the gold—*i.e.*, the value at which gold may be sold in case *all of* the existing quantity had to be employed as trinkets will then be *less* than its *current value*, which is the same thing as the *market value* of the gold ; gold is kept at a value, at which only a far smaller supply (in casu 100 units) can be sold for trinkets.

Graphically any person's subjective price curve for gold may be expressed as a curve, which on its early part corresponds to the curve of gold as employed for trinkets, but suddenly, when the limit has been reached of what the person in question would use for trinkets, becomes flat—*i.e.*, corresponds to the curve of " the general good," to his money-curve.

Originally the natural value of gold (as a good) according to the existing quantity has determined its money value ; but once it has become money, its value will be determined by entirely different circumstances, the natural value of the gold completely disappearing in the market value, where it can never again be traced.

The price of gold for trinkets must, however, be expressed in the gold itself: the criterion for how much gold the individual will use for trinkets must then be sought in the prices of all goods. If the necessary cost of living at one time is £50 in gold and at another time £100 in gold, one is more willing to employ £5 for trinkets in the latter than in the former case, because £5 would mean 1/20th part of the cost of living, when this is £100, but 1/10th, if it is £50. In spite of the rising prices of goods (*i.e.*, the reduction in the purchasing power of gold) the price of the gold (expressed in £ sterling) as a raw material is *unchanged*; leaving out of consideration the expense of conversion, the price of trinkets will therefore be unchanged—*i.e.*, cheaper than before, in proportion to the value of other goods, which have gone up in price. If rising prices often give certain classes special income, at least until the rise has been completed, these classes will direct a stronger demand for the luxury article, *in casu* ornaments of precious metal, and through this temporarily raise their price.

When we have the choice between using a piece of gold for ornament or for money, we will employ it in such a way that it will yield us the *greatest* utility, which it only can when our last 10s., the last part of each good which costs 10s., and the last trinket of the value of 10s., yield us the same utility and satisfy an equal desire. If a man grows poorer and the utility of his last shillings increases, he will reduce his purchase of gold. Likewise he will buy fewer trinkets when the prices of goods as well as his income are reduced. Gold in its capacity of money then attains greater value and greater utility, representing, as it will then, more goods. In other words, we buy gold for technical use or for trinkets without thinking of the fact that gold is also the substance of the coin.

**99. Peculiarities of the Value of Gold.**—Now the difference between the value of gold and that of other goods is apparent; while the value of consumers' goods is decided according to their utility, the value of gold as a commodity is determined according to its value as money. As the value of gold is not determined according to its utility, the question arises: What then decides the market value of gold? The *Credit-theory* which has arisen out of the *Quantity-theory* must give us the reply; here we will only say: there is a value-determining interaction between the total of *all* means of circulation and the total of circulated goods measured in money.

With the two employments of the gold, for money and for trinkets, the causes which affect the value of gold in the most frequent employment will be those affecting the value of gold the most, whatever the employment for which it is used The greater or smaller demand for gold as an article of consumption will not be very important for the valuation of gold, even if not without effect, because the gold employed for trinkets, in any case in Europe, is far from being as much as the quantity stored in the vaults of the banks or employed in circulation.

Finally, a general increase of prices (the depreciation of gold), and a subsequently greater demand for gold to be employed for ornaments may cause that the circulation or the bank reserve must do without some gold; by this a reduction in the amount of money-gold will certainly take place, even if not a very great one, but this will lead to lower prices of commodities, or, in other words, to the gold value again being increased. It is through this process that the yield of an increased production of gold is distributed between the bullion reserves of the banks and industry. The practical proof of the fact that the *natural value* of the coin metal is lower than the market value, which it attains because it is money, has been supplied by *silver* since 1870. The value of silver decreased gradually from 60d. per ounce to 23d. per ounce, when it was demonetised in Western Europe; this reduction in value has perhaps been the case more in proportion to gold than to other goods. The price of silver was supported by the fact that silver was money. If millions of Asiatic people, who still have silver as the principal coin metal, would abolish silver coinage and adopt the gold basis, the white metal would drop enormously in price, down to its *natural* value, at which all silver could be sold, solely as an article of consumption; the liberated silver would then have to be used for ornament and utensils, for which purpose its present price makes it too expensive. The price of silver is not only supported by the fact that it is used for standard coins, but also by its employment for small change, which has been proved during 1917, when silver, under the pressure of larger coinings of token money, among other causes also, again passed beyond 60d. (although this was only in paper). For silver we may point out the difference between the *natural value*, the *current value*, which is higher, and the usually still higher *function-value* of the stamped silver coin.

The value of gold from 1873 to 1895 had been rising, both in proportion to silver and to other goods. This rise had been caused by the fact that gold had become the *sole* principal coin-metal of the Western countries, which fact created a relative scarcity o fgold, which would *not* have taken place if the report of the Paris Commission of 1867 to the respective Governments, about the advantages of the gold basis in preference to Bimetallism, had not been carried so quickly into effect in the Latin Mint Union, in Scandinavia and in Germany. By the introduction of the gold basis in the Western countries, and by the triumphant progress of the gold to Eastern Europe, the difference between the natural value of gold and its market value was further *increased*, and the difference between the natural value of silver and its market value was further *decreased*.

As even the most superficial observer must deny that the existing quantity of gold can be sold for trinkets in the same proportion of exchange with other goods as now, he must also grant the *incorrectness* of the contention that the value of gold as *merchandise* determines its *money* or *market-value*; if we know that the market value of gold is higher than its natural value, it is really immaterial whether 90 or 80 per cent. higher, or only 5 per cent.; what is of importance is that it *is* higher.

The fashion might alter in such a way that gold was not demanded as an article of consumption—*i.e.*, became valueless in this respect, and still gold coins might be valuable. That a greater or smaller number of units of gold are demanded for the purpose of being used for trinkets cannot conceal the difference between the natural value and the market value of gold.

Naturally the value of gold would fall, if the fashion turned away from gold for employment as ornaments; *not* because its *natural* value would become nil, but *only* because the gold liberated from the employment as trinkets would increase the amount of money, and therefore have the effect of a further quantity of gold mined—*i.e.*, to decrease the purchasing power of gold; the same is the case with the gold hoarded in Asia. As the Western countries presumably buy more goods from Asia than this continent buys from Europe and America, a continual stream of precious metal goes to Asia, and apparently does not return, but is hoarded as gold and silver treasures. If Asia should once become able to detect that a hoarding of this kind is actually of little value, such quantities of precious metals would go to Europe that would cause a price revolution. Normally, however, the great or small demand for gold ornaments will have an indirect effect on the price of gold, inasmuch as it increases or decreases the quantity of gold employed for *money*, and it is not effective in the same proportion, because, as stated, the quantity of gold employed for trinkets is small (at present probably not one-third of the world's supply of gold is employed for ornaments or in industry). The demand for gold as ornaments is similar to the demand for any other raw material which may be employed in two or more ways : the greater or smaller consumption by the artist does not alter the prices of canvas materially.

On the other hand, with free coining rights gold must have the same market value, whether sold as a good or as money, as otherwise the profits of the goldsmiths would be too high (or too low). Competition, through the reduction (or increase) of the quantity of gold offered as goods, forces the prices of gold articles so far down that the goldsmith will only have ordinary profits left, when the expenses of conversion have been covered ; but *then* the price of gold must be alike without regard to its employment.

**100. The Value of the Money Substance.**—It is therefore *now* the value of gold as money which determines its value as a good, not *vice versa*.

*The demand for gold for ornaments* has therefore, in the first instance, only *influence upon how much* will be employed for ornaments at the given gold value, which has been determined by special causes, but only in a minor degree on the *price*, and that only indirectly.

If there was only one coining authority in the entire world, and if it was impossible for private persons to have gold coined, we would have two valuations of this metal : (1) *function value*, which would be influenced by the quantity of gold, which the holders of the coining privilege had coined, and (2) the *value of gold as a good*, which would be determined by the quantity of gold left for employment for ornaments. We would then meet with the anomaly that a gold coin, if the stamp were removed, would perhaps lose one half of its value, as two different causes would then determine the value of gold as merchandise and as money respectively (as actual examples we may mention the American silver dollar, the French 5-franc and the German thaler). The fact that it is easy to melt down coins would make improbable the opposite case, that the value as merchandise would be the higher of the two.

It would be desirable if we could completely overcome the error maintained by many economists, that the value of gold as merchandise determines its value as money, and that its value as merchandise is a condition for its employment as money, and even that its substantial value is a condition. For at the very moment gold ceased to be money, and we had to revert to the security which the value of the substance presumably would yield, we would discover that the gold value had fallen from the high current value to the lower natural value.

Presuming that the entire world would maintain the bi-metallic basis, we might very well maintain an unchanged proportion between the value of the two metals, not only of 1 to 16, but even of 1 to 8. The market value of both metals because they are money, is so much higher than the natural value, that the difference, which undoubtedly is present between the natural value of these metals, would not be sufficiently effective.

An equilibrium would then be attained, by the value of gold decreasing heavily, not only in proportion to silver, but also in proportion to other goods, while that of silver would rise. Some silver, which is now used by private persons, would then be coined, while on the other hand some gold coins or bars would be required for turning into ornaments. Even with the proportion of exchange of 1 to 2 F do not believe that *all* gold would be used for ornaments, or all silver as money, even if the annual production of silver is 15 times as large as the annual production of gold.

Silver is still the principal coin metal for millions of people, and is accepted by them according to its *market value* ; but even if silver were entirely demonetised, and only employed for small change—*i.e.*, was accepted in coin without consideration of its market value, and consequently according to the promise of the stamp, that it is a *representative* of the gold—this employment would naturally have some influence on the price of silver, because so much less would be left for industrial use. The public authorities would in this case take in advance the silver which is required for coins at the market price, a price which is fixed in consideration of other employment.

We may now advance the following rules for precious metal employed in a stamped condition, according to whether it is *standard* coin or only token coin.

The value of gold as money as well as *qua* ware, is determined by the *relative total* of the means of circulation (that is, of all the means of circulation, which besides gold serve as means of payment). The distribution between the employments, as goods and money, takes place by the value of gold in relation to all goods determining how much is bought for industrial use. With *completely demonetised silver*, which then only serves as small change, the price is determined by the quantity of silver left *after* the purchase by the Governments of their requirements for coining. The price of *gold* (in money) determines the *quantity* of gold, which is employed in industry ; but the *quantity* of silver left for useful employment, *after* the State has coined as much as required, determines the price of *silver*. The gold price is determined by the position of gold as money, the price of silver would be determined by the position of the metal as a good. All this only holds good under the presumption that the value of gold coined is equal to its value uncoined, while silver takes a higher value coined (as token money) than uncoined.

We have mentioned gold as " money " because gold before 1914—at least in the European-American communities—was the international means of payment. Division of labour and international trade had developed to such an extent that whatever is the standard coin of a country, a large part of its turnover—*i.e.*, the entire international turnover, which nowadays amounts to an amount equal to the annual net income of the country—will be settled in the international currency, or rather accounted for in this currency (because the settlement takes place by a kind of transfer or " giro "). But if a large part of the turnover has to be settled in gold, the prices of goods in the country must be dependent upon the fluctuations of the gold, because the test of the value of the local currency will be its exchangeability for gold.

Conditions have then entailed that although the separate country, of course, decides which standard it will employ—there is yet an European-American *international standard*, the gold basis. Realising this, the Eastern European countries have followed the lead of Western Europe. The international standard need not be the gold currency; it is quite plausible that a written agreement between the leading commercial nations might prefer international bimetallism, or, as Marshall terms it, "Symmetallism."

The acceptance of gold as an international currency is then not due to the natural value of the gold—*i.e.*, to the human desire for the gold as a good, and *not to the command of a Government* either; it is due solely to an international, unwritten agreement of the *communities*, imposed upon us by conditions, and which we therefore do not completely command, and which results in a general confidence that this metal in coined or unstamped condition will be accepted as the equivalent of goods or human labour.

If this confidence fails, gold must fall to its natural value, which therefore is the limit, beyond which the value of gold cannot fall—*i.e.*, the limit where all gold is employed for ornaments or for technical auxiliaries. How far the price of gold may rise cannot be proved; up till now it has, anyhow, never been so far above its natural value, that all gold was coined and nothing was left for use as trinkets. In the first case the natural value of gold and its market value would correspond; in the latter case they would be as far from one another as possible, as then not one grain of gold would be saleable for ornaments, because as a good it does not yield anybody as great utility as in its capacity of money—*i.e.*, as any other goods which may be bought for gold.

Both cases are theoretically possible: the *former* if gold were demonetised, or *if*—as about A.D. 1000—gold grew so scarce that it would be *too* valuable to be employable as money; the *latter*, either in a completely communistic society, where nobody commanded an income of more than, say, £100, or in a secteric community, which regarded the use of gold ornaments as *sinful*, and therefore did not attribute any utility to *gold as a commodity*.

**101. A Scrap of Leather as Money.**—If we say that gold has *become* money on account of its small volume in proportion to its value, its power of resistance against wear, its divisibility and its quality of being always unchanged, we have only replied to the question why, in preference to many other goods, it became money and has been maintained as such, but not to the question whether gold only may be the money substance, nor whether, in its capacity of money, it may be above its market value. In this case we should have three values for gold—the function value, the market value of the substance, and the natural value. The war has replied to the last question in the affirmative; but only presuming that the *free right of coinage has been stopped,* and the Government is able to *maintain a favourable balance of trade,* thereby making it unnecessary to melt down the gold or sell it abroad by weight. It is otherwise immaterial how this balance of trade is maintained, whether by forcing the export of goods by contracting loans abroad or by mortgaging or selling assets abroad, to which the banks may force the population through their credit or note policy.

If we grant that *all* gold may be money so that nothing is left for ornaments or industrial use, and, on the other hand, that the value of gold would be much lower if gold was demonetised, we have opened the question of the value of a *scrap of leather* if this were to become the money substance. As a good leather would somehow increase in value, because some leather must be withdrawn from the usual employment. Naturally, free coinage would be out of the question, because, if otherwise, the stamped scrap of leather would fall to the bootmaker's price. But if public authorities have the sole right to issue money, the stamped scrap of leather would start with the printed value, and if a wise policy of issue were maintained, it would retain its purchasing power. The difference between leather money and gold coins would only be that arising out of the fact (1) that the difference between the function value of the natural price would be much greater than in the case of gold; (2) and that the quantity of gold in proportion to the quantity of leather scraps procurable is relatively small, so that the employment of a good like leather to be the money substance would *not* raise the leather price very much above the natural value. *In common* they would have the fact that the purchasing power of the scrap of leather would not, any more than that of coined gold, be affected by an increase of production of the material under the *same* presumption that one authority *only* directs the coining; the purchasing power of both would be weakened if we allowed free coining, presuming that more material could be procured at a lower expense than the face value.

But the Governments might issue too many scraps of leather; in this case they would affect the level of prices, first at home and afterwards everywhere, until the time when a balance of exchange to be settled causes a disagio on the abused leather scraps of the country. This possibility for abuse by one state, or by all states simultaneously, will cause that gold, in spite of the interests of Central Europe in not allowing the mining countries this trump card, will be maintained as the international means of exchange, but possibly in some combined form (gold transfer policy).

Any good—whatever its natural value—may rationally be money. The ideal substance of money would, however, be a good whose place in the scale of values never changed, and which fluctuated, for instance, in accordance with corn prices or the wages of labour; but inside a period of a few years the said two prices do not fluctuate in the same direction or with the same strength. A dreamer might perhaps imagine the stamping of a materially valueless coin, which at any time could be exchanged for 4 kilos of wheat or one working hour; if the proportion between corn and standard working hours could be fixed, it would be possible to realise the idea of employing corn as a measurement of value. The law of ground rents would show us the difficulty in fixing this proportion when the ground rent is privately owned.

Let us state at once that most money is "scraps of leather," *i.e.*, promises issued by the public, by private parties, as with most means of credit, which, in whatever proportion used, excellently effect the purpose of money, to be the means of exchange. But they do not pretend to be anything in themselves; they only *represent* the coin of the realm, and stand in the same relation to this as does the state-money to the goods which they are intended to buy. Means of credit are secondary representatives.

**102. The Cost of Production and Gold Price.**—A mine pays when so much gold is gained from it that the productive forces are paid for their work; how much is paid will, however, depend upon the level of prices—*i.e.*, the purchasing power of money or of the gold itself. The same mine will pay to-day and perhaps not to-morrow, in proportion as the purchasing power of gold is high or low; if therefore a mine is being worked, we presume that the gold extracted will pay the productive forces. If the quantity of gold is now increased to such an extent that its purchasing power is reduced, those mines where only sufficient gold had been produced to pay the productive forces, now rising in price, will no longer be able to do so, and ought, in any case, to stop production when the capital invested in implements has been used up; if, however, more gold is required, and the purchasing power of gold is, therefore, again increased, these mines will again pay and be worked regularly. During the war all kinds of money depreciated (expressed in the rising level of prices): after the Armistice several gold mines closed down, not being able to pay their way. Then gold detached itself from the paper money, remembered it was a commodity, and rose in price expressed in paper notes, and some mines, working below the margin, could again pay dividends. (In this we leave out of consideration the fact that a mine will actually be worked, even if it cannot pay interest on the capital originally invested, but can only cover the current expenses and the necessary renewals. We must further not forget that in mining the element of chance plays a very great part; only a small percentage of the "claims" worked will become permanent mines.)

With regard to the influence of price on the output, gold will therefore follow the same rule as other goods.

The last necessary expense of production must, therefore, correspond to the market price; but a factor which is independent of the expense—*i.e.*, the amount and strength of demand—determines *which* of the different possible production-expenses will be the *last necessary*.

This rule is, however, somewhat altered as far as gold is concerned, inasmuch as the value of gold is determined, not by the year's output, but by the *existing supply of all kinds of money*, affecting, among others, the prices of implements and labour used in mining; from those costs the owners decide whether a mine is to be worked or not.

But working a mine increases the world's supply of gold and, provided that this more than corresponds to the increase in the population or turnover of goods, the mines are working against their own interests—*i.e.*, by reducing the purchasing power of gold.

As long as this is relatively high, many mines will pay; the production will be forced, and new mines prospected for. In itself falling prices of goods (= increasing purchasing power of gold) should cause an increased production of gold, because gold and all production of metal in a way comes within the rule of decreasing return. The production is, however, increased irregularly. Suddenly new, rich, and easily-accessible deposits of gold are found, as, for instance, was the case in Klondike. This may cause the purchasing power of gold to fall so much that the gold mines elsewhere must discontinue unless, by a better technique, the expenses can be reduced. The latter is continually the case: from gathering gold-carrying earth and sand in pans and shaking the sand away in current water, through the next stage of mixing mercury in the sand to take up the gold, and again to detach the mercury, we have reached the methods of the 'nineties to add cyanide of potassium to the sand, and by the chemical combination to extract the gold by electric currents.

It will best be seen, however, how the value of the precious metal determines the amount of production, if we consider the influence which the demonetising of silver in the Western countries had upon the production of silver of the United States and Mexico. Many mines were obliged to discontinue, by which the mine rent (*i.e.*, the miner's differential profits) disappeared. Their owners, therefore, steadily besieged the Congress in Washington in order to have the silver-standard re-introduced, for the purpose of increasing the value of silver, and through this the rent of silver mines.

The contention that *the cost of production of gold determines its value* is quite *as wrong* as is the statement that it is *the value of gold as a good* which determines its market value—*i.e.*, its purchasing power. The influence of both factors is only indirect, inasmuch as they may have influence upon the existing supply of gold, and through this again upon the supply of money, the total of which, in relation to the demands of the turnover, will again decide the level of prices. *Only such mines in which the cost of production of the precious metal is smaller than or equal to the market value, which is influenced by the total supply of money, will be worked; others not.* And they will only be utilised to the point where a further utilisation will yield less gold than the quantity which is the price of the productive forces.

During the war gold economics have apparently collapsed; we find that some neutral states could keep their paper money above the value of gold, while all belligerent countries kept theirs below, and the settlement by means of gold of the differences in the balance of exchange did not take place at all, or only under much value-confusing friction, leaving out of consideration that the difficult shipping and transport conditions caused the two gold-points to come very far apart. And yet I will maintain that this collapse is mostly apparent only: gold is still, in 1917, the standard by which the quality of the several national currencies are judged, and gold shall again come into its own.

# BOOK V.

## MANIPULATED PRICES.

### CHAPTER XVIII

### Customs Duties and Prices

**103. Constant Return.**—The theory of *Customs Duties* must be treated collectively as a chapter in the theory of International Trade; but its *immediate* effects must be mentioned in the theory of price.

While an embargo on imports would entirely shut the national market, an import duty will only strengthen the barrier, which in a way is always present, because of the price-increasing transport expenses. These expenses will, if the raw material is imported, be a kind of *negative* protection for the goods, of which the raw material in question forms a technical component. A duty on a raw material will act, for the buyer, as an increase of the expenses of transport of the said raw material, or, in other words, as a tax on production, and in case he exports the finished article, as an export duty on this.

In the case of constant return foreign goods will, in the first instance, be increased in price by the amount of the duty; this will increase the prices at home; the decrease in turnover caused does *not* hurt the production in the country itself, which had just been *insufficient* to cover the consumption of the country and which thereby would gain an extra profit or a rentability which did not previously exist. Additional productive forces are attracted, and the price will fall to the expenses at home; these expenses will, however, be *somewhat increased* if, for instance, the special labour on account of increased demand becomes more expensive. This will be the case if the workers of the trade are a comparatively close circle—*i.e.*, that the trade for social or technical reasons is relatively closed. For the handicrafts the duty may mean an assistance against a *lower wage per unit* abroad.

This lower wage may be due to the fact that the wages per hour are low abroad as, for instance, in the ladies' dressmaking trade of Berlin—or that the wage abroad certainly is high, but that this wage, on account of a higher technique abroad, will be spread over the quantity produced in the hour and in the end be smaller per unit. In the first case we speak of a sensible protection against a foreign *parasitical trade*; in the latter case it can only be class and social reasons that make a state keep alive a national handicraft which is technically inferior to that of foreign countries. The protection may, however, be an encouragement for some artisans at home to venture the higher technique.

If the home country produces at 9s., and the foreign country at 7s. per unit, a duty of 3s. will immediately make possible a price at home of 10s. with the limitation that the turnover will be smaller than the *total* sales of the home and foreign product, previous to the imposition of the customs duty. The home production may now be extended, and supply the total home consumption, which has certainly been reduced, and the price will fall to 9s. The duty has therefore only been shifted on to the buyer by 2/3rds of its amount; perhaps *somewhat more* will be shifted on if a raw material produced at home forms one of the components of the good, or if the workers of the trade, on account of the greater demand, can claim a higher wage. The duty has then (1) balanced an inferior development; (2) caused a frequently desirable increase in the price of the components of the article, and (3) restricted the home consumption. The first is perhaps not an advantage, and it must be maintained that a proper defence for the customs duty can only be put forward in trades, where a higher technique is possible, and simply has to be induced by securing the market for the increased production necessary to employ the higher technique.

**104. Industry.**—Let us, in the case of increasing return, take the example (page 218), where we have shown the fight between two producers, and let the smaller, G, represent the home producer and the larger, N, the foreign producer.

If we require in all 11 units at a price of 9s., of which 7 units are produced by a manufacturer *abroad*, N, at the price of 9s. and 4 units by a manufacturer *at home*, G, at the price of 9s., G's cost of production will correspond to the market price. Now the foreign country may first have started the production of the good in question and have gained a good start, so that producers at home dare not venture to start an establishment of such dimensions, that they can successfully compete with foreign countries—*i.e.*, can produce at the same relatively small expenses. According to the law, which generally holds good for establishments working under the rule of increasing return, that the inferior producer will be defeated by the stronger, the home producer, G, who has the smaller establishment, is in danger of being ruined. He dare not venture an extension of his business, because in that case he would increase the output and thereby press down the prices at home, perhaps below his own expenses of production.

If now a duty of 3s. per unit is imposed on the good when imported, this could not be supplied within the customs boundaries at less then $8 + 3 = 11$s., while G can still produce his 4 units at 9s. The price will then rise to nearly 11s., but as this makes the production of the good in question a profitable business, whose market is secured, the productive forces in the country will be attracted by the national industry. G will then dare to extend his establishment; he may increase his production to 7 units, and thereby reduce his expenses to 8s.; other manufacturers at home are attracted and, in order to keep the lead, G is tempted to increase as far as to 11 units, and to supply the entire home consumption. But the price of demand for 11 units is now 9s., for which reason the market price will be 9s. The producer has therefore gained a profit without a permanent increase in the market price, although this has temporarily been increased; in the present case a profit of 2s. per unit, as 11 units may be produced for 7s. each. The home factory will perhaps further increase its production sufficiently to be able to produce under the same conditions as the larger factories abroad, and may now attempt to compete with these in their own market.

When there are several factories in the country, of which some produce at the same price as factories abroad, but most have a higher expense, the duty will give to the former a differential rent, which is immediately equal to the amount of the duty per unit, but which will later fall when they themselves or their competitors are tempted to extend and drive one another out of the market by competition, which has been explained in Chapter XVI.

This will particularly be the case when the expenses of a home industry are high, because it is not able to utilise its full capacity. With full utilisation the Swedish boot factories are able to produce boots for four times the number of people which they supply; the duty may in this case simply by reserving the market without new establishments automatically produce lower expenses, which again make it possible for the factories to attempt competition with the foreigners in their own market, instead of being competed out of their own. *Wieth Knudsen* has pointed out that the world war has given large industries, for the first time in their existence, an opportunity to produce to their *full capacity* without fear of reduction in prices; this is the secret of the enormous extension of production effected by numerous war industries.

The development of the American and German Steel industries have fully proved the correctness of the so-called "*education theory.*" The customs duty has *educated* the home industry to find a higher technique *through extension,* and this was in the above cases further supported by the two countries being able to develop their production of ore.

The advocates of pure Free Trade presume that every country will of its own accord find which production is the relatively most profitable; they overlook the law of inertia, that he who has gained the lead has a chance to keep it, and will keep it because a higher development technically presumes a mass production, for which a national industry, just starting, cannot expect to have the sales. On the other hand, the protective duty will be more likely to have this effect in a large than in a small country, in which even *all* of the home market is not sufficient for the turnover presumed by a higher technique. In Denmark it has been the unprotected industries which, anyhow before the war, have proved to be capable of export.

For certain goods the fact is so fortunate that the technically perfect large establishment *can* be brought about with the turnover attainable; but here the existence of many middle-sized concerns will often prevent each of them from attaining the turnover which is requisite in order to work at the same low expenses as the foreign manufacturers. A small country will therefore often only be able to work at as low a cost as foreign countries by means of much concentration, which can only be effected by a trust or an amalgamation. However high the

Danish protection duty for textiles may be put it will not be sufficient, unless followed by concentration and by the discontinuation of several concerns. In a way the education theory, as well as the observation, that protective duties are the resting pillow of inefficiency may be true. On the one side protection will maintain a number of technically imperfect establishments, the numbers of which prevent each of them from attaining the necessary turnover. At the same time we have before 1908 experienced in our textile industry that the certainty of turnover, created by the duty, has made the employers unwilling to scrap unsuitable machinery and try new methods. This may often be wrong, but in certain cases it is an advantage if the scrapping of *still useable machinery* actually reduces the capital of the country.

**105. The Education Theory.**—On the other hand, there will also be many cases, especially in the long run, where the theory of education is confirmed. England has, on the strength of the lead once gained and on account of her coal mines, had a preferential position in industry. The Continent, as well as America, have proved that they could equal their competitor once their industry had been forced to experiment. The Scandinavian peninsula has in the " white coal " (the waterfalls) a source of power which may some day gain the industrial monopoly from England, who has already been weakened by the cheapening of coal transport. Northern Italy and other countries near the Alps have even more " white coal."

The great importance of protection is perhaps to be found in its relation to the feeding and auxiliary industries of the protected industry. The protection of a finished article means more employment for its technical components, the prices of which are thereby increased in the home country. Suppose that a country has a raw material, the price of which is low, because it must pay the expenses of a long-distance transport to a foreign country. If now an industry arises which can employ this raw material, this may perhaps gain an opportunity for sale, which will permit a rational extraction; not only is a raw material industry secured hereby, but the plentitul output of the raw material may perhaps make possible a totally different industry in which the raw material is also a component. Repair shops and auxiliary industries arise round a manufacturing centre. Cloth factories may cause dye works to be established by giving them a market; many sufficiently large plants make possible the establishment of a factory for the special machinery required. A machine shop of this class may become capable of export for its specialities, and may, once it has been erected, venture the construction of other machines.

Finally, it may happen that one industry does not only react upon industries at an earlier stage of development of production, but also upon industries at the same stage, as, for instance, when the protection of low-class chinaware provides a factory with the the economic basis that permits it to develop an art-industry which, to start with, may not be profitable. We must remember that where joint production is present—*i.e.*, that the production of several goods is more or less connected—an advantage meant for one good may easily benefit another, provided that they are *related in production*, either have raw materials in common or are produced by the same process, or by one good forming part of the other. By granting subsidies for the transport of mail, the transport is often made possible of a large variety of goods which might not otherwise be able to bear the expense of transport.

The judgment of protection will often be faulty for anybody, who simply judges a separate concern according to its rentability and does not understand that the gross profits of a factory *may* very well be tantamount to national net profits, the expenses dissolving themselves into net incomes for others—and who does not remember that one trade affects another, and will feel the indirect effects. For instance, the criticism of the subsidies of mercantilism has been unfair, because only the loss to the exchequer has been taken into consideration.

The war has given prominence to the often quoted, but rarely read argument of *Carey*: the necessity of a nation *not* being solely dependent upon the state of a certain trade on the manufacture of the articles of which it is without influence. England, therefore contemplates after the war to give government support to the so-called " key-industries." If a country produces a certain good in quantities to the value of £5,000,000, this industry cannot be entirely left to foreign mercy for an auxiliary material, the value of which is only a few per cent. of the total, and it is then preferable to maintain an auxiliary industry of this nature at home, even at a loss; besides the education theory, the so-called "autarchic" theory will then come in; that a country in certain respects must be self-supporting—partly in order not to be cut off, and partly for the social-political reason, that a variety of possibilities of employment creates occasion for using *all* the aptitudes of a people, while a national specialising not only makes the people one-sided, but also makes the nation's livelihood dependent on fashion, taste, income, and the state of markets, over which the country has no influence.

The opposite effect may also be met with. A good is often the finished article in one relation, and the raw material in another. The protection of cloth factories may destroy the exporting ready-made garments industry. We find the classical instance of this in the German corn and cattle policy. In 1908 the price for rye in Berlin was 50 marks higher than the subsidised export price quoted in Copenhagen. The offal, rye-bran, was quoted higher in Germany than German rye in Denmark, who therefore imported and ground German rye and used the Danish rye for fodder. The German export premium, which kept German rye at the foreign price with the addition of the 50 marks duty per ton, indirectly provided us a cheap fodder, while the artificially increased corn price in Germany increased the price of fodder. The consequence was that the small farmers in Germany could not afford to buy fodder for a larger number of animals than could be fed on the produce of the land, while the opposite was the case in Denmark. The German corn policy increased the amount of live stock in Denmark and decreased it in Germany. Certainly there was a high import duty on cattle in Germany corresponding to the corn duty; but this did not benefit the small farmer, who had to buy his fodder; the fact that German fodder was expensive caused that the cost of production of cattle by the small German farmers became too high, and furthermore the duty kept young cattle at high prices; the consequence was that the number of cattle and *eo ipso*, the production of meat, could not keep up with the consumption, although the high prices of meat cut away some consumers, just as the high prices of fodder and breeding cattle cut away some producers. The high meat prices, which a limited, but well-situated number of consumers could offer, caused that Denmark could export cattle to Germany in spite of the duty. If Germany adopted free trade in agricultural produce, we would profit in the first instance (and therefore believe that the meat duty had been borne by us) but in the long run our price of rye, which would no longer be kept low by German export-premiums, would rise, our fodder would be more expensive, while the cattle breeding of Germany, owing to the lower prices of fodder, would be increased, and the German cattle prices would fall. In other words, the effect of protection can never be judged by a snapshot or through the relations of the protected article itself only.

Finally, the protection of a good, by increasing the price of its components, may make difficult the production of another thing, which in itself is natural, and of which the same technical components form part.

Conditions are not as clear as the doctrinaire Free Traders and Protectionists imagine. A Danish politician, *Anders Nielsen*, once said on the subject of abolishing some extraordinary subsidies to agriculture, that all protection and *government support* must aim at making itself *unnecessary*; if this was not attained, the support would be a failure. To abolish a protective duty, when an industry has really developed, is, however, difficult, owing to the capitalisation of the advantage gained by the cheaper production and the price, which, on account of the duty, is still high. A reduction of the duty will in this case have the effect of a reduction of the sale price of the factory in question, and while this reduction certainly does not take away the possibility of existence for the factory, it may ruin the owner, who must pay interest on the high sale-price of the factory. Finally, there will often be smaller concerns working in the shelter of the protection with their expenses on the margin of the market price, and the larger producers, who fear to lose a differential rent through the duty being abolished, will mobilise these in their endeavours to prevent this.

The duty will, as stated, certainly increase the price in the first instance by its full amount, but under increasing return the expenses will gradually be cheapened, and where no Pool or Trust (with the support of duty) maintains a monopoly price in the country, the price at home may even fall below that abroad if latent natural conditions for the trade in question are present.

The education may become too violent as, for instance, when the protection attracts too many forces from the other trades, and increases the production in such a way that the good cannot be sold at the price increased by the duty. We have a classical example in the sugar industry of Austria, in which the bounties forced the production, and where the utilisation of the protective duty through a high price, stabilised through export premiums, made impossible the sale of the article in the country itself. The Austrian production, previous to the Brussels agreement, could not have covered consumption if it had been equal per head to that of England. When a protective duty becomes too high, it naturally does not only provide room for a technically advantageous mass production, but also shelter for establishments of small capacity working at high expenses.

For raw materials protection may, to start with, be warranted, but, as a rule, the way to proceed is to protect the trades which utilise raw materials produced at home, and it will even often be correct to impose an export duty on the raw materials in order to further employment at home. Sweden may some day come to regard her export of ore as disadvantageous; as, besides water power, coal is also needed for the conversion into iron and steel, it may, of course, happen that an English or German export duty on coal may make this conversion difficult for Sweden, so that the observation that the iron goes to where the coal is, and not *vice versa*, will again hold good.

Import premiums on the raw material may be just as rational as import duties on the finished article; one is a direct, the other an indirect, state-support. An export duty may be the means for a state to acquire the monopoly which arises by a trade commanding the raw materials of a country. This duty prevents the low level of prices in the country from amalgamating with the higher prices abroad, as the export price, less the export duty, must be equal to the market price at home.

**106. Agriculture.**—In decreasing return the market price will be increased, but not by the entire amount of the duty; how much will, of course, depend on the schedule of demand, which is often steep for raw materials and agricultural produce. A duty on corn will, provided that much is not used as fodder, be nearly completely utilised. Suppose the schedule of demand to be 18, 16, 14, 12, 11, 10, 9s., and the schedule of supply to be 7, 8, 9, 10, 11, 12, 13s.; the state of the market will then be 5 units, sold at a price of 11s. Suppose, now, that the first 4 units are produced abroad, and the last 3 at home,—*i.e.*, that of 5 units sold the 4 are foreign ($s_1$, $s_2$, $s_3$, $s_4$) and one home produce ($s_5$), while 2 units produced at home ($s_6$ and $s_7$) are returned unsold. If we impose a duty of 3s. on each unit the schedule will read:

| D | S | |
|---|---|---|
| 18 | 7 + 3 | (foreign produce) |
| 16 | 18 + 3 | — |
| 14 | 11 | (home produce) |
| 12 | 12 | — |
| — | — | — |
| 11 | 9 + 3 | (foreign produce) |
| 10 | 10 + 3 | — |
| 9 | 13 | (home produce). |

The price will then be 12, and 4 units will be sold, of which 2 are produced at home and 2 abroad; the home production has then been increased, the purchase of foreign goods has decreased; the unit which is produced at 12s., and which, before the duty was imposed, was the 6th in the schedule and could not be sold, because the price of the 6th buyer was below 12s., has now, when the duty has been imposed, become the 4th, as the foreign units, which were previously cheaper, have now, on account of the duty, a price of supply which makes them come later in the schedule.

Where the country in question does not need to import much grain, the customs barrier will cause that the price at home will immediately be equal to the price on the world market with the addition of the duty. In the long run, however, this will not quite hold good, inasmuch as the duty and the higher price arising thereby will result in the taking up of soil which is on the margin of what will pay to cultivate for the production of corn. To make this rule effective it is necessary that there must be land to take up for cultivation, and there must be no agreement to the contrary between the farmers. Until Germany had her duty system supplemented by an export premium, it proved that the East Prussian corn prices did not reach the world prices with the addition of the duty.

**107. The Corn Duty and the Consumer.**—The protection which the consumers have, in abstinence or substitution, against rising prices is very weak for corn, which satisfies the most necessary demand. If, therefore, the corn duty does not lead to a production which exceeds the consumption of the country itself, the duty will be fully utilised.

Corn is the raw material of labour, and through this is a factor in the price of most goods. A duty of 5s. on 100 kilos. of grain will cause that the yearly expenses of a working class family for bread and flour will be increased from £7½ to £10½; but it will increase the price of ordinary food in the same proportion. The corn duty has the effect of a capitation tax—a tax on the many and poor to the advantage of the large farmers, because the small farm uses its own corn and, therefore, is indifferent to price-fluctuations. Another fact is, that the small farmer cannot always calculate this but, for instance in Germany, looks at the high prices obtained for the crop, but is not aware of the fact, that just as much more money is required for his bread and for fodder for his cattle, nor of the general increase in the prices of goods caused by the corn duty.

That the duty leads to an increased cultivation and better utilisation of the soil cannot be denied, in any case in countries where large farms prevail; but here also it does not necessarily mean more intensive working.

Just because corn is the raw material for so many other productions, the corn duty may have many other disagreeable additional effects by hampering other production.

It is therefore dangerous to resort to the corn duty, even as a temporary expedient, especially if there is no certainty for abolishing it again. Agricultural interests are always very strong politically, and people who have been accustomed to get high prices for their produce will, even if these prices are higher than the cost of production, not easily be contented with a lower price; this will be remembered from the days of the Napoleonic wars. Further, the corn duty will be capitalised as an increase of the ground rent. As soon as the property changes owner, the corn duty will have entailed a sale price, which is so much higher that the new owner will not be better situated with the higher corn prices than was the previous owner with the lower prices. From being a surplus, the increase in price has become a debt. In order to pay interest on this debt the new owner must maintain the protective duty, an experience which has been amply confirmed by the history of German agriculture during the last generation.

In Denmark a corn duty would hardly increase the area under cultivation, while a duty on special crops, for instance, wheat or sugar beet, would increase the cultivation of these crops at the expense of others. The fluctuations in the prices of wheat have in Denmark largely affected the proportion between the areas of wheat and rye. We must, however, remember, that the separate crop is grown in joint production, as the rotation of crops must be considered as a whole—*i.e.*, the employment for one crop partially influences the crops which naturally are grown in rotation with the protected crop, even if it is possible, to a certain extent, by addition of the requisite manure to give the protected crop a larger share in the rotation than it would normally have.

On account of the joint production, it is very difficult to calculate the cost of production. For this reason the statements of beet growers must be incorrect, because the intensive treatment and cultivation of beet areas will actually also benefit the following crops.

While the agricultural duty, as against the industrial duty, does not lead to lower but to higher marginal expenses, because the national limit of cultivation is extended, it may lead to a cultivation of new crops, which in itself is advantageous, and which has only been prevented by lack of skill and initiative, and it may at times lead to the introduction of a higher technique.

The millers are wrong in their statement that by protecting the finely-ground flour only, the price of coarse flour will not be increased, for the latter is only imported in smaller quantities beforehand; the fact that the two articles stand in a substitutionary relation to one another, and that the finer flour is better able to bear the cost of transport, will cause that the coarse flour, the price of which is now kept down by the finely-ground American flour, will rise, even if the duty only affects the finer grade. The flour duty would probably increase the price of corn by part of its amount by creating a market for good bread corn at home.

I am assailed by one doubt: Can the corn price be so low that the farms will not be able to continue production without the starvation of the farm labourers? In this case a corn duty may possibly become necessary.

The corn duty can therefore hardly be rejected as a purely temporary expedient, the time of discontinuation of which should be decided simultaneously with the introduction of the duty; it would, however, be advisable to attempt the substitution of the middle sized farm for the large scale farming before starting to protect agriculture, and if the agricultural duty is actually adopted in order to gain the important object, to make the country self-supporting as far as food is concerned, this protection ought to be accompanied by a tax on the increased ground-rent after a couple of rotations of crop. Otherwise the ruinous see-saw movement will be started: Even when a government realises that the agricultural protection is obsolete, it dare not reverse, because the duty has been capitalised, detached from agriculture in the form of mortgages, so that the abolition of the duty would mean ruin for those farmers who are unable to shift the reduction in price on to the previous owners, who again through the capitalisation of the ground rent have become creditors.

**108. Shifted to the Foreigner.**—Another side of the question is the fact that a protective duty does not necessarily mean that the burden of the home consumer will be *equal* to the duty. The duty, which increases the price at home, will often depress the world-price. The consumers of the importing country, who must now pay import-duty, are not able to pay as much for the good, duty unpaid, as they were before, while the duty has further caused an increase in the quantity grown in the country itself, which again means a smaller demand on the world market. The process takes the following form:—If the price before the imposition of the duty is, say, 100s., a duty of 30s. will have the effect of depressing the prices of the world market from 100s. to, say, 95s., the inland price in a protected country will be increased by the amount of the duty 30s. or to 125s.—*i.e.*, the duty has increased the inland price to 30s. more than the world price, but as an offset depressed the latter by 5s. The result is that the burden of the consumer is actually only 25s. The effect on the world market is still more noticeable where the duty has been supplemented by export premiums, which prevent an excessive inland production from falling below the price abroad, with the addition of the duty, but which, on the other hand, directly and heavily depresses the world price—a fact of which flour and sugar have provided perfect instances.

We are now in the heart of the question: How can the foreign countries be made to bear the duty?

Suppose that in the country, the export of which it is desired to prevent, there are several producers, of which some produce with a differential rent and others are just at the margin. The importing country will, by imposing a duty, cut away the marginal producers of the foreign country; an earlier producer will become the marginal producer and is able to sell cheaper—*i.e.*, to continue the export. The price in the importing country is higher (on account of the duty, and of the consumption being limited to the rather well-situated), the price in the exporting country is lower than before, and it will, consequently, by continued export not have the entire duty covered, but must bear part thereof. This the exporter does not know, however, because the inland prices of the exporting country, of course, will adjust themselves in such a way that they correspond to the prices of the importing country less the duty.

Something similar may be said of an export duty. Suppose that the price of production in Denmark is 100s. and the market price 120s., because, for instance, Sweden for some reason buys up at that figure. If we now impose an export duty of 20s. the price in Denmark will fall—more goods will be offered on the inland market, and it will pay the exporter to sell at 101s. instead of sending the good out of the country and obtain 120s., less 20s. export duty. In the second instance, this will cause smaller imports to Sweden, where the price will consequently now rise, for instance, to 125s. The price in Denmark will now be 105s.—*i.e.*, the export duty has increased the price abroad, and the foreign country will now pay more for the (reduced) part of the Danish export than before—*i.e.*, the export duty will, in this case, partially be paid by the *foreign* consumer.

This shifting on of the duty to a foreign country then takes place indirectly, and on account of the law of indifference in such a manner that this is not *immediately* apparent; and the extent to which this takes place is, of course, dependent on the relative position of monopoly of the country in question to the good. If England should impose a duty on the import of butter, we would probably have to pay part thereof; should England impose an export duty on coal, we would also have to pay. But if England should impose an export duty on cloth, that country itself would have to bear it, because it is possible to buy cloth elsewhere. During the war Denmark had the chance to impose export duties, but politicians as well as merchants let it pass, for one reason, because it is a "liberal" catechism that export duties are one of the expedients of the "foul mercantilism."

Concerning *differential* duties the question arises: Will the home price of the good be decided by the minimum or by the maximum rate, when both are employed? If, for instance, the rest of the world must pay 5s. duty on a quarter of wheat, while Canada has free import into England? In the first instance, the price will rise by 5s. in England. Canada will then force her export until the price in Canada has risen. Now it is the question if Canada is able to supply England after having supplied herself, in which case the price would fall nearly to the previous level in England and Canada. The English consumers may perhaps have to pay 6d. or 1s. more for 1 cwt. than before. The Canadian farmers will not only from England, but also from the town population of Canada herself, obtain a couple of shillings more. This may extend the limit of cultivation, and thereby result in a further reduction in price. If, however, Canada is not able to provide sufficient supplies for England, the price will continue for a long time to be 5s. higher in both countries, until an extension of the margin of cultivation will at last force the price somewhat down. The farmers of the preferred country will in this case reap the same advantage as the farmers of the importing country, and the consumers in *both* places will have to pay more. A *punitive* duty will, if the supplies of the exporting country are necessary, be borne by the consumers in England; if the said supplies are superfluous, the punitive duty may stop the imports, as, for instance, when the French differential rate for sugar, produced in the French colonies, entailed that European beet sugar could not be employed at all in France as the material for refining.

Differential duties will further change the proportion of the exchange of goods between the two countries, and may thereby alter the tendency of their production, leaving out of consideration the fact that also the proportion of exchange between the preferred country and other countries, with which it usually trades, will be altered. This is all the more evident because the differential duty is nearly always a link in a mutual system; when a system of this nature is carried into effect, it unites the countries who are parties to the agreement in a kind of common customs district, but with the local protection which corresponds to the lowest mutual rate; if this is sufficiently high, as is the case with many of the rates granted before the war by Canada to England, the preference will be illusory.

**109. The Theory of Solidarity.**—A protectionistic author once maintained that a new inland production worth, say, £5,000,000, does not only mean a gain of the 10% to 15%, which is the profit of the last seller, but actually the full amount of £5,000,000, as this amount can be dissolved into so and so much net gain to employer, labourer, capitalist, supplier of raw material, etc. To a certain extent this view is correct; in any case when it is not argued that the £5,000,000 will in all cases appear as a new net gain for the citizens; otherwise, an example will show how much he is wrong.

A consumption of £5,000,000 worth of Danish flour—as against imported flour—will not give the nation a larger gain than those 15% which are gained by the millers and their auxiliaries (labourers, building artisans). The raw material, wheat, can as an international commodity be sold, whether there is an inland milling industry or not. (If, however, the population is educated to eat bread made from Danish wheat, the price of this article may rise). Only by employing labour, which was previously unemployed, can a new trade enrich the community. Similarly with the raw material; only inasmuch as this was previously unsaleable or only saleable at a lower price, will there be a net gain in the specific employment. Further must be deducted the interest on the capital invested in the milling industry and its auxiliaries, because this might actually be invested outside the borders of the country, if a duty on flour does not ensure the requisite rentability of inland investment.

The result will therefore be that from the gross profits of the production must be deducted the *substitution prices of all the components employed.* It must, however, be maintained, that the abolition of protection once introduced, if the technical capital invested has not been written off, and is thereby reduced to the value of scrap iron, may become a national loss, and that such a reduction in the rate of duty ought to take place with notice permitting the wearing out of the capital once invested.

The same author advances a conception, which he terms the *ratio of solidarity*, stating how much a member of the community employs out of his income for the purchase of home-made goods. If a production creates a new class of consumers, or increases the income of the existing classes of consumers, the author maintains that, for instance, 60% of this income is employed in the purchase of home-made goods—*i.e.*, in starting new production ; but here again the fact applies that the components employed in new production were of value before the protection was introduced, and that they only act as an increase of income with the difference in their value before and after the introduction of protection.

Leaving out of consideration that the introduction of protection will at once create a boom in the protected trades, and thereby have the effect of an increase in the means of circulation, the productive forces in a country will, in the long run, be fairly well employed, so that the principal effect of protection will be to *rearrange the employment of these forces to the detriment of the existing trades* ; this may be an advantage if there are possibilities for technical development in the new trades ; but in any case the advantage will only be a difference—*i.e.*, between what the components were able to earn before, and what they are able to earn afterwards. But from this it will also appear that the protection must not be too general, and must be limited to a few trades, as it is only as an exception that a large part of the productive forces of the country are unemployed ; a uniformly adjusted duty on all goods, the " solidarity protection "—as a Swede, Dr. Brock, terms it—may be compared to Baron Munchausen's attempt to lift himself by his pigtail, and the only effect will be increased prices, at least temporarily.

It is, of course, conceivable that the industry of a *small* country may be destroyed by the abolition of protection, because it will not immediately be able to adjust itself to the changed conditions, and because the industry of foreign countries will suddenly carry it off its legs, and create a violent industrial crisis. Even if other industries will have better opportunities as a set-off, some years will elapse before the changed conditions can be taken advantage of, and it is economically as well as politically wise to accept an interim period.

Inasmuch as the duty increases the prices of goods and thereby increases the expenses of the *consumers*, it will cause a loss for these, and this loss must be deducted from the net gain of imposing the duty. (Before 1908 the increase in the price of the article—caused by Danish protection—was in some instances more than the total wages of labour.)

Inasmuch as the import continues in some measure, the increase in the price of the good for the consumer will not mean a national loss, as this is then only a tax, which otherwise would have to be paid in some other way.

*Schulze-Gavernitz* is of the (surely wrong) opinion that more than three-fourths of the world's steam power is employed in transport ; it is possible that an European customs policy, restricting the foreign trade, may create a net gain through the saving in the cost of transport (?).

A manufacturer once called my attention to the fact that merchants in their purchase of goods will prefer the foreign good, if this is only a farthing cheaper ; in comparison with the total trade profits, this increase in price is so immaterial that it may very well be justified to overcome it by imposing a moderate duty. The objections to the solidarity protection are weakened if this is only a nominal impost of a few per cent. of the value.

The question, whether a duty is to be imposed or not, can only be answered by a concrete investigation for each separate good. Science cannot acknowledge pure protectionism or pure free trade, because the economic forces are never allowed to act according to their inherent strength, and because the world does consist of national groups, whose interests are not identical, even if perhaps they are not antagonistic, as the doctrinary protectionist will contend.

So far we have only treated the direct effects ; it is possible that our results will be modified when the customs duty is considered as a factor in the theory of international commerce.

# CHAPTER XIX

## THE MONOPOLY PRICE.

**110. The Monopolised Market.**—At a time when prices are not determined through free competition and by the unhampered effects of the forces, but when the producers to an increasing extent have amalgamated, and one will is commanding the output, the principal task of the theory of value will be to find the rules governing the state of the monopolised market.

The monopolist of course commands the output to a greater or smaller extent ; in any case he will, within his sphere of power, manipulate the market with maximum profits in view.

In case the price has remained fluctuating between the small margin from $p_n$ and $s_n$, the monopolist will immediately appropriate this difference without needing to decrease his production in order to carry the market price as high as $p_n$.

But not satisfied with this he will *increase his price further* ; in order to do this he must, however, *reduce his production—i.e.*, put his price so high and his output so low that his *differential rent reaches its maximum*, that is, that the *difference between what he actually obtains* by the higher price and the smaller output, and his *total expenses in producing the reduced quantity of goods*, will be the maximum.

Expressed in symbols this reads : When he reduces his output from $n$ to $m$ units and the $m$-th buyer's price is $p_m$ ($> p_n$),

$$m \cdot p_m - t_{s(m)} > \begin{matrix} (m+1) \cdot p_m & - t_{s(m+1)} > n \cdot p_n - t_{s(n)} \\ (m-1) \cdot p_{m-1} & - t_{s(m-1)} > 1 \cdot p_1 - s_1 \end{matrix}$$

(in which $p_m$ is the $m$-th buyer's price, which *corresponds* to the monopoly-price, in which $m$ is the number of units which can be *sold* at this price, and in which $t_{s(m)}$ is the total expenses in the production of $m$ units, while $p_n$ is the natural market price and $t_{s(n)}$ the expenses of production of $n$ units.)

Or : *the monopoly-price, multiplied with the quantity sold,* must *with the deduction of the total expenses,* involved in producing this quantity, yield the highest possible differential rent to the seller, and *therefore be more than any higher price, multiplied by the smaller quantity, less the total expenses—and it must also be more than any lower price, multiplied with the corresponding larger quantity, less the total expenses of the larger quantity.*

If we describe the seller's differential rents, as $r_{s(m)}$ with a quantity of $m$ units sold, and with a quantity of $m + 1$ and $m - 1$ respectively as $r_{s(m+1)}$ and $r_{s(m-1)}$, we know that he will restrict his production to $m$ units if

$$r_{s(m)} > \begin{matrix} r_{s(m+1)} \\ r_{s(m-1)} \end{matrix}$$

How much he will reduce his production in order to attain the maximum will depend on the form of the curve of demand; if this *is flat* a considerable reduction will be needed in order to increase the price appreciably; for the luxuries of the poor, or for goods which have a substitute, the monopoly will be difficult to exploit, because the curve of demand is a limit, beyond which the seller cannot go; our ability to substitute one good for another in our consumption, and thereby avoid an overcharged good, is the worst enemy of the monopoly. If an increase in price drives a whole class of buyers out of the consumption, and when this will further result in increased expenses per unit for the manufacturer, the monopoly will be of little value to the holder. If, however, the curve is steep, as for necessaries of life, the customary consumption of the rich, raw materials, and goods, which are sold in small quantities, a monopoly will be very lucrative, because no great reduction in production is needed in order to obtain a high price of demand. A monopoly on luxuries is not as lucrative as one on necessaries. A monopoly on spices, sewing thread and other goods, which are bought in small quantities for relatively unimportant small change, is an excellent source of income.

Dr. Dalton has pointed out to me that we only get a position of equilibrium when demand is elastic or in the case of inelastic demand when the supply curve rises by diminishing output. But in other cases a further restriction of output will always increase monopoly profit. Raw materials obey the law of decreasing return and the demand is very inelastic on a great part of the curve; a monopoly on raw materials is then very valuable and the more dangerous, because he who commands one step of the ladder of production is actually as strong as if he commanded all the stages of the production of the good, and consequently a monopoly of raw materials gives power over *all the goods* in which *the raw material in question forms a component* without having a substitute.

**111. Monopoly and Schedule of Supply.**—Naturally the form of the curve of supply will also be of importance. When a reduction of the production in itself will entail lower expenses, as is the case with decreasing return, there is an advantage in the reduction itself; not so with increasing return, where the reduction will entail higher expenses per unit, and therefore take away some of the advantage gained by the higher sale price.

A special case arises when the production cannot be decreased, but the sales may be reduced, as the higher price is then obtained either by throwing away the surplus quantity or by selling it in another market than the one monopolised. On one side of the accounts is then added the expenses of the larger production, and on the other the income from the sale of part of the production in one market and of the surplus in another.

Regarding the effect of a reduction of production we must distinguish between the several ways in which this reduction takes place, whether through the restricted working of the existing factories—*i.e.*, by not utilising the full capacity as is the case when a cartel decides its division between its factories—or whether by simply closing the poorest concerns. In the latter case lower marginal expenses will be arrived at—*i.e.*, besides the advantage of the higher prices the monopolist will also gain the advantage of ridding himself of that part of his production which does not yield him any particular profit; in the first case he will have higher expenses at all his factories, because a smaller turnover must be spread over the same plant. This has led to the fact that even when a cartel distributes its production, the least successful concerns are actually closed by selling their share—*i.e.*, they are paid a lump sum to cease working in order to enable the best factories to work to their full capacity. In the latter case the compensation must be part of the socially (although not technically) necessary expenses, which must be covered in order to continue.

What is said above may be stated in the rule that *a monopolistic trust as a rule will decrease the expenses per unit, while the distributing cartel will increase them.* Both may, however, obtain a reduction by distributing the production according to *speciality* between the existing factories instead of reducing the production. Danish textile factories would undoubtedly gain much by distribution according to the nature of the production—*i.e.*, by specialising; only by adopting such measures can the factories of a small country hope to attain the level of effectivity of the large factories abroad (compare, for instance, the distribution of the various grades of paper between the Danish paper factories). The distribution may also be undertaken in order to reduce transport expenses; in this case a distribution of the grades as well as distribution of the customers into groups takes place. The transport expenses for raw material to the factory as well as the dispatch of the goods to distant customers will, besides the purely technical optimum, put a limit to the possible concentration. A fully capable weaving mill, which will not manufacture too many different sorts of goods, would hardly need more capital before the war than about £50,000 in order to be fully equipped. A concern may, however, technically gain by having a much larger capital, but it must in that case seek its customers far outside its natural rayon, for which reason it would stop the concentration before the *technical optimum* had been reached. This would not in the latter case correspond to the economic optimum.

**112. Taxation and Monopoly.**—These considerations will be of importance when we ask what will be the *effects* of a tax. A *fixed* tax on each concern without consideration of the amount of production—*i.e., corresponding to an increase in the expenses of establishment*—will on the expense side act as a strengthening of the tendency towards mass production. A *proportional or progressive tax on the price* will also increase the expenses per unit when the production is reduced in order to obtain a higher price. *A uniform tax per unit* will obviously not have this effect.

Suppose $a$ to represent an increase in the cost of production or a tax, *proportional* to the *quantity* produced; the *total tax* claimed —when the tax is $a$ on each unit sold—will be $m \cdot a$, if $m$ units are sold, but only $(m - 1) \cdot a$ if only $m - 1$ units are sold. In the latter case the taxes paid will be $a$ *less* than if $m$ units are produced; $a$ will then represent the *amount of tax saved* by the reduction in production. But if this amount is more than the difference between the differential rent of the monopolist, when he produces $m$ and $m - 1$ units respectively, *i.e.*, if $r_{s(m)} - a <$

$r_{s(m-1)}$, he will gain by reducing his production from $m$ to $m-1$ units and thereby increase the price.

He will perhaps gain by reducing his production to $m-x$ units; in this case the amount of tax saved is $x \cdot a$. With a tax of $a$s. per unit his gain $r_{s(m)}$ when producing $m$ units, will be reduced to $r_{s(m-x)}-(m-x) . a$. The difference between $m . a$ and $(m-x) . a$ is now $x . a$, *i.e.*, the *amount of tax saved*. If now $x . a > r_{s(m)} - r_{s(m-x)}$ then $r_{s(m)} - a . m < r_{s(m-x)} - (m - x) . a$, *i.e.*, the profit left after the tax has been imposed is more when he produces $m-x$ than when he produces $m$ units.

*If, in the case of the imposition of a uniform tax per unit, the amount of tax saved by a reduction of the production is larger than the difference between the producer's differential rent at a turnover of m and m — x respectively, the monopolist will derive advantage by a further reduction of his production and a further increase in price; but by the further increase of price, part of the tax is shifted on to the consumers.*

The monopoly has actually not done the harm it might, as a tax may, in certain cases, be shifted on to the consumer. The contention that a tax on a monopolised good cannot be shifted on is theoretically incorrect—even if it often proves correct in practice, because it is not possible for the monopolist to reduce his production suddenly. There can be no doubt that if the cost of production of a monopolised good is doubled, the price must rise—how much will depend upon the schedule of demand; the steeper this is the greater is the probability that the tax will make the monopolist decrease the production further.

A tax of 1s. per unit will yield £5 for 100 units, and £4 10s. for 90 units; by producing 90 units only the monopolist will in this case save 10s. in taxes. If the tax is 5s. per unit the difference in the total amount of tax, when the sale is 100 and 90 units respectively will be £2 10s.; in the latter case it is more plausible that the *amount of tax saved* will balance the difference between the differential rent at a production of 90 units and of 100 units—*i.e.*, the higher the tax the greater the probability for further reduction of production and shifting on to the buyer.

*Knut Wicksell* and *Westergaard* maintain in support of *Cournot* the same view; Westergaard has expressed this in *Nordisk Tidsskrift* for 1898 in the following manner: " If, in the case of a tax, proportional to the quantity sold, the monopolist increases the price a little, the net profits, less the tax, will be reduced a little ; but, as the increase of price causes a smaller consumption, the tax will be less in amount, and a thorough investigation will reveal that this will be able to balance the loss mentioned. Sometimes the increase in price will be less than the tax, but at times even more than this, according to circumstances ; but in any case it will prove to be a fact that the producer will lose more than the exchequer will gain."

The monopolist actually loses by a tax because his differential rent is decreased ; but as he would lose more by keeping his price unchanged, he further reduces his production in order to shift part of the tax on to the consumers through the higher price.

**113. Various Taxes.**—Suppose the schedules to read as follows :—

| D | | | | TECHNICAL SCHEDULE. |
|---|---|---|---|---|
| 7 units demanded at | 13s. | can be produced at | | 11s. |
| 10 ,, ,, | $11\frac{1}{2}$s. | ,, | ,, | 10s. |
| 14 ,, ,, | 10s. | ,, | ,, | $9\frac{1}{7}$s. |
| 16 ,, ,, | 9s. | ,, | ,, | 9s. |

The normal market condition is 16 units at a price of 9s. ; the producer gains no differential rent ; in the monopolised market the conditions yielding the producer the maximum advantage will be 10 units at a price of $11\frac{1}{2}$s. This appears from the following scale in which Column 1 is the number of units multiplied with the sale price, Column 2 the cost of production, and Column 3 the differential rent (in this case arisen as a monopoly rent) :—

| COLUMN 1. | COLUMN 2. | | COLUMN 3. |
|---|---|---|---|
| 7 . 13 | — 7 . 11 | = | 14s. |
| 10 . $11\frac{1}{2}$ | — 10 . 10 | = | 15s. |
| 14 . 10 | — 14 . $9\frac{1}{7}$ | = | 12s. |
| 16 . 9 | — 16 . 9 | = | 0s. |

A tax of 1s. per unit will now decrease the differential rent in the four cases by 7, 10, 14 and 16s. respectively ; this will thereafter amount to 14 — 7 = 7s., 15 — 10 = 5s.; 12 — 14 and 0 — 16 are negative.

The uniform tax has altered the condition for maximum profit to 7 units at a price of 14s., out of which the tax must be paid.

The differential rent is certainly 1s. less at a production of 7 units $(14 < 15)$; but the tax of 10 . 1s. is more than $7 \times 1$. This is not a proper case of shifting on, as the price has certainly been increased by the amount of the tax, and even by more; but, on the other hand, the producer has lost more than the amount of the tax; the net profit is reduced from 15s. to 14 — 7s.

A progressive tax, or a tax proportional to the amount of the monopoly price exceeds the price of the free market, will *not* reduce the production, and it is plausible that it may even *break the monopoly* and force the producer to extend. Suppose the price under free competition to be 9s., the overprice in the four above cases will then be 4, $2\frac{1}{2}$, 1 and 0s. (13 — 9, $11\frac{1}{2}$ — 9s., etc.). A tax of $33\frac{1}{3}$% on the overprice will yield $1\frac{1}{3}$, $\frac{5}{6}$, $\frac{1}{3}$ and 0s. per unit respectively. We must multiply this tax by the turnover, and deduct the result from the differential rent—*i.e.*:

| | $r_s$ | — $n$ . TAX. | | = PRODUCER'S NET PROFIT. |
|---|---|---|---|---|
| ( 7 units) | 14s. | — 7 . $1\frac{1}{3}$s. | = 14 — $9\frac{1}{3}$ | = $4\frac{2}{3}$s. |
| (10 units) | 15s. | — 10 . $\frac{5}{6}$s. | = 15 — $8\frac{1}{3}$ | = $6\frac{2}{3}$s. |
| (14 units) | 12. | — 14 . $\frac{1}{3}$s. | = 12 — $4\frac{2}{3}$ | = $7\frac{1}{3}$s. |
| (16 units) | 0s. | — 16 . 0s. | = | = 0s. |

In this case the progressive tax has forced the monopolist to extend his production from 10 to 14 units, and to let the price *drop* from $11\frac{1}{2}$ to 10s. The monopolist's differential rent was originally 15s., and after the imposition of the progressive tax it is $7\frac{1}{3}$s. The government gains $4\frac{2}{3}$s. in all. The consumers gain, on the first 10 units, $1\frac{1}{2}$s. (the difference between $11\frac{1}{2}$ and 10s.), in all 15s., and for the 4 additional units the (smaller) advantage of the difference between their subjective price and the 10s. The tax has been beneficial socially; it has nearly *broken the monopoly* and transferred *part of the monopolist's profit to the State* and further increased the *consumer's rent.*

With increasing return it is besides not easy to advance rules generally, because the seller's profit is too largely dependent upon the actual appearance of the technical schedule—*i.e.*, to which extent an alteration in the quantity produced will alter the cost.

Where a monopoly has been established in a trade, obeying the rule of increasing return, a tax, *progressive* on the price, will probably break the monopoly; with decreasing return it will probably not have this effect, because it is counteracted by increasing expenses.

When the Danish Government granted a private electricity company the *actual* monopoly of landing a cable on the north of Zealand, the rent paid by the company to the exchequer ought not to have been dependent on the quantity consumed only, but also progressive on the price, at which the electricity is resold to the consumers.

This is the right form for the treatment of monopolies by the State; together with the establishment of a trust commission, which should have authority to make investigations and possibly regulate prices, the progressive tax per unit will supply the Government with means to prevent abuse of monopolies and yet be able to take advantage of its good points.

As, in the case of increasing return, on many points the price of demand will be higher than the corresponding price of supply, it is feasible if the difference between two such points is rather large that a uniform tax will make the monopolist reduce his production even considerably. This will often be the case, when the marginal consumption of a good fluctuates between two classes; an increase in price will drive the lower class out of the market. The production must be reduced considerably, which again may lead to a very high cost of production. The production can now be continued only if the higher class has a price of demand for the good, which is sufficiently high to cover not only the tax, but also the increase in the cost caused by the considerable reduction of the production. If the price of tickets on the Copenhagen tramways were increased by 3d. (from 2d. to 5d.) a large number of the public would partly cease to use the tramways—*i.e.*, the town would grow smaller; the electrical power, which is based on cars following quickly after one another, would then not pay, and when the electrical plant had been worn out the old horse-trams would again be worked—*i.e.*, the working would be more expensive.

A proportional tax on the *surplus* of monopoly would reduce all possible differential rents in the same proportion and not alter the production, but only transfer part of the profits to the public. The monopolist will, on the other hand, when a tax per unit is not too high, be forced to bear part thereof; if a reduction in production will reduce the cost by a considerable amount, and if at the same time a reduced output does not meet with very much higher prices of demand, it will cause the producer the smaller loss to keep his production unchanged and pay the tax himself out of his differential rent. *Lindberg* proposes that from the dividends of a limited company, and accumulation of reserves and payment of bonus under *normal* conditions, must be calculated the net profits per unit produced, and a progressive tax collected on what the actual profits amount to beyond this.

If, for instance, 7 units are demanded at 12s., and 10 units at $11\frac{1}{2}$s., while 7 units are produced at 11s. and 10 units at 10s., the monopoly price will be $11\frac{1}{2}$s., at which price 10 units are sold. A tax of 1s. per unit will increase the cost of production for 7 units to $11 + 1$, which corresponds to the price of demand; the differential rent has consequently disappeared; but the cost of production for 10 units is increased to $10 +$ 1s., or $\frac{1}{2}$s. less than the corresponding price of demand; the producer will consequently bear the tax and not increase the price.

A fall in the cost of production will in all cases, where an increase causes an increase in the market price, lead to a reduction of the price, as can be seen by taking our example, on page 268. A tax of 1s. has made the monopolist reduce his production to 7 units, offered at a price of 12s. If the cost of production per unit is now reduced by 1s., the position will be the same as it was before the tax was imposed, and the monopolist will, in order to gain the maximum advantage, reduce the price to $11\frac{1}{2}$s. with a turnover of 10 units.

**114. Alterations in Demand.**—When the expenses are decreasing, the price will most often be altered in the opposite direction to the alteration in the *demand*. If, for instance :—

4 units are demanded at 10s. and produced at 5s.
5 ,, ,, 7s. ,, ,, 4s.

the monopoly price will be 10s., at which are sold 4 units, because $4 . (10 - 5) > 5 . (7 - 4)$. If now the 5th buyer's means are altered, so that he is able to give $8\frac{1}{5}$s. per unit, the monopoly price will fall to $8\frac{1}{5}$s., at which price 5 units can be sold; because $4 . (10 - 5) < 5 . (8\frac{1}{5} - 4)$.

If, therefore, a class of buyers, who had hitherto not been able to afford an effective demand for a thing, have their income increased and, consequently, can demand it at a higher price than before, even if this does not reach the previous monopoly price, the monopolist will often gain by extending his production, reducing his price and thereby gaining a new class of buyers. What he loses on the lower price of the quantity previously sold, he will gain by profits on the increased sale. (This possibility often arises as to railway tariffs).

As the expenses of production are reduced in the case of a decreasing return, the incentive to decrease the production, which a monopolist has in the generally steep curve of demand for raw materials, is strengthened. His differential rent will not only increase through the monopoly profits, but those units which he gives up producing gave him beforehand little or no differential rent, because they were produced at the highest expenses. A tax also need not be as heavy as where the *schedule of supply* is constant or even falling, in order to make him reduce his production beyond the quantity of the monopoly condition.

In case the coal mines should come under monopoly management—government or private—the prices might go very high; no great reduction is needed in order to bring about the high price of demand. A strike of the coal miners does not harm the mine owners, provided they have stock, for by the interruption of working the value of this is doubled. After the war we must reckon with the possibility that the great powers will exploit their own raw material deposits and those of their colonies with a view to a maximum profit; an easily realisable and profitable taxation of the nations which do not produce raw materials will then be feasible.

A corn monopoly would be dreadful; this can hardly be imagined otherwise than as a commercial monopoly. The exploitation of this by the state or under the state control would hardly be dangerous for the population, for the vote would reject a government which exploited the home market. But against foreign countries it can be employed with great advantage (compare coal and corn prices during the war.)

A temporary monopoly on representatives of goods often arises as a commercial monopoly. By a *corner* the price of corn, coffee, cotton, etc., can be driven very high, but only for a time; for the hidden supplies will at last appear and finish the corner. This will not show the heaviest fluctuations in price until the "bears" must cover the parcels, which they have sold for later delivery in the hope of a lower price, and the "bulls" are able to "squeeze" the "bears" by securing the actual supplies and at the same time holding the contracts which the latter have undertaken. In my book, *Vigtige Varer* (*Important Commodities*) I have given examples of the actual cornering of the bears as far as sugar and corn are concerned. (Business for future delivery can also be done in shares, and consequently a corner may be effected in the shares of a company, and the actual holder can force those who have promised delivery without being able to procure the shares, to free themselves from the unfulfillable contracts by paying an enormous compensation.)

**115. Dead Capital.**—The artificial monopoly is most likely to occur in industries with increasing return, where the conditions of production in themselves invite the large producer to compete the small producer out of the market. This competition may at times take such forms that the largest producer may gain by temporarily selling at prices below his cost of production in order to finish his competitors more quickly ; when only a few producers are left, they form a cartel and distribute their production, or a Trust buys up the remaining concerns. This development takes time ; even after the establishment of the cartel, trust or fusion, it will not be possible immediately to start the most advantageous method of production, because the capital of the poor factories must first be worn out or written off. In Denmark the paper factories as well as the breweries have rather large capitals sunk in " dead " plant and not written off ; the interest and writings off of these capitals therefore form part of the cost of production, although technically they do not count. In other words, part of the current expenses saved by the formation of the trust are employed in paying interest upon a not worn out, but scrapped capital, the economic destruction of which was, however, a *condition* for the improved working ; in order to pay interest thereon it is, however, necessary that sales are *not* based on the actual expenses after the alteration, but that the power of monopoly is exercised ; in case, however, it should become a *necessity* to sell at the new cost, it would still be possible to continue when the " dead " capital had been wiped out as a loss. This will explain one side of the financing of the trust : that in the " scrapped dead capitals " invested in unsuitable factories, we have an expense which, on one hand, is a condition for the establishment of the trust—in the same manner as stones must be removed in order to make soil suitable for cultivation—and which, in a way, is socially necessary, but which, on the other hand, is not *technically* necessary—*i.e.*, necessary in the sense that production would not be continued, even if the writings off on the "scrapped capital" are not covered by profits. In other words, it must, as in the case of removal of stones from the soil, be probable that interest can be paid on the scrapped capitals; but if this presumption fails the production will still be continued.

**116. Dumping**—Very few producers produce *one* good only; the monopolist thus often works with a joint production; where two goods produced in this manner may further be substituted for one another, as is the case with the various classes on the railway, or the different stages of a journey, peculiar facts will appear. *Warming* has, in the report of a committee to the municipality of Copenhagen, made some interesting observations on the discontinuance of the penny rates on the tramways; undoubtedly a number of people will continue to ride, but a not inconsiderable part of the public will prefer to walk the short distance instead of paying twopence; if now experience tells us that passengers leave the tram before this starts on the short distance for which a penny was paid, the discontinuance of this rate may entail that the tramcars will be empty for this distance, and this would cause a loss for the tramways. In other places and at other times of the day the penny rate may prevent long distance passengers from finding a place on the tram.

The monopoly will often gain by keeping two prices, when it is possible to divide the customers in two markets; whether this will be done depends upon how easily the customers of one class may slip over into the other.

The theory of monopoly contains—as stated by *Edgeworth*—rules of so paradoxical a nature that an "eminent economist" with good reason wrote to Edgeworth, who had shown him his peculiar theory about the imposition of a tax on first-class railway tickets, which might in certain cases make the company reduce the fares for first as well as second class: "It is not likely that anything in the monopoly system will surprise me."

The fact that an industry by reducing production will increase expenses against itself creates the problem, how at the same time to maintain the large production, which is a condition for low expenses, and the high monopoly price, which means reduced sales. The means are, as stated before, to divide the market into two or more parts ; now the goods will be divided into two classes at different prices, the goods being actually alike although they may give the impression of being different, and of which one good seeks its customers in the richer classes and the other in the poorer (soap, tobacco). Where there are import duties we have the possibility of producing much, and yet of selling part only in the country itself, but throwing the remainder beyond the customs borders. Of course nothing will be sold at below the expenses per unit (otherwise it would be more advantageous not to produce), but sales will be effected below the average expenses. Suppose the schedules to be

| | D | | |
|---|---|---|---|
| (1) | 18 | produced at | 10s. |
| (2) | 16 | ,, | 10s. |
| (3) | 14 | ,, | $9\frac{1}{2}$s. |
| (4) | 12 | ,, | 9s. |
| (5) | 11 | ,, | 9s. |
| (6) | 10 | ,, | 9s. |
| (7) | 9 | ,, | 9s. |
| (8) | 8 | ,, | $8\frac{1}{2}$s. |
| (9) | $7\frac{1}{2}$ | ,, | 8s. |

The equilibrium is 7 units at 9s., which does not leave a differential rent ; the monopoly, when operating in one market only, will produce 3 units, sold at 14s., produced at $9\frac{1}{2}$s., which leaves a monopoly rent of $3 \times 4\frac{1}{2} = 13\frac{1}{2}$s.

If now we produce 9 units, we may reduce the expense per unit to 8s. If we throw 6 units across the customs boundary (dumping) and keep three at home, the latter being sold at 14, we have $3 \times 14 + 6 \times 7\frac{1}{2} = 42 + 45 = 87$ ; from this must be deducted $9 \times 8 = 72$ ; in other words, the differential rent has been increased to 15s.

The producer gains by dumping and the community does not lose as much as it would if the producer exploited his monopoly *without* dumping. The community loses by the *monopoly* which robs the consumer of more differential rent than it yields the producer ; but dumping does not harm the exporting nation beyond this, it is even an advantage ; the profit by the lower expenses on the three first units (previously produced at $9\frac{1}{2}$s., but now, as part of the larger production at 8s.) is not only a private but also a national gain.

For the *importing* country dumping is in itself not detrimental; when German sugar in England fell in price to 15s. per cwt., on account of the German export premium, an English paper wrote: "Just a small increase of the premium, and Germany will dump us all our sugar for nothing!"

When the article is a raw material dumping may entail that a finishing industry is moved from the dumping country across the frontier. The Cadbury factories were, before 1902, able to export chocolate to Germany, manufactured from German sugar. English shipyards have benefited by the dumping of German steel plates. This applies when the dumped article is a raw material; if, however, it is a fully finished article, dumping may destroy the industry of the importing country.

If dumping is not a permanent measure, but stops immediately when the industry of the importing country has been destroyed, so that the exporting country gains a monopoly over the country to which it previously made presents, this country may be entitled to guard itself against too cheap imports by "countervailing duties."

But in other cases the cheap supplies will not cease, for they are to the advantage of the seller; the ability to utilise a concern to its full capacity reduces the expenses very much. *Scharling* mentions in his book, *Trade and Customs Policy*, that a firm, working at its full capacity, produced certain steel goods at a cost of 14¼s., and had a consumption of fuel of 1½ tons coal per ton goods, but that a production of 2/3rd of the capacity demanded expenses of 17¼s. and 2 tons coal; in 1901 German sugar factories sold loaf sugar in Switzerland at 23 marks, while in Germany the price was 38¼ marks; but then Germany and Austria exported one half of their production, which would not have been sufficient for the home demand in case the consumption had been as large as in Denmark. *Scharling* also mentions a German firm, which was able to produce 114,000 tons of certain metal goods at 85s., but at full capacity produced 152,000 tons at 70s. The proposition runs as follows:—

WITHOUT DUMPING.

| | |
|---|---|
| 114,000 tons at 100s. = | 11,400,000s. |
| Less expenses at 85. | 9,690,000s. |
| | 1,710,000s. |

WITH DUMPING.

| | |
|---|---|
| 114,000 tons at 100s. = | 11,400,000s. |
| 38,000 tons at 70s. = | 2,660,000s. |
| | 14,060,000s. |
| Less expenses at 70s. | 1,064,000s. |
| | 3,420,000s. |

The profit was in this case doubled, without the home consumers paying more than they would have had to pay if their consumption only had been produced.

*Brock* denies in his book *On Duties* that dumping may harm the importing country to any great extent; his argument is that 10 or 20% of the production of a factory may be dumped, but one cannot sell, for instance, more than one half of one's production below cost.

This is hardly completely correct. What the monopolist desires, when he splits his market, is to avoid the rule attending increasing return, that *the price of supply is the average expense.* If in the dumped market the *minimum* price only covers the expense of *increasing the total production by the quantity of goods* which he dumps—*i.e.*, sells below his average cost, he may make a distribution of what is the cost *beyond* this (the general costs) between the two markets according to an estimate of their sensitiveness.

The producer of raw materials may easily have a dumping ground *at home* when he has obtained the monopoly, by calculating his prices of raw materials according to what the different industries can give, thereby exploiting one industry, but selling to others at a low price. This is termed " discrimination " by American legislation, which is adverse thereto. We know the same thing from the tariff policy of American railroads, in favouring certain towns and industries by giving a discount.

A monopoly has thus a tendency to work the best factories only, to work these to their full capacity, to sort their customers in groups, which they make pay different prices, working on the principle from the tariff policy " what the traffic can bear."

International monopolies may either be due to the fact that a single concern (for instance, The Standard Oil Co.) commands also the foreign markets and exploits these according to the special conditions, or as in the Cement and Sewing Thread industries, to international agreements between several national monopolies; in the latter case the industry of each country is allowed to exploit the local market; the surplus, which might force the price down, is then shipped to Asia as a joint undertaking.

**117. The Monopoly Rent.**—Suppose the schedule of demand to be 18, 16, $14\frac{1}{6}$, 12, 11, 10, and 9s. for from 1 to 7 units, and suppose the expenses of a constant schedule of supply to be 10s. per unit; the buyers will get 6 units at a price of 10s. (= 60s.) although they would have paid for these $t_d = 18 + 16 + 14\frac{1}{6} + 12 + 11 + 10 = 81\frac{1}{6}$; the consumer's rent, $r_d$, is, therefore, $81\frac{1}{6} - 60 = 21\frac{1}{6}$s. In the free market the producer gains no differential rent under constant return; the gain of the community is, consequently, $21\frac{1}{6} + 0$s.

The monopoly condition is 3 units at $14\frac{1}{6}$s. and the highest possible differential rent is $3 \cdot 14\frac{1}{6} - 3 \cdot 10 = 12\frac{1}{2}$s. (4 units would only have given the producer a differential rent of 48 — 40 = 8s.: 2 units would have given him 12s. (2 . 16 — 2 . 10). If 3 units are sold $t_d = 18 + 16 + 14\frac{1}{6} = 48\frac{1}{6}$; $n \cdot p_n = 3 \cdot 14\frac{1}{6}$s. The consumer's rent has thus fallen to $48\frac{1}{6}$s. -- $42\frac{1}{2} = 5\frac{2}{3}$, that is, by $15\frac{1}{2}$s., of which $12\frac{1}{2}$s. are converted into producers' rent, and 3s. are completely lost.

The more the production is reduced, the smaller, of course, will be the buyer's differential rent, $r_d$, which, for 6, 5, 4, 3, 2 and 1 units respectively is $21\frac{1}{6}$, $16\frac{1}{6}$, $12\frac{1}{6}$, $5\frac{2}{3}$, 2 and 0s. The monopoly will therefore principally be to the disadvantage of the buyers. But what is worse, the *community loses by the monopoly, for the buyers lose more* ($15\frac{1}{2}$s.) *than the monopolist gains by reducing his production* ($12\frac{1}{2}$s.).

As the monopoly is most common when it acts under the rule of increasing return, we will consider the position under this condition.

In Diagram XXIII*a* D is the curve of demand, S the curve of supply. We presume in this that the monopoly is owned by a trust with a single factory, which is worked to its full capacity; further, we presume that the factory produces so cheaply that its expenses are equal to $p_n$. With the price $p_n$ and a turnover of $n$ we have $r_{dn} = a + b + c + d + e + i + h$, while $r_{sn} = 0$, because $p_n \cdot n = f + g$. The monopolist now reduces his production to $m$ units, which he produces at $x$ more than $p_n$, but

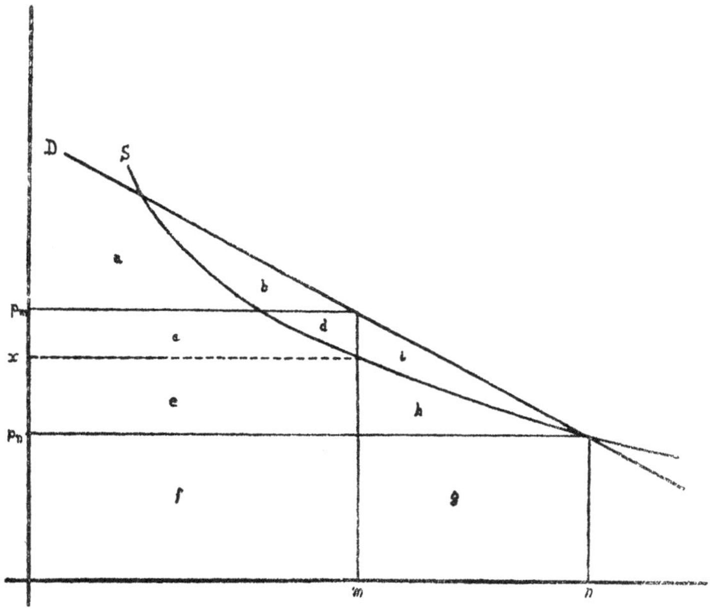


Diagram XXIIIa

sells at the higher price $p_m$; we now have $r_{dm}' = a + b$; $r_{sm} = c + d$; the buyer has consequently lost $c + d$, which have been

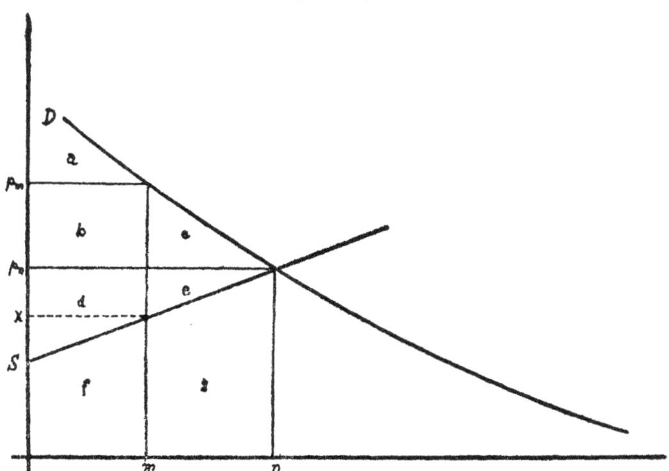


Diagram XXIIIb

gained by the seller, $e$ has been lost by the more expensive production and $i + h$ by the turnover being smaller.

It is, however, only an exception that the production is concentrated in one factory. The rule is that the monopolist has the production distributed over several plants, which are not equally well fitted. He will then reduce his production by ceasing to work the poorest factories and working the others to their full capacity. In Diagram XXIII$b$, $m$ is the quantity produced in the best factories, $n - m$ the production in the poor factories; in the best factories the cost of production is $x$, in the poor it is $p_n$. With a turnover of $n$ the price is $p_n$, $r_{dn} = a + b + c$ and $r_{sn} = d + e$. If now the monopolist abandons his poor factory, he will only produce $m$ units at a price of not above $x$ and sell these at $p_m$; we therefore arrive at $r_{dm} = a$, $r_{sm} = d + b$, the buyer has lost $b + c$, of which $b$ has been gained by the seller and $c$ has been lost by smaller consumption. The seller, who gains $b$, will, on the other hand, lose $e$ by the smaller turnover; $b > e$.

The diagram also holds good with decreasing return, the abandoned field being substituted for the discontinued factory.

The community will, however, not only lose under monopoly conditions, but also, if production is forced beyond the natural equilibrium.

If, in the example on page 278 the producer manufactures 7 units instead of 6, the market price obtained can only be 9s. The producer's differential rent will then be negative. He will obtain for the 7 units $7 . 9 = 63$s., and thereby lose 7s. ($63 - 70$). The buyers will certainly gain a larger consumer's rent than before; they would have been willing to pay for the 7 units $t_d = 18 + 16 + 14\frac{1}{8} + 12 + 11 + 10 + 9 = 90\frac{1}{8}$s. At a price of 9s. they only pay 63s. The buyers' differential rent, $90\frac{1}{8} - 63$ will then be $27\frac{1}{8}$s. The gain of the community will be $27\frac{1}{8} - 7 = 20\frac{1}{8}$s. With a turnover of 6 units at 10s. the gain would have been $21\frac{1}{8}$s.

From this a likely conclusion would be: *With a given distribution of income the community will gain most when the market price and the quantity sold are determined on the open market under full and free competition. If the quantity sold is decreased, the producer will gain, but not as much as the buyer loses; if the quantity sold is increased, the buyer will gain, but not as much as the producer loses.*

Neither the interests of the producer nor those of the buyer are separately identical with those of the community. The monopoly is exploited in such a way that a limited circle of buyers pay a higher price, while the final object of free competition is the larger quantity of goods sold at the small profit.

**118. The Ideal Price.**—*Westergaard* contended that the above rule was not correct. I must admit that he was right ; for, first of all, money is not the correct measurement for the consumer's rent, as shown in Chapter XIII, the rent being a psychical entity —*i.e.*, utility.

To return to our figure example, it may be that the 6s., which the buyer gains in differential rent by an increase in the turnover to 7 units at a price of 9s., in comparison with a turnover of 6 units at 10s., are worth far more for him in utility than the 7s., which the producer loses by the increased turnover, are for the latter. Because the actual distribution of income is not equal, it may happen that by producing beyond the natural point of equilibrium a larger total satisfaction measured in utility will be gained by the community, although the seller will lose more than the buyer will gain, when measured in money. The question becomes of practical interest when the State is the holder of the monopoly, as by giving its service without remuneration, the government actually *redistributes* the incomes ; the government will perhaps reason that there will be a gain in utility by everybody having a share in certain goods, and make them pay through *taxation* and not through a price per unit. The question is, if the people who enjoy the goods, and thereby receive the gift, will thereby obtain greater utility than those who pay the taxes ; if the latter are richer than the former, this is unquestionable, but then it is a case of redistribution of incomes by the government, and this is only defensible to the extent to which the existing distribution is considered unjust.

The same will appear from a figure example, which I will leave to the reader to work out. Suppose that the means of three persons, A ,B and C are such that 100 units of utility correspond to 100, 80, and 60s. respectively, and that the *utility series* of a good, is equal for all three persons, viz. : 100, 90, 80, 60 and 50 units of utility for 1, 2, 3, 4, 5 and 6 units respectively. Find how many units A, B and C respectively will buy at the prices 70, 50, and 80s. (market, distress and monopoly price) and the differential rents in money and utility at the three prices, for the three persons separately and together. The result will be that at a price of 70s. only A and B will buy, together 6 units (C buys nothing); the consumers' rent in money will be 72s. (in utility 75 units). At a price of 50s. A, B and C will buy 12 units; the consumer's rent will be 236s. in money, but 263½ units of utility; at a price of 80s. A and B will buy 4 units; their consumer's rent is 30s in money and 30 units in utility. We can deduce from this that when the price falls the consumer's rent will increase, but *more* in utility than in money, as long as new poorer buyers come in.

Now the utility calculation is faulty; but *Westergaard* has also thought of something else, of the "ideal price" which may be very far from the price of free competition, and even farther from the monopoly price. *Warming* maintains that the "ideal price" corresponds to the free market price in the case of constant or increasing expenses, but not for concerns which work with *decreasing expenses* per unit, and especially not, if the general expenses (*i.e.*, establishment expenses, etc.), are very considerable in proportion to the variable expenses; for here the ideal price will be *below* the free market price, in which the general expenses as well as the variable expenses are distributed over the quantity produced, and which therefore is considerably higher than the cost of the last units produced. The ideal price would, however, often be only *cover for the variable expenses*, as the deficit appearing will be more than balanced by an increase in the consumer's rent. Ideal price is actually related to dumping, because the production is in both cases extended beyond the equilibrium of the average cost—in the case of the ideal price through the producer himself covering the general expenses, in the case of dumping by these expenses being paid preferentially by the safest buyers, who are best able to pay.

Naturally the ideal price can only be maintained in spheres where the state is the producer, and the principle can only be fully realised in the *socialistic state*. But here the government will also command productions, which yield a *surplus*—*i.e.*, those which work with increasing expenses and where the market price will correspond to the cost of production of the last unit, and, consequently a producer's differential rent will be gained (especially the ground rent).

In a controversial commentary to Warming's above views *Riis-Hansen* quite correctly points to the important point that when treating the consumer's differential rent (or utility) one must take into consideration the *distribution of incomes.* A reduction of prices and fares may in many cases benefit principally the rich, but even if the advantage, that is, the increase of the differential rent, is the same in money, it will, on account of the smaller marginal utility of money, from a subjective point of view be smaller for the well-to-do, so that the *loss* which is caused the state, for instance, by a reduction of railway fares, will *not* mean a *corresponding gain* in the differential utility of the public. (Marshall speaks here of compromise of benefits.)

Warming's idea should, however, be further worked out, also because the question of, and principles for, *state exploitation* of public undertakings is becoming more and more burning. Where ought the state monopoly to be exploited—where should the state produce at a loss ?

Suppose the schedule of demand for from 100 to 1,000 passengers on a railway to be as specified below (the second column contains the subjective prices for a varying number of passengers, Column 1).

TABLE A.

| 1 | 2 | 3 | 4 | 5 | | 6 |
|---|---|---|---|---|---|---|
| NUMBER. | ORE. $p_n$ | IF THE NUMBER OF PASSENGERS IS | THE VALUE OF $t_d$ MONEY. | LESS $n.p_n$ | | CONSUMER'S RENT, $r_d$. KR. |
| The first 100 | 130 | 100 | 130 | 130 | = | 0 |
| The following 50 | 104 | 150 | 182 | 156 | = | 22 |
| ,, 50 | 86 | 200 | 225 | 172 | = | 53 |
| ,, 100 | 70 | 300 | 295 | 210 | = | 85 |
| ,, 50 | 60 | 350 | 325 | 210 | = | 115 |
| ,, 50 | 50 | 400 | 350 | 200 | = | 150 |
| ,, 100 | 40 | 500 | 390 | 200 | = | 190 |
| ,, 150 | 30 | 650 | 435 | 195 | = | 240 |
| ,, 150 | 20 | 800 | 465 | 160 | = | 305 |
| ,, 200 | 10 | 1 000 | 485 | 100 | = | 385 |

The third column states the varying number of passengers ; the fourth column is the total amount of their subjective prices ($t_d$), the fifth column is the number of passengers multiplied by the marginal price for their number ($n \,.\, p_n$) ; the sixth column is the difference between $t_d$ and $n \,.\, p_n$, *i.e.*, the consumer's rent expressed in money.

In order to approach actual conditions, we now presume that

the general expenses of the railway vary slightly only, for instance, from 104 with 100 passengers to 140 with 1,000, and we suppose that the expense per unit is constant, say 30 öre for each passenger. In Column 1 of Table B we again state the varying number of passengers; in the second column the gross income of the railway, $n \cdot p_n$; the third column states the general expenses for the varying numbers; the fourth column the amount of the proportional expenses per passenger; the fifth column the total expenses, and the sixth column the profit of the railway.

TABLE B.

| 1<br>NUMBER | 2<br>$n \cdot p_n$. | 3<br>GENERAL EXPENSES | + | 4<br>UNIT-EXPENSES PER PASSENGER 30 ÖRE. | 5<br>TOTAL EXPENSES. $t_s$ | 6<br>PROFITS OF THE RAILWAY, $r_s$ (Col. 2—5).<br>KR. |
|---|---|---|---|---|---|---|
| 100 | 130 | 104 | + | 30 | 134 | — 4 |
| 150 | 156 | 105 | + | 45 | 150 | + 6 |
| 200 | 172 | 110 | + | 60 | 170 | + 2 |
| 300 | 210 | 116 | + | 90 | 206 | + 4 |
| 350 | 210 | 116 | + | 105 | 221 | — 11 |
| 400 | 200 | 120 | + | 120 | 240 | — 40 |
| 500 | 200 | 122 | + | 150 | 272 | — 72 |
| 650 | 195 | 127 | + | 195 | 322 | — 127 |
| 800 | 160 | 131 | + | 240 | 371 | — 211 |
| 1,000 | 100 | 140 | + | 300 | 440 | — 340 |

If the railway is conducted with a view to exploiting the monopoly, we would stop at a ticket price ($p_m$) of 104 öre and carry 150 passengers. If the railway is only required to cover expenses we would put the price of the ticket at 70 öre and carry 300 passengers (we may probably be able to put the price somewhere between 60 and 70 öre, and carry about 325 passengers, in which case the railway will just pay.)

If, now, like Warming, we would try to find the "ideal price" at which the total of the consumer's rent and the surplus of the railway together make the maximum, we arrive at the following schedule :—

TABLE C.

| | $p_n$ | $r_d$ | + $r_s$ | = | R<br>KR. |
|---|---|---|---|---|---|
| 100 passengers at... | 130 ÖRE | 0 | — 4 | = | — 4 |
| 150 „ ... | 104 „ | 22 | + 6 | = | + 28 |
| 200 „ ... | 86 „ | 53 | + 2 | = | + 55 |
| 300 „ ... | 70 „ | 85 | + 4 | = | + 89 |
| 350 „ ... | 60 „ | 115 | — 11 | = | +104 |
| 400 „ ... | 50 „ | 150 | — 40 | = | +110 |
| 500 „ ... | 40 „ | 190 | — 72 | = | +118 |
| —— „ ... | — „ | | | | —— |
| 650 „ ... | 30 „ | 240 | —127 | = | +113 |
| 800 „ ... | 20 „ | 305 | —211 | = | + 94 |
| 1,000 „ ... | 10 „ | 385 | —340 | = | + 45 |

When seeking the maximum profit for the community, our producer will stop at a price of 40 öre and 500 passengers carried, by which the State certainly loses 72 kr., but the consumers, on the other hand, gain 190 kr. At the equilibrium of the free market (300 passengers at 70 öre) the State would have gained 4 kr., but the passengers only 85 kr.; at the monopoly price (104 öre) the state would have gained 6 kr., the passengers only 22 kr.

The appearance of the ideal price is due to the special condition that the general expenses only increase slightly with the increase of transport, while the expenses per unit are the same. If we had presumed that the general expenses had been unchanged, a calculation would have shown that the ideal equilibrium would be 30 öre and 650 passengers; in other words, the community derives the greatest advantage of a public undertaking, when the price is put at the approximate expenses per unit, provided that the general expenses only increase slightly with an extended use.

**119. State Management.**—When the expenses per unit are very low, and decrease with an increasing production, the controlling apparatus and collection may often be so costly that the community is the gainer by yielding the services free of charge, as the latter expenses, from a productive point of view, are wasted. We may now give the following rules for prices under State management.

(*a*) To sell below the expenses per unit causes a loss for the community unless the collection and controlling apparatus is very expensive.

(*b*) The maximum advantage for the community is when the plant is expensive, of long duration, and worn out more by the effect of weather than by use, that the State sells below its cost price, and approximately at the variable expenses per unit.

(*c*) The *gain* by the cheap sale falls to those who have the highest subjective prices; that is, on the *strictly necessary* units of the poor marginal buyers and on the excess consumption of the rich.

To the same extent, as the general expenses are the most important, it is correct to supply free of charge, and to the same extent as the variable expenses are the largest, it is correct to take full payment; as long as the expenses are not considerably increased by an increase of use, the community ought to be willing to bear the loss.

*Wicksell* points out that, as far as roads and bridges are concerned the use can be increased immensely from 100 to 10,000,000 people, without any considerable increase of the expense; once the bridge has been built, it is right that it should be employed as much as possible.

These considerations have increased validity where the use of a good is not in proportion to the user's income, but poor and rich consume approximately the same.

But the deficit in the State accounts must be covered by taxes. To return to our tables, in this case it must also be presumed, that the 190 kroner which the buyers gain also in utility, will more than balance the 72 kroner collected from the taxpayers. But, on the other hand, the persons who take advantage of the facilities in question must be compared with the persons who pay the tax; as long as rates are imposed on the consumption of essentials it is a doubtful gift to procure for the users the good produced by the state, for instance, a journey below the cost.

But the railways have also other purposes, for instance, to reclaim new agricultural land in the rayon of the centre of consumption; the gain through the railway will then appear, not as much from the dividends of the railway as on quite different accounts, for instance, those of industry which thereby obtains a cheaper transport of raw materials, or in the increase of land values in the regions through which the railway passes. It would therefore be reasonable to make the increasing land values bear the cost of establishment.

What has been stated here by a figure example can be illustrated by the following curves :—

The difference between Diagrams XXIV *a* and *b* is that the curve of demand (D) in one case is steep, in the other flat. The curve S states the falling average expenses; *g* is the number of passengers when the railway must pay, *n* when only the expenses per unit must be covered, $p_g$ is the natural market price = the average expenses with a production of *g* units, *e* is the average expenses for *n* units, the sale price of which is $p_n$ only. With a turnover of *g* units and a price of $p_g$ the consumer will gain the differential rent A; the railway will only have expenses covered. At a price of $p_n$ and the greater turnover of *n* the buyers will have in consumer's rent besides A also $G + N + B_g + B_n$, but the State, which produces at *e* and sells at $p_n$, will lose $B_g + B_n +$

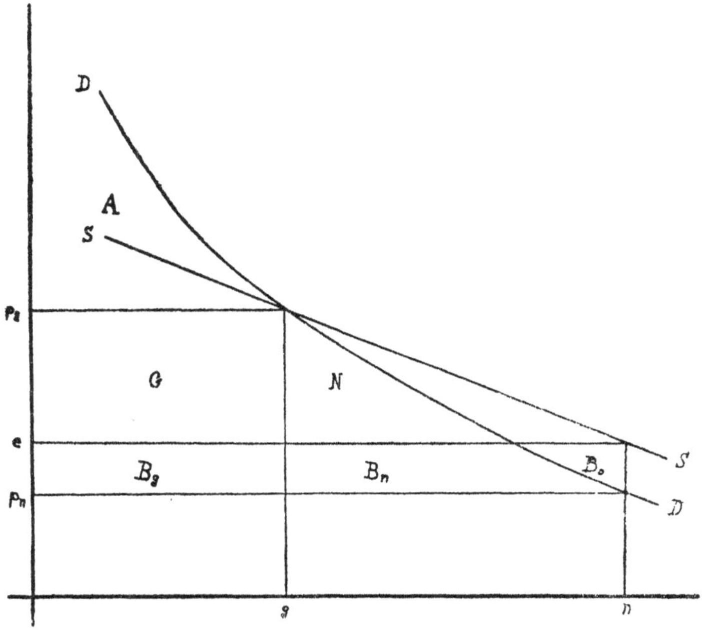


Diagram XXIVa

$B_o$, of which the previous consumers will gain $B_g$, and the new consumers $B_n$, while $B_o$ is completely lost; at the same time the additional users will gain N and the old ones will gain G (the latter on account of falling expenses). The community will gain G + N and lose $B_o$. With the flat curve of demand G + N will be much more than $B_o$; but if the curve is very steep $B_o$ will be larger than G + N (compare Diagram XXIV*b*).

*The more even the curve of demand and the greater the rate of fall in the technical curve of expenses*, the better will it pay from the social point of view to extend the production beyond the conditions of the free market.

As the State, in order to meet its expenses, must appropriate part of the income of the citizens, it has, of course, on the other hand the right to *exploit* a monopoly, and must in this case also consider who are the consumers of the produce of the State concern, and who will gain by paying less taxes on account of the profits of the monopoly. In this case the state is entitled to employ all the means which the monopolist employs in order to obtain a high price and at the same time keep expenses low; for

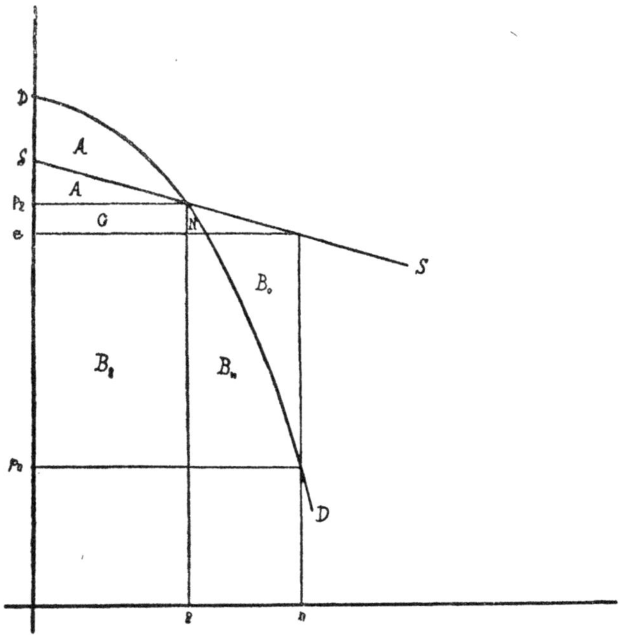

Diagram XXIVb

instance, divide its services into classes and its customers into groups, so that the service varies more in appearance than in substance and reality. Where the liking for social distinction comes into the enjoyment of the consumer, the State may, of course, by ornaments and packing, or by the place in rank or position, sort its goods in several qualities, in other words, sell part of its production at the highest price, which more than covers the loss by selling cheaply to those who are less able to pay. This has been done during the war; otherwise the State must often in this follow the rule to charge " what the traffic can bear "; this applies to freights, and we have further in this a criterion for the calculation of freights. The freight, as charged in proportion to the value of the commodity, is partly an expression for " what the traffic can bear "; if it is charged in proportion to volume and weight, it tends towards becoming a cost price, while on the other hand the low freights for marl probably correspond to Warming's ideal price. In the principle, " what the traffic can bear," is however not only considered the value of the commodity transported, but also the strength of the railway's monopoly in relation to the commodity; has the article other opportunity for transport; is the article itself monopolised, etc.?

Which policy to follow with regard to State monopolies will depend very much upon whether this is considered fiscally—*i.e.*, as a source of income for the State, or socially — *i.e.*, that the undertaking has been made a State monopoly for social advantage.

**120. Justum Pretium.**—The ideal price is not identical with "justum pretium," which comes nearest to being the price of the long market. The definition, however, does not cover exactly. During the war raw materials have often risen far beyond the price at which even the reduced supplies could be sold, if the powerful position the holder of raw materials could maintain in relation to the *other* productive factors did enable him to appropriate part of their normal profits. When ten factories all compete for a stock, which is only sufficient for seven, every one of them will bid more than they can strictly speaking, because the raw material will then not only represent the value which it adds to the good, but even the possibility of continuing production and retaining the *clientele*; the subjective price is therefore arrived at in the same manner as if I had both the blades of the scissors but wanted the screw to keep them together; in case of need I would then pay nearly the entire value of the scissors for the screw.

The retention of stocks by cornering in order to sell part at an overprice and then run the risk of losing on the stored quantities must be said to be "unjust and unreasonable restraint of trade."

The question which is often before the price regulating authorities is the following:—If 8 units can be procured at 4s. and the 9th at 10s. (and there are buyers at that price), should it then be permitted that not only the 9th unit, but also the remaining 8 are sold at 10s. In normal conditions the reply would be in the affirmative, as for a temporary inconvenience one would not regulate and interfere with the effects of the rule of indifference. Another matter is that the consideration that there must not be too flagrant a disproportion between profits and social usefulness, may lead to the said rise in price not being allowed—*i.e.*, that the State either expropriates the 9th unit and sells it at a loss (in this case it will often be necessary to ration in order to bring about an equilibrium between demand and supply) or imposes a tax on the remaining 8 units of 6s. each.

At the end of Book II. I have attempted to give a definition of " fair price " as a customary price, which does not alter the accustomed standard of living of the lower and middle classes. *Ashley* accepts the definition, that " just price " is a *normal price* which corresponds to the cost of production, in contradistinction to a price which is determined by the accidental chances of the market with the modification, however, that the cost of production is determined by a " fixed standard of living on the part of the producers."

*St. Thomas Aquinas* maintains in his *Summa Theologica* as the fundamental rule of exchange that the values exchanged are equivalent. It is unjust to sell a thing at a higher price than it is worth. On account of the special utility which the good may have for certain buyers, you must not increase the sale price ; for this utility is not inherent in the thing and does not concern the seller ; by taking a higher price for the special utility, I am selling something which I have no title to, and which does not belong to me. But by this he actually says that the vagaries of the short market (for instance, on account of war) create a utility for these goods on which the seller's action has had no influence, for which reason he has no right to make himself paid therefor. The exploitation of a monopoly of any nature, therefore, becomes a sin, as it is against " justum pretium " ; compare further the principle of " common law " that the price of services and goods of *general* importance must be " fair and reasonable " (harbours, tramways, railways, power and light-plants), but also for instance bakers and butchers.

**121. The Retail Monopoly.**—*The retail price* is often decided by custom—*i.e.*, is a fixed price which once was reasonable, as, for instance, when the boot dealer maintains the same price for his boots as when he made them himself, and thereby often earns *more* by retailing the machine-made boots than he did when he sold his own hand-made article; ( he individual net profit will, however, not be more, because competition has caused the boot store to keep a large stock and a smart shop).

If now an additional seller comes into the market, the price should fall according to general principles; as a rule, this does not happen, because the retailers find that the smaller turnover does not cover the unchanged general expenses, and therefore come to a tacit agreement to keep a higher price. The same applies to the various handicrafts, the addition of more people who are to exist by the trade, therefore, means that the general expenses for each must be distributed over a smaller quantity. The competition has therefore led to an increase in prices and often to an inferior quality because the competition in this case only acts through attempts to catch the eye and ear of the buyers, but not by supplying the best article, or by cheapness of price in proportion to quality. When free competition is no longer conducted on the principle of serving the public best, but on the principle—poorer goods or more advertising—*i.e.*, that the man who best can cheat the consumer will survive in the competition, free competition is no longer "the goad on the neck of the bullock," which make the producers eager to serve "His Highness the Consumer," but a blinding hood thrown over the head of a consumer who actually is not able to judge his own interest. Competition in relation to the consumer is too often substituted by the *common intention* of the retailers, created by their common need, to drive up the prices, and this is far more effective than any positive cartel agreement, because the reduced turnover is the incentive forcing each of them to do so. For the small artisans with a certain total turnover (bakers) for the suppliers of services, the limits for extension of which is rather restricted (lawyers, brokers) and often for the trade (merchants, intermediaries and retailers) the free access to the trade does *not* mean the same as free competition, because the necessity of everyone obtaining a living entails a tacit agreement to increase prices in the same manner as a cartel, which simply increases the price of and distributes a limited production. It is peculiar that where the multitude of retailers fixes a high profit on sales, the large concerns do not attempt to beat down the price. The large department stores of Copenhagen must—apart from certain specially advertised articles—be said to keep even higher prices than the middle-sized retail shops. The competition between insurance companies indirectly forces premiums up, through the competition for clever agents who must be enticed by ever-increasing commission Something similar is the case with the wholesalers, the number of whom is often too large, and who in certain cases superfluously interpose themselves between the factory and the retailer (for instance, between miller and baker).

Both the public and the private monopoly are still at an early stage of development. What is outlined here in an experimental and scattered manner must in the future be approved of or rejected when put to the test of facts. The day will come when the theory of value under monopoly, if it is to treat all the possible cases of exploitation, will be quite a comprehensive volume, and even of the proportions of a Bible, when not only the theory of distribution under monopoly, but also its *financing* is included—that is, when the conditions for trade in the free market will only be treated as *propaedeutics*, because they will be the exception, and for study only the means to understand the ruling manipulated market.

## CHAPTER XX

### Connected Prices

**122. Competing Demand.**—In Chapter XI we found that the simple price rules in a number of cases do not unconditionally hold good. We cannot always start with a schedule of demand, found directly through a valuation of utility, and compare this to a schedule of supply, arisen from prices fixed for the technical components required to produce the good. A thing will in many cases either in demand or in supply be connected with others—*i.e.*, their conditions of production, schedules of demand or market conditions are interacting or directly interdependent.

By *competing demand* the same thing is subject to demand from several mutually independent sides, owing to different applicabilities, so that the appearance of a new applicability or the alteration of one already existing will immediately alter the state of the market for the article.

Suppose that our article has only one employment, for which the schedule of demand is 13, 11, 9, 7, 6 and 5s., at a price of 9s. only 3 units can be sold, and a sale of 6 units presumes a price of 5s. Suppose that a new employment, B, arises, and that the schedule of demand for the article for this purpose is 16, 15, 14, 10, 9, 8, 7 and 6s., a price of 9s. would entail a turnover of 3 units to A and 5 to B, in all, 8 units, and, as will appear from the composite schedule of the two employments, 6 units will attain a price of 10s. or 5s. more than was the price when the article could only be employed in the one way, A. The joint schedule will be 16, 15, 14, 13, 11, 10, 9, 9, 8, 7, 6, 6, 5s. If the schedule of supply is constant, the increased applicability will, in the long run, simply lead to an increased turnover at unchanged prices, if it is falling, the greater applicability may even lead to *lower prices in spite of* the increased turnover ; but if the schedule of supply is rising, the greater applicability will not only lead to a higher price at the first moment, but also when the conditions of production have adjusted themselves to the new demand. If the schedule of supply is 4, 4, 5, 5, 6, 6, 7, 7, 7, 7, 8 and 9s., there must, as long as A is the only employment, be sold 5 units at 6s., but when employment, B, is added, the turnover will be 11 units at a price of 7s. While all 5 units sold previously were bought by A, only 4 of the 11 are now bought by A, but 7 by B—*i.e.*, the appearance of B has caused that some units have been taken away from their previous employment.

If a tax is put upon one employment, because this is considered detrimental or superfluous (for instance, a tax on horses for luxury, on silk for dress) the demand for this application will be reduced by the amount of the tax. We will therefore have a smaller sale of the article, accompanied by a fall in price, which in the case of decreasing return will continue; of what is now sold, the employment, which has not been taxed, will claim a larger quantity.

Competing demand is of most importance for raw materials; we have shown on page 155 how the appearance of a new finished article, in which the raw material may form a component, will inflate the joint schedule of demand for the raw material.

**123. Joint Demand.**—Suppose two goods, A and B, which supplement one another, and the use of enjoyment of one of which cannot be realised, unless the other is also at our disposal. Suppose now the joint schedule of demand for the pair of goods to be 10, 9, 8, 7 and 6s. for from 1 to 5 pairs (compare Sec. 64). If the article A is produced at 4s. and the article B at 3s., 4 units will be bought of each at the total price of 7s. The conditions of production of the goods will decide how the total price of demand must be distributed between the two goods, which stand in complementary relation to one another. The joint prices of demand are split up into two, of which one is a function of the other. If the price of A is fixed, the price of B will be the difference between the schedule and the price of A. The schedule is given below:—

| JOINT SCHEDULE OF DEMAND. | SCHEDULE OF SUPPLY A + B. |
|---|---|
| 10 | 4 + 3 |
| 9 | 4 + 3 |
| 8 | 4 + 3 |
| 7 | 4 + 3 |
| 6 | 4 + 3 |
| — | — — |

If A's expenses are increased from 4s. to 5s., the schedule of B would be 10 — 5, 9 — 5, 8 — 5 and 7 — 5s. instead if 10 — 4, 9 — 4, 8 — 4 and 7 — 4s.—*i.e.*, the 4th unit of B would be demanded at 2s. only, not as before at 3s.; we must go back as far as the 3rd unit of B (8 — 5) in order to arrive at a price, which will cover expenses. Consequently only 3 units of both goods are sold, as against 4 units in the first instance, but A's price has been increased by 1s.

An increase in the cost of production of one good will then cause a reduction in the sale of both goods. The equilibrium equation is $p_n = a_n + b_n$, in which $a_n$ and $b_n$ are the marginal cost of the goods A and B, and $p_n$ the joint marginal price of demand. If $a_n$ is increased the equilibrium is disturbed, and the turnover decreases for A as well as for B.

If A's expenses are reduced, the schedule of demand for B will rise, and the sale of A and B will be increased to the same extent; the price of B will at once be increased, and the increase will be maintained if B is produced under the rule of decreasing return, but is substituted by a fall if B is produced under increasing return.

The demand for the handle of a knife is, for instance, equal to the price of demand for the finished knife, less the cost of production of knife blades. If the cost of production of the latter is increased, the price of demand for knife handles will fall; this will entail a reduction in the production of handles, and, some time later, also in the production of blades.

This can be graphically stated as follows:—

In Diagram XXV, the mutually independent curves of supply for three goods are given, A and B being produced under decreasing and C under increasing return; the curves. for the first two goods are rising; for the latter the curve is falling.

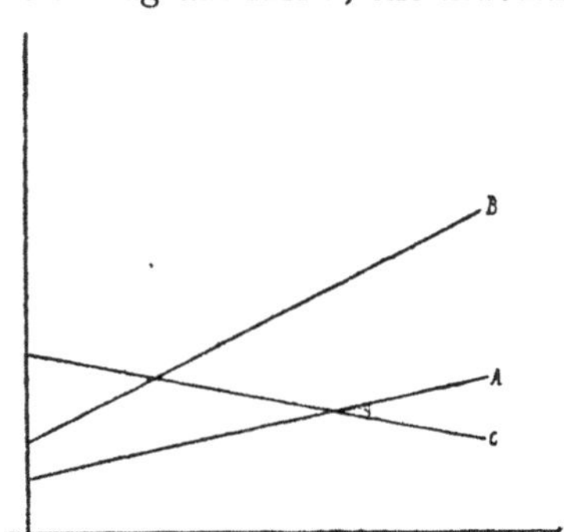

Diagram XXV

Suppose, now, that there is a joint demand, D, for the pair of goods, A and B; in Diagram XXVI we then first draw the curve of the good A; with this for basis we draw the curve for B, so that this line

($B_1$ in Diagram XXVI) is at the same distance from A as B in Diagram XXV was from the base. $B_1$ therefore states the total expense in producing varying quantities of the pair of goods A + B. D now intersects $B_1$ at *b*; *n* units of each of the components of the pair of goods will be produced; the cost of production of A will be *n a*, of B *a b*, and of A + B, *n b*.

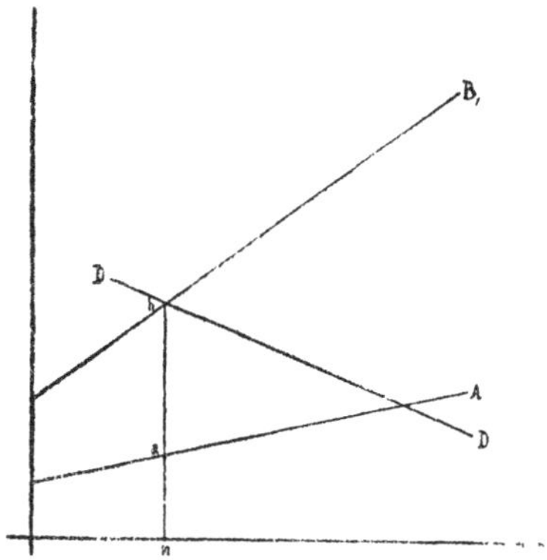


Diagram XXVI

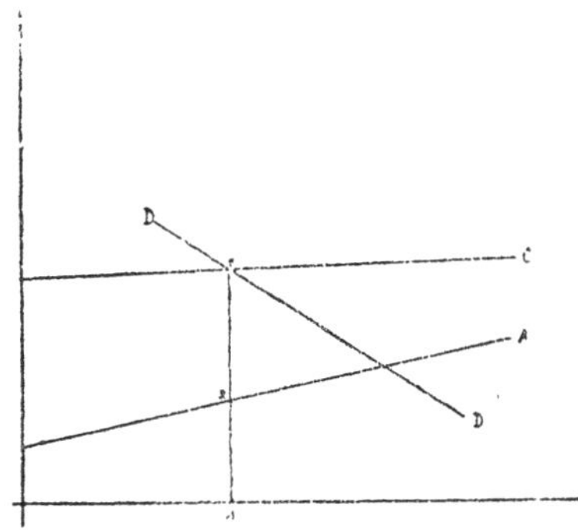


Diagram XXVII

In Diagram XXVII D is directed against the pair of goods, A + C; again we first draw A, and with this as basis C at the same distance from A as C was from the base in Diagram XXV, and we call this curve $C_1$; it appears not to be falling; that it actually is will be apparent from the fact that the distance between the two curves is decreasing. D intersects $C_1$ at *c*; *n* units are produced of A and of C, the cost of A is *a . n*, of $C_1$ *a . c*, and the marginal cost of the pair of goods is *n . c*. Where one component has a falling and the other a rising curve, the joint curve of supply of the pair of goods will approximately be constant. (The student will, by varying the form of the curves, and by comparing the demand for A + B to the demand for A + C, and by increasing the demand or imposing a tax on the three goods, find information on many interesting points.)

A tax on one good will, presuming that none of the two goods can be used in other compositions, act as if the tax had been put on the other good with regard to the sale of both goods and to their joint market price, and even as a tax on the pair of goods as such. It is immaterial in this connection on which of the components the tax is imposed, or whether this is imposed on the pair of goods.

If the mutually supplementing goods are raw materials, the tax on one of the goods is distributed in such a way that, by reducing the price of the other raw material, it is partly shifted on to the supplier of this, and will not entirely be paid by the consumer of the finished article of which both are components.

The commodity A may be supplementary to two other goods, B and C; together with B A satisfies one demand, together with C another. Suppose, for instance, the schedule of demand for A + B to be 10, 9, 8, 7 and 6s., and for A + C, 13, 12, 11, 10, 9, 8s. If, now, A is produced at 5s., B at 4s., and C at 3s., 2 units will be sold of B, 6 units of C and 6 + 2 = 8 units of A. If, now, a tax of 1s. per unit is imposed upon A, the turnover of B and C, as well as that of A, will be reduced, in the present case tol unit of B, 5 units of C, and 5 + 1 units of A.

If, now, A is produced under the rule of increasing return, a tax may cause an increase of price which amounts to more than the tax on A, and thereby cause a still further reduction in the sales of B and C. If $b$ units of B are sold and $c$ units of C, and, consequently, $b + c$ units of A, the following conditions of equilibrium must hold good: the subjective price for the composite good A + B of the $b$-th buyer must be equal to the marginal cost of producing $b + c$ units of A, with the addition of the marginal cost of $b$ units of B. The subjective price of demand of the $c$-th buyer for the good A + C must be equal to the marginal cost of production of $b + c$ units of A with the addition of the marginal cost of production of $c$ units of C. An increase in the cost of B will reduce the production of B and of A, but not of C; if, however, A is produced under increasing return, the price of A may also rise, and the sale of C also decrease, provided that the price of the combination A + C is increased.

We may now advance the rule that the value of the elements in a group of goods, which are related in production, is determined by their marginal value in each of their compositions, and they *must* be distributed in such a manner that this holds good.

A monopoly on one of two goods, which supplement one another, entails a reduction in the sale of both goods. Concerning the price we have the important rule that *the monopolist of the article A may fix his price at such a level that he obtains the same monopoly profit as he would have obtained if he alone controlled the output of both goods.* With a schedule of demand for A + B of 10, 9, 8, 7, and 6s., and a cost of production of A of 4s., of B 3s., the total *monopoly* price, if our producer commands the output of A and B, will be 9s., at which two pairs of goods can be sold.

If, now, he commands the good A, and the price of B, as decided by free competition, is still 3s., and if he puts the sale price of A at 6s., at which 2 units can then be sold, the monopoly profit will be 2 . 6 — 2 . 4 = 4s., *i.e.*, the same profit as if he had commanded both components.

It is immaterial to the public which of the two goods are commanded by a monopolist, or whether both are. The same will apply, even if the prices of the schedule of supply are falling and not constant, as presumed in this.

If I have the monopoly on the millstones by which the grain *must* be ground and there is no substitute for the stones, I may actually appropriate the possible monopoly of the baker and miller, and partly that of the farmer, as no corn to be ground can reach the public except through me.

Joint demand is also met with on other points than where it is immediately apparent; while tea and coffee may be substituted for one another, sugar is supplementary to the two. When American firms in East Asia have common agents for ink, nibs and writing paper, which are produced in separate factories, this is due to their realisation of the fact that these goods are in complementary relations to one another; while books and cycles stand in substitutionary relations to one another, cycles and summer restaurants are in complementary relation to one another. In this another rule comes in and counteracts the rule, that the increase in price of a thing reduces the price of demand for the complementary article—*i.e.*, that the demand for a thing, which has a complementary product, will also create a demand for the latter. An increase in the price of cigars will create a chance for pipe tobacco and cause an increase in the price of this, but also in the price of pipes. This is not against the natural rule that an increase in the price of tobacco will drive down the price of the pipe, for this holds good only for an unchanged demand and presuming that the increase in the price of tobacco is due to an alteration in the supply; while what happens when the demand is changed from cigars to pipe tobacco is an increase of the joint demand, by which, of course, the pipe as well as the tobacco will benefit.

**124. Competing Supply.**—In Sec. 66 we found the rule for the connection between two goods, which essentially cover the same demand; if $h$ units are produced of the finer quality and $s$ units of the second, the price of the latter must be determined by the total output $(h + s)$ of both goods. (The price of a thing of second quality will on the separate market be the same, when there are, say, 15 units on the market, however these are distributed between the two qualities.)

The price of the simpler good corresponds to what the $h + s$-th *buyer will pay* for the substitute, if there were no goods of a finer grade; while the following conditions must at the same time be fulfilled—*i.e.*, that the price of the second quality *must correspond to the necessary cost of this quality when* s *units are produced, and* the price of the first quality must firstly *cover the necessary cost of this quality when* h *units are to be produced* and secondly *correspond to the price obtained for the substitute* (X) *with the addition of the amount, by which the marginal buyer of the finer good expresses the difference in utility, which he attributes to the first quality in preference to the second.*

The best situated and most eager purchasers will always have all the goods of the first quality; if there are so many units of the main good that the less well situated can have some thereof, they may obtain some, and the price of the main good will then be put so low that the poor are able to buy; this will, in the long run, only be possible in case the cost of production is also sufficiently low; the substitute may then be used less or completely disappear.

The cheapening of the cost of production of the first quality will cause that whole classes of buyers leave off buying the substitute; an increase in price of the main article will make the marginal buyers thereof purchase the substitute instead. This may, in contradistinction to the main good, lose customers of the best situated as well as of the poorest. If the price of the substitute is increased, the poorest buyers thereof must reduce their consumption, and at the same time some of the better situated buyers will turn to the finer good. Goods which have a substitute have their marginal consumers on the margin between two classes, and the substitute has its first consumers placed in a similar manner.

In the figure example in Sec. 66 we have found an equilibrium, because when the schedule of demand for the essential consumption (which is satisfied also by the substitute) is 10, 9, 8, 8, 7, 7, 6, 6, and 5s., and the additional schedule for the difference in utility yielded by the main article is 6, 5, 4, 3, 3, 2, 1, 7 units of the second grade will be sold at a price of 5s. (which corresponds to the presumed cost) and 2 units of the first grade at 10s. (the cost of this grade = the price of the substitute + the additional price of the second buyer).

If the cost of the first quality falls to 9s., 3 units can be sold of the first quality at 9s. (= 5 + 4s.) and 6 of the second quality at 5s., as the total sales still cannot amount to more than 9 units, 5s. being the price of the 9th buyer, if there is no main article.

(In this we leave out of consideration the fact that the purchasing power of the buyers of the first quality will increase as they obtain their article so much cheaper than the price they would be willing to pay (for instance, the first buyer would be willing to pay 10s. for the second quality and further 6s. for the advantage of obtaining the first quality instead, 16s. > 10s.) ; the consequent fall in $u_{pm}$ makes the addition somewhat larger than the original 6, 5, 3, 3, 2, and 1s.)

If, now, the cost of the substitute ($x$) is increased from 5s. to 6s. for instance, through a tax of 1s., only 8 units of both goods can be sold in our example from Sec. 66 (6s. being the 8th buyer's price of demand) ; as $x$ is increased by 1s., the subjective prices for the main good must also be increased by 1s. to 12, 11, 10, 9, 8 and 7s. ; as long as only 2 units are in the market of this quality, the price will be 11s. ; but presuming that the cost of production is still 10s., the market will *in the long run* again adjust itself, and 3 units will be produced at 10s., which will be sold as well as 5 units of the second quality at 6s. The substitute has *lost* 2 *units*, one to the main good, and one which *completely disappears from the consumption.* If the cost of the substitute had remained unchanged at 5s. while that of the main good had been increased to 11s., the latter would lose 1 unit to the substitute, the price of which in the first instance would rise, but, presuming that the cost remained 5s., would in the long run drop again to 5s., but with an *increased turnover*.

Finally, we have during the war seen examples of the substitute completely failing (margarine) ; then the following alteration will take place in the schedule of demand for the main good, through the fact that $x$ (the price of the substitute) is substituted by what each of the buyers would have given also for the original satisfaction yielded by the substitute (the brackets state the prices of demand for the main good, when the price of the substitute, $x = 5$s.)

Column 1 is the curve of the original satisfaction, Column 2 the curve of additional utility both expressed in money.

$$10 + 6 = 16 \ (11)$$
$$9 + 5 = 14 \ (10)$$
$$8 + 4 = 12 \ (9)$$
$$8 + 3 = 11 \ (8)$$
$$7 + 3 = 10 \ (8)$$
$$7 + 2 = 9 \ (7)$$
$$6 + 1 = 7 \ (6)$$
$$6 + 0 = 6 \ (5)$$
$$5 + 0 = 5 \ (5)$$

Presuming that there are 2 units on the market, the price will, in the first instance, rise from 5 + 5 to 9 + 5s., what the second buyer would actually be willing to pay for the utility of the substitute with the addition of the further utility supplied by the finer good. If the main good can still be produced at 10s., the price will gradually fall back, so that 5 units will be sold, but if the supply of the main good cannot be increased, the price must remain at 14s. as long as the substitute cannot be procured, which will yield the producer of the first grade an extra profit of 14 — 10s. per unit; in other words, of the two prices, which make up the price of demand of the main good, the schedule of additional price will remain as before, but instead of $x$ (the price of the substitute) will be added what the buyers would actually pay for the satisfaction yielded by the substitute.

We may add that the question can be further complicated, if the production of one of the goods is subject to the rules of increasing or decreasing return. An increase in the price of the main good, by forcing the consumers to buy the substitute, may make possible an increased production of this, possibly at a lower cost than before. The effect of the increase in price of the main good or a tax on this will then in the first instance be that the price of the substitute will be increased, but in the long run that it may even fall *below* what it was before, and that the sale may even increase by more than the quantity gained from the main good.

If the main good is produced under the rule of decreasing expenses, a tax on the second quality, by increasing the possibilities for sale of the first grade and consequently also the production, will certainly increase the price of this in the first instance, but in the long run lead to a decline in price. If the main good is subject to the rule of increasing expenses, a tax on the substitute will lead to an increase in the price of the main good, not only immediately, but also in the long run. If, for instance, the supplies of vegetable products, from which oil may be extracted, should fail, the greater consumption of butter could probably only be satisfied at a higher cost per lb.

Suppose that a holder of monopoly in our example increased the price of the main good from 9 to 10s., reducing the turnover to 2 units ; after a temporary increase in price of the substitute, this would settle down at the old price with an increased turnover ; a monopoly on a thing, which has a substitute, is therefore not so very dangerous.

If, however, a substitute is monopolised, and pieviously 6 units had been produced and sold at 5s., and the holder of the monopoly will sell at 7s. only, he will, in the first instance, sell 3 units only ; but at the same time the demand for the main good is increased, because $x$ is increased from 5s. to 7s., and therefore makes the schedule of demand for the first 6 units of the main good read, 13, 12, 11, 10, 10 and 9s. ; if, now, the cost of production of this is unchanged (9s.) 6 units will be sold instead of 3 ; if, now, the producer of the substitute will continue to sell 3 units, there will be on the market 9 units in all of both grades ; but this means that the 7th, 8th and 9th buyer should buy the substitute, which they are not able to, because their marginal price is below 7, *i.e.*, the production of the substitute must be further reduced. Where the prices of the two goods come relatively near to one another, the monopoly on the substitute *cannot* therefore be exploited to any great advantage, as some customers are driven out of the market, and others will use the first grade ; only where there is a material difference between the cost of production of the two goods, and where the curve of demand for the substitute is very steep can the monopoly be made lucrative ; compare, for instance, the monopoly on chicory.

The relations between the substitute and the fine article are illustrated by the proportion between the different rents which are demanded for flats or shops. A town is divided into zones; if the price of a shop in Tooting is £50 and a shop in Oxford Street of the same size and outfit will yield the holder £100 more income, the latter is worth £150.

We may illustrate the comparison between two zones graphically by Diagram XXVIII.

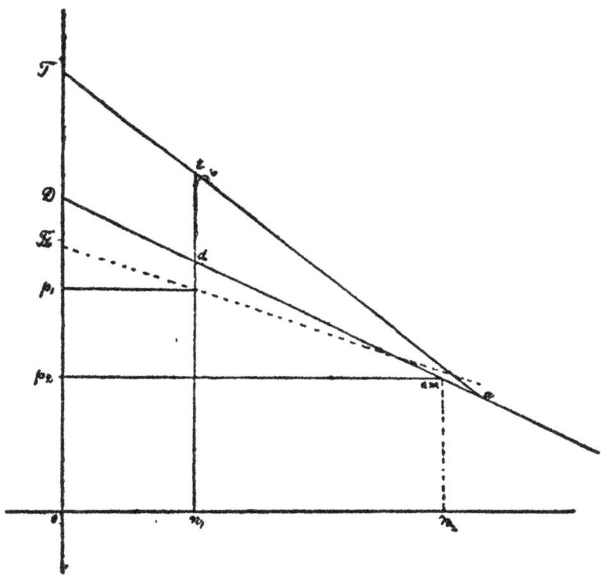

Diagram XXVIII

Suppose the cost of erection to be $o\,p_2$; suppose the land in the second zone to be no-rent land; the house-rent in this zone will then in the long run be equal to the cost of building ($o\,p_2$). Further the number of rooms in the first zone is $= n_1$; the curve D states the price of demand of the tenants for housing accommodation in the second zone, while the curve T states the addition which each separate tenant would pay for living in the first zone. First we mark off $o\,p_2$ along the ordinate. By drawing a line parallel to the base from $p_2$ we find the point n the curve of demand where the subjective price is equal to $o\,p_2$; by this we find $n_2$, *i.e.*, the number of tenants who will be accepted at this price From the point $n_1$(which states the marginal tenant in the first zone, as determined by the existing accommodation) we draw a parallel to the ordinate up to the curve T. We now know that an overprice can be obtained for accommodation in the first zone, as expressed by the difference between T and D for the first tenant and, for instance, the difference between $t$ and $d$ for the $n_1$-th tenant. We must then deposit the triangle D T$a$ on the line $p_2m$, and thereby we obtain the new curve T$b$, by which we express the *now* altered subjective prices of the tenants for accommodation in the first zone; where the line $n_1t$ intersects the dotted curves T$b$ we find the rent in the first zone, which is $p_1$.

The above diagram illustrates the relations between substitutes and finer goods also for other cases than housing accommodation. With regard to variations in the prices of dwellings I would further refer to my book, *Land Taxes and Land Prices*.

A peculiar case arises when the good in one application is a substitute and in another is the main article. Suppose that in ordinary conditions 10 units are produced, of which 2 are indispensable for medical use, while 8 are employed as an unimportant substitute, which only fetches a low price, for instance, 1s., while the price of the corresponding finer article is 5s. Suppose, now, that a scarcity arises so that only 2 units can be produced, which are indispensable and are bought by the chemists at the very high price of 10s.; the previously despised substitute has become more expensive than the good which it substituted.

The cheaper article is said to substitute the finer; not only separate goods, but entire groups may substitute one another. Not only different kinds of meat, but fish and meat and even meat and vegetables substitute one another; wool and cotton, petroleum and electric light, paintings and colour prints may substitute one another. In production several raw materials may, as a rule, substitute one another, as also mechanical power and human labour. The war has shown the endless possibilities for substitution in consumption as well as in production of goods, which it would hardly be thought possible could have substitutes.

The appearance of a substitute is of importance for many by practically increasing their purchasing power; the cost of the substitute is perhaps less than was the cost of the main good—*i.e.*, more is left to be spent on other articles; it may also happen that the introduction of a substitute may create quite new consumers who could not afford the main article. The appearance of the substitute may thus alter the marginal utility of income upwards as well as downwards.

In some cases the substitute actually represents less enjoyment, but in many cases it is only prejudice that causes a difference between the value of an article and its substitute; in this case the introduction of the latter is an actual gain for the community, acting as a cheapening of the satisfaction of the demand in question (*cf.* the introduction of "coney seal skin").

**125. Joint Supply.**—Joint supply is present when several goods which satisfy different demands are manufactured by the same process, some goods being by-products. Perhaps 100 different goods are extracted from coal and petroleum, and they continually change in relative importance; the progress of chemistry creates every day new applicability for hitherto valueless refuse. When slaughtering animals this fact has always been appreciated; the cost of the animal must be distributed over skin, horn, chest, shoulder, back, head, tongue, the liver and lungs, the entrails, blood, etc.; the increasing scarcity of foodstuffs in connection with an increasing ability to employ every part of the animal has turned refuse, which might even be troublesome, into valuable products; the manufacture of cheese rennet has turned calves' stomachs into a valuable good. What was previously refuse has become a by-product and has in some cases even almost become the main article.

Suppose now that a certain good A has the following schedule of demand; 12, 10, 9, 8, 7, and 6s. for from 1 to 6 units; if now the cost of producing 1 unit is 10s., 2 units will be sold.

It now proves, however, that a hitherto neglected by-product B can be used, and that the schedule of demand for this is as follows:—5, 4, 3, 2, 2, and 1s. for from 1 to 6 units. In the production of 2 units at 10s. the producer will obtain 2 units of the good B, which may be sold at 4s.; in other words, his gross income has been increased to 14s. This will tempt him and others to continue the production until the total of both prices of demand is equal to the cost of production; finally 4 units of the good A will be sold at a price of 8s., and 4 units of the good B at a price of 2s. The employment of the by-product has therefore caused an increased turnover and a cheapening of the good A.

The schedules are given below :—

| SCHEDULE OF DEMAND. A + B | THE TOTAL COST OF PRODUCTION OF THE SCHEDULE OF SUPPLY. |
|---|---|
| 12 + 5s. | 10s. |
| 10 + 4s. | 10s. |
| 9 + 3s. | 10s. |
| 8 + 2s. | 10s. |
| —— | —— |
| 7 + 2s. | 10s. |
| 6 + 1s. | 10s. |

If now the applicability of the by-product is increased, so that the schedule of demand for this is extended, for instance, to 6, 5, 4, 3, 3 and 2s., the sale of both goods will increase ; in our example 5 units will now be sold of the good A at 7s. and 5 units of the good B at 3s. ; in other words, on account of the greater applicability of the by-product the sale of the good A has been increased, the price has fallen and the sale of the by-product B has been increased with a rise in price. Provided that the goods are produced under the rule of increasing return, it is possible that the increase will entail a lower cost of production and a further increase of the turnover ; the price of both goods will then fall as an effect of the increased demand for the by-product.

If the cost of production is increased, the sale of both goods will decrease and their price will rise ; a tax on one of the two goods produced in the process will, of course, affect the price of the other good, because it has the effect of an increase in the total cost of production. The condition of equilibrium is : $a_n + b_n = s_n$ in which $a_n$ and $b_n$ are the $n$-th buyer's prices for each of the two goods, and $s_n$ is the marginal cost of producing $n$ units of the joint product.

It must be remembered that every good has its own schedule, and that the form of one may be steep and that of another flat ; how the altered cost will affect the turnover will depend upon this, as well as which of the two goods will fall most in price. Above we have taken the clear case ; but most frequently several goods which are produced jointly have only part of the expenses in common, and the by-product may, for instance, require further working up, and the expenses of this must therefore be deducted from that price of demand of the by-product which forms a factor of the total demand.

In *joint production* we must consequently distribute the common expenses over each of the goods produced jointly. Very few goods are not manufactured in joint production, and have in any case some expenses in common, for instance, when several goods are produced in the same factory; also in agriculture the different crops are produced in rotation—*i.e.*, in joint production. In the distribution of goods, and especially in the forwarding business, where the transport of goods of various descriptions and passengers are effected by services which may only partly be separated, or by transport of goods from two towns on the same railway line to a common centre, the same relations will again be present. The solution, "what the traffic can bear," remains the most practical, modified by social considerations, as the expenses caused by yielding a certain service can only be found out as far as a small part is concerned—*i.e.*, the varying expenses per unit.

When the schedule of demand for one of the goods is steep, it may sometimes pay to destroy the last units of the good in question; the monopolist will then attempt to sell the two goods in different quantities—*i.e.*, in another proportion than the one in which they are produced; this particularly applies where the production comes under the rule of increasing return.

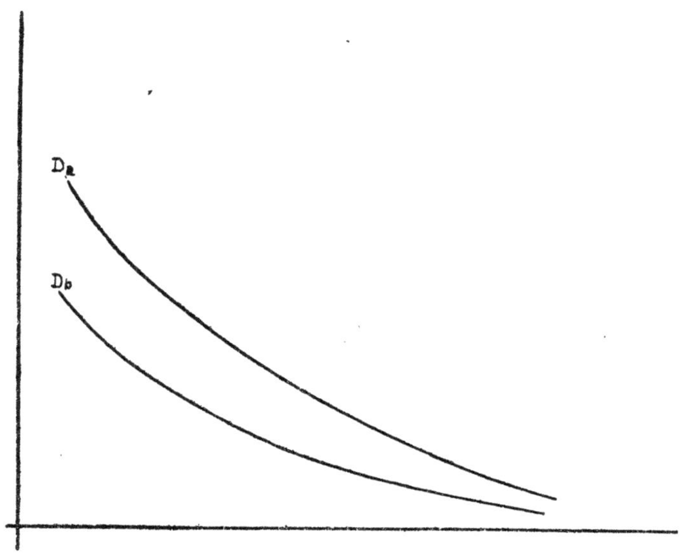


Diagram XXIXa

In joint production the monopoly has a very enormous number of possibilities to choose between in its search for the maximum profit, because the different goods each have their own schedule of demand.

We presume that each time when a unit of A is produced, a unit of B will also be produced at a total expense stated by the curve S in Diagram XXIX*b*. We now take the two curves of demand for the goods in Diagram XXIX*a* $D_a$ and $D_b$, and draw the curve $D_b$, with the curve $D_a$ as basis; the curve $D_{a+b}$ in Diagram XXIX*b* then states what the producer obtains for each pair, consisting of 1 unit of the good A and 1 unit of the good B. Where the topmost curve and the curve of supply intersect we find the market condition.

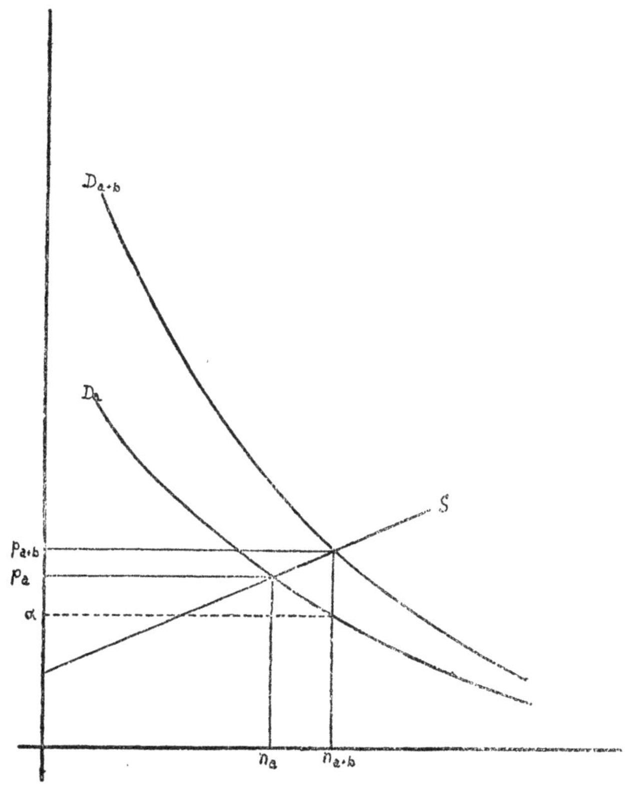


Diagram XXIXb

If only the good A of the joint product can be sold, the price of this will be $p_a$ and the sale $n_a$. Now the by-product B is introduced; $n_{a+b}$ units of A and $n_{a+b}$ units of B are now produced. The price of A will now be $a < p_a$; the price of B will be $p_{a+b} - a$. As shown by the diagram, $p_{a+b}$ is the marginal cost of $n_{a+b}$ units of production, and at the same time the sum of the marginal prices of the two goods.

**126. Petroleum.**—*Ussing* points out in his book on petroleum the possibilities of application of the raw oil; from this is produced oil for illumination, for lubrication and for motors. Further the raw oil may be used for motors, without refining. This has the following consequences :—

" 1. The raw oil is much *cheaper*, the price per lb. before the war being between 1d. and 1⅜d., while that of petroleum was between 1¾d. and 2¼d.

" 2. By using the raw oil the *refining monopoly*, which is the most important point in the organisation of the oil production, *is avoided*.

" 3. The increased demand for raw oil only *indirectly* affects the price of the refined product by increasing the price of the former."

Concerning the character of the demand he states :—

" 1. *Decreasing* demand for petroleum for *illumination* in Western and Northern Europe and the United States, *increasing* demand in states which are less far developed; generally a certain, although slow, increase in the world consumption of petroleum for illumination can be expected.

" 2. *Strongly increasing* demand for petroleum for *technical* use; this development causes that the *total* consumption of petroleum is not reduced in the more developed countries either.

" 3. Strongly increasing consumption of *raw and by-products*, especially fuel and lubricating oil and motor spirit."

*Considered jointly all this must have price-increasing effects.*

*Ussing* further states, with regard to the increasing use of benzine—which was previously a valueless by-product—that according to general principles it would be presumed that the introduction of benzine would force the price of petroleum down; the opposite is the case.

" Inasmuch as the quantity of raw oil in any case cannot be

increased except at increased expenses, while at the same time the *refining* may be varied in such a way that, more or less respectively of petroleum and benzine is obtained from the same quantity of raw oil, *the two products will compete for the raw oil,* and the strong demand for benzine and the higher prices thereof will then *force the prices of raw oil upwards and, consequently, also the price of petroleum* '

The postulate that the producer is able to increase profits, presuming it is possible to alter the proportion between the main and the by-product, by increasing the latter at the expense of the former, is only *partly* correct. The fact is that if we produce from each unit of the base product, not 1A and 1B, but ½A and 1½B, we arrive at the following schedule :—

| | | | | |
|---|---|---|---|---|
| 1st | unit of the base product yields | | | $\frac{1}{2}A_1 + (1B_1 + \frac{1}{2}B_2)$ |
| 2nd | ,, | ,, | ,, | $\frac{1}{2}A_1 + (\frac{1}{2}B_2 + 1B_3)$ |
| 3rd | ,, | ,, | ,, | $\frac{1}{2}A_2 + (1B_4 + \frac{1}{2}B_5)$ |
| 4th | ,, | ,, | ,, | $\frac{1}{2}A_2 + (\frac{1}{2}B_5 + 1B_6)$, etc. |

The foot number states the place of the good in the schedule of demand.

In producing 1½ units of B instead of 1 unit in each unit of production we will arrive at a comparatively large production of B from a relatively small number of units of production, and, consequently, B can be sold at a low price only. In working up 6 units of the base product, we thus obtain 3 units of A and 9 units of B instead of 6 units of each. Therefore the question must arise for the producer : Is $3a_3 + 9b_9 > 6a_6 + 6b_6$ ($a_3$ and $a_6$ being the third and sixth buyer's price of demand for A, $b_6$ and $b_9$ the sixth and ninth buyer's price of demand for B, $a_3 > a_6$, $b_9 < b_6$. From this it will be apparent that the following conditions must be present to make Ussing's statement correct.

1. A must have a steep and B a flat curve of demand (unless the curve of B is higher than that of A right through) so that a reduction in the quantity of A will greatly increase the price thereof. The greater the difference in the rate of fall of the curves the better will it pay to substitute the production of B for that of A.

2. The producer must have a monopoly. If this is not the case he will, of course, adjust his production of the two goods in proportion to the market prices ; *but* if he is a sufficiently large producer, he will beat down the price of B by increasing the production thereof at the expense of A.

Under these two conditions the manufacturer will *not only gain* by altering his production in favour of the previous by-product, but he will force the price of the main product upwards, and will finally, in certain cases, gain by employing more units of production (in the present case raw oil) than before.

(The student is advised to make experiments ; take a schedule of demand for petroleum and benzine, but suppose the latter to be on a higher level than the former, starting the schedule of petroleum at, say, 30s., and that of benzine at 32s.

Then we presume that from each unit of production 4 gallons are produced (3 gallons of petroleum and 1 gallon of benzine) and we also presume an increasing cost for each gallon of raw oil, say 50, 55, 65, 70, 75 and 80s.

We now first find the market price and the monopoly price, presuming that the benzine cannot be employed, and afterwards the prices when the benzine becomes useable and has a schedule of demand. We now make the same productive unit produce 2P and 2B instead of 3P and 1B, and find the monopoly price.)

**127. The Derived Price.**—Only as an exception is the indirect price the same as the price of the good actually desired ; as a rule, it will take time to realise the good, the utility of which is indirect, as the utility-giving good (by exchange or manufacturing), and consequently a time and risk account must be deducted from the price of this.

The indirect price, however, does not come within personal economics and does not rest on a valuation of utility, because it is fixed by a *merchant*, who buys in order to re-sell ; his actual minimum price is the producer's price, and what he at most will pay for the good himself is determined by the buyer's prices. The brain of a merchant is like a concave mirror, which reflects a distorted picture ; the producer's price is represented by him in increased proportions, the customer's price of demand in diminished measurement.

When the good is bought in order to be re-sold unchanged, the merchant only adds time or place-utility ; often his activity consists in exploiting a monopoly position, to which he had had an idea that the good would come ; consequently, when he is a merchant only, we may say that the finished article has one technical *component* only ; when he adds form utility—*i.e.* manufactures the good which he buys, for instance, by his own labour, we say that the good has two *components* ; if, for instance, he adds raw materials together with labour and machine power, etc., the good has many components—*i.e.*, he buys the finished article in its dissolved condition in the shape of the separate components, and sells it in the finished condition. This must be emphasised, because we will then understand that for the modern producer the essential is not the *purely* technical, but the *mercantile* side of the question ; even the greatest manufacturer may be ignorant of the technique of a concern, but he *must* understand how to find the economically best composition of the technical components and to throw them into the right market. He is principally a merchant, for instance, not an *employer*, but a *purchaser of labour*.

When there are two components—say labour and raw material—the derived price is a difference : (1) Finished article, less Labour = Raw Material, and (2) Finished Article, less Raw Material = Labour, and finally (3) Finished Article = Labour + Raw Material. But all three forms are the same equation, in which there are two unknown factors. Only if we know the price of labour can we deduce the price we are at most able to pay for the raw material, and *vice versa*. The third formula is the one which is understood by the individual producer, starting with the prices of raw materials and labour as fixed and known amounts. But none the less the influence is in the opposite direction from the social point of view—*i.e.*, from the price of demand of the finished article to the price of demand for its components.

In Sec. 65 we have shown how a simple schedule of demand for the raw material is formed, when the expense of conversion is supposed to be known. This schedule of demand is as usual compared with the schedule of supply, which states the cost of production for various quantities. This is unfortunately not a simple matter ; first of all, there is not one, but several, components (the law of joint demand) ; secondly, one raw material may be substituted for another, just as human and machine labour may substitute one another (competing supply) ; thirdly, raw materials are often produced by the same process from the same base material (joint supply) ; and finally the same raw material may be a component of several finished articles (competing demand).

We have shown the rule for the latter in Sec. 65.

If leather is demanded for saddlery and for boots, there will be one schedule of demand for boots and another for saddlery. These two reduced schedules are intermixed, as shown in the section treating competing demand. The price of leather must be *deduced* from the two, and even from three or four schedules of demand (boots, saddlery, travelling bags, leather upholstery). But through this these goods become *related in production, and price-connected.*

This war has witnessed the competition between saddlery and boots: the employment which most brutally comes to the fore with the strength of *economical* necessity (*i.e.*, paying ability) will increase the price of the raw material, attract it and reduce the consumption of other goods, in which the raw material forms a component. But the boot is again dependent on its leather; for this reason the price of boots again must rise with a decreased turnover. For the separate producer the *highest price he will pay* for leather is not only dependent upon how much he *can obtain for boots*, but the *lowest price he will accept* for boots is dependent upon and derived from the price he must pay for the leather. At one end of the process are the three schedules of demand of the consumers for boots, saddlery and trunks, arisen from an estimate of utility, at the other extreme is a series of increasing prices of production of the leather, according as a greater or smaller quantity is to be procured.

Somewhere between these is the schedule of demand-prices for leather—exactly where, will for instance, be determined by the expenses of conversion, which are required in order to add to the leather the other components, which make it into a finished article.

Provisionally we may establish the following rule:—When a raw material forms a component in the production of several goods, for instance, in the goods A and B, the following conditions for equilibrium must hold good: if $a$ units of the good A and $b$ units of the good B are sold, the market price of the raw material must correspond to the marginal expense in extracting $a + b$ units of the raw material, as well as to the price which the last buyer of the good A will pay, less the marginal expense of converting $a$ units of the raw material into the good A—a price which again tends to be equal to the price, which the last buyer of B will pay, less the marginal expense of converting $b$ units of the raw material into the good B.

Even these brief suggestions will show that the price rules of the technical components require a special analysis, the means to make which has been given in this and the preceding chapter.

**128. Competition in Production.**—Of the finished articles which have the same raw material we may, to some extent, say that they compete in production ; this is quite clear for goods which may be employed at various stages of their development, as, for instance, milk, cream, butter and cheese ; if one of these goods is produced, the means to produce the others will no longer be present ; for these goods we have the double relation, firstly, that they substitute one another, secondly, milk is the principal substance of them all. In normal conditions the milk of the cow is distributed between the four employments in such a manner that the price of the milk is the same ; an improvement of the cheese-production will draw the other prices upwards as well, because this will shift some milk on to the production of cheese. During the war this relation has caused difficulties, because the attempts to regulate the price of milk have caused the milk to be employed in the other ways not regulated. An impost on each pound of butter produced would have been more effective by reducing the production of butter and leaving more milk for consumption as milk and cheese (presuming that the export had been stopped).

When a good has several employments it will certainly attain the same price in all of them, provided that it is a case of the good being applicable for more than one purpose ; in case one employment excludes the other, the good will, besides the actual price, have a *latent* price—*i.e.*, its *substitution price*, on which it would have to fall back in case of the secondary employment.

In the theory of the wages of labour we will see that many of us have a substitution price in the possibility of seeking other employment ; this will then decide a limit, below which our present employment must not remunerate us. In the theory of the ground-rent we find the same ; by carrying on gardening in the vicinity of a large town I gain a gardener's rent, which is created by the price of the products (and in the second instance by the vicinity of the market) ; I would work without gaining this rent ; but if the soil for ordinary purposes of agriculture would yield me a rent of 50s. for each acre, I would not employ my soil for gardening unless the yield from this would be a differential rent of 50s; the ground rent, which is derived from the corn-price and which therefore is not *price-determining, but determined by the price,* will be an expense in case the land is employed for *other* purposes (garden, building site, or railway) and this expense *must* be covered. The ground rent in the inferior employment will therefore become a substitution price for the land when this is to be employed for a higher grade purpose. Most raw materials have in this manner a substitution-price, on which they may fall back in case of a different employment; when we speak of the natural price of a factor, we are, as a rule, thinking of its substitution-price.

## CHAPTER XXI

### THE PRICE OF THE TECHNICAL COMPONENTS.

**129. The Cost of Extracting Raw Materials.**—Raw materials are often extracted under the law of decreasing return; an increased demand must be covered by the working of new deposits, which are difficult of access, or by more intensive working of those already in existence; there is, of course, an element of hazard, inasmuch as the richness of the deposit and the difficulties of working are not known when a " claim " is discovered, and new deposits are often found by accident. But under normal conditions a larger consumption of a given raw material, whether this is due to increased applicability or simply a larger demand, will meet with increased difficulties of production—*i.e.*, the probability is that the raw material will be more and more scarce and thereby attain an increasing value. This is, of course, counteracted by the fact that new and more easily workable land and deposits may be taken up for working when our technique improves and the cheapening of transport draws hitherto unused rich deposits into the rayon of supply of the Western European consumption. Accident and need co-operate in this. Very often the press of population is necessary in order to make us go beyond our accustomed rayon of supply, but once we have ventured out and sunk the capitals required for clearing, for making the deposits workable, etc., we find that we may even extract the newly discovered treasures cheaper than the old ones.

Finally, industrial progress will *in itself* affect the *expenses of extraction* in the same manner as the expenses of conversion; evidently an ever-increasing quantity of energy (technical cost) is needed to extract raw materials; but this *technical cost may on account of the higher technique* again be supplied cheaper. (Otherwise it would hardly be feasible that the production of ore and coal could have been increased to nearly four times as much as 30 years ago.) An increased demand for a raw material is in any case not immediately accompanied by a higher technique, and will only gradually produce this through the effect of prices.

Although for a time we may obtain foodstuffs as well as raw materials cheaper in this manner, the law of *decreasing return* is still effective, owing to our *increasing need of raw materials.* The increase of this need is partly due to the *press of population*, and partly to our increasing ability to find *new applications* for the raw materials, partly to our greater *lavishness*, because they are manufactured more with a view to a *varying taste* than to *durability*, and, finally, the improvement in the *circumstances of the lower classes* act in the same direction. The consumption of the poor claims more raw material than work. The capacity of stomach and width of chest of rich and poor are alike ; in any case the same quantity of raw material will be required for the consumption of necessaries. It is the work applied that makes the difference ; the *real income* of the *rich man* (or at least that part he consumes) consists to a large extent of *services*, that of the *poor man of slightly worked raw materials.*

The different yield of the deposits causes that there is always a differential rent which, in a manner, is permanent and increasing ; yet the deposits are not inexhaustible; even the soil may for a time be robbed of valuable qualities. While the English deposits of salt will suffice for the time within our vision, many of the oil wells of Pennyslvania are already exhausted ; without the continued detection of new wells, petroleum and its by-products would not play the part in the technique which they do. But the consequence of this is that even if the richness of the deposits are given by nature, amortisation must be taken into consideration in the same manner as for other temporal goods. The yield of the deposit of raw material, which in a technical sense is gratuitous, will *economically* be split up into differential rent and amortisation.

(Suppose the yield to be $a$, the time until the deposit is exhausted, $n$, and the rate of interest, $r$, we now have the capital value $\frac{a}{r} . (1—(1+r)^{-n})$, which yields the interest $a(1 \div (1+r))$. Suppose, for instance, that a capital is doubled in 15 years and that the deposit will last for 60 years. The yield will then be $\frac{15}{16} . a$, because the rate of amortisation will be $\frac{1}{16} . a$. This amortisation accumulates into a capital, the interest on which after 60 years will be $\frac{15}{16} . a$.)

We may also say that a deposit of raw material gradually

changes place in the schedule of supply; to a certain extent its curve of expenses is decreasing at the beginning of the exploitation of the deposit, but after a time it is increasing.

There is another peculiarity in the production of the raw material—*i.e.*, that new deposits cannot quickly be made ready for working, and that therefore a period of high prices will give a raw material a temporary position of monopoly, and, consequently, for a time cut off the daily market from its connection with the long market. The price of the raw material will therefore fluctuate much in our time, where technical tradition has lost strength, and new applications of a certain raw material as well as substituting raw materials are continually found.

**130. The Expense of Conversion.**—In Chapter XI we have stated that the prices of the derived schedule of demand for the raw material are the *difference* between the price of the finished article and the expenses of conversion, the latter being considered to comprise *all* the other expenses for labour, machinery and such other raw or auxiliary materials, as are required in order to turn the raw material in question into the finished article. *Now* the raw material under consideration may economically play the most important part, and *now* the other technical components. A new application of a raw material has the same effect as a new class of buyers has on the consumer's good—*i.e.*, the joint schedule of demand is swelled, the joint schedule being composed of the schedules of demand for a multitude of different applications, the prices of which are all differences. If the raw material is of comparatively small economic importance for a given finished article, this may of course bid a higher price for it than if it is of great importance. The new employment will, of course, react against the price of the raw material, but only little in proportion to the other applications, which demand larger quantities. In the application for arc-lights a very high price may on one hand be offered for coal because the value of coal is so insignificant in proportion to the other expenses in producing the lamp and the electricity; on the other hand the quantity of coal employed for this purpose is so small in proportion to the consumption of coal for other purposes that the price of coal is only in theory affected by that of the arc-lamp.

The expenses of conversion change incessantly, because the prices of the other components continually fluctuate; but hereby is also altered the price difference, which is the price of demand of the raw material; alterations in the expenses of conversion, therefore, have just as much effect as alterations in the price of the finished article, the *shadow of which gives the derived price* to the raw material. If the value of one finished article is altered, or its expenses of conversion, the demand for its raw material will be altered, and, consequently, also the schedule. The resulting alteration in price entails that the raw material is differently distributed, and is attracted by the finished article whose expenses of conversion are falling, and drawn away from those whose expenses have remained unaltered.

Again we may immediately see that when the *expenses of conversion* are increased the price of demand for the raw material *falls,* and also its market price and the quantity sold. If, however, the *expenses of extraction* are increased, the price of the raw material will *rise,* although with a *decreased* consumption—*i.e.,* the *expenses of extraction and conversion have opposite effects on the price of the raw material,* but the same effect on the amount of *production.* If the price of demand for the finished article is increased, *or* if the raw material becomes applicable for more goods than before, the prices of the schedule of demand for the raw material will rise.

Finally, when several raw materials are employed together, a fall in the price of one will increase the price of demand for the others,—*i.e.* raw materials are related with regard to price in the same manner as is the separate raw material to the expenses of conversion, these being in a complementary relation to the raw material. When two raw materials are in *complementary* relations to one another, *the prices of demand for them vary in opposite directions.*

This confirms the law maintained by *Carey*—that industrial progress entails that the difference between the prices of the raw material and the finished articles is reduced; the greater the command which man gains over nature, the lower will be the expenses of conversion and the higher the price which can be paid for the raw material—*i.e.,* at the same price a larger number of units will be demanded, or the same quantity will be demanded at a higher price. At the same time the raw material itself has a tendency to rise in price, from the causes arising through the expenses of extraction. When the technique of tanning is improved, the price of hides will rise; similarly raw silk when the expense of converting it into silk material is decreased, or if it becomes more difficult to produce the raw silk; a much higher wage for sewing silk gowns causes that the price of silk material as well as of raw silk decreases.

In the struggle with nature for the raw materials, the producer must respond by reducing the expenses of conversion

**131. Wieser's Law.**—It has been attempted to find the value of the separate components by employing the so-called theory of marginal productivity and imputing to a component that part of the total value of the finished articles produced which the last additional unit of the component in question has added to the total value.

It is, however, impossible to find the specific productivity of the separate *technical* component. This is not only due to the fact that the factors do not each give a certain utility to the main product, but the useful finished article is produced by the *factors in co-operation.* When 10,000 yards of yarn, a loom and a working day together yield a certain quantity of cloth, who will then be able to say how much of this cloth is due to the yarn, and how much to the man and the loom? Is a hammer more useful than an anvil, the needle than the thread, the man than his spade, the fly-wheel than the piston rod, the shipowner, who makes the contract, than the sailor, who tends the winch? They are all equally indispensable. Air is also a technical component, so is water, and both are indispensable, and contribute undoubtedly to the applicability of most products; and yet, as long as they are not scarce and cost nothing, we forget their share in the result of production.

From the technical productivity we can, therefore, conclude *nothing* as to the value of a component, and in a way a "just" distribution of the gross result of a production between its factors is a chimera, and is only supported by those who are satisfied with this or that distribution.

By the expression "productivity" the adherents of the theory of marginal productivity mean something different—*i.e.*, what I term *rentability*, the net result of the effort expressed in money.

Suppose, now, that in order to produce a certain quantity of a finished article, the value of which is £100, the following composition of the components A, B and C is required: $4A + 5B + 2C$.

If we eliminate 1A in order to find what is its economic contribution and consequently employ 3A + 5B + 2C, the resulting product may be worth, say, £95. If instead we eliminate 1B, making the composition 4A + 4B + 2C, we may have a product, the value of which is, say, £90, *i.e.*, 1B = £10, and if, finally, we do without one C (4A + 5B + 1C) and find the value of the produce to be £60, C = £40. We therefore arrive at the absurd result that although 4A + 5B + 2C in co-operation create £100, their value as found by alternately eliminating 1 unit is found to be £150—*i.e.*, 4 . 5 + 5 . 10 + 2 . 40.

Let us take another example: X + Y = £50, but X alone produces values for £5, while Y alone produces values for £10. We may now proceed in two ways: start with the value of the components separately—in all 5 + 10 = £15, or from the value lost in the result of their co-operation in case one of them is eliminated, we find a value of £45 for Y and of £40 for X, total, £85; both are absurd.

(*Zeuthen* criticises the above examples, and is of the opinion that in these there are no price-determining marginal units for any of the factors, the technique being presumed to give a certain composition of the factors; but if the production is sufficiently large and subject to the rule of substitution (that one component may be substituted for another according to the comparative prices of the two) one may actually, by withdrawing 1 unit of each of the components of the thing, *find a price for this component corresponding to its addition to the total of the product value in each of its employments.* If the last ton of steel is withdrawn from the production of rails, from the production of ships or machines, the result of each of these activities will be reduced by the value of 1 ton of steel; for otherwise the distribution of steel between the numerous employments would have been another. In the same manner the marginal workers in a large number of trades (theoretically in all of them) will only earn their wage for the concern.)

If now there are two components, and the value of their produce is 50, we have only *one* equation with two unknown factors, which makes possible a series of different amounts for these. The theory of marginal productivity will find the missing equation by alternately withdrawing the marginal unit of the two components—we know the result. In order to get further, *Wieser* advances the following equations to find the value relations of several goods, which are related in production :

The three raw materials, $x$, $y$ and $z$ are components in three finished articles, A, B and C in the following combinations :—
$A = x + y = £100$ ; $B = 2x + 3z = £290$ ; $C = 4y + 5z = £590$.

$x$, $y$ and $z$ represent the raw materials (the technical components as well as their price, the figures prefixed being the technical co-efficients) while the £ figures are the prices at which the three finished articles are sold. We arrive at the result : $x = £40$, $y = £60$ and $z = £70$.

Leaving out of consideration the fact that *Wieser's* exposition does not show that we deduce the price of the raw material from that of the finished article, this does not tell us very much beyond what we already know : that the price of the good is equal to the sum of the prices of the components, and that those are equal in all applications. Some links are missing—*i.e.*, the inherent relations of the *components*, independent of the finished article—in the present case the difficulty in procuring the components. We will therefore correct the exposition of the Austrian economist :

When $a$ units of the thing A are to be produced, $b$ units of B and $c$ units of C, $a(x + y)$ must be employed for A, $b(2x + 3z)$ for B and $c(4y + 5z)$ for C, or of the three raw materials respectively of $x$, $(a + 2b)$, of $y$, $(a + 4c)$ and of $z$, $(2b + 5c)$. D and S in the schedule represent prices of demand and supply respectively :

SCHEDULES OF THE FINISHED ARTICLES.

| | $A = (1x + 1y)$ | | | $B = (2x + 3x)$ | | | $C = (4y + 5z)$ | |
|---|---|---|---|---|---|---|---|---|
| | D | S | | D | S | | D | S |
| 1st unit | | | | | | | | |
| $a$-th unit | $p_a$ | $1x_p + y_p$ | $b$-th unit | $p_b$ | $2x_p + 3z_p$ | $c$-th unit | $p_c$ | $4y_p + 5z_p$ |

SCHEDULES OF THE RAW MATERIAL.

| | X | | | Y | | | Z | |
|---|---|---|---|---|---|---|---|---|
| | D | S | | D | S | | D | S |
| 1st unit | | | 1st unit | | | 1-st unit | | |
| $a$-th | | | $a$-th | | | $b$-th | | |
| $a + b$-th | | | $a + c$-th | | | | | |
| $a + 2b$-th | $x_p$ | The price of the marginal technical cost in the extraction of $(a + 2b)$ units | $(a + 4c$-th) | $y_p$ | The price of the marginal technical cost in the extraction of $(a + 4c)$ units | $3b + 5c$-th | $Z_p$ | The price, of the marginal technical cost in the extraction of $(3b + 5c)$ units |

$p_a$, $p_b$ and $p_c$ are the price of demand of the $a$-th, $b$-th and $c$-th buyer respectively of the finished articles A, B and C; $x_p$, $y_p$ and $z_p$ are equal to the marginal prices of demand for respectively $a + 2b$ units of X, $a + 4c$ units of Y and $3b + 5c$ units of Z. The marginal expense for, say, the $a + 2b$-th units of X is the price of the marginal technical cost, involved in extracting this unit. The deciding factors are—leaving out of consideration the expenses of conversion, which in themselves must be regarded as equal to the cost of a raw material—the extremes: *the curves of demand for the finished article and the cost of production of the raw materials.* Apart from the expenses of conversion there is, consequently, *a reaction from the demand for the finished article*, and an effect in the opposite direction from the *technical cost* in producing the raw material. What makes the case complicated is the fact that the effect is neither on the *demand* for one finished article nor for three, but for the many possible technical costs of hundreds of co-operating raw materials, which cost does not only vary proportionally to the quantity, and the composition of which may even be altered for the same quantity, but the price of which is in itself not only dependent on the application, on the technical form, but also and *not least* on the price of the finished article. For even if we know both the form and amount of the technical cost in producing different quantities of the raw material, we can *not*, through this know the schedule of supply of the raw material, because the corresponding prices for the marginal cost are directly dependent upon the prices of demand for the finished article.

The schedule of demand of the thing A has, as shown, a direct effect on the schedules of demand for X and Y, but these again have influence upon which is to be the marginal unit of the raw materials X and Y, and even on the price of the marginal unit; but through this the price, and the quantity sold of the goods B and C are again affected, and this will not only react on Z, but also on X and Y, in a continuous oscillation until equilibrium is attained; but if this is disturbed even in one place, the ingenious adjustment of price and turnover between the six goods will be disturbed; a new series of oscillations, continuing from one good to another, from main articles to raw materials and *vice versa*, and tending towards a new equilibrium, will again start.

It ought, perhaps, to be emphasised that *v. Wieser's* equations—

which are here supplemented—give only *one certain solution* with regard to prices and turnover, provided that there are as many equations as there are unknown factors, *presuming* free competition—*i.e.*, that monopoly does not create causes of disturbance.

By comparing the schedules of demand and supply for the three finished articles as well as for the three raw materials, we have made sensible *Wieser's* exposition, and thereby shown the intimate relations and interactions, besides showing by our exposition that the technical relations also become different, according as a greater or smaller number of units are produced, which also affects the formation of prices.

Of the finished articles A, B and C respectively, must be sold so many units, and so many units of the raw materials (X, Y and Z) that the marginal prices of demand of the former $p_a$, $p_b$ and $p_c$, and the marginal cost of production of the latter ($x_p$, $y_p$ and $z_p$) are in such relation to one another that with the given co-efficients they cover one another (in $2x + 3z$, $x$ and $z$ are the components, and 2 and 3 the co-efficients) ; otherwise the employment of all the raw materials extracted is not attained, nor also is exactly the quantity in question of each raw stuff sold and at the *same* price, irrespective of the employment. From the six equations we further gather that an alteration in any of the prices must alter all the other prices and the turnover of all the main articles as well as of all the raw materials—and that how they are altered depends partly on the schedules of demand for the finished articles and partly on the expenses of extraction of the raw materials, which differ according to the quantity produced, as well as according to the technical curves of the finished articles.

In this example, where joint demand and competing demand are both present, the *problem of imputation of value* already appears, the values *imputed* to the technical components being actually not found for each component separately, but only for the components in co-operation. If the formula had been : Finished Article = Raw Material X + Raw Material Y, and there had only been one equation, anybody would have been able to see that in order to find $x$ and $y$ we would need some further determining factor—and this is found in the conditions of production of these materials ; but in these conditions there are elements of scarcity and of monopoly. We can, *a priori*, see that the scarcity must either be overcome by increasing cost, or else cannot be overcome, and whether it is *inherent* or *intended* we must in any case speak of the economic position of power of the component in question, or, rather, about that of its owner, as an important price-determining factor. Our analysis of the problem of imputation is, therefore, only at an early stage as long as we have not examined the *position of power* of the components.

In a subsequent volume we will return to the theory of the expenses of production behind which we find the technical cost, the sacrifice of energy incorporated in the different components. We know about their price, how their derived schedules of demand and their schedules of supply are formed. We have mentioned that also a *new* element comes in—*i.e.*, the relative scarcity, the position of monopoly of the components : in their mutual struggle to obtain a share of the price which the public will pay for the finished article, their share is determined by their economic position of power, not by their technical utility—*i.e., rentability is not determined by technical productivity.*

**132. Interaction.**—The cost of production of a thing (*i.e*, the quantity of technical components, multiplied by their price) is then a rather more complicated conception than its prices of demand, because the former are affected by four different causes : (1) the market condition for the finished article ; (2) the price conditions of the other components ; (3) the technical cost in producing the components, and (4) the economic position of power of these components, or, rather, of their owners, mutually as well as in relation to the producers of the finished article.

We can neither solve the problem of price by pointing to the cost of production as something objectively determined and evident, nor rest content with its being *derived from the price of the finished article.* A quotation from the Norwegian *Aarum* really explains it all :

The value of the technical components employed in a thing (say raw material, productive goods, including labour in all its forms) is not ' simply a reflection of the value of the consumer's good ' in the same manner as the utility of the former is derived from that of the latter ; there is ' no *absolute* relation of cause and effect but a *mutual relation of dependency and interaction* between the two classes of goods.'

*Wieser's* law of the prices of goods which are related in

production (the goods A, B and C and the raw materials) states that the marginal utility of the least useful employment in the group determines the value of the raw material. But *Aarum* points out that this value again " by reflection " has a determining effect on the value of the other goods, which have become related in production through the common raw material. First of all, the common producer's good will have a value which is determined by the marginal produce—in the present case the *b*-th unit of the good B—but secondly the value of this good will affect the value of the other goods in which it is a component. In the open market the raw material must have the same price in all applications ; the dress manufacturer and the manufacturer of dynamos pay the same price for silk thread. Each application finds the price of the raw material apparently given *from without* ; the manufacturers in each application produce so far down (provided that they are not the exploiters of a monopoly) that this price of the component on the margin is just covered by what is left of the sale price of the finished article when the other components have been paid for.

A rise in price of the raw material entails a reduction in the production of all the goods, in which the raw material forms a component, even if to a *different extent—i.e.*, according to the *relative importance of the raw material* in the production of the thing in question, and the form of the *price curve of this thing* ; in some trades this will be of practically no importance, but in others it will entirely stop production.

Further it is difficult to point out the *direct* connection between the value of the finished article and its technical components—*i.e.*, the producers' goods, because (apart from the expenses of extraction) the mutual price relations of several components, or raw materials, which are employed in the production of *one* good —*i e.*, the proportion in which they divide the amount, which the finished article can offer (its own price of demand), is dependent upon their *relative position of power* or monopoly.

The fact that *one raw material or component* is employed in the production of *many different finished articles*, and that *one finished article* contains *many different components* causes that the simple contention that the technical components—the producers' goods —have a value derived from that of the finished article, tells us just as little as, for instance, the often misunderstood rule that capital and labour are paid according to their marginal productivity (this ought to be marginal rentability).

**133. Alterations in Demand and Supply.**—Suppose that in our example we increase the demand for the good A, the price schedule of which therefore rises; the $a$-th price of demand will now be more than $p_a$ and consequently larger than $x_p + y_p$. The equilibrium must now be sought for an increased turnover of A, which increases the demand for its components X and Y, and thereby, in any case in the first instance, also increases their price. X and Y must now be withdrawn from B and C, in the production of which they are also employed, and the production of which must therefore be reduced. But thereby there will be less employment for the good Z, which in B is employed together with X and in C together with Y; the price of Z will fall. In the second instance the production of X and Y will be increased, presumably with somewhat increased marginal expenses. Besides an increase in the production of A we then have an increased production of X and Y and a rise in price of A, X and Y, and also often of B and C, whose effort to attain the previous production will, however, be hampered by the fact that the demand for these finished articles is unaltered, while the expenses of production for B and C have been increased, because the prices of X and Y have risen more than that of Z has dropped.

Suppose, now, that we impose a tax on the raw material X, the cost of production of which will therefore be increased, while the turnover will decrease. As the price of demand for the finished articles A and B, in which X forms a component, is unaltered, a lower number of units of these must be sold at rising prices. Y and Z are also reduced, even if their producers are willing to bear some of the tax out of their differential rent, for which reason the price of the finished articles A and B will not be increased by the *full* amount of the tax—*i.e.*, part of the tax on X has been shifted on to the producers of Yand Z, presuming that these goods are produced under the law of decreasing return. The good C finds its raw materials Y and Z cheaper and increases production. The goods in which the taxed raw material X forms a component rise in price, and their turnover is decreased. The raw materials, which are components together with X, have their value decreased, and the finished articles, in which they form components *without* connection with X, fall in price and have an increased turnover, while the raw materials which are connected with the co-components of X (the prices of which are reduced) will rise in price with an increased turnover. If another raw material can be substituted for X the price of this will rise.

Many raw materials have emanated from a process by which the original raw materials of the first order have been adapted, the current raw materials being often the outcome of a conversion; these converted raw materials (of the second order) are nearly all produced in a joint production, which complicates the matter. An increased demand for, say, tar on account of a new application, may in the first instance reduce the price of coke, as this is a differential price, and in the second instance it will increase the price of demand for coal—*i.e.*, coke, tar and tar preparations, gas and ammonia—all raw materials of the second order—are affected by the increased demand for tar. A tax on a raw material of this class does not only affect the *finished articles in which it forms a component*, not only the *other raw materials*, which, together with it, form components in the finished article, not only the raw materials which are produced together with it in *joint production*, but also the raw materials which, if required, may *substitute* it. Add to this that some materials are in themselves *direct consumers' goods as well* as components in other goods, and it will be understood how infinitely complicated the formation of price of the raw materials is, and how unstable their equilibirum. Imagine a tax on tar! It will reduce the direct consumption of that good, increase the price, decrease its application, decrease the production of the goods in which tar forms an important technical component, increase the prices of these, reduce the prices of all goods, which, together with tar, are raw materials in tar preparations, increase the price of gas and coke and decrease the price or freight of coal. Against coal the tax on tar means a weakening of the schedule of demand for tar, as against tar preparations a strengthening of the schedule of supply; for the goods which, together with tar, are the subject of joint demand it means a fall in the schedule of demand; for goods which are produced in the same process as tar, it means a rise in their schedule of supply, and for the goods which may substitute tar it means a rise in their schedule of demand.

Suppose that, besides the raw materials, X, Y and Z there is a fourth, Æ, which cannot form a component of A, B and C, but of another group of finished articles, which we collect under the joint description D, the price of Æ being $æ_p$. We now discover that Æ may be substituted for X. If $æ_p > z_p$ it is of no avail that Æ and X may technically be substituted for one another. But if $æ_p < x_p$, the producers of A and B will direct a demand on Æ, which will entail that $p_a$ and $p_b$ (the prices of A and B) will be higher than the expenses, which are reduced by the amount $(x_p - æ_p)$; the production of A and B may then be forced; the prices of the components of these goods—*i.e.*, Y and Z, will rise; a larger quantity of these will also be produced, probably at in-reased expenses; the expenses of the good C will be increased, and consequently the sale and production will be reduced. Now the price of the good Æ rises, which permits an increase in the quantity produced, but the increased price causes that Æ is no longer profitable in all the employments included in D, the production of which must therefore be decreased. The final result is that the quantity of Æ, which *technically substitutes* a unit of X, must have the same price as 1X. The discovery that Æ may substitute X has therefore increased the price of Æ and depressed that of X. This is still more complicated if X may be substituted by Æ in some applications, but not in others. The result *may* be that X is not used at all in the applications where it is ousted by its substitute, but remains in the applications where it cannot be substituted. This is the case when 1X is technically = 1Æ, but the cost of production of X cannot fall as far as to the price of Æ, even if this has been increased

**134. The Monopoly.**—If the production of or trade in a raw material becomes the subject of a monopoly, this will, as a rule, be profitable, because the schedule of demand is relatively steep, and because the separate raw material is employed together with so many other components (labour, machinery, power, etc.) that its value in proportion to that of the finished article is often small (*i.e.*, the raw material is in many applications of relatively small economic importance). Further a monopolist may easily put out of action the law of indifference by dividing the purchasers into groups. If A can pay 13½, B 12½, C 11⅓, and D 11s., and the cost of production of the raw material is 11 (which consequently will be the price of the open market for 4 units) the monopoly price will be 12½, at which 2 units are sold. But if the monopolist can differentiate between the various applications and make them pay according to their capacity, he will not reduce production, but keep four different prices. The holder of a monopoly of an indispensable raw material is, to a large extent, able to *appropriate the differential rent, which the producer of the finished article would otherwise obtain,* and is even able to force the producers of the finished article to trade in the same manner as they would if they held a monopoly, only that *all of them surrender the profit thereby to him.* When the raw material in question has no substitute, the power of the monopoly is absolute; when substitution is possible, the limit for the exploitation is, of course, determined by the price of the substitute in proportion to its technical utility; as the substitution of another raw material as a rule will cause a loss in effective utility and often requires alteration of the machinery, a raw material monopoly will even in this case be valuable.

In the same manner as the raw material may force the producer of the finished article to produce according to the rules of monopoly, in order afterwards to confiscate his monopoly rent, one raw material may also appropriate the differential rent of a weaker raw material. But many raw materials, as far as a large part of their produce is concerned, and provided that they are produced under the rule of decreasing return, will be in a position of monopoly, and therefore there will, in the relations between the raw materials, be a struggle for the gross profits of the finished article; this profit will not be reduced because the turnover of a strong monopoly raw material is reduced so much and its price put so high that the producer of the finished article is forced to work under monopoly conditions and collect a monopoly rent, which the supplier of the raw material may appropriate through his prices. In this struggle between the raw materials for the monopoly profit of the finished article, the relative strength of the monopolies of the former will decide the share which each of them will obtain. This struggle will, after the war, probably take such forms and lead to so much new experience that the chapter dealing with the formation of prices of raw materials will become one of the most interesting in economics. Every raw material has the weakness that, even if in order to obtain a higher price it should have its production reduced, it *still wants a sale, and must,* on the other hand, *co-operate* with other raw materials, as they are of no value without this co-operation. Besides the limit to the exploitation by the monopoly on a raw material of another raw material co-operating with it—*i.e.*, that the technical cost of the extraction of the latter must also be paid, there is consequently also the limit that the other raw material, even if its position of monopoly is weaker by being retained and made difficult to obtain, may force the stronger raw material to give up part of its monopoly profit. Coal and iron cannot therefore in a struggle give one another the knock-out, but are forced in some way to divide the monopoly profit which these two powerful raw materials—the principal substances of technical capital—can enforce on the strength of the rather concentrated position of the deposits With the raw material policy, which the raw material producing powers appear to intend to follow, it would not be surprising if coal and iron, even if the level of prices otherwise dropped to what it was before the war, would after this still maintain prices twice as high as those of 1913. In a subsequent volume we shall revert to the price theory of the raw materials and their relative position of monopoly, because we may therein find the key to the theory of distribution.

Besides the monopoly of the seller we have that of the *buyer, the consumer*; this is of next to no importance for articles of consumption, but very important for raw materials and other components, because these are not only sold by, but also *bought* by merchants who manipulate the market. In the same manner as the seller's monopoly is held in check by the buyer's ability to substitute other goods in the consumption, or to resign, the *buyer's monopoly* is balanced, partly by the ability of the raw material to find other applications, and partly by the cost of extraction of the raw material; but as the latter obeys the rule of decreasing return, a producer who holds a position of monopoly as against the component he requires, will be able to force the producer of the latter to reduce production in order to sell cheaper. A finished article in a strong position may force the component to accept a distress price in the short market, and to resign any monopoly profit gained and be content with simply having expenses covered in the long market. As the minimum of existence for labour is paramount to its expenses of produc-duction, a concentrated industry may force the wages of labour far down, persuming that the labourers themselves have not a position of monopoly in special training, expert knowledge or ability to boycott the industry for additional labour from the outside.

There may be free competition in the relation between the finished article and the consumer, and yet monopoly relations between the finished article and the raw material—and *vice versa.* It is also possible that the buyer's monopoly only applies to some suppliers whom he can force to give " discriminating " discounts, while other suppliers on account of situation, possibilities of sale, etc., are themselves in a relative position of monopoly to the same buyer.

While a producer, even if he is in a position of monopoly as against the consumers, will always try to force down his supplier of raw materials, this interest on his part ceases when his profit is limited, as, for instance, when war time contracts with the army make the conditions " cost price + 15% " a fair price. His interest will even be in the opposite direction, partly because of the merchant's general liking for large profits, if only they do not have to contribute thereto themselves, and partly because, for instance, a trust or a government contractor whose profits are limited, may often by directly, or indirectly through the banking group which finances both undertakings, acquiring an interest in the business of their suppliers of raw materials, neutralise the limitation of profits by paying a high price for their raw material or semi-manufactured article.

**135. The Derived Price of Machinery.**—In the same manner as that of the raw material, the price of the *machinery* is derived either from the price of a finished article—reduced by passing through the brain of a merchant—which there, when the price of the other technical components have been deducted, becomes the *price of demand* for the machine ; but the merchant may also arrive at the indirect price by comparing the machine with the labour substituted by it.

Suppose that a machine, before being worn out, will enable a man to produce 300 units ; its maximum value is these 300 units ; but first of all the raw material is not obtained for nothing, and secondly the machine will require some human tending and auxiliary materials and power ; the expenses for all these things must, according to the theory of joint demand and indirect price, be deducted from the value of the finished articles ; this maximum limit must further be reduced according to the law of substitution, because one cannot pay more for the machine than the wages of the labourers which it substitutes, presuming that the consumption of raw material is the same in both cases.

The price of demand for the machine will therefore be the lower of the two prices, the price of the good less the prices of the various components mentioned, and the wages of the labour substituted. Further must be deducted a time discount, because I must pay for the machine at once, while its yield and, consequently, its amortisation, is spread over some length of time. The interest to be covered by the machine is not only the ordinary market interest, but the interest which the employer of the machine must pay in consideration of his special credit—*i.e.*, the security given, the time of repayment and his general " standing." The price of demand for the machine, reduced in this manner is consequently calculated on the basis of the quantity produced of the finished article and its selling value.

The machine is included in the cost of production of the article produced, not only with the cost of its tending and the labour required to work it, its maintenance and power, its labourers and auxiliary materials, but also with its rate of amortisation and interest.

The manufacturer of machines will at least have his cost of production covered, including interest for the time he has had an outlay of capital ; if he lets the machine he must at least have the rate of amortisation covered besides an interest for the period of lease ; this interest must, of course, be calculated for the entire value of the machine, and not only for the part written off during the period of lease, for the machine cannot be made successively as it yields utility. The interest on the entire value of the machine must, therefore, be paid from first to last to the person who is waiting for his payment, whether this is the manufacturer of the machine or the capitalist who has lent the amount to the manufacturer, or the employer himself.

Now this price of demand of the producer of goods for the machine must be equal to or higher than the price of supply of the manufacturer of the machine, and when a new machine is introduced, it must even be more than this in order to break the law of inertia. The machine must, to start with, yield an additional return, which can be collected either by the manufacturer of the machine or by the producer of goods employing it.

**136. The Victory of the Machine.**—Let us now take the schedule of demand for a certain finished article, and find, by deducting the price of raw materials and time discount, the price which a producer of goods, who is the only one in the market, will pay for a machine, including its tending and the power required.

Suppose that in one week 50 labourers at a wage of 20s. each can produce 10 units, and that each additional machine will increase the production by 1 unit, after which it is worn out.

The schedules will then have the following appearance :—

| PRICE OF DEMAND FOR THE FINISHED ARTICLE. | | | TOTAL VALUE PRODUCED. | THE MACHINES HAVE COLLECTIVELY INCREASED THE PRODUCTION BY: ABSOLUTELY. | AVERAGE | EACH MACHINE HAS INCREASED THE VALUE OF THE PRODUCTION BY |
|---|---|---|---|---|---|---|
| 10 | units at | 100s. | = 1,000s. | | | |
| 11 | ,, | 96s. | = 1,056s. | 56 | 1 at 56 | 56s. for first machine |
| 12 | ,, | 92s. | = 1,104s. | 104 | 2 ,, 52 | 48s. for 2nd machine |
| 13 | ,, | 88s. | = 1,144s. | 144 | 3 ,, 48 | 40s. for 3rd machine |
| 14 | ,, | 84s. | = 1,176s. | 176 | 4 ,, 44 | 32s. for 4th machine |
| 15 | ,, | 80s. | = 1,200s. | 200 | 5 ,, 40 | 24s. for 5th machine |
| 16 | ,, | 76s. | = 1,216s. | 216 | 6 ,, 36 | 16s. for 6th machine |
| 17 | ,, | 72s. | = 1,224s. | 224 | 7 ,, 32 | 8s. for 7th machine |
| 18 | ,, | 68s. | = 1,224s. | 224 | 8 ,, 28 | 0s. for 8th machine |
| 19 | ,, | 64s. | = 1,216s. | 216 | 9 ,, 24 | —8s. for 9th machine |

The amount by which the machines increase the value of the production, presuming that the same number of labourers is required, is exactly the selling value of the *produce* of the marginal machine, which consequently will be the price of demand for the marginal machine. It should be noted that while the *productivity* of each additional machine is the same (1 unit) its *rentability* is decreasing, not only because the value of each unit is lower (the greater the quantity of goods produced, the cheaper the price at which they must be sold), but also because, for instance, it is not only the unit produced by Machine No. 3 (the 13th), which only fetches 88s. (while the price for 12 units was 92s.), but also *all the remaining* 12 *units when the* 13*th is added, are reduced in price from* 92s. *to* 88s. The 5th column will therefore represent the price of demand for the machine (including, for instance, the labourer who tends the machine, power, auxiliary materials, oil, etc.). The fall in the schedule need not be regular ; it may rise when the schedule of demand for the good produced at some point becomes more flat than before; for instance, if the schedule of demand for the finished good from being steep suddenly becomes even, because the good from being consumed by the rather well-to-do finds a regular market in wider circles and maintains this; in this case it is quite feasible that the schedule of demand for machines may rise on a certain part. Suppose that an increase of the production from 16 to 17 units did not bring about a fall in price from 76 to 72s., but only to 75s., the toal value of the production of 17 units would not be 1,224, but 1,275, which would mean that the return of the 7th machine would be 59s. instead of 8s.

The producer of goods, however, cannot and will not increase his price for the 7th machine to 59s. because the 7 machines would, in the present instance, increase the value of his production by 216 + 59s., which, distributed between 7 machines would mean 39s. for each, which amount would be his maximum price. It may therefore happen that the succession is interrupted, and that a higher price than the former is inserted. This would, however, tempt him to increase his purchase of machines until equilibrium had again been attained. The result is a schedule of demand for the machine which is mainly falling, but with interruptions, which again give the machine a higher value—*i.e.*, increase the demand temporarily.

But from this we may also gather that the return of the machine decreases; a machine is not only a material object; it is the realisation of a new method of working as well. If our machine costs nothing (*i.e.*, is practically speaking, a method only) our producer will continually acquire machines until he has obtained 8; if the machine may be produced for 24s. and only 2 are employed, he *would be able to* pay 48s. for the machine, and has therefore earned a differential rent of 24s.; the differential profit will continue—even if decreasing—until he has acquired the 5th machine, which just pays. At this point the price of the finished article has fallen from 100s. to 80s.—*i.e.*, *in the long run the return of the machine will benefit the consumers in the form of cheaper prices of the goods produced by machinery.* What happens is that the socially necessary expenses change character; from being based on hand-power they become based upon machine power. When the machine for a long time has given now its manufacturer and now its employer a differential profit, it will finally cover for the former only the cost of production, and after a further period the latter will only have the cost of the machine, with the addition of interest, covered by the price of the finished article.

We have said that finally the return of the machine will benefit the consumer, but this contention must be qualified.

(1) First of all, the producer of goods may stop the acquisition of machinery *before* the natural point, at which the machine does not more than pay. In this case the employer may keep the price of his *goods* so high that the machine yields a differential rent. In this case the technique will *not even temporarily* benefit the producer.

(2) A not inconsiderable part of the advantage of employing machinery is left to the *intermediary merchant*. In order to sell the increased quantity of goods produced by using machine power instead of hand power, the producer must first of all make the intermediary traders interested by offering them a higher commission or discount. In many trades investigations have even been made to ascertain the profits per unit for the artisan, and an offer has then been made to him of the same amount or more as *trading* profits. In my opinion, a great part of the effects of technical progress—cheaper cost of production—has been absorbed by the increase in the expense of distribution—*i.e.*, the men whose work has been saved by a higher technique have been employed, not so much in increased production (they may have had their working hours shortened) as in an increase of the number of persons engaged in the distribution of goods.

(3) Finally, even that part which benefits the consumers is not tantamount to an improvement in the state of the community, because the technique will benefit certain classes of consumers before the others, and inasmuch as the advantage is *evaporated* through the *exchange* of goods. When a technical advance reduces the expenses of industry, but agriculture is working with an unchanged technique and unchanged prices, the latter will have an advantage in their capacity of buyers of the industrial products. But this will have the same effect as a cheapening of the *doses of energy* required for the cultivation of the soil, inasmuch as implements, semi-manufactured articles and the maintenance of labour can be bought cheaper. This again means an extension of the *limit of cultivation* and a higher *ground rent*, always in kind and in most cases also as expressed in money.

(4) In our example the employer will earn a differential rent, even if he employs 5 machines at 24s. each and obtains a price of 80s. for the goods ; this appears from the 5th and 6th columns

of the table ; his additional income from the 5 machines is 200s., and they cost him 5 . 24 = 120s. only. The differential rent is, therefore, 80s. But our producer of goods has no sensible reason for paying more for any machine than it will earn *itself*. By employing 5 machines instead of 4, he only increases the value of the goods produced by 24s., and even if in a way he might obtain balance by paying 40s. for each machine, he would not do this. This differential profit will, however, disappear, because it will entice others to produce by machinery, and thereby reduce the price of goods, so that the additional yield of the last machine will not cover its price. The separate producer will not be able to detect this as long as the price of goods is sufficient to make *all* his machines pay, taken collectively. Only the monopolist is able to detect that also in *consideration* of the selling value of his product will he gain by not purchasing more machines.

But our producer may proceed in a different manner—*i.e.*, keep his production constant and reduce his number of labourers only. He will then still produce 10 units, but instead of employing 50 labourers, he would employ 1 machine and 45 labourers. The machine will then be worth the wages of 5 labourers = 100s. ; this will tempt him to continue to substitute machines for labourers until all 10 units are produced by 10 machines (at a value of 100s. each) ; if he buys the machines at the cost of production, 24s., he will gain on each machine a differential rent of 76s.

This state is not stable, partly because our producer of goods, by his increased demand for machines, will press the price of these upwards against himself, and partly because the wages of labour will fall when the labourers are gradually discharged, the labourers attempting to compete with the now more expensive machine by reducing their demand for wages ; all this apart from the fact that the producer will not, in the long run, be content with the quantity originally produced, and that his competitors will follow his example.

Consequently the machine will gain ground also in the open market ; first of all, on the basis of the *existing* prices of the finished article, which are reduced by the machine itself creating a differential profit at first, and reducing it itself.

(*a*) The example given in the table may be criticised, inasmuch as we have presumed that *each* additional machine will increase the production in the same proportion ; if all other conditions, say space, management, etc., are unchanged, this will not hold good ; when an *optimum* has been attained—the technically most advantageous proportion between the quantities of the various components, of which the machine is one—and when another distribution would yield less profit, an increase in the machine power will yield a decreasing return. This causes that the point at which the separate factory cannot continue to increase its machine power with advantage will be arrived at earlier than in the example ; this, however, does not alter our conclusions.

(*b*) It may also be said that when the early stages of development have been completed and a new machine has made good, and the production of the good in question has thereby been multiplied, this will in itself increase the schedule of demand for the finished article—because habit and the knowledge in wider circles of the existence of the good creates a previously non-existing demand for this—whether this be a new demand created by the good or only the substitution of the good for another article. This has the opposite effect to the peculiarity mentioned under (*a*), that the fall in value of the machine is increased by the fact that increased employment of the machine can only within a certain limit be presumed to increase the production of goods to a corresponding extent. But here again we may leave out of consideration the fact that by leading to mass production the machine will often create an increased demand, which delays the fall in the demand for the machine itself, through the increased demand for the good produced.

(*c*) By increasing the production of goods, the machine also increases the consumption of raw material and the price thereof ; but just because of the fact that the schedule of demand for the machine is *a difference between a falling price of demand for the finished article and an increasing cost of extraction of the raw materials*, and, consequently, is an expression for the variations of the differences between these two factors, it will often fall at a quicker rate *later on than at the beginning*, when the increase in the quantity of raw material required is not of the same relative importance as it is when the machine is generally employed and has perhaps multiplied the production.

To sum up : The quantity of goods made by machinery is increased, the price of them falls, thereby reducing the price of the machine, until this has made good and the men producing by the old methods have either been competed out or have been forced to alter their methods; the result of this process, which may take a long time, will be that the machine is sold at its cost of production, and that the price of the good produced has fallen to the new cost, which is determined by the employment of the machine. In the price of the good the wages of labour have become a *smaller* part, while the *amortisation of the machine* and interest on it have become a *larger part*, and a differential rent, which had arisen and which may often have been high, has disappeared; the machine has become the auxiliary of the *representative firm* and the *socially necessary* expenses are based on the new technique.

Up to the point where the price of the goods covers expenses only, the purchase price of the machine and interest thereon being now included in these, the machine will yield a differential profit, which, in case the manufacturer of the machine holds a patent, will be appropriated by him, because he can maintain a price for the machine far above the cost; part of this profit, however, will generally be lost in the costly propaganda to introduce the machine, but once the market is created, he may later be allowed to keep his monopoly rent uncurtailed, although this will now be less on account of the fall in the schedule of demand for the machine and, consequently, in its selling price, in proportion as it increases the production of goods. If the manufacturer of the machine does not hold a patent, the price of the machine will fall more quickly—*i.e.*, lower than is necessitated by the fall in price of the finished article, because the competition between several producers of machines transfers the profits to the employer of the machine, from whom the profit will gradually pass on to the purchasers of the finished article in the form of reduced prices of the latter.

What has been said of the machine in relation to hand labour also applies when a more complicated machine supersedes the machine of an inferior technique.

But before this the price-movements of the machine have possibly ceased, inasmuch as such fluctuations are due to the increase in production of goods caused by the machine itself or to its position of monopoly. Afterwards its price is only altered for the same reasons as those of all other goods: Its cost of produc-duction may be altered, the machine may be antiquated or superseded, and naturally the good produced by the machine may be subject to violent price-fluctuations, which may temporarily place the machine in a position of need if the movement is a downward one, or of monopoly if the movement is an upward one.

**137. Interest and the Machine.**—We have stated that the producer of goods will finally only have covered the amortisation and interest on the machine ; the latter must be covered if he is to work without a loss, and the amount of interest together with the purchase price of the machine will therefore decide whether he will employ a machine or not.

But the machine need not yield a *money* profit at all ; in the example in Sec. 136 the machines No. 8 and 9 will yield a return which, expressed in money, is nil and negative respectively, that is, they do not yield a rent, although they, as well as the other machines, increase the production by 1 unit each (*i.e.*, are equally productive). The interest, therefore, seems to be a feature *apart* from the employment of the machine ; if we presume the interest to be given and the employment of machines to be variable, we will find that the extent to which machines are introduced is a function of the rate of interest.

If the interest amounts to 8s., and out of the calculated cost of the machine (24s.) 16s. is the purchase price and 8s. the interest, the dropping of the interest demanded will cause our producer to increase the number of machines employed from 5 to 6, because the 16s., by which the 6th machine increases his return, will then be sufficient for him. If the interest is increased to 16s. he will stop at the 4th machine (32s.). If, with this rate of interest, he would already stop after acquiring the 3rd machine, the earning capacity of which is 40s., he would, beyond the purchase price (16s.) and the interest (16s.), also earn an extra profit of 8s. which he may turn into a permanent monopoly profit, if he commands the number of machines which should be bought by the industry in question.

From this we may immediately advance the rule that the interest *does not directly arise from the yield of the machine*, and therefore cannot be said to be the yield of the technical capital. The interest existed before the machine ; it influences the number of machines to be employed ; it is a regulator, without which a larger number of machines would be used. The machines increase our productivity in the same manner as improved methods of production, but we cannot deduce any lasting *rentability* from this.

The technical gain, which is increased by an increase of productivity, is quite a different matter from the money gain, which need not have anything to do with productivity. On the part of the lender (or rather the saver of money) the demand for interest is maintained from subjective considerations, but the *further specification* is determined by his economic position of power as an individual, or as member of a class. The simple theory that interest can be paid because the economic capital is productive has justly been termed the " naïve " theory of productivity. Interest exists without the machine, and the capital represented by the machines claims interest for the same reasons as those which are represented by raw materials and stocks of goods: that the lender makes a sacrifice of waiting and has an economic position of power.

Another matter is that the machine for a time yields monopoly and differential rent, which may attract capital to certain industries, and through this draw it away from those which are less productive, and thereby increase the marginal rentability, which corresponds to the interest.

Economic rentability is related to technical rentability in the same manner as value to usefulness: technical productivity and usefulness respectively are conditions for rentability and value, but do not determine the amount thereof. In the same manner as the maximum of utility causes the value to be nil, and for the same reason *a maximum of productivity may cause the interest to become negative*. Owing to this law the larger productivity of the machine itself causes its rentability to decrease.

**138. Amortisation of the Machine.**—The machine has a certain period of life and, normally, it must be written off according to this; but it may happen that a new invention appears *before* the existing machine has been worn out. In this case the yield of the machine must not only pay the writing off on the new machine, but also the amount to be earned by the scrapped machine, which has not been worn out, in order to pay its book-value—*i.e.*, the price of demand for the machine—found in the manner previously described—must be reduced by an amount corresponding to that part of the old machine which has not been written off.

Suppose that a set of machines worth £50 is able to produce 100 units at 10s. each before being worn out, all other expenses being left out of consideration; when 40 units have been sold at 10s., a better machine is invented which costs £65 and produces 200 units; to this must be added the £30 which have not been written off on the first machine; the cost of the new machine will therefore be £65 + £30. In order to pay expenses, the cost of 200 units must therefore be 9½s. each.

When now we have produced 50 units with the new machine and sold these for £23 15s., another machine is invented, at a price of £75, and producing 360 units; to the cost of this machine must be added the £71 5s., which have not yet been earned by the second machine—*i.e.*, the cost of the third machine is £146 5s., and the cost of production of the 360 units is therefore 8⅛s. This might continue under the incentive of competition. Although the first machine would not yet have been worn out at the time when the third machine was acquired, and *without* new purchases of machinery the factory in question would only have absorbed £50 of the national capital, it would in the process mentioned here have absorbed £50 + £65 + £75 = 190.

Incidentally a protective duty might in certain cases have been useful; by keeping out a competition, which would have forced our manufacturer to scrap the first machine too early, it would have made it possible for him to have worn it out and enabled him to avoid acquiring the second machine and buy the third when the first was worn out; his expenses in the future would then be 5s. per unit only, as the third machine would not have to pay off what was left of the first and second machines. Thanks to the old protective duty certain Danish industries have been able to go direct from very out-of-date machines to ultra modern ones, when the new Customs Act came into force. In a period when the frequency of inventions makes the machines out of date, directly they have been acquired, the separate manufacturer, who can have no idea of the capital resources of the country, will therefore bind more capital in his trade than he is entitled to relatively. In our example it is possible that the manufacturer will gain by purchasing the third machine for £75 and even add to this the part of the second machine, which has not been written off, and yet it may be that it is not convenient for the community, at a time when the second machine might suffice, to spare £75 for a plant which, even if it pays, is not necessary. The £75 are withdrawn from another employment, which may actually be more necessary, which will gradually appear through that increase in the rate of interest, which always succeeds too quick a change to a longer period of investment favouring the future at the expense of the present.

(In case a new machine does not only mean greater effectivity, but also a saving of the other components, for instance, power and labour, the value of the savings must, of course, be added to the value of the machine, just as the amount with which a scrapped machine is included in the cost of a new machine must be reduced by the value of the former for other purposes, say as scrap iron.)

We generally measure the capital of a country according to its earning capacity, but, after all, a machine which may last a hundred years represents essentially future value; if we do *not* measure the capital of a country *as an income-yielding medium*, but as *incorporated energy*, which is quite defensible when the country can spare the energy at its disposal for establishments, which only in time can reproduce the quantity of energy corresponding to their own technical cost, it cannot be denied that to scrap machinery which is not worn out is to reduce the *total energy* available.

**139. Labour and the Machine.**—Of the labourers who have lost their employment through the advance of the machine, some who have possibility of substitution will go into other trades, perhaps to the building of the machines which superseded them, or to the increase of the raw materials which has been entailed by the increased production of goods. Other workers will be called in to tend the machines; nowadays they will often obtain a higher wage than the hand worker, while particularly in old times, when the machines were less complicated, they obtained a lower wage (inferior labour, women, children and unskilled labourers were called in to substitute the dismissed artisans). Some labourers go into the large industrial reserve army, and others who are just as badly situated remain in the trade and must sell at the terms of the machine industry, and, consequently, they only gain a wage which approaches the lowest individual minimum of existence (the toy industry of Silesia); the wage per unit, which yields 1s. an hour to the man who tends the machine, may not yield the handworker 2d.

In the long run conditions will be equalised and the machine will benefit many in the community, but in the trade where the machine gains ground the intermediate period may be very disastrous to the hand worker and show an apparent " over-production " of hands; just as the displaced machinery, the displaced worker may become "scrap-iron," and both represent a loss in actual producing power.

**140. The Interdependence of the Prices of the Components.**—The price I will pay for the machine depends upon what it can produce—*i.e.*, upon the difference between the value of the finished good which it yields, and the expenses for the necessary raw materials and other components. In a narrower sense its value is also a function of the value of its own auxiliaries, coal, oil, etc., and its cost of repairs and amortisation, to which the first cost of the machine stands in complementary relation and therefore varies in the opposite direction. The form in Sec. 131, which corrects Wieser's formula must then be extended to comprise 20 or 30 components, between which the gross profits of the finished article must be distributed. The relations become so complicated that it is impossible to establish a general covering formula.

Still more difficult is it to calculate from the price of raw materials the price of the components, in the form of which the technical energy required for the production of the former must be applied. We must content ourselves by presuming a state of absolute equilibrium, and then take some point of the complicated price mechanism in order to investigate the effects and reactions. The price of demand for a component is a difference, but in order to find this the subtrahend and minuend must both be known. But now the subtrahend (the expenses of conversion) consists itself of different components, the prices of which are also differences of which the subtrahend is *just the price of the first component we are seeking.*

Labour is also a component obeying *Wieser's* law. We have previously employed the expression " the marginal productivity of labour " (expressed in *money*, not in kind) as determining the value of the labour applied. The expression is not exhaustive, because it does not state anything beyond the fact that equal labour and equal raw material must obtain the same price in all applications, and therefore economically, at any rate on the margin, must yield the same, for otherwise it would be attracted from one application to another. Labour, like other components, has an indirect schedule of demand, and is therefore related in the same interacting manner as these to the price of the finished article and to the price of the co-operating components as well as to those which substitute labour. Labour as well competes with and is complementary to the machines.

The task to find the price of labour becomes difficult, because labour unites with all imaginable components in the production of all goods ; it would be quite easy if the price of supply of labour was fixed, say, just covered the minimum of existence. Even if this is the case in some trades, it does not apply in all. With regard to labour the same fact applies as for the *raw material*, that an element outside the market comes in—*i.e.*, the relative position of monopoly of the branch of labour in question. As a general good, labour is faced with the buying monopoly of capital; capital in this sense is not technical capital, but the command of the producers' goods which is inherent in the capitalist's purchasing power. And this, whether owned or borrowed, is only the lot of relatively few.

Wieser's revised law therefore is not adequate as a means of finding the prices of the components and undertaking the *imputation*; in order to know this process we must examine the *importance of the relative position of monopoly of the components*, and we will then find confirmation for the contention that the distribution of income is not dependent upon the technical utility of the components, but on their relative position of monopoly—*i.e.*, of the extent to which the owner or producer of the components in question commands the market. *Oppenheimer* is right in his observation that the distribution is the result of a position of power, and not of inviolable economic rules, which further should be just, because "the components are postulated to be paid according to their productivity." It certainly does take place according to economic rules, but among many effective causes the position of power is not the least, and this has nothing to do with productivity or " justice."

If we comprise all the components : labour, raw material, machinery and power in the description dose of energy, we know *vide* Chapter XV, that the value of a dose of energy is its yield in its poorest (marginal) application—*i.e.*, the price of its marginal product—decreasing if the production obeys the rule of decreasing return, and decreasing, because an increase of production causes that the separate units are worth less. The difference between what is produced by the first doses of energy and the last will be the share in kind which is appropriated by the employers, and these must again give up part thereof to the land and its owners. (We shall examine in due course, if through the determining of prices and the exchange for industrial produce part of the gain imputed to the land is not transferred to others than the owners of the land).

Now the conception, " a dose of energy," is abstract only, and must be dissolved into the different forms, in which energy must be applied, machinery, raw materials, labour, etc. . . . It is the task of imputation to find out how the yield of the dose is distributed between the different forms of energy. The altered *Wieser's* law together with the law of *monopoly* have given us the means to solve the problem.

By dissolving the raw material and the machine into their components, we will finally return to *labour*, and to this we must add the *sacrifice of waiting*. But this will not give the correct picture, because the goods, in which the labour and the sacrifice of waiting are incorporated, have their price determined, not even according to this labour and sacrifice of waiting, but, once they are produced, they obey the law of relative position of monopoly. Capital is not present in the form of sacrifice of waiting and accumulated labour, but in the form of concrete goods.

Now the position of monopoly may be directly connected with these goods, but it may also be connected with their *purchasing power*, when their producer gives them up for a *compensation* which pays out the producer and consequently commands the components necessary for production—that is, the position of monopoly may be connected with capital in an abstract sense. But the man whose yes or no decides whether I shall obtain the necessary components or not is able to appear, not as a technical, but as an *economic* component ; he represents the sacrifice of waiting, even if his compensation may be quite out of proportion to this sacrifice ; his compensation is similarly to that of all other components determined by his position of power, as this arises from the ability of the capitalist to retain or choose between several applicants in proportion to his need for employment of his capital, and, on the other hand, the relative position of distress of these applicants.

This chapter is the intermediary between the theory of price-formation and the theory of imputation ; in order to investigate the latter we must first analyse the *machinery of the economic circulation and the organisation of the production of the community*—the subject of the next volume.

**141. Theories.**—In this book we presume that the cost of production is something decided by outside influences, and we therefore find that with the given distribution of income and the existing technical and social arrangement the last necessary expenses, by corresponding to the subjective price of the last buyer, form the market price, presuming the absolute rule of free competition.

While even the older authors have corrected the theory of the cost of production and adopted the theory of the last necessary expenses (which are something different from the "socially necessary" expenses in *Karl Marx's* theory), they still fail to observe that which of many possible are the last necessary expenses (the marginal expenses) must be determined by the schedule of demand, for in relation to the expenses this is primary.

We learn from the schedule of demand that each quantity sold commands its corresponding price, and similarly the schedule of production shows us that each unit has its price without which it will not appear—*i.e.*, it shows us the quantity and price as equally legitimate factors on the part of the supply and on the part of the demand.

*Schäffle* states in *Bau und Leben des Socialen Körpers* : The market price is *not* the average of the cost of production, but the "*separate cost of the last saleable unit.*" *N. C. Frederiksen* expresses the same idea in the *Ideas of Political Economy* : "It is the extreme utility, the smallest utility which is sufficient for the buyers, which decides the demand that turns the scale ; it is the extreme sacrifice—*the cost* which the sellers who have least advantage of the business are just able to yield— which determines the supply."

In the meeting of the schedules we have found the connection between the prices of demand and supply, inasmuch as the conditions of exchange of the parties must be manifested by this ; but at the same time we have, by analysing the schedules, found the connection between the primus motor, *our desire,* materialised through the distribution of income and the *technical cost,* nature's resistance against satisfying our desire—two in themselves incommensurable entities, a feeling and a necessary effort, which can only be compared when both are converted into a common standard—*the price.*

But now the "Open, Sesame" of the liberal school of economics, demand and supply, ceases to be a phrase only; we know the nature of their being, how they arise and their effects. Through our double theory we have reached that reconciliation between the subjective and the objective theory—the theories of utility and cost—which has in vain been sought in the famous controversy in *Conrad's Jahrbücher* between v. Bohm-Bawerk and Dietzel, in which Simon Patten supported the former and Scharling's great treatise on value was counted in favour of the latter.

The theories advanced in the present work are different from the classical theory of value. While *Locke, Macleod and Malthus* maintain that the exchange value depends upon the proportion between demand and supply, alterations in the former being due to alterations in this proportion, we have shown that this theory holds good for the short market when torn away from its general connection. *Malthus* appears to believe that a rise in price is due to an increase of the demand, which alters the proportion between demand and supply, and through this makes possible a higher cost of production, and this idea is partly right; but apart from the fact that it can be misunderstood, it is far from being exhaustive.

Starting with this formula—demand and supply—which does not tell us very much, and the distinctness of which is only attained by leaving out of consideration all difficulties—we have attempted, through the laws advanced for the effects of desire and the distribution of income, to substantiate the conception of demand, and to determine this demand we have found some guidance in *Sismondi and Malthus. Roscher* has understood the nature of demand, inasmuch as he knows that the purchasing power of the individual—*i.e.*, the distribution of income, is determining for demand.

By calling attention to the technical cost (which is something different from *Scharling's* "efforts saved") supplemented by the price laws for this cost, which will be advanced in the following volume, we have also shown that the supply, as far as the long market is concerned, does not mean an accidentally existing quantity, but certain technical and economic conditions, without the presence of which the quantity desired cannot be produced.

We have also turned against the theory of labour, which entirely ignores the subjective elements of the price and is blind to the importance of the distribution of income, and our reason for this is the fact that it is impossible to point to the substance of labour, which is incorporated in the good, and because none of the adherents of the theory, from *Ricardo* to *Marx*, really maintains that the goods are *actually* exchanged according to their inherent value (the substance of labour applied), but, for instance, *Marx* states that this is done according to rules which are determined by the unconscious necessity of the rate of profit being alike everywhere.

*Adam Smith*, whose *philosophic* theory of value (to quote the expression of *Wieser*) corresponds to *Ricardo's* theory of labour, in his *empiric* theory takes up the theory of the cost of production. Some authors describe this cost as being the total of the capital spent in the production, to which, for instance, *Senior* adds an average rate of profit, while the great majority of " empiric " authors treat the expenses completely as a matter of book-keeping. To the theory that the value of the raw materials, labour and machinery, which are incorporated in a good, determine its value, *James Mill* has already replied that this theory is quite unfertile, and he has in vain attempted to explain the exchange value of a good by pointing to the exchange value of other goods. The cost of production must be analysed in another manner than as a supplement to the theory of distribution.

We shall later show the relations between the " effective demand " and the price of the technical cost, and within the different forms of this we shall find the solution of the question of price, by means of the *theory of imputation*. Besides appropriating the *admissions of Scharling* in his controversy with *Bohm-Bawerk*, that the theory of marginal utility is all-comprising (against *Stuart Mill's* theory of value, which does not cover all cases, but must be supplemented by exceptions and special rules) we shall only point out that besides on the two points mentioned, we have also disagreed with the objective theories of value by pointing to the *technical cost*—as this may take different forms, and as the components may be put together differently in our search, not only for a technical, but also for an economical optimum—as well as by pointing to the fact that the value of the components themselves is a function of the value of the finished article and, consequently, of the demand for this. Finally, we have, by continually taking monopoly into consideration, kept the theory in closer agreement with actual conditions.

Of course the theory of marginal value does not mean as great a difference from past theories as its men often believe; but it is stamped by a unity and firmness which is due to the fact that we have found a method which permits us to carry through the analysis.

The science has undoubtedly lost popularity; it demands of its man a special training in the same manner as Law and Mathematics; it has to an increased extent become a theoretical analysis and has come farther and farther away from what has been termed "merchants and bank economics"—this branch of the liberal school which seems to have been created by and for the business men in honour of themselves.

Our method is deductive; our deduction rests on certain of the results of Psychology (the law of maximum satisfaction and decreasing utility) and on certain objective outside relations, which observation has made into material for our purpose; we have treated our subject as a problem of equilibrium. We start from a given economic equilibrium, which is repeatedly disturbed and must be re-established; we must do so, because the laws of equilibrium apply everywhere where life is. Life itself is the disturbed equilibirum and an effort to regain it. Biology terms this the law of *adaptation*; we are working with this law when we examine how men would act under certain economic, technical and social conditions from the motives which Psychology ascribes to them. Knowing these conditions we understand that our rules are not absolutely valid; they do not claim to be eternal truths, but only historical categories.

Induction can only be used as a test, the observations are too many. We are forced to isolate in order to find the causal connections; for every effect is the product of a thousand causes, and every cause has effect on a thousand points, and because no cause is allowed its full chain of effects, as other causes become effective, either the direction will be altered or the original force will be the more effective, and finally every effect will return by a roundabout route to weaken its own cause.

For this reason the theories are not immediately disproved, even if apparently they are at variance with observations ; before we dismiss them we must trace the disturbing causes, and then, on the strength of the apparently disproved theories, we may find " the new planet " whose existence confirms them. Our method is also mathematical, not so much in the algebraic armament, which we have reduced to a minimum as in the method of thought.

Our object is not to champion or attack any economic arrangement or policy, only to state the connection between economic phenomena. What the practical men, politicians and merchants, will deduce from these does not concern us.

For Product Safety Concerns and Information please contact our EU representative GPSR@taylorandfrancis.com
Taylor & Francis Verlag GmbH, Kaufingerstraße 24, 80331 München, Germany

www.ingramcontent.com/pod-product-compliance
Lightning Source LLC
LaVergne TN
LVHW011109300926
849160LV00008B/327
*9780415607162*